EZRA–NEHEMIAH

WISDOM COMMENTARY

Volume 14

Ezra–Nehemiah

Deborah Ann Appler
and Terry Ann Smith

Amy-Jill Levine
Volume Editor

Barbara E. Reid, OP
General Editor

A Michael Glazier Book

LITURGICAL PRESS
Collegeville, Minnesota

litpress.org

A Michael Glazier Book published by Liturgical Press

Library of Congress Cataloging-in-Publication Data

Names: Appler, Deborah Ann, author. | Smith, Terry A., 1962- author.
Title: Ezra-Nehemiah / Deborah Ann Appler and Terry Ann Smith.
Description: Collegeville, Minnesota : Liturgical Press, [2025] | Series: Wisdom commentary ; volume 14 | "A Michael Glazier Book." | Includes bibliographical references and index. | Summary: "Deborah Appler and Terry Ann Smith offer a sustained investigation and feminist critique of Ezra-Nehemiah that moves beyond traditional historical and theological interpretations. Their intersectional analysis engages themes of gender, power, economics, and social justice and demonstrates how ancient and modern communities grapple with community formation and identity amidst ever-evolving social and cultural challenges"— Provided by publisher.
Identifiers: LCCN 2025004487 (print) | LCCN 2025004488 (ebook) | ISBN 9780814681138 (hardcover) | ISBN 9780814681381 (epub) | ISBN 9780814669631 (pdf)
Subjects: LCSH: Bible. Ezra—Commentaries. | Bible. Nehemiah—Commentaries.
Classification: LCC BS1355.53 .A67 2025 (print) | LCC BS1355.53 (ebook) | DDC 222/.707—dc23/eng/20250401
LC record available at https://lccn.loc.gov/2025004487
LC ebook record available at https://lccn.loc.gov/2025004488

Contents

Abbreviations

AARAS	American Academy of Religion Academy Series
AASOR	Annual of the American Schools of Oriental Research
AB	Anchor Bible
AIL	Ancient Israel and Its Literature
ANEM	Ancient Near East Monographs
AYBRL	Anchor Yale Bible Reference Library
BAR	*Biblical Archaeological Review*
BASOR	*Bulletin of the American Schools of Oriental Research*
BDB	F. Brown, S. R. Driver, and C. A. Briggs, *Hebrew and English Lexicon of the Old Testament*
BHS	*Biblical Hebraica Stuttgartensia*
Bib	*Biblica*
BibInt	*Biblical Interpretation*
BibInt	Biblical Interpretation Series
BLS	Bible and Literature Studies
BSac	*Bibliotheca Sacra*
BTB	*Biblical Theology Bulletin*
BW	Bible and Women
BZAW	Beihefte zur Zeitschrift für die alttestamentliche Wissenschaft
CBQ	*Catholic Biblical Quarterly*
CHANE	Culture and History of the Ancient Near East

CurBR	*Currents in Biblical Research*
DBI	*The Dictionary of Biblical Interpretation*
EJL	Early Judaism and Its Literature
ExpTim	*The Expository Times*
FAT	Forschungen zum Alten Testament
FCB	Feminist Companion to the Bible
GBS	Guides to Biblical Scholarship
GPBS	Global Perspectives on Biblical Scholarship
HALOT	L. Koehler and W. Baumgartner, *The Hebrew and Aramaic Lexicon of the Old Testament*
HCOT	Historical Commentary on the Old Testament
HTR	*Harvard Theological Review*
HUCA	*Hebrew Union College Annual*
IBC	Interpretation: A Bible Commentary for Preaching and Teaching
IEJ	*Israel Exploration Journal*
IFT	Introductions in Feminist Theology
ITC	International Theological Commentary
IVBS	International Voices in Biblical Studies
JBL	*Journal of Biblical Literature*
JBQ	*Jewish Bible Quarterly*
JCS	*Journal of Cuneiform Studies*
JES	*Journal of Ecumenical Studies*
JETS	*Journal of the Evangelical Theological Society*
JFSR	*Journal of Feminist Studies in Religion*
JNES	*Journal of Near Eastern Studies*
JPS	Jewish Publication Society
JRH	*Journal of Religion and Health*
JSJ	*Journal for the Study of Judaism in the Persian, Hellenistic, and Roman Periods*
JSNTSup	Journal for the Study of the New Testament Supplement Series
JSOT	*Journal for the Study of the Old Testament*

JSOTSup	Journal for the Study of the Old Testament Supplement Series
JTS	*Journal of Theological Studies*
LAI	Library of Ancient Israel
LHBOTS	The Library of Hebrew Bible/Old Testament Studies
LSTS	The Library of Second Temple Studies
LXX	Septuagint
MT	Masoretic Text
NEA	*Near Eastern Archaeology*
NICOT	New International Commentary on the Old Testament
NPR	National Public Radio
NRSV	New Revised Standard Version
NRSVue	New Revised Standard Version Updated Edition
OBT	Overtures to Biblical Theology
OCM	Oxford Classical Monographs
OTE	*Old Testament Essays*
OTG	Old Testament Guides
OTL	Old Testament Library
PEQ	*Palestine Exploration Quarterly*
PL	Patrologia Latina
ProEccl	*Pro Ecclesia*
RevQ	*Revue de Qumran*
SAC	Studies in Antiquity and Christianity
SBL	Society of Biblical Literature
SBLMS	Society of Biblical Literature Monograph Series
SemeiaSt	Semeia Studies
SFSHJ	South Florida Studies in the History of Judaism
SJOT	*Scandinavian Journal of the Old Testament*
STDJ	Studies on the Texts of the Desert of Judah
SymS	Symposium Series
USQR	*Union Seminary Quarterly Review*
VT	*Vetus Testamentum*

VTSup	Vetus Testamentum Supplement Series
WBC	Word Bible Commentary
WCS	Wisdom Commentary Series
WTJ	*The Westminster Theological Journal*
WW	Word and World
ZAW	*Zeitschrift Für Die Alttestamentliche Wissenschaft*

Contributors

Sonya S. Cronin is a lecturer at Florida State University and teaches for their international programs in London and Florence. She is author of *Raymond Brown, "the Jews," and the Gospel of John*, and a forthcoming book on Mark's Gospel with Fortress Press. She is the founder of *The Carrier Pigeon Post*, a nonprofit periodical that sends humanities education into prisons and collects and archives the childhood stories of the incarcerated.

Suzanne Wenonah Duchesne, PhD, is the assistant professor of worship and preaching at New Brunswick Theological Seminary and an ordained elder in the United Methodist Church. Her relationships with members of the Kiowa, Cherokee, Mvskoke, Choctaw, Chickasaw, Abenaki, Penobscot, Shinnecock, Southern Ute, Lenape, and Yuchi Nations guide her scholarship in antiracism and decolonized preaching and worship, curriculum resources, and liturgies.

Adde Gross is a fine artist based in Baltimore, Maryland. She is always looking for the next opportunity to translate life experiences into art. She hopes that viewers not only appreciate her work but also think about how the work is relevant to them and the space they occupy. Receiving her BFA in painting from Salisbury University, she has continued to develop her skills and love of creation.

Zo Gross is a graduate of the MFA in creative writing and publishing arts program at the University of Baltimore and author of *Our Own Gods*. They spend their time playing video games, making soup, and sitting under trees. They are vehemently opposed to the American status quo. They live by moving water.

Leslie Maro is a former executive assistant (and New Brunswick Theological Seminary student) who worked in the corporate offices of a newspaper publisher in northern New Jersey. Leslie is driven by a desire to grow closer to God through understanding the history and experiences of God's people and the nuances of scriptural language. Now retired, she uses her studies to foster a welcoming community at Old North Reformed Church, Dumont, New Jersey, where she volunteers at the thrift shop—a ministry raising funds for local nonprofits. She is also committed to animal rescue and usually has a senior dog enjoying its own retirement in her home with the resident cat who endures the seemingly endless parade of old dogs.

Kathleen McCallie serves as associate professor of ministerial leadership and ethics at Phillips Theological Seminary in Tulsa, Oklahoma. Before joining the Phillips faculty she served twenty-six years in pastoral ministry and is ordained in the United Church of Christ. In addition to her experience leading congregations, she worked as a denominational officer in the UCC, social activist, and community organizer in various justice-seeking movements.

Reverend Crystal Paul-Watson is the senior pastor of the United Methodist Church of Hartford, Connecticut, the parish coordinator of eight churches in the Greater Hartford area, and a trainer for the Global Ministries Earthkeepers. Rev. Paul-Watson received a BS in education from Cortland University and earned an MA in education leadership from New Paltz University. A published author, Rev. Paul-Watson is the cofounder and codirector of Creators' Haven, a group of multicultural women artists who come together to support one another and address justice issues through art.

Rabbi Sonja K. Pilz, PhD, earned her doctorate from the Department of Rabbinic Literature at Potsdam University in Germany and holds a Rabbinic Ordination from Abraham Geiger College in Germany. Before becoming Congregation Beth Shalom's spiritual leader in Bozeman, Montana, she worked for the Central Conference of American Rabbis (CCAR) as editor of CCAR Press. She also taught Worship, Liturgy, and Ritual at Hebrew Union College-Jewish Institute of Religion in New York and the School of Jewish Theology at Potsdam University, and she served as a rabbinic intern, adjunct rabbi, and cantorial soloist for congregations in Germany, Switzerland, Israel, and the United States. Not surprisingly, she loves to write poetry, midrashim, and prayers. Her work has been published in *Ergon*, *Liturgy*, *Worship*, the *CCAR Journal*, *Ritual Well*, and a number of anthologies.

Charles M. Rix, PhD, MFA, is the dean and vice president of Academic Affairs at New Brunswick Theological Seminary. His research focuses on the application of Mikhail Bakhtin's literary theory and the phenomenology of Emmanuel Levinas to feminist and post-Shoah readings of the Hebrew Bible. His chapters appear in *Representing the Irreparable: The Shoah, the Bible, and the Art of Samuel Bak* (Syracuse University Press, 2008), as well as the *Oxford Handbook of Feminist Approaches to the Hebrew Bible* (Oxford University Press, 2021). He is also a playwright whose short plays have been performed in New York City and Los Angeles at Short Play Festivals (2022–2024).

SuJung Shin serves as a pastor for the Hurdtown's United Methodist Church and Lake Hopatcong UMC in New Jersey. She received a ThM from Yonsei University in Seoul and earned an MDiv at Wesley Theological Seminary in Washington, DC, and a PhD in biblical studies at Drew University. She has been teaching the Old Testament in a number of seminaries, including Wesley Theological Seminary, Moravian Theological Seminary, and New Brunswick Theological Seminary. She has served various congregations as an educator, youth pastor, social worker, and Bible instructor. She is passionate about the living word of God in Scripture and believes we can make it relevant to our lives.

Mila Díaz Solano is a Dominican sister of Springfield, Illinois, born in Peru. She ministered in a rural parish of the Central Andes, in a diocesan program of formation for young adults in Catholic Social Teaching, and in the Theology Department of the Instituto Bartolomé de las Casas (IBC), and she taught Scripture at the Seminary Juan XXIII in Lima, Peru, and at Mundelein Seminary in Illinois between 2018 and 2019. She is currently serving in the leadership team of her congregation.

Foreword

"Tell It on the Mountain"— or, "And You Shall Tell Your Daughter [as Well]"

Athalya Brenner-Idan

Universiteit van Amsterdam/Tel Aviv University

What can Wisdom Commentary do to help, and for whom?

The commentary genre has always been privileged in biblical studies. Traditionally acclaimed commentary series, such as the International Critical Commentary, Old Testament and New Testament Library, Hermeneia, Anchor Bible, Eerdmans, and Word—to name but several—enjoy nearly automatic prestige, and the number of women authors who participate in those is relatively small by comparison to their growing number in the scholarly guild. There certainly are some volumes written by women in them, especially in recent decades. At this time, however, this does not reflect the situation on the ground. Further, size matters. In that sense, the sheer size of the Wisdom Commentary is essential. This also represents a considerable investment and the possibility of reaching a wider audience than those already "converted."

Expecting women scholars to deal especially or only with what are considered strictly "female" matters seems unwarranted. According to Audre Lorde, "The master's tools will never dismantle the master's house."[1] But this maxim is not relevant to our case. The point of this commentary is not to destroy but to attain greater participation in the interpretive dialogue about biblical texts. Women scholars may bring additional questions to the readerly agenda as well as fresh angles to existing issues. To assume that their questions are designed only to topple a certain male hegemony is not convincing.

At first I did ask myself: is this commentary series an addition to calm raw nerves, an embellishment to make upholding the old hierarchy palatable? Or is it indeed about becoming the Master? On second and third thoughts, however, I understood that becoming the Master is not what this is about. Knowledge is power. Since Foucault at the very least, this cannot be in dispute. Writing commentaries for biblical texts by feminist women and men for women and for men, of confessional as well as non-confessional convictions, will sabotage (hopefully) the established hierarchy but will not topple it. This is about an attempt to integrate more fully, to introduce another viewpoint, to become. What excites me about the Wisdom Commentary is that it is not offered as just an alternative supplanting or substituting for the dominant discourse.

These commentaries on biblical books will retain nonauthoritative, pluralistic viewpoints. And yes, once again, the weight of a dedicated series, to distinguish from collections of stand-alone volumes, will prove weightier.

That such an approach is especially important in the case of the Hebrew Bible/Old Testament is beyond doubt. Women of Judaism, Christianity, and also Islam have struggled to make it their own for centuries, even more than they have fought for the New Testament and the Qur'an. Every Hebrew Bible/Old Testament volume in this project is evidence that the day has arrived: it is now possible to read *all* the Jewish canonical books as a collection, for a collection they are, with guidance conceived of with the needs of women readers (not only men) as an integral inspiration and part thereof.

In my Jewish tradition, the main motivation for reciting the Haggadah, the ritual text recited yearly on Passover, the festival of liberation from

1. Audre Lorde, "The Master's Tools Will Never Dismantle the Master's House," in *Sister Outsider: Essays and Speeches* (Berkeley, CA: Crossing Press, 1984, 2007), 110–14. First delivered in the Second Sex Conference in New York, 1979.

bondage, is given as "And you shall tell your son" (from Exod 13:8). The knowledge and experience of past generations is thus transferred to the next, for constructing the present and the future. The ancient maxim is, literally, limited to a male audience. This series remolds the maxim into a new inclusive shape, which is of the utmost consequence: "And you shall tell your son" is extended to "And you shall tell your daughter [as well as your son]." Or, if you want, "Tell it on the mountain," for all to hear.

This is what it's all about.

Editor's Introduction to Wisdom Commentary

"She Is a Breath of the Power of God" (Wis 7:25)

Barbara E. Reid, OP

General Editor

Wisdom Commentary is the first series to offer detailed feminist interpretation of every book of the Bible. The fruit of collaborative work by an ecumenical and interreligious team of scholars, the volumes provide serious, scholarly engagement with the whole biblical text, not only those texts that explicitly mention women. The series is intended for clergy, teachers, ministers, and all serious students of the Bible. Designed to be both accessible and informed by the various approaches of biblical scholarship, it pays particular attention to the world in front of the text, that is, how the text is heard and appropriated. At the same time, this series aims to be faithful to the ancient text and its earliest audiences; thus the volumes also explicate the worlds behind the text and within it. While issues of gender are primary in this project, the volumes also address the intersecting issues of power, authority, ethnicity, race, class, and religious belief and practice. The fifty-eight volumes include the books regarded as canonical by Jews (i.e., the Tanakh); Protestants (the "Hebrew Bible" and the New Testament); and Roman Catholic, Anglican, and Eastern

Orthodox Communions (i.e., Tobit, Judith, 1 and 2 Maccabees, Wisdom of Solomon, Sirach/Ecclesiasticus, Baruch, including the Letter of Jeremiah, the additions to Esther, and Susanna and Bel and the Dragon in Daniel).

A Symphony of Diverse Voices

Included in the Wisdom Commentary series are voices from scholars of many different religious traditions, of diverse ages, differing sexual identities, and varying cultural, racial, ethnic, and social contexts. Some have been pioneers in feminist biblical interpretation; others are newer contributors from a younger generation. A further distinctive feature of this series is that each volume incorporates voices other than that of the lead author(s). These voices appear alongside the commentary of the lead author(s), in the grayscale inserts. At times, a contributor may offer an alternative interpretation or a critique of the position taken by the lead author(s). At other times, they may offer a complementary interpretation from a different cultural context or subject position. Occasionally, portions of previously published material bring in other views. The diverse voices are not intended to be contestants in a debate or a cacophony of discordant notes. The multiple voices reflect that there is no single definitive feminist interpretation of a text. In addition, they show the importance of subject position in the process of interpretation. In this regard, the Wisdom Commentary series takes inspiration from the Talmud and from *The Torah: A Women's Commentary* (ed. Tamara Cohn Eskenazi and Andrea L. Weiss; New York: URJ Press and Women of Reform Judaism, The Federation of Temple Sisterhoods, 2008), in which many voices, even conflicting ones, are included and not harmonized.

Contributors include biblical scholars, theologians, and readers of Scripture from outside the scholarly and religious guilds. At times, their comments pertain to a particular text. In some instances they address a theme or topic that arises from the text.

Another feature that highlights the collaborative nature of feminist biblical interpretation is that a number of the volumes have two lead authors who have worked in tandem from the inception of the project and whose voices interweave throughout the commentary.

Woman Wisdom

The title, Wisdom Commentary, reflects both the importance to feminists of the figure of Woman Wisdom in the Scriptures and the distinct wisdom that feminist women and men bring to the interpretive process. In the Scriptures, Woman Wisdom appears as "a breath of the power of God, and a pure emanation of the glory of the Almighty" (Wis 7:25), who was present and active in fashioning all that exists (Prov 8:22-31; Wis 8:6). She is a spirit who pervades and penetrates all things (Wis 7:22-23), and she provides guidance and nourishment at her all-inclusive table (Prov 9:1-5). In both postexilic biblical and nonbiblical Jewish sources, Woman Wisdom is often equated with Torah, e.g., Sirach 24:23-34; Baruch 3:9–4:4; 2 Baruch 38:2; 46:4-5; 48:33, 36; 4 Ezra 5:9-10; 13:55; 14:40; 1 Enoch 42.

The New Testament frequently portrays Jesus as Wisdom incarnate. He invites his followers, "take my yoke upon you, and learn from me" (Matt 11:29), just as Ben Sira advises, "put your neck under her [Wisdom's] yoke, and let your souls receive instruction" (Sir 51:26). Just as Wisdom experiences rejection (Prov 1:23-25; Sir 15:7-8; Wis 10:3; Bar 3:12), so too does Jesus (Mark 8:31; John 1:10-11). Only some accept his invitation to his all-inclusive banquet (Matt 22:1-14; Luke 14:15-24; compare Prov 1:20-21; 9:3-5). Yet, "wisdom is vindicated by her deeds" (Matt 11:19, speaking of Jesus and John the Baptist; in the Lukan parallel at 7:35 they are called "her [wisdom's] children"). There are numerous parallels between what is said of Wisdom and of the *Logos* in the Prologue of the Fourth Gospel (John 1:1-18). These are only a few of many examples. This female embodiment of divine presence and power is an apt image to guide the work of this series.

Feminism

There are many different understandings of the term "feminism." The various meanings, aims, and methods have developed exponentially in recent decades. Feminism is a perspective and a movement that springs from a recognition of inequities toward women, and it advocates for changes in whatever structures prevent full flourishing of human beings and all creation. Three waves of feminism in the United States are commonly recognized. The first, arising in the mid-nineteenth century and lasting into the early twentieth, was sparked by women's efforts to be involved in the public sphere and to win the right to vote. In the 1960s and 1970s, the second wave focused on civil rights and equality for women. With the third wave, from the 1980s forward, came global feminism and the emphasis on the contextual nature of interpretation. Now a fourth wave is emerging, with a stronger emphasis on the intersectionality of women's concerns with those of other marginalized groups and the increased use of the internet as a platform for discussion and activism.[1] As feminism has matured, it has recognized that inequities based on gender are interwoven with power imbalances based on race, class, ethnicity, religion, sexual identity, physical ability, and a host of other social markers.

Feminist Women and Men

Men as well as nonbinary people who choose to identify with and partner with feminist women in the work of deconstructing systems of domination and building structures of equality are rightly regarded as feminists. Some men readily identify with experiences of women who are discriminated against on the basis of sex/gender, having themselves had comparable experiences; others who may not have faced direct discrimination or stereotyping recognize that inequity and problematic characterization still occur, and they seek correction. This series is pleased to include feminist men and nonbinary persons both as lead authors and as contributing voices.

Feminist Biblical Interpretation

Women interpreting the Bible from the lenses of their own experience is nothing new. Throughout the ages women have recounted the biblical stories, teaching them to their children and others, all the while interpreting them afresh for their time and circumstances.[2] Following is a very brief sketch of select foremothers who laid the groundwork for contemporary feminist biblical interpretation.

One of the earliest known Christian women who challenged patriarchal interpretations of Scripture was a consecrated virgin named Helie, who lived in the second century CE. When she refused to marry, her

1. See Martha Rampton, "Four Waves of Feminism" (October 25, 2015), at https://www.pacificu.edu/magazine/four-waves-feminism; and Ealasaid Munro, "Feminism: A Fourth Wave?," *Political Insight* (September 2013), https://journals.sagepub.com/doi/pdf/10.1111/2041-9066.12021.

2. For fuller treatments of this history, see chap. 7, "One Thousand Years of Feminist Bible Criticism," in Gerda Lerner, *The Creation of Feminist Consciousness: From the Middle Ages to Eighteen-Seventy*, Women and History 2 (New York: Oxford University Press, 1993), 138–66; Susanne Scholz, "From the 'Woman's Bible' to the 'Women's Bible,' The History of Feminist Approaches to the Hebrew Bible," in *Introducing the Women's Hebrew Bible*, IFT 13 (New York: T&T Clark, 2007), 12–32; Marion Ann Taylor and Agnes Choi, eds., *Handbook of Women Biblical Interpreters: A Historical and Biographical Guide* (Grand Rapids: Baker Academic, 2012).

parents brought her before a judge, who quoted to her Paul's admonition, "It is better to marry than to be aflame with passion" (1 Cor 7:9). In response, Helie first acknowledges that this is what Scripture says, but then she retorts, "but not for everyone, that is, not for holy virgins."[3] She is one of the first to question the notion that a text has one meaning that is applicable in all situations.

A Jewish woman who also lived in the second century CE, Beruriah, is said to have had "profound knowledge of biblical exegesis and outstanding intelligence."[4] One story preserved in the Talmud (b. Ber. 10a) tells of how she challenged her husband, Rabbi Meir, when he prayed for the destruction of a sinner. Proffering an alternate interpretation, she argued that Psalm 104:35 advocated praying for the destruction of sin, not the sinner.

In medieval times the first written commentaries on Scripture from a critical feminist point of view emerge. While others may have been produced and passed on orally, they are for the most part lost to us now. Among the earliest preserved feminist writings are those of Hildegard of Bingen (1098–1179), German writer, mystic, and abbess of a Benedictine monastery. She reinterpreted the Genesis narratives in a way that presented women and men as complementary and interdependent. She frequently wrote about the Divine as feminine.[5] Along with other women mystics of the time, such as Julian of Norwich (1342–ca. 1416), she spoke authoritatively from her personal experiences of God's revelation in prayer.

In this era, women were also among the scribes who copied biblical manuscripts. Notable among them is Paula Dei Mansi of Verona, from a distinguished family of Jewish scribes. In 1288, she translated from Hebrew into Italian a collection of Bible commentaries written by her father and added her own explanations.[6]

Another pioneer, Christine de Pizan (1365–ca. 1430), was a French court writer and prolific poet. She used allegory and common sense

3. Madrid, Escorial MS, a II 9, f. 90 v., as cited in Lerner, *Feminist Consciousness*, 140.

4. See Judith R. Baskin, "Women and Post-Biblical Commentary," in *The Torah: A Women's Commentary*, ed. Tamara Cohn Eskenazi and Andrea L. Weiss (New York: URJ Press and Women of Reform Judaism, The Federation of Temple Sisterhoods, 2008), xlix–lv, at lii.

5. Hildegard of Bingen, *De Operatione Dei*, 1.4.100; PL 197:885bc, as cited in Lerner, *Feminist Consciousness*, 142–43. See also Barbara Newman, *Sister of Wisdom: St. Hildegard's Theology of the Feminine* (Berkeley: University of California Press, 1987).

6. Emily Taitz, Sondra Henry, and Cheryl Tallan, *The JPS Guide to Jewish Women 600 B.C.E.–1900 C.E.* (Philadelphia: JPS, 2003), 110–11.

to subvert misogynist readings of Scripture and celebrated the accomplishments of female biblical figures to argue for women's active roles in building society.[7]

By the seventeenth century, there were women who asserted that the biblical text needs to be understood and interpreted in its historical context. For example, Rachel Speght (1597–ca. 1630), a Calvinist English poet, elaborates on the historical situation in first-century Corinth that prompted Paul to say, "It is good for a man not to touch a woman" (1 Cor 7:1). Her aim was to show that the biblical texts should not be applied in a literal fashion to all times and circumstances. Similarly, Margaret Fell (1614–1702), one of the founders of the Religious Society of Friends (Quakers) in Britain, addressed the Pauline prohibitions against women speaking in church by insisting that they do not have universal validity. Rather, they need to be understood in their historical context, as addressed to a local church in particular time-bound circumstances.[8]

Along with analyzing the historical context of the biblical writings, women in the eighteenth and nineteenth centuries began to attend to misogynistic interpretations based on faulty translations. One of the first to do so was British feminist Mary Astell (1666–1731).[9] In the United States, the Grimké sisters, Sarah (1792–1873) and Angelina (1805–1879), Quaker women from a slaveholding family in South Carolina, learned biblical Greek and Hebrew so that they could interpret the Bible for themselves. They were prompted to do so after men sought to silence them from speaking out against slavery and for women's rights by claiming that the Bible (e.g., 1 Cor 14:34) prevented women from speaking in public.[10] Another prominent abolitionist, Isabella Baumfree, was a former slave who adopted the name Sojourner Truth (ca. 1797–1883); she quoted the Bible liberally in her speeches[11] and in so doing challenged cultural assumptions and biblical interpretations that undergird gender inequities.

7. See further Taylor and Choi, *Handbook of Women Biblical Interpreters*, 127–32.

8. Her major work, *Women's Speaking Justified, Proved and Allowed by the Scriptures*, published in London in 1666, gave a systematic feminist reading of all biblical texts pertaining to women.

9. Mary Astell, *Some Reflections upon Marriage* (New York: Source Book Press, 1970, reprint of the 1730 edition; earliest edition of this work is 1700), 103–4.

10. See further Sarah Grimké, *Letters on the Equality of the Sexes and the Condition of Woman* (Boston: Isaac Knapp, 1838).

11. See, for example, her most famous speech, "Ain't I a Woman?," delivered in 1851 at the Ohio Women's Rights Convention in Akron; Modern History Sourcebook, https://sourcebooks.fordham.edu/mod/sojtruth-woman.asp.

Another monumental work that emerged in nineteenth-century England was that of Jewish theologian Grace Aguilar (1816–1847), *The Women of Israel*,[12] published in 1845. Aguilar's approach was to make connections between the biblical women and contemporary Jewish women's concerns. She aimed to counter the widespread antisemitic notion that women were degraded in Jewish law and that only in Christianity were women's dignity and value upheld. Her intent was to help Jewish women find strength and encouragement by seeing the evidence of God's compassionate love in the history of every woman in the Bible. While not a full commentary on the Bible, Aguilar's work stands out for its comprehensive treatment of every female biblical character, including even the most obscure references.[13]

The first person to produce a full-blown feminist commentary on the Bible was Elizabeth Cady Stanton (1815–1902). A leading proponent in the United States for women's right to vote, she found that whenever women tried to make inroads into politics, education, or the work world, the Bible was quoted against them. Along with a team of like-minded women, she produced her own commentary on every text of the Bible that concerned women. Her pioneering two-volume project, *The Woman's Bible*, published in 1895 and 1898, urges women to recognize that texts that degrade women come from the men who wrote the texts, not from God, and to use their common sense to rethink what has been presented to them as sacred.[14]

Nearly a century later, *The Women's Bible Commentary*, edited by Carol A. Newsom and Sharon H. Ringe (Louisville: Westminster John Knox, 1992), appeared. This one-volume commentary features North American feminist scholarship on each book of the Protestant canon. Like Cady Stanton's commentary, it does not contain comments on every section of the biblical text but only on those passages deemed relevant to women. It was revised and expanded in 1998 to include the Apocrypha/Deuterocanonical books, and the contributors to this new volume reflect the global face of contemporary feminist scholarship. The revisions made in the third edition, which appeared in 2012, represent the profound

12. The full title is *The Women of Israel or Characters and Sketches from the Holy Scriptures and Jewish History: Illustrative of the Past History, Present Duties, and Future Destiny of the Hebrew Females, as Based on the Word of God.*

13. See further Eskenazi and Weiss, *The Torah: A Women's Commentary*, xxxviii; Taylor and Choi, *Handbook of Women Biblical Interpreters*, 31–37.

14. While Cady Stanton's work was groundbreaking in its feminist approach, it nonetheless reflected racist and antisemitic attitudes she and the like-minded white Christian women who worked with her held.

advances in feminist biblical scholarship and include newer voices (with Jacqueline E. Lapsley as an additional editor). In both the second and third editions, *The* has been dropped from the title.

Also appearing at the centennial of Cady Stanton's *The Woman's Bible* were two volumes edited by Elisabeth Schüssler Fiorenza with the assistance of Shelly Matthews. The first, *Searching the Scriptures: A Feminist Introduction* (New York: Crossroad, 1993), charts a comprehensive approach to feminist interpretation from ecumenical, interreligious, and multicultural perspectives. The second volume, published in 1994, provides critical feminist commentary on each book of the New Testament as well as on three books of Jewish Pseudepigrapha and eleven other early Christian writings.

In Europe, similar endeavors have been undertaken, such as the one-volume *Kompendium Feministische Bibelauslegung*, edited by Luise Schottroff and Marie-Theres Wacker (Gütersloh: Gütersloher Verlagshaus, 2007), featuring German feminist biblical interpretation of each book of the Bible, along with Deuterocanonical apocryphal books, and several extrabiblical writings. This work, now in its third edition, was translated into English.[15] A multivolume project, The Bible and Women: An Encyclopaedia of Exegesis and Cultural History, edited by Charlotte Methuen, Irmtraud Fischer, Mercedes Navarro Puerto, and Adriana Valerio, is currently in production. This project presents a history of the reception of the Bible as embedded in Western cultural history and focuses particularly on gender-relevant biblical themes, biblical female characters, and women recipients of the Bible. The volumes are published in English, Spanish, Italian, and German.[16]

15. *Feminist Biblical Interpretation: A Compendium of Critical Commentary on the Books of the Bible and Related Literature*, trans. Lisa E. Dahill, Everett R. Kalin, Nancy Lukens, Linda M. Maloney, Barbara Rumscheidt, Martin Rumscheidt, and Tina Steiner (Grand Rapids: Eerdmans, 2012). Another notable collection is the three volumes edited by Susanne Scholz, *Feminist Interpretation of the Hebrew Bible in Retrospect*, Recent Research in Biblical Studies 5, 8, 9 (Sheffield: Sheffield Phoenix, 2013, 2014, 2016).

16. The first volume, on the Torah, appeared in Spanish in 2009, in German and Italian in 2010, and in English in 2011 (Atlanta: SBL). The other available volumes are as follows: *Feminist Biblical Studies in the Twentieth Century*, ed. Elisabeth Schüssler Fiorenza (2014); *The Writings and Later Wisdom Books*, ed. Christl M. Maier and Nuria Calduch-Benages (2014); *Gospels: Narrative and History*, ed. Mercedes Navarro Puerto and Marinella Perroni; Amy-Jill Levine, English ed. (2015); *The High Middle Ages*, ed. Kari Elisabeth Børresen and Adriana Valerio (2015); *Early Jewish Writings*, ed. Eileen Schuller and Marie-Theres Wacker (2017); *Faith and Feminism in Nineteenth-Century Religious Communities*, ed. Michaela Sohn-Kronthaler and Ruth Albrecht (2019); *The Early Middle Ages*, ed. Franca Ela

Another groundbreaking work is the collection The Feminist Companion to the Bible Series, edited by Athalya Brenner (Sheffield: Sheffield Academic, 1993–2015), which comprises twenty volumes of commentaries on the Old Testament. The parallel series, Feminist Companion to the New Testament and Early Christian Writings, edited by Amy-Jill Levine with Marianne Blickenstaff and Maria Mayo Robbins (Sheffield: Sheffield Academic, 2001–2010), contains thirteen volumes. These two series are not full commentaries on the biblical books but comprise collected essays on discrete biblical texts.

Works by individual feminist biblical scholars in all parts of the world abound, and they are now too numerous to list in this introduction. Feminist biblical interpretation has reached a level of maturity that now makes possible a commentary series on every book of the Bible. In recent decades, women have had greater access to formal theological education, have been able to learn critical analytical tools, have put their own interpretations into writing, and have developed new methods of biblical interpretation. Until recent decades the work of feminist biblical interpreters was largely unknown, both to other women and to their brothers in the synagogue, church, and academy. Feminists now have taken their place in the professional world of biblical scholars, where they build on the work of their foremothers and connect with one another across the globe in ways not previously possible. In a few short decades, feminist biblical criticism has become an integral part of the academy.

Methodologies

Feminist biblical scholars use a variety of methods and often employ a number of them together.[17] In the Wisdom Commentary series, the authors will explain their understanding of feminism and the feminist reading strategies used in their commentary. Each volume treats the biblical

Consolino and Judith Herrin (2020); *Prophecy and Gender in the Hebrew Bible*, ed. L. Juliana Claassens and Irmtraud Fischer (2021); *Rabbinic Literature*, ed. Tal Ilan, Lorena Miralles-Maciá, and Ronit Nikolsky (2022); *Ancient Christian Apocrypha*, ed. Outi Lehtipuu and Silke Petersen (2022); *The Jewish Middle Ages*, ed. Carol Bakhos and Gerhard Langer (2023); and *Nineteenth-Century Women's Movements and the Bible*, ed. Angela Berlis and Christiana de Groot (2024). For further information, see https://www.bibleandwomen.org.

17. See the seventeen essays in Caroline Vander Stichele and Todd Penner, eds., *Her Master's Tools? Feminist and Postcolonial Engagements of Historical-Critical Discourse* (Atlanta: SBL, 2005), which show the complementarity of various approaches.

text in blocks of material, not an analysis verse by verse. The entire text is considered, not only those passages that feature female characters or that speak specifically about women. When women are not apparent in the narrative, feminist lenses are used to analyze the dynamics in the text between male characters, the models of power, binary ways of thinking, and the dynamics of imperialism. Attention is given to how the whole text functions and how it was and is heard, both in its original context and today. Issues of particular concern to women—e.g., poverty, food, health, the environment, water—come to the fore.

One of the approaches used by early feminists and still popular today is to lift up the overlooked and forgotten stories of women in the Bible. Studies of women in each of the Testaments have been done, and there are also studies on women in particular biblical books.[18] Feminists recognize that the examples of biblical characters can be both empowering and problematic. The point of the feminist enterprise is not to serve as an apologetic for women; it is rather, in part, to recover women's history and literary roles in all their complexity and to learn from that recovery.

Retrieving the submerged history of biblical women is a crucial step for constructing the story of the past so as to lead to liberative possibilities for the present and future. There are, however, some pitfalls to this approach. Sometimes depictions of biblical women have been naïve and romantic. Some commentators exalt the virtues of both biblical and contemporary women and paint women as superior to men. Such reverse discrimination inhibits movement toward equality for all. In addition, some feminists challenge the idea that one can "pluck positive images out of an admittedly androcentric text, separating literary characterizations from the androcentric interests they were created to serve."[19] Still other feminists find these images to have enormous value.

18. See, e.g., Alice Bach, ed., *Women in the Hebrew Bible: A Reader* (New York: Routledge, 1999); Tikva Frymer-Kensky, *Reading the Women of the Bible* (New York: Schocken Books, 2002); Carol Meyers, Toni Craven, and Ross S. Kraemer, eds., *Women in Scripture* (Grand Rapids: Eerdmans, 2001); Irene Nowell, *Women in the Old Testament* (Collegeville, MN: Liturgical Press, 1997); Katharine Doob Sakenfeld, *Just Wives? Stories of Power and Survival in the Old Testament and Today* (Louisville: Westminster John Knox, 2003); Mary Ann Getty-Sullivan, *Women in the New Testament* (Collegeville, MN: Liturgical Press, 2001); Bonnie Thurston, *Women in the New Testament: Questions and Commentary*, Companions to the New Testament (New York: Crossroad, 1998).

19. J. Cheryl Exum, "Second Thoughts about Secondary Characters: Women in Exodus 1.8–2.10," in *A Feminist Companion to Exodus to Deuteronomy*, FCB 6, ed. Athalya Brenner (Sheffield: Sheffield Academic, 1994), 75–87, at 76.

One other danger with seeking the submerged history of women is the tendency for Christian feminists to paint Jesus and even Paul as liberators of women in a way that demonizes Judaism.[20] Wisdom Commentary aims to enhance understanding of Jesus as well as Paul as Jews of their day and to forge solidarity among Jewish and Christian feminists.

Feminist scholars who use historical-critical methods analyze the world behind the text; they seek to understand the historical context from which the text emerged and the circumstances of the communities to whom it was addressed. In bringing feminist lenses to this approach, the aim is not to impose modern expectations on ancient cultures but to unmask the ways that ideologically problematic mind-sets that produced the ancient texts are still promulgated through the text. Feminist biblical scholars aim not only to deconstruct but also to reclaim and reconstruct biblical history as women's history, in which women were central and active agents in creating religious heritage.[21] A further step is to construct meaning for contemporary women and men in a liberative movement toward transformation of social, political, economic, and religious structures.[22] In recent years, some feminists have embraced new historicism, which accents the creative role of the interpreter in any construction of history and exposes the power struggles to which the text witnesses.[23]

20. See Judith Plaskow, "Anti-Judaism in Feminist Christian Interpretation," in *Searching the Scriptures: A Feminist Introduction*, vol. 1, ed. Elisabeth Schüssler Fiorenza with Shelly Matthews (New York: Crossroad, 1993), 117–29; Amy-Jill Levine, "The New Testament and Anti-Judaism," in *The Misunderstood Jew: The Church and the Scandal of the Jewish Jesus* (San Francisco: HarperSanFrancisco, 2006), 87–117.

21. See, for example, Phyllis A. Bird, *Missing Persons and Mistaken Identities: Women and Gender in Ancient Israel* (Minneapolis: Fortress, 1997); Elisabeth Schüssler Fiorenza, *In Memory of Her: A Feminist Theological Reconstruction of Christian Origins* (New York: Crossroad, 1994); Ross Shepard Kraemer and Mary Rose D'Angelo, eds., *Women and Christian Origins* (New York: Oxford University Press, 1999).

22. See, e.g., Sandra M. Schneiders, *The Revelatory Text: Interpreting the New Testament as Sacred Scripture*, rev. ed. (Collegeville, MN: Liturgical Press, 1999), whose aim is to engage in biblical interpretation not only for intellectual enlightenment but, even more important, for personal and communal transformation. Elisabeth Schüssler Fiorenza (*Wisdom Ways: Introducing Feminist Biblical Interpretation* [Maryknoll, NY: Orbis Books, 2001]) envisions the work of feminist biblical interpretation as a dance of Wisdom that consists of seven steps that interweave in spiral movements toward liberation, the final one being transformative action for change.

23. See Gina Hens-Piazza, *The New Historicism*, GBS, Old Testament Series (Minneapolis: Fortress, 2002).

Literary critics analyze the world of the text: its form, language patterns, and rhetorical function.[24] They do not attempt to separate layers of tradition and redaction but focus on the text holistically, as it is in its present form. They examine how meaning is created in the interaction between the text and its reader in multiple contexts. Within the arena of literary approaches are reader-oriented approaches, narrative, rhetorical, structuralist, post-structuralist, deconstructive, ideological, autobiographical, and performance criticism.[25] Narrative critics study the interrelation among author, text, and audience through investigation of settings, both spatial and temporal; characters; plot; and narrative techniques (e.g., irony, parody, intertextual allusions). Reader-response critics attend to the impact that the text has on the reader or hearer. They recognize that when a text is detrimental toward women there is the choice either to affirm the text or to read against the grain toward a liberative end. Rhetorical criticism analyzes the style of argumentation and attends to how the author is attempting to shape the thinking or actions of the hearer. Structuralist critics analyze the complex patterns of binary oppositions in the text to derive its meaning.[26] Post-structuralist approaches challenge the notion that there are fixed meanings to any biblical text or that there is one universal truth. They engage in close readings of the text and often engage in intertextual analysis.[27] Within

24. Phyllis Trible was among the first to employ this method with texts from Genesis and Ruth in her groundbreaking book *God and the Rhetoric of Sexuality*, OBT (Philadelphia: Fortress, 1978). Another pioneer in feminist literary criticism is Mieke Bal (*Lethal Love: Feminist Literary Readings of Biblical Love Stories* [Bloomington: Indiana University Press, 1987]). For surveys of recent developments in literary methods, see Terry Eagleton, *Literary Theory: An Introduction*, anniversary ed. (Minneapolis: University of Minnesota Press, 2008); Janice Capel Anderson and Stephen D. Moore, eds., *Mark and Method: New Approaches in Biblical Studies*, 2nd ed. (Minneapolis: Fortress, 2008); Michal Beth Dinkler, *Literary Theory and the New Testament*, AYBRL (New Haven: Yale University Press, 2019).

25. See, e.g., J. Cheryl Exum and David J. A. Clines, eds., *The New Literary Criticism and the Hebrew Bible* (Valley Forge, PA: Trinity Press International, 1993); Elizabeth Struthers Malbon and Edgar V. McKnight, eds., *The New Literary Criticism and the New Testament*, JSNTSup 109 (Sheffield: JSOT Press, 1994).

26. See, e.g., David Jobling, *The Sense of Biblical Narrative: Three Structural Analyses in the Old Testament*, JSOTSup 7 (Sheffield: University of Sheffield Press, 1978).

27. See, e.g., Stephen D. Moore, *Poststructuralism and the New Testament: Derrida and Foucault at the Foot of the Cross* (Minneapolis: Fortress, 1994); *The Bible in Theory: Critical and Postcritical Essays* (Atlanta: SBL, 2010); Yvonne Sherwood, *A Biblical Text and Its Afterlives: The Survival of Jonah in Western Culture* (Cambridge: Cambridge University Press, 2000).

this approach is deconstructionist criticism, which views the text as a site of conflict, with competing narratives. The interpreter aims to expose the fault lines and overturn and reconfigure binaries by elevating the underling of a pair and foregrounding it.[28] Feminists also use other postmodern approaches, such as ideological and autobiographical criticism. The former analyzes the system of ideas that underlies the power and values concealed in the text as well as that of the interpreter.[29] The latter involves deliberate self-disclosure while reading the text as a critical exegete.[30] Performance criticism attends to how the text was passed on orally, usually in communal settings, and to the verbal and nonverbal interactions between the performer and the audience.[31]

From the beginning, feminists have understood that interpreting the Bible is an act of power. In recent decades, feminist biblical scholars have developed hermeneutical theories of the ethics and politics of biblical interpretation to challenge the claims to value neutrality of most academic biblical scholarship. Feminist biblical scholars have also turned their attention to how some biblical writings were shaped by the power of empire and how this still shapes readers' self-understandings today. They have developed hermeneutical approaches that reveal, critique, and evaluate the interactions depicted in the text against the context of empire, and they consider implications for contemporary contexts.[32] Feminists also analyze

28. David Penchansky, "Deconstruction," in *The Oxford Encyclopedia of Biblical Interpretation*, ed. Steven McKenzie (New York: Oxford University Press, 2013), 196–205. See, for example, Danna Nolan Fewell and David M. Gunn, *Gender, Power, and Promise: The Subject of the Bible's First Story* (Nashville: Abingdon, 1993); David Rutledge, *Reading Marginally: Feminism, Deconstruction and the Bible*, BibInt 21 (Leiden: Brill, 1996).

29. See David Jobling and Tina Pippin, eds., *Ideological Criticism of Biblical Texts*, SemeiaSt 59 (Atlanta: Scholars Press, 1992); Terry Eagleton, *Ideology: An Introduction* (London: Verso, 2007).

30. See, e.g., Ingrid Rosa Kitzberger, ed., *Autobiographical Biblical Criticism: Between Text and Self* (Leiden: Deo, 2002); P. J. W. Schutte, "When *They*, *We*, and the *Passive* Become *I*—Introducing Autobiographical Biblical Criticism," *HTS Teologiese Studies / Theological Studies* 61 (2005): 401–16.

31. See, e.g., Holly E. Hearon and Philip Ruge-Jones, eds., *The Bible in Ancient and Modern Media: Story and Performance* (Eugene, OR: Cascade Books, 2009).

32. E.g., Gale Yee, ed., *Judges and Method: New Approaches in Biblical Studies* (Minneapolis: Fortress, 1995); Warren Carter, "Matthaean Christology in Roman Imperial Key: Matthew 1.1," in *The Gospel of Matthew in Its Roman Imperial Context*, ed. John Riches and David C. Sim (London: T&T Clark, 2005); Warren Carter, *The Roman Empire and the New Testament: An Essential Guide* (Nashville: Abingdon, 2006); Elisabeth Schüssler Fiorenza, *The Power of the Word: Scripture and the Rhetoric of Empire* (Minneapolis:

the dynamics of colonization and the mentalities of colonized peoples in the exercise of biblical interpretation. As Kwok Pui-lan explains, "A postcolonial feminist interpretation of the Bible needs to investigate the deployment of gender in the narration of identity, the negotiation of power differentials between the colonizers and the colonized, and the reinforcement of patriarchal control over spheres where these elites could exercise control."[33] Methods and models from sociology and cultural anthropology are used by feminists to investigate women's everyday lives, their experiences of marriage, childrearing, labor, money, illness, etc.[34]

As feminists have examined the construction of gender from varying cultural perspectives, they have become ever more cognizant that the way gender roles are defined within differing cultures varies radically. As Mary Ann Tolbert observes, "Attempts to isolate some universal role that cross-culturally defines 'woman' have run into contradictory evidence at every turn."[35] Some women have coined new terms to highlight the particularities of their socio-cultural context. Many African American feminists, for example, call themselves *womanists* to draw attention to the double oppression of racism and sexism they experience.[36] Similarly, many US Hispanic feminists speak of themselves as *mujeristas* (*mujer* is

---

Fortress, 2007); Judith E. McKinlay, *Reframing Her: Biblical Women in Postcolonial Focus* (Sheffield: Sheffield Phoenix, 2004).

33. Kwok Pui-lan, *Postcolonial Imagination and Feminist Theology* (Louisville: Westminster John Knox, 2005), 9. See also Musa W. Dube, ed., *Postcolonial Feminist Interpretation of the Bible* (St. Louis: Chalice, 2000); Christl M. Maier and Carolyn J. Sharp, eds., *Prophecy and Power: Jeremiah in Feminist and Postcolonial Perspective*, LHBOTS 577 (London: Bloomsbury T&T Clark, 2013); L. Juliana Claassens and Carolyn J. Sharp, eds., *Feminist Frameworks and the Bible: Power, Ambiguity, and Intersectionality*, LHBOTS 630 (London: Bloomsbury T&T Clark, 2017).

34. See, for example, Carol Meyers, *Rediscovering Eve: Ancient Israelite Women in Context* (New York: Oxford University Press, 2013); Luise Schottroff, *Lydia's Impatient Sisters: A Feminist Social History of Early Christianity*, trans. Barbara and Martin Rumscheidt (Louisville: Westminster John Knox, 1995); Susan Niditch, *"My Brother Esau Is a Hairy Man": Hair and Identity in Ancient Israel* (New York: Oxford University Press, 2008).

35. Mary Ann Tolbert, "Social, Sociological, and Anthropological Methods," in *Searching the Scriptures*, 1:255–71, at 265.

36. Alice Walker coined the term (*In Search of Our Mothers' Gardens: Womanist Prose* [New York: Harcourt Brace Jovanovich, 1967, 1983]). See also Katie Geneva Cannon, "The Emergence of Black Feminist Consciousness," in *Feminist Interpretation of the Bible*, ed. Letty M. Russell (Philadelphia: Westminster, 1985), 30–40; Renita J. Weems, *Just a Sister Away: A Womanist Vision of Women's Relationships in the Bible* (San Diego: Lura Media, 1988); Nyasha Junior, *An Introduction to Womanist Biblical Interpretation* (Louisville: Westminster John Knox, 2015).

Spanish for "woman").[37] Others prefer to be called "Latina feminists."[38] As a gender-neutral or nonbinary alternative, many today use Latinx or Latine. *Mujeristas*, Latina and Latine feminists emphasize that the context for their theologizing is *mestizaje* and *mulatez* (racial and cultural mixture), done *en conjunto* (in community), with *lo cotidiano* (everyday lived experience) of Latina women as starting points for theological reflection and the encounter with the divine. Intercultural analysis has become an indispensable tool for working toward justice for women at the global level.[39]

Some feminists are among those who have developed interpretations from the perspectives of lesbian, gay, bisexual, transgender, queer and/or questioning, intersex, asexual, and other ways people choose to identify (LGBTQIA+). These approaches focus on issues of sexual identity and use various reading strategies. Some point out the ways in which categories that emerged in recent centuries are applied anachronistically to biblical texts to make modern-day judgments. Others show how the Bible is silent on contemporary issues about sexual identity. Still others examine same-sex relationships in the Bible by figures such as Ruth and Naomi or David and Jonathan. In recent years, queer theory has emerged; it emphasizes the blurriness of boundaries not just of sexual identity but also of gender roles. Queer critics often focus on texts in which figures transgress what is traditionally considered proper gender behavior.[40]

37. Ada María Isasi-Díaz (*Mujerista Theology: A Theology for the Twenty-First Century* [Maryknoll, NY: Orbis Books, 1996]) is credited with coining the term.

38. E.g., María Pilar Aquino, Daisy L. Machado, and Jeanette Rodríguez, eds., *A Reader in Latina Feminist Theology* (Austin: University of Texas Press, 2002).

39. See, e.g., María Pilar Aquino and María José Rosado-Nunes, eds., *Feminist Intercultural Theology: Latina Explorations for a Just World*, Studies in Latino/a Catholicism (Maryknoll, NY: Orbis Books, 2007). See also Michelle A. Gonzalez, "Latina Feminist Theology: Past, Present, and Future," *JFSR* 25 (2009): 150–55. See also Elisabeth Schüssler Fiorenza, ed., *Feminist Biblical Studies in the Twentieth Century: Scholarship and Movement*, BW 9.1 (Atlanta: SBL Press, 2014), who charts feminist studies around the globe as well as emerging feminist methodologies.

40. See, e.g., Bernadette J. Brooten, *Love Between Women: Early Christian Responses to Female Homoeroticism* (Chicago: University of Chicago Press, 1996); Mary Rose D'Angelo, "Women Partners in the New Testament," *JFSR* 6 (1990): 65–86; Deirdre J. Good, "Reading Strategies for Biblical Passages on Same-Sex Relations," *Theology and Sexuality* 7 (1997): 70–82; Deryn Guest, *When Deborah Met Jael: Lesbian Biblical Hermeneutics* (London: SCM, 2005); Teresa J. Hornsby and Ken Stone, eds., *Bible Trouble: Queer Reading at the Boundaries of Biblical Scholarship*, SemeiaSt 67 (Atlanta: SBL, 2011); Joseph A. Marchal, "Queer Studies and Critical Masculinity Studies in Feminist Biblical Studies," in *Feminist Biblical Studies in the Twentieth Century*, ed. Schüssler Fiorenza, 261–80.

Feminists have also been engaged in studying the reception history of the text[41] and have engaged in studies in the emerging fields of disability theory and of children in the Bible.

Feminists also recognize that the struggle for women's equality and dignity is intimately connected with the struggle for respect for Earth and for the whole of the cosmos. Ecofeminists interpret Scripture in ways that highlight the link between human domination of nature and male subjugation of women. They show how anthropocentric ways of interpreting the Bible have overlooked or dismissed Earth and Earth community. They invite readers to identify not only with human characters in the biblical narrative but also with other Earth creatures and domains of nature, especially those that are the object of injustice. Some use creative imagination to retrieve the interests of Earth implicit in the narrative and enable Earth to speak.[42]

Biblical Authority

By the late nineteenth century, some feminists, such as Elizabeth Cady Stanton, began to question openly whether the Bible could continue to be regarded as authoritative for women. They viewed the Bible itself as the source of women's oppression, and some rejected its sacred origin and saving claims. Some decided that the Bible and the religious traditions that enshrine it are too thoroughly saturated with androcentrism and patriarchy to be redeemable.[43]

In the Wisdom Commentary series, questions such as these may be raised, but the aim of this series is not to lead readers to reject the authority of the biblical text. Rather, the aim is to promote better understanding of the contexts from which the text arose and of the rhetorical effects it has on people in contemporary contexts. Such understanding can lead to a deepening of faith, with the Bible serving as an aid to bring flourishing of life.

41. See Sharon H. Ringe, "When Women Interpret the Bible," in *Women's Bible Commentary*, ed. Carol A. Newsom, Sharon H. Ringe, and Jacqueline E. Lapsley, 3rd ed. (Louisville: Westminster John Knox, 2012), 5; Taylor and Choi, *Handbook of Women Biblical Interpreters*; Yvonne Sherwood, "Introduction," in *The Bible and Feminism: Remapping the Field*, ed. Yvonne Sherwood with Anna Fisk (New York: Oxford University Press, 2017).

42. E.g., Norman C. Habel and Peter Trudinger, *Exploring Ecological Hermeneutics*, SymS 46 (Atlanta: SBL, 2008); Mary Judith Ress, *Ecofeminism in Latin America*, Women from the Margins (Maryknoll, NY: Orbis Books, 2006).

43. E.g., Mary Daly, *Beyond God the Father: A Philosophy of Women's Liberation* (Boston: Beacon, 1985).

Language for God

Because of the ways in which the term "God" has been used to symbolize the divine in predominantly male, patriarchal, and monarchical modes, feminists have designed new ways of speaking of the divine. Some have called attention to the inadequacy of the term *God* by trying to visually destabilize our ways of thinking and speaking of the divine. Rosemary Radford Ruether proposed *God/ess*, as an unpronounceable term pointing to the unnameable understanding of the divine that transcends patriarchal limitations.[44] Some have followed traditional Jewish practice, writing *G-d*. Elisabeth Schüssler Fiorenza has adopted *G*d*.[45] Others draw on the biblical tradition to mine female and non-gender-specific metaphors and symbols.[46] In Wisdom Commentary, there is not one standard way of expressing the divine; each author will use her or his preferred ways. The one exception is that when the tetragrammaton, YHWH, the name revealed to Moses in Exodus 3:14, is used, it will be without vowels, respecting the Jewish custom of avoiding pronouncing the divine name out of reverence.

Nomenclature for the Two Testaments

In recent decades, some biblical scholars have begun to call the two Testaments of the Bible by names other than the traditional nomenclature: Old and New Testament. Some regard "Old" as derogatory, implying that it is no longer relevant or that it has been superseded. Consequently, terms like Hebrew Bible, First Testament, and Jewish Scriptures and, correspondingly, Christian Scriptures or Second Testament have come into use. There are a number of difficulties with these designations. The term "Hebrew Bible" does not take into account that parts of the Old Testament are written not in Hebrew but in Aramaic.[47] Moreover, for Roman Catholics and Eastern Orthodox believers, the Old

44. Rosemary Radford Ruether, *Sexism and God-Talk: Toward a Feminist Theology* (Boston: Beacon, 1993).

45. Elisabeth Schüssler Fiorenza, *Jesus: Miriam's Child, Sophia's Prophet; Critical Issues in Feminist Christology* (New York: Continuum, 1994), 191n3.

46. E.g., Sallie McFague, *Models of God: Theology for an Ecological, Nuclear Age* (Philadelphia: Fortress, 1987); Catherine Mowry LaCugna, *God for Us: The Trinity and Christian Life* (San Francisco: HarperCollins, 1991); Elizabeth A. Johnson, *She Who Is: The Mystery of God in Feminist Theological Discourse* (New York: Crossroad, 1992). See further Elizabeth A. Johnson, "God," in *Dictionary of Feminist Theologies*, ed. Letty M. Russell and J. Shannon Clarkson (Louisville: Westminster John Knox, 1996), 128–30.

47. Gen 31:47; Jer 10:11; Ezra 4:7–6:18; 7:12-26; Dan 2:4–7:28.

Testament includes books written in Greek—the Deuterocanonical books, considered Apocrypha by Protestants.[48] The term "Jewish Scriptures" is inadequate because these books are also sacred to Christians. Conversely, "Christian Scriptures" is not an accurate designation for the New Testament, since the Old Testament is also part of the Christian Scriptures. Using "First and Second Testament" also has difficulties, in that it can imply a hierarchy and a value judgment.[49] Jews generally use the term Tanakh, an acronym for Torah (Pentateuch), Nevi'im (Prophets), and Ketuvim (Writings).

In Wisdom Commentary, if authors choose to use a designation other than Tanakh, Old Testament, and New Testament, they will explain how they mean the term.

Translation

Modern feminist scholars recognize the complexities connected with biblical translation, as they have delved into questions about philosophy of language, how meanings are produced, and how they are culturally situated. Today it is evident that simply translating into gender-neutral formulations cannot address all the challenges presented by androcentric texts. Efforts at feminist translation must also deal with issues around authority and canonicity.[50]

Because of these complexities, the editors of the Wisdom Commentary series have chosen to use an existing translation, the New Revised Standard Version Updated Edition (NRSVue),[51] which is provided for easy reference at the top of each page of commentary. The NRSVue was produced by a team of ecumenical and interreligious scholars, is a fairly literal translation, and uses inclusive language for human beings. Brief discussions about problematic translations appear in the inserts labeled "Translation Matters." When more detailed discussions are available, these will be indicated in footnotes. In the commentary, wherever Hebrew

48. Representing the *via media* between Catholic and reformed, Anglicans generally consider the Apocrypha to be profitable, if not canonical, and utilize select Wisdom texts liturgically.

49. See Levine, *The Misunderstood Jew*, 193–99.

50. Elizabeth Castelli, "*Les Belles Infidèles*/Fidelity or Feminism? The Meanings of Feminist Biblical Translation," in *Searching the Scriptures*, 1:189–204, here 190.

51. The volumes of Wisdom Commentary produced through 2023 use the edition of NRSV published in 1989; subsequent volumes use the updated edition, NRSVue, released in 2021.

or Greek words are used, English translation is provided. In cases where a wordplay is involved, transliteration is provided to enable understanding.

Art and Poetry

Artistic expression in poetry, music, sculpture, painting, and various other modes is very important to feminist interpretation. Where possible, art and poetry are included in the print volumes of the series. In a number of instances, these are original works created for this project. Regrettably, copyright and production costs prohibit the inclusion of color photographs and other artistic work.

Glossary

Because there are a number of excellent readily available resources that provide definitions and concise explanations of terms used in feminist theological and biblical studies, this series will not include a glossary. We refer you to works such as *Dictionary of Feminist Theologies*, edited by Letty M. Russell and J. Shannon Clarkson, and volume 1 of *Searching the Scriptures*, edited by Elisabeth Schüssler Fiorenza with the assistance of Shelly Matthews. Individual authors in the Wisdom Commentary series will define the way they are using terms that may be unfamiliar.

A Concluding Word

In just a few short decades, feminist biblical studies has grown exponentially, both in the methods that have been developed and in the number of scholars who have embraced it. We realize that this series is limited and will soon need to be revised and updated. It is our hope that Wisdom Commentary, by making the best of current feminist biblical scholarship available in an accessible format to ministers, preachers, rabbis, teachers, scholars, and students, will aid all readers in their advancement toward God's vision of dignity, equality, and justice for all.

Acknowledgments

There are a great many people who have made this series possible: first, Peter Dwyer, retired director of Liturgical Press, and Hans Christoffersen, editorial director of Liturgical Press, who have believed in this project and have shepherded it since it was conceived in 2008. I am grateful to Therese L. Ratliff, the Press's director and CEO, who is now championing this project.

Editorial consultants Athalya Brenner-Idan and Elisabeth Schüssler Fiorenza have not only been an inspiration with their pioneering work but have encouraged us all along the way with their personal involvement. Volume editors Mary Ann Beavis, Mahri Leonard-Fleckman, Amy-Jill Levine, Linda M. Maloney, Song-Mi Suzie Park, Ahida Pilarski, Sarah J. Tanzer, and Lauress Wilkins Lawrence have lent their extraordinary wisdom to the shaping of the series, have used their extensive networks of relationships to secure authors and contributors, and have worked tirelessly to guide their work to completion. Others who have contributed greatly to the shaping of the project are Linda M. Day, Carol J. Dempsey, Gina Hens-Piazza, Mignon Jacobs, Seung Ai Yang, and Barbara E. Bowe of blessed memory (d. 2010). Editorial and research assistant Susan M. Hickman provided invaluable support with administrative details and arrangements at the outset of the project. I am grateful to Brian Eisenschenk and Christine Henderson who assisted Susan Hickman with the Wiki. I am especially thankful to Lauren L. Murphy and Justin Howell for their work in copyediting; and to the staff at Liturgical Press, especially Colleen Stiller, retired production manager; Angie Steffens, production manager; Elizabeth Elin, production coordinator; Stephanie Lancour, production editor; Julie Surma, desktop publisher; and Tara Durheim, marketing director.

Authors' Introduction

In 1982, the Weather Girls recorded their hit disco single "It's Raining Men." This song gained international acclaim for joyfully declaring an unprecedented surplus of men. While the Weather Girls likely did not have Ezra–Nehemiah or an ancient audience in mind when composing the lyrics, this catchy tune prompts reflection on gender, power, and privilege within these biblical texts. Considering the scarcity of women in Ezra–Nehemiah, we pondered how to approach a feminist reading of these books. Admittedly, we were not aiming to identify explicitly female aspects of the text. Instead, we wanted to uncover any thread that could shed light on women's roles, behaviors, or perspectives beyond their roles as wives and daughters during the period in which Ezra–Nehemiah was written. For instance, how do we interpret the presence of the prophet Noadiah (Neh 6:14)? What do the depictions of foreign wives reveal about the status of women in general? Despite women often being overlooked in narratives of nation formation, are there hints in Ezra–Nehemiah suggesting otherwise? Our exploration extends beyond a narrow focus on women to include considerations of class and ethnicity, particularly concerning justice for both women and men. We aim to uncover what Ezra–Nehemiah communicates about power, privilege, and difference. As we read Ezra–Nehemiah we seek to take into account the challenges raised by Amy-Jill Levine to ensure that our readings are good for Jews as well as for women.[1] Levine recounts

1. Amy-Jill Levine, "Multiculturalism, Women's Studies, and Anti-Judaism," *JFSR* 19 (2003): 119.

the dangers multicultural readers of biblical texts face when we fail to take into account the voices of all marginalized communities. Ezra–Nehemiah, as a formative text of Judaism, deserves a reading that seeks to avoid "culturally inscribed bigotry."[2]

Yet, we must admit that we struggled with writing this commentary. How much can one say about the endless number of lists and genealogies? Sometimes we did not like the characters or the texts of Ezra or Nehemiah. We spent long hours conversing about how to tease out the intersectional aspects of an extremely patriarchal text. Each new question either raised other questions, which the text did not necessarily answer, or made us uncomfortable. For example, how do we deal with the possibility that the text advocates for creating homeless children, women, and men with its threat to remove foreigners and their families from the community? At times, we grappled with issues of justice when leaders seemed indifferent to the effects of their actions on their communities. As scholars, preachers, and professors, we encountered the challenge of deciphering how the writers addressed the cultural and religious concerns of their day while acknowledging that issues of belonging, identity, and religious solidarity amid partisan politics remain relevant today. We approach this work with the awareness that it will be utilized by a contemporary audience, including preachers, teachers, and laity, who will employ it to illuminate their existing social and religious conditions as well as foster hope within their respective spheres of influence. The task has been daunting as our own biases were revealed while interpreting Ezra–Nehemiah for the communities in which we serve. We journeyed with those returning as they sought answers on how to be God's people renewed in their ancestral land and experienced anew a deep appreciation for how God renews and illuminates what it means to remain faithful during periods of social, political, and religious upheaval and transformation.

Feminist Method and What Makes This a Feminist Commentary

At present, scholars have not undertaken the challenge of reading the entirety of Ezra–Nehemiah through a feminist or womanist lens with concern not only for gender but also for intersectional connections (e.g., gender, sexuality, race, class, ethnicity, ableness). In 2005, Roland Boer noticed this and criticized feminists for ignoring Ezra–Nehemiah and 1 Chronicles and

2. Levine, "Multiculturalism," 128.

2 Chronicles due to the lack of appearances of women to explore in these texts.[3] He lamented feminist interpreters' "hermeneutics of recovery," where they engage in "micro-readings" of those women present rather than grapple with women's absence from the text and its historical context.[4] Julie Kelso, writing in 2013, joined Boer in criticizing feminist readings that latch on to women in Ezra–Nehemiah and ignore that women are intentionally written out of the text—the society has no need for women.[5] Kelso noted, like Boer, that feminists have not sustained an argument on the entire book of Ezra–Nehemiah, nor have they called out the silencing of women.[6] Those scholars who do engage in feminist readings of these books engage in what Kelso called "at-first-glance-ism," which recognizes the absence of women and then highlights women present in the text to paint a portrait of the importance of women in the text.[7] Reading biblical texts in churches and synagogues, Kelso suggested, influences feminist interpreters who want the texts to empower women. In reality, she argued, when women in these texts are heard they often "mimic the masculine."[8] Therefore, Kelso called on feminists to analyze how women's absence from these texts silences women and maintains the patriarchy.

Given that feminist discourses involving gender predominantly emphasize the feminine, we acknowledge that such discussions are incomplete absent a critical examination of masculinity since neither may be understood apart from the other. Moreover, patriarchal, hierarchal, or dominant structures that encode various forms of masculinity over and against this dichotomy tend to do so at the expense of women. In other words, the gendered aspects of femininity are heightened mainly because the gendered aspects of masculinity are hidden or culturally encoded as normative. Thus, we concur with Todd Reeser that the tendency to normalize masculinity as nongendered or unmarked and therefore absent in discussions of gender has detracted from understanding how

3. Roland Boer, "No Road: On the Absence of Feminist Criticism of Ezra–Nehemiah," in *Her Master's Tools? Feminist and Postcolonial Engagements of Historical-Critical Discourse*, ed. Carolyn Stichele and Todd Penner, GPBS 9 (Atlanta: SBL, 2005), 233.

4. Boer, "No Road," 234–35.

5. Julie Kelso, "Reading Silence: The Books of Chronicles and Ezra–Nehemiah, and the Relative Absence of a Feminist Interpretive History," in *Feminist Interpretation of the Hebrew Bible in Retrospect*, ed. Suzanne Scholz, Recent Research in Biblical Studies 5 (Sheffield: Sheffield Phoenix, 2013), 268–69.

6. Kelso, "Reading Silence," 269.

7. Kelso, "Reading Silence," 269.

8. Kelso, "Reading Silence," 289.

masculinity as a "stable and impermeable surface"[9] functions discursively as a form of domination in the guise of patriarchy. Here too, we are acutely aware of the multiplicity of definitions and tensions that arise when broaching the subject of maleness and masculine identity (or multiple masculine identities). Nevertheless, we are interested in one particular form of masculinity, which, as an embedded ideological construct, serves conceivably as the dominant model for maleness, national identity, and cultural coding in Ezra–Nehemiah. According to R.W. Connell, hegemonic masculinity refers to the "hegemonic position in a given pattern of gender relations."[10] Hegemony, thus understood, refers to the ideological, economic, cultural, and political interests of a dominant majority or groups who, by the status afforded to them in society, represent a particular idea that has become universally accepted by society. As a form of cultural dominance in Ezra–Nehemiah, the concept of hegemonic masculinity suggests that the textual ambivalence toward women, the emasculation of powerful women, or the construction of foreign women (and men, particularly eunuchs) as others occur out of a paradigm that idealizes and privileges this particular form of masculinity from which others are then measured and recast.

While we do not overtly address hegemonic masculinity as a theme we explore in Ezra–Nehemiah, this dynamic informs our reading and analysis. For us, it is important for our feminist reading and analysis that we address where, how, and in what way these books speak to issues of marginalization, vulnerability, and the power dynamics encoded in the final form of the text. We are deeply indebted to and grateful for the impact that gender studies have made on the field of biblical studies and the vast body of scholarship now available by gifted men and women who laboriously provide fresh insights on a complex subject.

History of Feminist and Gender Interpretations of Ezra–Nehemiah

General Readings

Tamara Cohn Eskenazi is among the first to provide a feminist reading of Ezra–Nehemiah in *The Women's Bible Commentary* (3rd ed.) and in her

9. Todd W. Reeser, *Masculinities in Theory: An Introduction*, 2nd ed. (Newark: Wiley-Blackwell, 2023), 9–11.

10. Raewyn Connell, *Masculinities* (Berkeley: University of California Press, 2005).

article "Out from the Shadows: Biblical Women in the Postexilic Era" (1992).[11] In both of these works, she recovers the women hidden in the texts of Ezra–Nehemiah and explores the Elephantine documents that suggest Jewish women in Persian Period Elephantine were property owners, which, she says, explains the fear of mixed marriages that allowed foreign women to inherit the land. Eskenazi's research, in spite of criticisms from Julie Kelso and Roland Boer (see above), provides a foundation for the few feminist readings of these books. Eskenazi's works focus more fully on the women in Ezra than in Nehemiah; Brigitte Rabarijaona makes up for this gap with her focus on the women embedded in Nehemiah's narrative.[12] Like Eskenazi, Christiane Karrer-Grube provides a feminist-theological reading of Ezra–Nehemiah that recovers the women who hide behind the narrative.[13] She intends to expose the weaknesses of Israel's identity that are based on separating out "others" who threaten the well-being of the community but instead undermine the community by breaking up families.[14]

Many other feminist and womanist interpreters have tackled the expulsion of foreign women in Ezra 9–10 and Nehemiah 13:23-29. Willa M. Johnson draws on Mary Douglas and other anthropologists to elucidate the importance of boundaries, especially the purity codes, for defining community and bringing order out of chaos in a chaotic postexilic Judah.[15] She argues that to maintain the purity of the community and not defile the "holy seed," the community must expel the foreign wives. Intermarriages are also forbidden to ensure that land does not transfer out of the repatriate community. Johnson reads Ezra 9–10 in tandem with

11. See Tamara Cohn Eskenazi, "Ezra–Nehemiah," in *Women's Bible Commentary*, ed. Carol A. Newsom, Sharon H. Ringe, Jaqueline Lapsley, 3rd ed. (Louisville: Westminster John Knox, 2012), 192–200; "Out from the Shadows: Biblical Women in the Postexilic Era," *JSOT* 54 (1992): 25–43.

12. Brigitte Rabarijaona, "Women in the Book of Nehemia," *Gender Agenda Matters: Papers of the "Feminist Section" of the International Meetings of The Society of Biblical Literature*, ed. Irmtraud Fischer and Daniela Feichtinger (Newcastle-upon-Tyne: Cambridge Scholars, 2015), 115–24.

13. Christiane Karrer-Grube, "Ezra and Nehemiah: The Return of the Others," in *Feminist Biblical Interpretation: A Compendium of Critical Commentary on the Books of the Bible and Related Literature*, ed. Luise Schottroff and Marie-Theres Wacker (Grand Rapids: Eerdmans, 2012), 192–206.

14. Kelso, "Reading Silence," 277.

15. Willa M. Johnson, *The Holy Seed Has Been Defiled: The Interethnic Marriage Dilemma in Ezra 9–10*, Hebrew Bible Monographs 33 (Sheffield: Sheffield Phoenix, 2011), 22–25.

modern discussions on race and ethnicity. Likewise, Harold Washington underscores the importance of purity laws in building identity but points out that, when society imposes these codes, women bear the burden of these laws.[16] Washington opines that by aligning the land with menstruating women with its use of *niddah* (unclean), the term for menstrual impurity (Ezra 9:11), the text parallels the foreign women and the polluted land and implies that neither one of them is fit for receiving the holy seed. Eva Feinstein understands the concerns of Ezra's community that the foreign women are not just polluted but are perpetually unclean and contaminate the community.[17] Claudia Camp argues that Ezra constructs foreignness as a strange woman who is dangerous to male identity and the patriliny.[18]

While the previous readings focus more fully on how Ezra 9–10 and Nehemiah 13:29 function in their ancient contexts, several scholars provide a cautionary message based on how applications of these texts to contemporary contexts have led to injustice. For example, Cheryl Anderson parallels Ezra–Nehemiah's expulsion of the wives from the Jewish community with the anti-miscegenation laws in the United States that forbade intermarriage between African Americans and whites, where African Americans were those usually sent away.[19] Gerri Snyman, reading Ezra–Nehemiah with apartheid, critiques South African scholars like J.N.K Mugambi who turn to Ezra–Nehemiah "benevolently," as a helpful model for reconstructing the new nation.[20] Like Anderson, Snyman raises parallels to the oppressive casting out of the wives with similar laws in

16. Harold C. Washington, "Israel's Holy Seed and the Foreign Women of Ezra–Nehemiah: A Kristevan Reading," *BibInt* 11 (2003): 429.

17. Eve Levavi Feinstein, *Sexual Pollution in the Hebrew Bible* (Oxford: Oxford University Press, 2014).

18. Claudia Camp, "Feminist- and Gender-Critical Perspectives on the Biblical Ideology of Intermarriage," in *Mixed Marriages: Intermarriages and Group Identity in the Second Temple Period*, ed. Christian Frevel, LHBOTS 547 (New York: T&T Clark, 2011), 303–15.

19. Cheryl Anderson, "Reflections in an Interethnic/Racial Era on Interethnic/Racial Marriage in Ezra," in *They Were All Together in One Place? Toward Minority Biblical Criticism*, ed. Randall C. Bailey, Tat-Siong Benny Liew, and Fernando F. Segovia, SemeiaSt 57 (Atlanta: SBL, 2009), 47–64.

20. Gerrie Snyman, "Collective Memory and Coloniality of Being, and Power as a Hermeneutical Framework: A Partialized Reading of Ezra–Nehemiah," in *Postcolonial Perspectives in African Biblical Interpretation*, ed. Andrew M. Mbuvi, Musa W. Dube, and Dora Mbuwayesango, GPBS 13 (Atlanta: SBL, 2012), 359–85.

apartheid South Africa, like the Prohibition of Mixed Marriages Act #55 of 1949 and the Immorality Amendment Act #21 of 1950 that tightened the apartheid system.[21] Reading the text benevolently justifies the actions of the colonial power, such as its racism, nationalism, religious intolerance, language requirements, and other oppressive strategies, basically rendering all the reconstruction projects "questionable."[22] Further, Robert Wafawanaka considers the entire narrative of Ezra–Nehemiah as a warning against intolerance. He suggests that the genocide in Rwanda and Burundi stems partly from the culture's tribalism and focus on differences. He writes: "One can argue that identity creates the very problem it seeks to avoid."[23] Grace Ji-Sun Kim parallels the expulsion of the foreign women in Ezra–Nehemiah with the exclusion and inhospitable treatment of Asian American women who, treated as "second-class citizens" or "perpetual foreigners," often feel unwelcome in North America.[24]

Other Readings

Wilda Gafney offers insight on the prophet Noadiah (Neh 6:14) while admitting the scarcity of biblical evidence that might develop who she is and what she accomplishes.[25] Gafney speculates that Noadiah is a prophet who opposes Nehemiah's policies, like the expulsion of women and children.[26] Further, she might be a leader or "mother" of a prophetic

21. Snyman, "Collective Memory," 362.

22. Snyman, "Collective Memory," 371, 382. Elelwani Farisani, writing from the same social context, critiques proponents of those drawing on Ezra–Nehemiah for their reconstructionist theology because they fail to expose the ideology of the text and how this biblical text suppresses the voices of the peoples of the land ("The Ideologically Based Use of Ezra–Nehemiah in a Quest for an African Theology of Reconstruction," in Mbuvi, Dube, and Mbuwayesango, eds., *Postcolonial Perspectives in African Biblical Interpretation*, 331–47). See editors' reflections on ideological-based interpretations in Bailey, Liew, and Segovia, eds., *They Were All Together in One Place?*, 47–64.

23. Robert Wafawanaka, "In Quest of Survival: The Implications of the Reconstruction Theology of Ezra–Nehemiah," in Mbuvi, Dube, and Mbuwayesango, eds., *Postcolonial Perspectives in African Biblical Interpretation*, 357.

24. Grace Ji-Sun Kim, "Foreign Women: Ezra, Intermarriage and Asian American Women's Identity," *Feminist Theology: The Journal of the Britain & Ireland School of Feminist Theology* 22 (2014): 241–52, https://doi.org/10.1177/0966735014523200.

25. Wilda C. Gafney, *Daughters of Miriam: Women Prophets in Ancient Israel* (Minneapolis: Fortress, 2008), 111–14.

26. Gafney, *Daughters of Miriam*, 111–12.

guild who has the power to undermine Nehemiah's agenda and frightens Nehemiah enough that he prays for God's intervention.[27]

Queer Readings of Ezra–Nehemiah

Michael Piazza, Ron Stanley, and Durrell Watkins offer queer readings of Ezra–Nehemiah.[28] Michael Piazza is the senior pastor of Cathedral of Hope, a gay and lesbian megachurch founded in Dallas in 1970. He reads Nehemiah as a model for servant leadership in the midst of the hostility and woundedness experienced by both Nehemiah's community and the contemporary queer community. Nehemiah's status as a cupbearer, suggesting he was a eunuch, provides an intersection with the queer community, who are often excluded from the wider church community.[29]

Ron Stanley engages with scholarship that supports the claim that Nehemiah was a eunuch because most cupbearers in Persia were. This makes Nehemiah a sexual outcast.[30] Stanley suggests that Nehemiah's preoccupation with being remembered (Neh 5:19; 13:14, 22, 31) stems from his fear of being forgotten after his death due to his gender and sexual status in a culture where legacy was typically passed down through progeny. Stanley reminds us, however, that faithful eunuchs were assured that they would be remembered as they received an everlasting name that was better than "sons and daughters" (Isa 56:4-5). Further, Nehemiah, the eunuch, is one of the "model leaders of the First Testament" who inspired the people to restore the city of Jerusalem.[31]

Durrell Watkins also designates Nehemiah as a eunuch and queer character who "comes out" when he calls himself a cupbearer.[32] He reads the expulsion of the foreign wives and children with expulsions experienced by many LGBTQ+ people today: "But what is also true is that LGBTQ+ people know what it is to be excluded from families, rejected from wor-

27. Gafney, *Daughters of Miriam*, 113–14.

28. Michael Piazza, "Nehemiah as a Queer Model for Servant Leadership," in *Take Back the Word: A Queer Reading of the Bible*, ed. Robert Goss and Mona West (Cleveland: Pilgrim Press, 2000), 115–23; Ron L. Stanley, "Ezra–Nehemiah," in *The Queer Bible Commentary*, vol. 1, ed. Deryn Guest et al. (London: SCM, 2006), 268–77; Durrell Watkins, "Ezra–Nehemiah," in *The Queer Bible Commentary*, ed. Mona West and Robert Shore-Goss, 2nd ed. (London: SCM, 2022), 235–41.

29. Piazza, "Nehemiah as a Queer Model," 113.

30. Stanley, "Ezra–Nehemiah," 271.

31. Stanley, "Ezra–Nehemiah," 275.

32. Watkins, "Ezra–Nehemiah," 239.

shipping communities, and denied marriage because 'religion' says they somehow pose a threat to tradition, to culture, or to social stability."[33] While recognizing Nehemiah's accomplishment of rebuilding Jerusalem, he wishes that he had liberated the people rather than destroyed families and held to unhelpful traditions. A queer reader is called to look beyond this to compassion and awareness of those harmed or excluded in the community and to respond with "a love ethic and a vision that affirms the sacred value of every child of God."[34]

While the feminist and intersectional scholarship that exists on Ezra–Nehemiah is helpful, we would have liked to draw on others who read the entire text with an intersectional lens. Recouping the narratives of women hiding behind the text is helpful and appreciated, but there is so much more left to do to construct rich feminist readings.

Ezra–Nehemiah in Jewish and Christian Worship and Prayer

Ezra–Nehemiah continues where 2 Chronicles leaves off, yet its canonical placement differs in Jewish and Christian traditions. In Judaism, Ezra–Nehemiah is part of the third section of the Tanakh: Torah (Law), Nevi'im (Prophets), and Ketuvim (Writings). The Writings are biblical books composed of many different genres (e.g., songs, theodicy, wisdom). While the Tanakh concludes with Chronicles, some medieval manuscripts place Ezra–Nehemiah at the end of the canon, where Nehemiah's call to be remembered for his good (טוב) actions (Neh 13:31) harks back to Genesis 1–2, where creation is good (טוב), creating a "sense of completion."[35] The Christian canon places Ezra–Nehemiah after 2 Chronicles among the historical writings, which constructs a sense of historical chronology. For Judaism and Christianity, the books recount theological history.

The New Testament does not quote either Ezra or Nehemiah, yet there are traditions about both of these men in the deuterocanonical texts and in the traditions of Judaism. Second Maccabees 2:13 credits Nehemiah with founding a library that includes books about the kings, prophets, and the writings of David, as well as kings' letters regarding votive offering. When Nehemiah is unable to secure some of the altar fire hidden

33. Watkins, "Ezra–Nehemiah," 237.

34. Watkins, "Ezra–Nehemiah," 241.

35. Douglas Knight and Amy-Jill Levine, *The Meaning of the Bible: What the Jewish Scriptures and Christian Old Testament Can Teach Us* (New York: HarperOne, 2011), 47.

by his ancestors, he orders the thick liquid (remnant of the fire) to be brought back and used instead (2 Macc 1:20-21). Sirach praises Nehemiah's building projects but ignores Ezra's accomplishments (Sir 49:13).

In Jewish traditions Ezra is the wise scribe and the creator of the Sanhedrin, or court system.[36] Ezra is credited with reading and preserving the Torah that might have been forgotten.[37] According to the *Mishnah Torah* ("Prayer and the Priestly Blessing"), Ezra continues Moses's tradition of praying facing the Jerusalem Temple from where people live.[38] Further, the Jerusalem Talmud describes how the fixed days for the Torah reading is set (Monday, Thursday, Shabbat).[39] To make prayer available to those speaking different languages, Ezra sets up eighteen sequential blessings—the first three praises, the last three thanksgiving, and the middle prayers requests of the community.[40] Ezra and his council also designated the three daily prayers—the morning prayer (Shacharit), the afternoon prayer (Minchah), and the evening prayer that is not obligatory—and the prayers recited at Sabbath, festivals, new moons, and Yom Kippur.[41]

Within Christianity, Ezra–Nehemiah are mostly absent in the Roman Catholic and Revised Common Lectionary (RCL) three-year cycles. Ezra's reading of the law (Neh 8:1-10) appears in Year C as a lection in Epiphany, the manifestation of the Lord. This text is read along with Luke 4:14-21 in the RCL, which emphasizes Jesus as the fulfillment of this Scripture in Isaiah 61:1-2.[42] Much of Nehemiah's communal prayer, often attributed to Ezra (Neh 9:6-37), appears only in the Episcopal lectionary.

36. Eran Viezel, "Ezra (Book and Person), Rabbinic Judaism," *Encyclopedia of the Bible and Its Reception*, vol. 8, ed. Brennan Breed et al. (Berlin: de Gruyter, 2014), 632–34.

37. Viezel, "Ezra (Book and Person)," 635.

38. Maimonides (Rambam), "Mishnah Torah: The Prayer and the Priestly Blessing 1," *Sefaria*, https://www.sefaria.org/Mishneh_Torah%2C_Prayer_and_the_Priestly_Blessing.1.5?lang=bi.

39. "Jerusalem Talmud Megillah 4:1-3," *Sefaria*, https://www.sefaria.org/Jerusalem_Talmud_Megillah.4.1.3?lang=bi.

40. Maimonides (Rambam), "Mishnah Torah: The Prayer and the Priestly Blessing 1."

41. Maimonides (Rambam), "Mishnah Torah: The Prayer and the Priestly Blessing 1." We offer thanks to Rabbi Michael Singer of Brith Sholom (Bethlehem, PA) for directing us to these sources. In addition, in the tradition, Ezra is responsible for the presence in worship of the two prayers, the Amidah and Shema (see Megillah 17b), *Sefaria*, https://www.sefaria.org/Megillah.17b?lang=bi.

42. Readings for the following lectionaries: Revised Common, Roman Catholic, Episcopal, Lutheran, and United Methodist in *The Text This Week. Lectionary, Scripture*

Nehemiah 9:6-15 is a lection for Easter Year A and is a part of the prayer that recounts God's acts of liberation for the people spanning creation through the exodus. Later in liturgical Year A (Proper 13A/Ordinary Time 18A) the portion of the prayer that indicts the ancestors for their unfaithfulness and remembers God's mercy for them is read (Neh 9:16-20).[43] Ezra and Nehemiah are venerated in the Roman Catholic Church and their feast day is July 13.[44] These two biblical persons are venerated by the Eastern Orthodox Church on the Sunday of the Forefathers (December 17).[45] So Ezra and Nehemiah have a place in Christian worship, but they do not have a very strong presence.

What Do We Call Them?

Here, we use the term "repatriates" as a generic descriptor that refers to exilic groups returning to Judah and the surrounding territories. This designation is to be distinguished from the Hebrew גלה, *golah* which refers to a specific group of exilic returnees.[46] At times, we use these terms interchangeably when a clear distinction is not possible. The terms used to define the territory and returnees vary across different Bible translations of Ezra–Nehemiah. Others have noted the problems of labeling and names in these books. Do we call them Judeans, Judahites, or Jews? Do we refer to the repatriates' homeland as Judah or Yehud? Yehud is the name in Aramaic of the Babylonian and Persian provinces that include most of the previous Kingdom of Judah. We chose to follow the NRSVue and refer to this territory as Judah. Are they the same group labeled "the people of the land" or "Israel"? The term "Jews," traditionally used to refer to "the people" or "Israel," poses some challenges in interpretation. The Hebrew word יהודים (*yehûdîm*), plural of יהודי (*yehûdî*), the Aramaic יהודיא (*yehûdāyēʾ*), and the Greek Ἰουδαῖος (*Ioudaios*) have multiple meanings, including residents of Judah, descendants of Judah,

Study, Worship Links, and Resources http://www.textweek.com/2_chron_neh_esther.htm, accessed December 30, 2024.

43. The Episcopal Lectionary, "Scriptures for Nehemiah," *The Text This Week*, http://www.textweek.com/2_chron_neh_esther.htm, accessed December 30, 2024.

44. Nehemiah and Ezra share the same feast day of July 13; Vatican, "Saint Esdras, Scribe," https://www.vaticannews.va/en/saints/07/13.html.

45. Orthodox Church of America, "Lives of All Saints Commemorated on December 17th," https://www.oca.org/saints/all-lives/2000/12/17.

46. The word "repatriates" does not appear in the text. We use this term to differentiate between the *golah* group that is named in the text and the other returnees.

and members of the tribe of Judah. Some scholars criticize the use of the word "Jews" before the second century BCE, arguing that it is anachronistic and more of a religious term than "Judahites," "Yehudites," or "Judeans," which capture ethnic or geographic designations.[47] Noting the significance of terminology for Jewish and Christian communities, we have chosen to use the terms "Jew/Jews" and "Israel/Israelites," respectively, throughout our analysis as translated in the NRSVue. Similarly, we follow the NRSVue to be consistent in our use of language for God. Here, we use "Lord" for *Adonai* (in place of the tetragrammaton YHWH) and "God" for *Elohim*.

Finally, a word on the terminology for the entire corpus of books referred to interchangeably as the Old Testament, Hebrew Bible, and First Testament. Concerning the Old Testament, Amy-Jill Levine and Marc Zvi Brettler comment,

> Only Christians have an "Old Testament," which itself differs among the various Christian communions. Jews have the Tanakh, and although the Old Testament and Tanakh share books, the communities interpret the shared verses differently. The Old Testament and the Tanakh are not, today for Christians and Jews, self-standing books. Christians read their Old Testament through the lens of the New Testament, and Jews read the Tanakh through the lens of postbiblical Jewish commentaries.[48]

We are also mindful that these works are the Sacred Scriptures of two great religious traditions: Judaism and Christianity. We seek to honor them as such, while also remaining faithful to the Christian traditions to which we both belong. To avoid what on the surface could be interpreted as a misrepresentation of the Old Testament as pejoratively Christian (the new superseding the old), some use the term "Hebrew Bible," given the language from which it emerges, which is also not without problems (what do we do with the Aramaic portions in Ezra?). Christopher Seitz rejects this titling, suggesting, "On this view, 'Hebrew Bible' is no more an inherently Jewish term than a Christian term. It might be better to refer to it as a minimal term, since it imposes very little (and some of what

47. For those arguing this position, see Shaye J. D. Cohen, *The Beginnings of Jewishness: Boundaries, Varieties, Uncertainties*, HCS 31 (Berkeley: University of California Press, 1999), 104; Tamara Cohn Eskenazi, *Ezra: A New Translation with Introduction and Commentary*, AB 14A (New Haven: Yale University Press, 2023), 19–20.

48. Amy-Jill Levine and Marc Zvi Brettler, *The Bible With and Without Jesus: How Jews and Christians Read the Same Stories Differently* (New York: HarperOne, 2020), 3.

it imposes, as we have seen, is inaccurate)."[49] Replacing the label First Testament for Old Testament is meant to remove the negative connotation of the word "old." We suspect that faith communities will continue to employ the labels that are familiar and comfortable for them. Here, following Levine and Brettler, we prefer and use the label "Scriptures of ancient Israel" recognizing that it too is not without its own problems as well.

Summarizing the Narrative of Ezra–Nehemiah

The narrative of Ezra–Nehemiah is a story of return, rebuilding, and restoration. It is the story of homecomings and new beginnings. Set within the Persian period, the narrative unfolds from King Cyrus's edict allowing exiled Jews to return to Judah to rebuild the temple in Jerusalem, to Nehemiah's reconstruction of Jerusalem's walls and infrastructure during the reign of King Darius. These reconstruction activities are not merely physical acts but also acts with religious import. As each project concludes (e.g., the altar, the foundation, the temple, and the walls of Jerusalem), the repatriates reaffirm the teaching of the Torah and celebrate the traditions of their ancestral past. Each activity represents the people's recommitment to their covenant with God and the recentering of religious life in their community. As Tamara Cohn Eskenazi observes, "In narrating these events, EN emphasizes the role of the people as the chief human agents, the power of documents as sources of authority, and the expansion of sanctity from the temple to the community and to Jerusalem as a whole."[50] Yet, their efforts are not without struggle and controversy as the repatriates encounter opposition from without and within, and overcome the challenges of returning to a homeland that has changed in their absence. The overall portrait of a community striving to reclaim and redefine their place in their ancestral homeland after a period of disruption and displacement speaks to the enduring resilience and legacy of both the people and the book.

Nevertheless, these books end with an emphasis on foreign women and their danger to the newly reconstituted Jewish community. The

49. Christopher R. Seitz, "Old Testament or Hebrew Bible? Some Theological Considerations," *ProEccl* 5 (1996): 6. See also Eugene Fisher's cogent response to Seitz, Eugene J. Fisher, "Hebrew Bible or Old Testament: A Response to Christopher Seitz," *ProEccl* 6 (1997): 133–36.

50. Eskenazi, *Ezra*, 4. Eskenazi abbreviates Ezra–Nehemiah as EN.

concern with identity is essential to Ezra–Nehemiah. We acknowledge, however, that constructing Jewish identity in the Persian period from the Bible in general is somewhat problematic. By this period, Jewish communities flourished in Babylon, Judah, and Egypt. We do not assume that designations of "Israel" and "Israelite" refer solely to Ezra and Nehemiah's group since the term גלה in Ezra 6:19; 8:35; and Nehemiah 8:17 is a clear indication that this group understands itself in contradistinction to other groups and persons in the territory of Judah.[51] Elsewhere, Ezra 3 and 4 document the disputes occurring between the "people in the land" and the "returning exiles" over the rebuilding of the temple. Ezra 9–10 and Nehemiah 13 display a concern with the communal practice of exogamy and its proliferation among the priesthood. While Ezra–Nehemiah seemingly only deals with the communities in Babylon and Judah, the books still grapple with the ambiguity of being one among the many. As such, the matter of identity in Ezra–Nehemiah is complicated as are the relational dynamics that accompany its claims of religious fidelity and exclusivity. Which of these groups is the authentic bearer of the religious traditions of ancient Israel? Which group constitutes the "true" people of the Jewish deity? Given the books' concerns, disputes involving Jewish identity appear in Ezra–Nehemiah as appeals to commonly held traditions, which competing groups use to validate their positions.

While we witness the struggle of this group of returnees transitioning from an identity "based on birth" to an "identity based on religion,"[52] we also observe that this transition cannot occur without establishing boundaries of inclusion and exclusion that categorically designate some persons and groups as ineligible for membership. We recognize that reconstructions of Jewish religious identity cannot be perceived as homogeneous since not all Jews of the period(s) in question viewed themselves as sharing the same practices, beliefs, and politics.

Economics behind Ezra–Nehemiah

Several texts in Ezra–Nehemiah reflect a changing economic system under Persian rule that impacted those living in Judah. Ancient Judah's

51. Joseph Blenkinsopp, *Judaism, the First Phase: The Place of Ezra and Nehemiah in the Origins of Judaism* (Grand Rapids: Eerdmans, 2009), 34.

52. Shaye D. Cohen, *From the Maccabees to the Mishnah*, 3rd ed. (Louisville: Westminster John Knox, 2014), 136.

economy relied on agriculture, and biblical texts demonstrate the community's strong commitment to the overall welfare of its members. The community's subsistence came from farming, viticulture, ceramics and textiles, and animal husbandry. For the most part, Judeans produced what they needed and distributed products among a close-knit community like the extended family, מִשְׁפחה, or the tribe, שֵׁבט—a local kinship economy centered on the father's house (בית אב). The father's house is the smallest unit that includes extended family. The mother's house is a subset of the father's house and plays a part in this economy, especially concerning matters of marriage and matrimony.[53] When the Assyrian and Babylonian empires controlled Judah, the economic system shifted to a foreign tributary model: Judah had to pay taxes to these conquering nations. Droughts and other agricultural crises often made it difficult for families to meet their responsibilities to the Persian king, a problem that continues in Ezra–Nehemiah's context.[54] Samuel Adams proposes that references to the father's house (Ez 2:59; 7:27; Neh 7:61; 12:22) in Ezra–Nehemiah reflect a local kinship economy.[55] He goes further to suggest that the nature of the household probably expanded as other fathers' houses banded together due to a need to respond to "foreign interest in their land and its resources, tensions between returnees from exile and those who stayed in the region, urbanization (esp. later in the Second Temple period), and the need to rebuild the temple."[56]

Our understanding of the economy of Judah under Persian imperial rule has only recently emerged as archaeological evidence from this historical period has been uncovered. Ezra–Nehemiah's Judah is part of the Jewish satrapy אבר נהרה (Aramaic meaning "across the river") that likely includes Gaza, Ashdod, and Samaria. Gale Yee, drawing on Charles Carter's archaeological study of the Persian period, suggests that Judah itself was small and stretched from Bethel to the north, Hebron to the

53. For more information on this topic, see Cynthia Chapman, *The House of the Mother: The Social Roles of Maternal Kin in Biblical Hebrew Narrative and Poetry*, AYBRL (New Haven: Yale University Press, 2016).

54. Bob Becking, "Drought, Hunger, and Redistribution: A Social Economic Reading of Nehemiah 5," in *The Historian and the Bible: Essays in Honor of Lester L. Grabbe*, ed. Philip Davies, Diana Edelman, and Lester Grabbe, LHBOTS 539 (New York: T&T Clark, 2010), 141–42.

55. Samuel L. Adams, *Social and Economic Life in Second Temple Judea* (Louisville: Westminster John Knox, 2014).

56. Adams, *Social and Economic Life in Second Temple Judea*, 11.

south, and the Judean desert to the east and was relatively poor.[57] When Persia defeated the Babylonians in 539 BCE, Cyrus and his son Cambyses divided the vast empire into twenty satrapies. They appointed Persian governors who would efficiently oversee the territory, collect capital, and organize defense systems. Leo G. Perdue and Warren Carter note that "tribute, taxes and treaty" define the Persian power structure.[58]

Ezra–Nehemiah describes an elite temple administration created under the patronage of the Persian kings which privileges some members of Judah over others. Jerusalem was a shadow of its former self as a result of the Babylonian army's destruction of the city in 586 BCE and was in great need of rejuvenation that came in the form of Persian benevolence as Persian kings allowed the exiles to return to build the temple, fortify the walls, and solidify the Torah (Ezra 1; Neh 2:7-8; 8). Yet behind this great generosity lurks a Persian imperial economic agenda that partners with the temple administration of priests, gatekeepers, singers, and other officials.

The Persian Empire under Darius I (c.550–486 BCE) fully implemented a tribute and export economy that integrated standardized minted coins along with the exchange of local agriculture and goods.[59] The temple became an essential part of Persian Judah's economic system, especially under an empire that demanded taxes and tributes to support its extensive infrastructure.[60] Priests, like Ezra, wanted to revive worship in this holy space, and the Persians wanted taxes and tribute especially to feed their military needs.[61] The temple provided a central place for collecting these tributes, not only in Jerusalem's temple, but at temples throughout the Persian Empire.[62] Persian officials charged Ezra with collecting the taxes, paying Persia its due, and then keeping the excess tribute to use

57. Gale Yee, *Poor Banished Children of Eve: Women as Evil in the Hebrew Bible* (Minneapolis: Fortress, 2003), 138.

58. Leo G. Perdue and Warren Carter, *Israel and Empire: A Postcolonial History of Israel and Early Judaism*, ed. Coleman A. Baker (London: Bloomsbury T&T Clark, 2015), 108.

59. For a discussion of coinage in Persian Judah, see Peter Altmann, *Economics in Persian-Period Biblical Texts: Their Interactions with Economic Developments in the Persian Period and Earlier Biblical Traditions*, FAT 109 (Tübingen: Mohr Siebeck, 2016), 168–73.

60. Herbert R. Marbury, "Reading Persian Dominion in Nehemiah: Multivalent Language, Co-Option, Resistance, and Cultural Survival," in *The Crucial Nature of the Persian and Hellenistic Periods: Essays in Honor of Douglas A. Knight*, ed. Alice Hunt and Jon Berquist (New York: T&T Clark, 2012), 158–76.

61. Marbury, "Reading Persian Dominion in Nehemiah," 167.

62. Yee, *Poor Banished Children of Eve*, 139.

at his own discretion (Ezra 7:17-18). Yee underscores the burden that this "two-tiered mode of extraction," temple and foreign taxes, had on the poor.[63] Collecting and dispersing these taxes gave this small community of priests and leaders headquartered in Jerusalem quite a bit of power and most likely fueled the opposition, who resented being cut off from a lucrative funding source. Yet collecting these monies could only happen when citizens were committed to supporting the temple.

When the repatriate community returned to Judah, the territory was smaller and parts of Judah, like the Shephelah, belonged in other satrapies. With the revival of the pilgrimage festivals—Sukkot ("Booths"), Pesach ("Passover"), Shavuot ("Weeks")—those of Israelite descent who returned home to areas outside of Judah might have been motivated to return to Jerusalem bearing the one-third shekel temple tax (Neh 10:33-34). The priests' concern was to unify the repatriate community in order to rebuild a strong religious identity and commitment to the God of Abraham and Moses that linked tithing to the ancestral traditions and law.[64] The biblical text relates that the temple taxes went to God but in actuality the priests controlled the funds.[65] Further, the priests, Levites, singers, doorkeepers, and temple servants received privilege by being tax exempt: "We also notify you that it shall not be lawful to impose tribute, custom, or toll on any of the priests, the Levites, the singers, the doorkeepers, the temple servants, or other servants of this house of God" (Ezra 7:24). Herbert Marbury reminds us that many clergy today have similar relationships with the state as they secure faith-based money to support programs that make them simultaneously beholden to the church and government.[66] It is a difficult dance.

Economic exploitation is a serious concern in Ezra–Nehemiah. Despite the appearance of Persia's generous support of the inhabitants of Judah, Ezra assesses the harsh reality of his people: "For we are slaves; yet our God has not forsaken us in our slavery" (Ezra 9:9). As Nehemiah prays to God he laments the loss of land: "Its rich yield goes to the kings whom

63. Yee, *Poor Banished Children of Eve*, 139.

64. "We also lay on ourselves the obligation to charge ourselves yearly one-third of a shekel for the service of the house of our God: for the rows of bread, the regular grain offering, the regular burnt offering, the Sabbaths, the new moons, the appointed festivals, the sacred donations, and the sin offerings to make atonement for Israel, and for all the work of the house of our God" (Neh 10.32-33).

65. Douglas Knight, *Law, Power, and Justice in Ancient Israel*, LAI (Louisville: Westminster John Knox, 2011), 240.

66. Marbury, "Reading Persian Dominion in Nehemiah," 175.

you have set over us because of our sins; they have power also over our bodies and over our livestock at their pleasure, and we are in great distress" (Neh 9:37). Concerns with economic matters permeate these texts (e.g. Ezra 2:69; 4:20; 7:18, 22; 8:27-37; Neh 5:4, 15; 7:70-72).

The Elephantine Papyri give examples of some members in the Jewish community taking our loans in the fifth century BCE.[67] Jehohen, daughter of Meshullach, borrowed four silver shekels from Meshullum, son of Zaccur (*TAD* B3.1; B34); and Gemariah, son of Ahio, three silver shekels from PN, son of Jathma (*TAD* B4.1; B48). Both contracts attest to interest rates beginning with 5 percent on the principle the first month, seizure of property collateral after one year, and, upon the borrower's death, the transfer of the loan to the borrower's children under the same terms yet with a larger burden of debt due to the addition of outstanding interest that becomes part of the capital.[68] Other loans began at an interest rate close to 60 to 75 percent.[69] The interest rates on these loans impacted the well-being of the borrower and family.

Daniel Smith-Christopher argues that Ezra–Nehemiah can serve as a text of resistance.[70] In contrast to those who believe that Ezra and Nehemiah are in collusion with their Persian overlords, Smith-Christopher argues that the text emphasizes the sovereignty of God and resists Persian hegemony when these officials can be stirred by God (Ezra 1:1), the temple is built under God's prophetic authority and not Persia's (Ezra 5:1-2), the text emphasizes that both Ezra and Nehemiah stand, not bow, before the king, an act of resistance, and these leaders acknowledge that the people are oppressed and make changes (e.g., Neh 5 and 9).[71] He concludes:

> . . . the attitude of the editors of Ezra–Nehemiah toward their Persian overlords is neither gratitude nor warmth. Their attitude is both the

67. Bezalel Porten et al., *The Elephantine Papyri in English: Three Millennia of Cross-Cultural Continuity and Change*, 2nd ed., Studies in Near Eastern Archaeology and Civilisation 22 (Atlanta: SBL, 2011), 203–5, 256–57.

68. Porten et al., *The Elephantine Papyri in English*, 203–5, 256–57.

69. Joseph Blenkinsopp, *Ezra–Nehemiah: A Commentary*, OTL (Philadelphia: Westminster, 1988), 257. The Torah prohibits the practice of charging interest on loans taken within the Jewish community (Exod 22:25; Lev 25:35-37; Deut 23:20). The practice seems to be disregarded in the Elephantine community in the 5th century among Jews and non-Jews.

70. Daniel Smith-Christopher, *A Biblical Theology of Exile*, OBT (Minneapolis: Fortress, 2002), 45.

71. Smith-Christopher, *A Biblical Theology of Exile*, 38–45.

> realistic assessment of forced subservience, and in response, a faithful non-violent resistance to any idea that Persian power or authority is greater than God's spiritual armament of the faithful. Thus, the editors of Ezra–Nehemiah represent a subversive theology, a hidden transcript, that reserves recognition of authority to God alone, while maintaining a necessary polite demeanor to the imperial representatives.[72]

As we explore Ezra–Nehemiah, we pay attention to the economic structures, particularly the impacts these often-oppressive systems have on women and other vulnerable citizens of Judah and the possible resistance that coexists with the struggle. We will illuminate places where Ezra–Nehemiah collude with Persia's economic system as well as where it offers a word of resistance and hope for Judah's and today's stratified societies.

Women's Role in the Economy of Persian Judah

It is difficult to get a clear picture of the roles that women play in Judah's economy in the Persian period because of gaps in both the material culture and the silence of women in the books of Ezra–Nehemiah. Tamara Cohn Eskenazi sheds light on the roles that women hold within Ezra–Nehemiah. Within the list of returnees is one named Hassophereth, meaning "the female scribe," who is head of a guild and might have maintained administrative records.[73] Although there are biblical examples of feminine nouns ascribed to male subjects, Ibn Ezra, a well-known Jewish philosopher and Torah commentator (1089–1164), is among those who believe that Hassophereth was both a scribe and a woman, and the grammar supports him.[74] Thousands of female servants returned from Babylon (Ezra 2:64-65; Neh 7:67) along with female singers (Ezra 2:65; Neh 7:67). Artaxerxes's queen sits beside him and perhaps advises when Artaxerxes holds court with Nehemiah to discuss rebuilding the Jerusalem walls (Neh 2:6). Further, Shallum's daughters helped to rebuild the Jerusalem walls (Neh 3:12). Women like Noadiah, who was possibly a Judahite, who powerfully opposed Nehemiah's rebuilding mission and

72. Smith-Christopher, *A Biblical Theology of Exile*, 45.

73. Tamara Cohn Eskenazi, "Hassophereth/Sophereth," in *Women in Scripture: A Dictionary of Named and Unnamed Women in the Hebrew Bible, the Apocryphal/Deuterocanonical Books, and the New Testament*, ed. Carol Meyers, Toni Craven, and Ross Shepard Kraemer (Boston: Houghton Mifflin, 2000), 91–92.

74. Eskenazi, "Ezra–Nehemiah," 196.

intimidated him (Neh 6:14), served as prophets. Shelomith, mentioned in Ezra 8:10, could be the daughter of Zerubabbel of the lineage of King David and charged with rebuilding the temple (see 1 Chr 3:19).[75]

Roles differed between elite and non-elite women, especially since those with wealth often relied on servants to do household chores. Still, for many women, the main focus of their day would have been on procuring and preparing food for the family.[76] One of the most important staples of the diet was bread (לחם, which can also be translated as "food") and one that required a great deal of work—threshing, winnowing, pounding grain in a mortar and pestle, grinding it into flour with grinding stones, kneading the dough, and then baking it.[77] Preparing bread and other foods consumed much of the day. Women were also the primary potters, spinners and weavers of cloth and baskets, midwives, child-rearers, healthcare providers, and viticulturists, among other roles.[78] Further, biblical evidence, specifically Proverbs 31:10-31 and Aramaic papyri from Elephantine, suggests that women had economic power outside of the domestic sphere.

Ellen Davis proposes that as adult males were conscripted for military service for long periods of time, women became the heads of the households and that Proverbs 31:10-31 reflects the multiple roles women needed to take on in this new economy.[79] Proverbs 31, dated by some scholars in the Persian period, describes a woman who fulfills the aforementioned household chores but who also transacts business by buying land and food (Prov 31:14, 16) and selling merchandise (Prov 31:18, 24). This resourceful woman, an אשת חיל, "strong woman," is married to a prominent man: "Her husband is known in the city gates, taking his seat among the elders of the land" (Prov 31:23), and she has servants (Prov 31:15). This woman has a great deal of stamina and economic capital.

Other Jewish women in Elephantine had access to land and other commodities.

75. Eskenazi, "Out from the Shadows," 37–38.

76. See Adams, *Social and Economic Life in Second Temple Judea*, 43.

77. Jennie R. Ebeling, *Women's Lives in Biblical Times* (London: T&T Clark, 2010), 49–50.

78. Ebeling, *Women's Lives in Biblical Times*, 45–59, 63–66, 100.

79. Ellen F. Davis, *Scripture, Culture, and Agriculture: The Agrarian Reading of the Bible* (Cambridge: Cambridge University Press, 2009), 149–50. Perdue and Carter explain that each satrapy needed to provide one thousand troops to Persia's army (*Israel and Empire*, 114).

Eskenazi's scholarship on Ezra–Nehemiah turns to the Elephantine Papyri to illuminate Jewish women's roles in the Persian economy. These documents provide evidence that prominent Jewish women in this community owned, sold, and inherited property and controlled their marital statuses. For example, through contracts we learn that Mibtahiah, the daughter of Mahseiah, inherited a house from her father that remained in her hands even when she divorced.[80] Mibtahiah brought wealth to her marriages (she has three), which was not allowed to leave her hands, as detailed in these contracts that she and each husband signed. In this same Elephantine community an Egyptian slave, Tapmut, married a Jewish man named Anani, son of Azariah, and she, too, could own property and make decisions about divorce. Eskenazi notes that her marriage gave Tapmut property rights and that both Tapmut's son and daughter, Yehoishma, could inherit.[81] Eskenazi, following Claudia Camp, suggests that Judah returned to the premonarchic kinship, more gender-egalitarian economy that Carol Meyers argues was lost when monarchs ruled.[82] While there might have been women in Judah who owned land, it is more likely that these women were foreign or part of the landed elite rather than members of the repatriate community. Still, intermarriage was possibly an economic act as members of the repatriate community who wished to secure land and wealth might have been motivated to marry the daughters of wealthy landowners, perhaps Persian or from Ammon, Moab, and Ashdod (Neh 13:23), in order to increase their status.[83] Our readings of Elephantine texts along with other clues will help us parse how women impacted or were impacted by the economy of Persian Judah.

Authorship, Dating, and Sources

Authorship, dating, and the sources used in the compilation of Ezra–Nehemiah have received a great deal of scholarly attention, and we point readers to the footnotes and bibliography for sources that explore

80. Eskenazi, "Out from the Shadows," 29 (reading contract C 8, 460 BCE).

81. Eskenazi, "Out from the Shadows," 29–30.

82. Eskenazi, "Out from the Shadows," 32–33. Both Camp and Eskenazi appeal to Meyers's argument that women have more power in the pre-monarchical household structure. See Carol Meyers, *Discovering Eve: Ancient Israelite Women in Context* (New York: Oxford University Press, 1988).

83. Johnson, *The Holy Seed Has Been Defiled*.

these areas in greater depth and detail. As such, we do not thoroughly examine the issues and arguments regarding its composition here, choosing instead to highlight and summarize the major debates and areas of consensus.

Early analysis of these compositions moved between single authorship and multiple authorship or between an independent work or a unified work. Should we treat Ezra–Nehemiah as one book or two? The Talmud maintains that Ezra and Nehemiah each authored their respective books.[84] Tamara Cohn Eskenazi and Sara Japhet support the theory that a single author wrote the texts without making assumptions about the identity of its author.[85] Others have proposed that the Chronicler (as a priestly school or circle) was responsible for all three compositions while holding to the position that Ezra–Nehemiah and Chronicles were developed over time as separate works.[86] They appear in the Septuagint as a single work titled *Esdras B*. These divergent views are rooted in textual arguments in which there appears to be some commonality in these works, and yet they display significant differences in their linguistic and thematic features. For our purposes, we concur with others who view these compilations as a unified work; however, in our analysis we treat them as separate books.

Related to the above is the issue of dating. When were these works compiled? Eskenazi and Japhet argue for a late Persian-period dating (360–350 and 370–360 BCE, respectively) with possible Hellenistic additions.[87] Lester Grabbe takes a similar position and places the book(s) in this same period.[88] Kyung-Jin Min suggests a late fifth-century date.[89] Overall, dating Ezra–Nehemiah remains a matter of debate. While important, we do very little with dating except where an explanation would

84. b. B. Bat. 15a.

85. Tamara Cohn Eskenazi, *In the Age of Prose: A Literary Approach to Ezra–Nehemiah*, SBLMS 36 (Atlanta: SBL, 1988), 11–14, and *Ezra*; Sara Japhet, "Composition and Chronology in the Book of Ezra–Nehemiah," in *Second Temple Studies*, vol. 2, *Temple Community in the Persian Period*, ed. Tamara Cohn Eskenazi and Kent H. Richards, LHBOTS (Sheffield: JSOT Press, 1994), 189–216. See also H. G. M. Williamson, *Ezra–Nehemiah*, WBC 16 (Waco: Word, 1985), xxxiii–xxxv. Cf. Lester L. Grabbe, *Ezra–Nehemiah*, OTR (London: Routledge, 1998), 94–105.

86. See Kyung-Jin Min's examination of these issues in *The Levitical Authorship of Ezra–Nehemiah*, JSOTSup 409 (London: T&T Clark, 2004).

87. Eskenazi, *Ezra*, 6.

88. Lester L. Grabbe, *Judaism from Cyrus to Hadrian*, vol. 1: *The Persian and Greek Periods* (Minneapolis: Fortress, 1992).

89. Min, *The Levitical Authorship of Ezra–Nehemiah*, 34.

help the reader interpret any inconsistencies in the chronological sequence presented by the narrated events.

The Scriptures of ancient Israel are written predominantly in Hebrew; there are two portions that are written in Aramaic in the books of Daniel (Dan 2:4b–7:28) and in Ezra (Ezra 4:8–6:18; 7:12-26). The Aramaic portions in Ezra capture dialogues or official correspondence between Babylonian and Persian monarchs, their representatives, and the exilic community. Aramaic was the *lingua franca* of the Persian Empire, and its use is attested during the period of the compilation of Ezra–Nehemiah. For example, the Elephantine Papyri (fourth and fifth centuries BCE) include letters written in Aramaic to a Persian governor. Much of Ezra and Nehemiah is written as first-person narration (Ezra 7:27–9:15; Neh 1–7; 12:27–13:31) with other portions appearing as third-person narration (Ezra 7:1-11; 10; Neh 8), lists of genealogies, and editorial comments. Various sources make up this composite work. Major sources include Ezra's memoir (Ezra 7:27–9:15), Nehemiah's memoir (Neh 1:1–7:5; 13:4-31), some Aramaic sources, and Cyrus's edict. These works have parallels in 1 Esdras (LXX), which was most likely compiled after Ezra–Nehemiah. There is also the matter of which of these books came first. It is widely accepted that the material in 1 Esdras is comprised of portions of Ezra–Nehemiah.[90] Ezra precedes Nehemiah in the chronological ordering of the books; however, there is no consensus on dating this material. Some suggest that Nehemiah's memoir predates Ezra's memoir, while others place Ezra first.[91]

The Importance of the City of Jerusalem for Ezra–Nehemiah

Jerusalem is central to Ezra–Nehemiah and is named over seventy-five times. Much of the activity in Ezra–Nehemiah occurs within the perimeter of this city. Jeshua, son of Jozadak; Zerubabbel, son of Shealtiel, and those who returned from exile rebuilt the House of God that was built by

90. See the scholarly discussions in Lisbeth Fried's edited volume, *Was 1 Esdras First? An Investigation into the Priority and Nature of 1 Esdras*, AIL 7 (Atlanta: SBL, 2011). For others who counter this view, see Deirdre N. Fulton and Gary N. Knoppers, "Lower Criticism and Higher Criticism: The Case of 1 Esdras," in Fried, ed., *Was 1 Esdras First?*, 11–29.

91. For contrasting views, see Aaron Demsky, "Who Came First, Ezra or Nehemiah? The Synchronistic Approach," *HUCA* 65 (1994): 1–19; Ulrich Kellermann, *Nehemia: Quellen, Überlieferung und Geschichte*, BZAW 102 (Berlin: de Gruyter, 2019); H. G. M. Williamson, *Ezra and Nehemiah*, OTG (Sheffield: JSOT, 1987).

King Solomon and destroyed by King Nebuchadnezzar of Babylon (Ezra 3:8–6:15). Later, Nehemiah and the community will rebuild Jerusalem's walls and gates (Neh 3–6). While Solomon's temple was consecrated or made holy by God (1 Kgs 9:3) and its inner sanctuary was deemed "the most holy place" (1 Kgs 6:16), the book of Nehemiah expands the temple's holiness to include all of Jerusalem as the "holy city" (Neh 11:1, 18). Maria Häusl contends that what makes the entire city of Jerusalem holy in Ezra–Nehemiah is not the presence of the temple; the city is the space where the people experience God.[92] They read and implement the Torah and celebrate the Festival of Booths at Jerusalem's Water Gate (Neh 8–10), sign a community commitment (Neh 10), and populate the city (Neh 11).[93]

When Jerusalem fell in 586 BCE, Gedaliah was appointed governor, and the Babylonian province of Judah in which Gedaliah served was in the Benjaminite city of Mizpah (2 Kgs 25:23-25; Jer 40:6–41:16). During the exilic period, Mizpah served as the center of power for the region of Judah.[94] Yet to strengthen their identity and connection to their Israelite ancestors, the repatriates sought to shift the power back to Jerusalem by rebuilding the city and its temple infrastructure and their connections to Kings David and Solomon. These kings are mentioned several times in Ezra–Nehemiah. David is evoked in the context of community worship and music (Ezra 3:10; Neh 12:24, 45, 46). Solomon becomes a cautionary tale to those priests who take foreign wives and follow their gods (Neh 13:26). Connecting to David's city (Neh 3:15; 12:36, 37) adds legitimacy to Ezra and Nehemiah's mission to rebuild the city of Jerusalem and cement their identity as a people. Ehud Ben Zvi refers to this phenomenon as a "social memory" of a particular community.[95] He notes that the repatriate community rebuilt Jerusalem because their social memories "required that YHWH's house be at the place the community remembered YHWH to have selected for this purpose."[96] In the community's

92. Maria Häusl, "Jerusalem, the Holy City: The Meaning of the City of Jerusalem in the Books of Ezra–Nehemiah," in *Constructions of Space*, vol. 5: *Place, Space and Identity in the Ancient Mediterranean World*, ed. Gert T. Prinsloo and Christl M. Maier, LHBOTS 576 (New York: T&T Clark, 2014), 105.

93. Häusl, "Jerusalem, the Holy City," 105.

94. John T. Strong, "Mizpah," *Eerdmans Dictionary of the Bible*, ed. David Noel Freedman (Grand Rapids: Eerdmans, 2000), 908.

95. Ehud Ben Zvi, "Exploring Jerusalem as a Site of Memory in the Late Persian Period and Early Hellenistic Periods," in *Memory and the City in Ancient Israel*, ed. Diana Vikander Edelman and Ehud Ben Zvi (Winona Lake, IN: Eisenbrauns, 2013), 201.

96. Ben Zvi, "Exploring Jerusalem," 202.

mind, this memory connected them to their past, as they looked forward with hope to their future.[97] Yet, archaeological evidence suggests that Jerusalem in Ezra and Nehemiah's time was sparsely populated.

The capital city of preexilic Judah that bustled with the presence of the temple and as the seat of the preexilic monarchy was reduced, says Warren Carter, to a skeleton-sized population of perhaps twenty-five hundred to three thousand people; Israel Finkelstein suggests an even smaller population and an area of approximately two to two-and-a-half hectares (1 hectare = 2.47 acres or 10,000 square meters).[98] Oded Lipschits argues for a five-hectare city with the inclusion of the Ophel.[99] Regardless of the exact dimensions or population, Jerusalem was a shadow of its former self as a result of the Babylonian army's destruction of the city in 586 BCE and was in great need of rejuvenation that came in the form of Persian benevolence, according to Ezra–Nehemiah (Ezra 1; Neh 2:7-8) as Persian kings allowed the exiles to return to build the temple, fortify the walls, and solidify the religious laws.

The Ungendering of Jerusalem?

Zion (i.e., Jerusalem) is gendered female throughout the Scriptures of ancient Israel. For example, Jerusalem appears as the ideal wife and nurturing mother (Isa 62:4-9; 66:7-13).

> Rejoice with Jerusalem, and be glad for her, all you who love her; rejoice with her in joy, all you who mourn over her—that you may nurse and be satisfied from her consoling breast, that you may drink deeply with delight from her glorious bosom. (Isa 66:10-11)

Jerusalem also appears as the unfaithful wife whose dalliances lead to the fall of Israel and Judah (e.g., Ezek 16 and 23) in about 722 BCE and 586 BCE, respectively. At times, the city is depicted as the suffering daughter (Mic 4:10; Lam 1:6, 15; 2:18; Isa 4:4) who eventually rejoices when the holy city is reestablished and the unclean and uncircumcised inhabitants have been evicted (Isa 52:1). Other depictions imagine Jerusalem as God's devoted bride (Jer 2:2) and mourning widow (Lam 1:1). Christl Maier traces

97. Ben Zvi, "Exploring Jerusalem," 217.

98. Israel Finkelstein, "Persian Period Jerusalem and Yehud Rejoinders," in Hunt and Berquist, eds., *The Crucial Nature of the Persian and Hellenistic Periods*, 49, 60.

99. Finkelstein, "Persian Period Jerusalem and Yehud Rejoinders," 60. The Ophel refers to the area between the Temple Mount and the City of David in Jerusalem.

biblical motifs of a gendered Zion/Jerusalem from preexilic through postexilic Israel/Judah and concludes that, by the postexilic period, this holy city became personified as mother (Isa 49:21-22; 66:8-11).[100] For Maier, this maternal designation makes sense for a sacred place that had once again become the "mother-city" in the reconstructed community.[101] Yet, Ezra–Nehemiah never refers to Jerusalem as "Zion," and depictions of Jerusalem as female are clearly absent. Ezra–Nehemiah, like Ezekiel, neuters Jerusalem. In her analysis of Ezekiel's portrait of a gendered Jerusalem, particularly as an unclean and unfaithful wife in chapters 16 and 23, Julie Galambush discovers that Jerusalem's female gender shifts when Ezekiel portrays the new temple-city in Ezekiel 40–48: "the lady vanishes" altogether.[102] Galambush argues that the shift away from the female personification of Jerusalem is intentional, as the priests do not wish to link the previous language of impurity ascribed to the old city to the new. While Galambush limits her study to Ezekiel, Ezra–Nehemiah, with its concern for the holy seed, male lineage, and endogamous marriage, follows suit and does not draw on the Zion tradition, thereby erasing the feminine from the holy city.

Concluding Thoughts about Ezra and Nehemiah

Many readers of Ezra–Nehemiah view this text as exclusive and unwelcoming. Ezra–Nehemiah sees fit to build boundaries and define what it means to be part of the holy community and to be God's people. The joy of returning to the ancestral land and the fear of being exiled once again may lead them to be especially attentive to protecting the fledgling community. To be sure, there are times when this community takes drastic measures to separate from those they fear will threaten their traditions, cultures, and claim to the land. We are clear throughout the commentary where we disagree with Ezra–Nehemiah's tactics of separation. Still, sometimes communities need to separate to define themselves, especially while living amid an intercultural society with

100. Christl Maier, *Daughter Zion, Mother Zion: Gender, Space, and the Sacred in Ancient Israel* (Minneapolis: Fortress, 2008).

101. Maier, *Daughter Zion, Mother Zion*, 216.

102. Julie Galambush, *Jerusalem in the Book of Ezekiel: The City as Yahweh's Wife*, SBLDS 130 (Atlanta: Scholars Press, 1992).

competing beliefs or ethics. Smith-Christopher reminds us that religions within Christianity, like the Quakers, Amish, the Mennonites, and the Moravians, all created "minority communities" for the very purpose of maintaining their identities and practices in the midst of the surrounding people who threatened their existence.[103] Many of these communities, once established, moved into the mainstream yet are able to maintain their core values and identity.

Our own communities struggle with identity and belonging. Ezra–Nehemiah becomes almost a reflection of who we are and who we want to be as a faith community that honors traditions yet is still able to maintain permeable boundaries. The reason we are willing to read beyond the male/patriarchal focus that is so evident in Ezra–Nehemiah is because we want to recognize that we, like this ancient community, grapple with issues of boundaries and how to secure our identities. How do we honor multiple voices without losing our uniqueness? Hopefully, we have raised significant issues that will encourage others to do further work on Ezra–Nehemiah in such a way that includes all people in the family of God.

About the Authors

I, Terry Ann Smith, currently serve as the associate dean of institutional assessment and associate professor of biblical studies at New Brunswick Theological Seminary. As a female African American biblical scholar, I am deeply passionate about issues of justice (gender, race, ethnicity, and the environment) as these topics intersect biblical texts. As an ordained minister and preacher in the Baptist tradition, I am equally concerned about how we embrace and live into the ethical and moral prescriptions they espouse with an acute attention to concerns for those whose voices are silenced or neglected. My scholarship reflects a nuanced understanding of these interconnected identities within biblical narratives and contemporary Christian, specifically urban, contexts. My teaching and writing focus on amplifying voices often overlooked in traditional biblical interpretations. My articles on Rachel and Leah, Sarah and Ishmael, and the prophet Isaiah demonstrate my commitment to exploring the intersections of gender and ethnicity. My forthcoming works, *God Help*

103. Daniel Smith-Christopher, *The Religion of the Landless: The Social Context of the Babylonian Exile*, 2nd ed. (Eugene, OR: Wipf & Stock, 2015), 208.

Us! The Bible and Pastoral Care Concerns for Black Churches and *Echoes of Dissent: Resistance and Protest—MLK, Malcolm X, and the Biblical Daniel*, further highlight my interest in examining these complex intersections, offering critical reflections designed to inspire students and readers to engage deeply with these vital issues. I hold a doctor of philosophy and a master of philosophy from Drew University in Madison, New Jersey; a master of divinity from New Brunswick Theological Seminary; and a bachelor of science in management and a master of science in information systems from Roosevelt University in Chicago, Illinois.

I, Deborah Ann Appler, serve as professor of the Hebrew Bible at Moravian Theological Seminary. I am an elder in the Eastern Pennsylvania Conference of the United Methodist Church and an Earthkeeper for the UMC Board of Global Ministries. Before teaching at Moravian, I served two local churches in Maryland in the Baltimore-Washington Conference during the late 1980s and early 1990s. In my role as pastor, I met with people who felt abandoned by the church because of their sexual and gender identities, because the church in general failed to address gender violence, or, even worse, because the Bible was used to justify remaining in toxic relationships. I began to realize that too many people in the world use the Bible as a weapon, and I longed to find ways to encourage ethical readings of this text for use in ministry, scholarship, teaching, and daily living. I am a white, cisgender woman feminist who cares passionately about social justice and inclusion. My teaching and scholarship focus on issues of community justice, especially as these issues intersect with gender, sexuality, race, age, class, and food justice. For example, my article on David's last days engages David's story in conversation with contemporary elder abuse issues. My article on Daniel 4 explores the predatory nature of the Persian economy in the context of global food justice issues. My commitment to collaborative work is evident through articles I have published on microaggressions and the need for atonement and creating a collaborative biblical resource for the Moravian Church with scriptural tools to eliminate violence against women. My fascination with digging in the dirt led me to excavate and serve on the staff at Tel Ramat Rachel and Tel Jezreel, the home of Jezebel and Ahab. Currently, I am revisiting my work on Jezebel, the food imagery in this text, to open conversations about gender, sexuality, and food justice. I hold a doctor of philosophy in Hebrew Bible from Vanderbilt University, a master of divinity from the Perkins School of Theology at Southern Methodist University, and a bachelor of science in chemistry from Western Maryland College (now McDaniel College).

Collaboration

As feminist biblical scholars, we recognize the power of working collaboratively to bring different perspectives and concerns to interpretations of biblical texts. Our Ezra–Nehemiah commentary is a result of taking this commitment to heart. When we began the writing process, we both took responsibility for creating a first draft of part of this book to get the conversation started. In our research, we read from a range of viewpoints on Ezra–Nehemiah while also paying attention to what this book has to say to us today. Together, we logged thousands of hours of Zoom time bouncing off ideas, editing, arguing with the text, and integrating essential questions and comments from our editor, Amy-Jill Levine, all while drinking lots of coffee and laughing and catching up. Both of us brought something different to the table. While we did not always agree with minor details, we mostly found consensus around the critical points we wanted to emphasize from the text. This agreement allowed us to team up with contributing voices who share their perspectives and experiences on intersectional issues Ezra–Nehemiah raises. Our collaborative writing process took time and intentionality, yet it also allowed us to learn from each other and create what we hope will be a helpful resource.

Acknowledgments

First, we want to acknowledge that a project of this magnitude could not be accomplished without the help and support of so many others. We are deeply grateful for the opportunity and challenge to contribute to this commentary series and collaboration of feminist interpretation of every book of the Bible. So many have been instrumental in our endeavors to bring this work to fruition. We want to thank Liturgical Press and Barbara Reid for their unwavering support and patience in giving us more grace and time to work through the demands of work and family, often at the expense of missed deadlines. We also want to express our extreme appreciation for our editor, Amy-Jill Levine, whose insights and questions challenged our implicit assumptions about our own ways of interpreting Ezra–Nehemiah, especially when seeking to articulate feminist readings of the text. Any failure to adequately address the text in this fashion has more to do with us than her guidance during this process. We thank our institutions, Moravian Theological Seminary and New Brunswick Theological Seminary, for their support in providing encouragement and access to resources necessary to research and write this volume. Our students have been invaluable as dialogue partners as we worked through this material in our classrooms. Finally, this work would not have been possible without the support of our families, who endured the emotional journey of endless rantings and ramblings about writer's block, and their gentle but insistent nudge that kept us heading toward the light at the end of the tunnel, which we now realize were not the headlights of an imminent collision but the end of the journey. This work would not have been possible without their sacrifices, encouragement, and love. In sum, words cannot fully capture our gratitude, but we offer a heartfelt thank you and our enduring love to everyone who supported us.

Ezra 1

There's No Place Like Home

Embedded in the cultural memories of countless individuals and groups are the shared values, traditions, and identities connected to particular places. For most people, the specific location is home and symbolizes a place of belonging. For example, the violent resettlement of mass groups outside their areas of origin (e.g., home) potentially leaves those displaced traumatized. In the words of Shelly Rambo, "Trauma is a story about the storm that does not go away. It is the story of remaining."[1]

The Scriptures of ancient Israel capture the witness of remaining by recounting a people's perceptions of God in their midst. In vivid detail, the narration and poetic artistry chronicle their ordeal of forced displacement (597–586 BCE), resettlement in the land of their captors (Babylon and Persia), and eventual return to the land of their ancestors, specifically Judah and Jerusalem (539–359 BCE). Within this story of remaining is the story of returning home—where rebuilding, restoring, and recovering reflect the crisis of survival in the aftermath of traumatic events (cf. 2 Kgs 25). In Ezra 1, we find the reframing of what it means to witness to remaining; Ezra 2 will continue this reframing.

1. Shelly Rambo, *Spirit and Trauma: A Theology of Remaining* (Louisville: Westminster John Knox, 2010), 143.

A Second Exodus (1:1-4)

Ezra 1 opens with a proclamation and edict from the Persian King Cyrus following his defeat of the Babylonians in 539 BCE. The mandate, issued during the first year of Cyrus's reign and foreshadowed by the prophet Jeremiah, allowed exiled Judeans and other groups living in Persian-controlled territories to return to Judah and Jerusalem (Ezra 1:1-3). Insertions from the book of Jeremiah point to an earlier prophetic tradition that promises Israel's restoration as a distinct people in a particular place.

> For thus says the LORD: Only when Babylon's seventy years are completed will I visit you, and I will fulfill to you my promise and bring you back to this place. . . . I will restore your fortunes and gather you from all the nations and all the places where I have driven you, says the LORD, and I will bring you back to the place from which I sent you into exile. (Jer 29:10, 14)

The stirring of Cyrus's spirit in 1:1 is reminiscent of other biblical passages where the spirit of God empowers Moses (Exod 31:3; 35:31), the Judges (Judg 3:10; 6:34; 11:29; 13:25; 14:6, 19; and 15:14), and the prophets (Isa 42:1; 44:3; Jer 51:11; Ezek 11:5; Joel 2:28; Mic 3:8; and Hag 1:14). The edict portrays Cyrus as a benevolent liberator of all diasporic peoples, particularly in the book of Isaiah, which aligns him with the משיח (messiah) or anointed one, the only non-Israelite referred to by this designation (cf. Isa 44:28; 45:1, 13). The term applies variably to the anointing of priests (Lev 4:3, 5, 16; 6:22; 1 Sam 2:35) and the anointing and reigns of Saul and David (e.g., 1 Sam 2:10; 12:3, 5; 16:6; 24:6, 10; 26:9, 11; and 2 Sam 19:21). A foreign ruler's assertion that the "God of heaven" (Ezra 1:2) gives him the world is found elsewhere in the Scriptures of ancient Israel, which characterizes Cyrus's reign as the will of God (Isa 44:28; 45:1; 2 Chr 36:23). While the narrator never claims that Cyrus is the משיח, reimaging Cyrus as a liberator rather than a conqueror suggests as much. This reimaging erases the historical realities of how Cyrus came to power and expanded his empire by waging war and confiscating the land and resources of a multitude of subjugated peoples.

Ezra 1:1-4

1In the first year of King Cyrus of Persia,
to fulfill the word of the LORD from the
mouth of Jeremiah, the LORD stirred up
the spirit of King Cyrus of Persia so that
he made a proclamation throughout all
his kingdom and also in writing, saying:
2"Thus says King Cyrus of Persia:
The LORD, the God of heaven, has
given me all the kingdoms of the earth,
and he has charged me to build him a
house at Jerusalem, which is in Judah.
3Let any of those among you who are
of his people—may their God be with
them!—go up to Jerusalem in Judah
and rebuild the house of the LORD, the
God of Israel; he is the God who is
in Jerusalem. 4And let all survivors
in whatever place they reside be assisted by the people of their place with
silver and gold, with goods, and with
livestock, besides freewill offerings for
the house of God in Jerusalem."

Cyrus Cylinder

Image from https://commons.wikimedia.org/wiki/File:Cyrus_Cylinder_back.jpg.

The Cyrus Cylinder is typical of imperial building inscriptions of the ancient Near East. The cylinder describes the return of various conquered groups and functions as a form of government-sanctioned media that constructs a flattering portrait of the ruler.[2] The cylinder's language suggests the ruler's goal was to retain the goodwill of conquered peoples by allowing them to return home and resume their religious practices, including reconstructing temples to their gods. This political strategy also facilitated the collection of tributes derived in part from temple treasuries. When understood as propaganda, the cylinder's language of chosenness (divine selection) reads as human hubris by a politician who seeks self-glorification and economic gratification at the expense of the populace.

2. Steven W. Holloway, *Aššur Is King! Aššur Is King! Religion in the Exercise of Power in the Neo-Assyrian Empire*, CHANE 10 (Leiden: Brill, 2002), xvii.

The incorporation of the edict in Ezra's account reframes the cylinder's original intent as a building inscription functioning as imperial propaganda. The editorial reframing builds on the message in which the king allows exiled peoples to return to their homelands. The proclamation puts forth a foreign policy initiative where Cyrus declares, "[A]ny of those among you who are of his people—may their God be with them!—[are now permitted to] go up to Jerusalem in Judah and rebuild the house of the LORD" (Ezra 1:3). Similar to the first exodus, with its mixed crowd of men, women, and children from multiple ethnic groups (Exod 12:38; Num 11:4), the "any of those among you" possibly includes men, women, and children even if it is unclear to whom "his people" refers. The inclusive nature of the edict suggests individuals and families can choose whether or not to participate in the pilgrimage to Judah and Jerusalem. Those who choose to return, these survivors from "whatever place they reside," are to receive donations from "the people of their place" (Ezra 1:4). Aramaic documents from ancient Egypt (Elephantine Papyri) contain the business transactions of Jewish women (including property ownership) during the postexilic period.[3] These transactions suggest the involvement of women in the socio-economic sectors of Jewish society. As solicited donors to the migratory cause, these women and their contributions are certainly plausible as they also represent "survivors" or the "people of their place."

The returnees as "survivors" captures the resilience of groups traumatized by forced displacement (Ezra 1:4). These survivors may represent exiles scattered throughout the Persian Empire or multiple ethnic groups displaced over time by imperial invasions and colonization. The diverse nature of the group explains the need for support from the "people of their place," which include the local inhabitants (non-Jews) and Jews choosing to remain. The assistance in the form of monies, material goods, animals, and offerings for "the house of God in Jerusalem" speaks to a thriving community rather than one merely surviving. On the one hand, the narrative portrayal of non-Judeans supporting the building of a religious edifice to a God not their own raises the concern of possible imperial coercion. On the other hand, we could be witnessing the solidarity garnered within an interfaith community called upon for support when needed.

3. Jehohen borrows four shekels at 5 percent monthly interest (*TAD B3.1* = Porter *B34*), and Mahseiah, son of Jedaniah, bequeaths his house to his daughter Mibtahiah (*TAD B2.3* = Porter *B25*). Bezalel Porten et al., *The Elephantine Papyri in English: Three Millennia of Cross-Cultural Continuity and Change*, 2nd ed., Studies in Near Eastern Archaeology and Civilisation 22 (Atlanta: SBL, 2011), 165–72, 203–5.

Overall, the editorial revision of the edict's message now reflects the theological promise of return articulated in ancient Israel's prophetic tradition together with a specific emphasis on exiled Judeans and their God. While the text does not explicitly mention possessing the land, the four references to Jerusalem in Ezra 1:2-4 suggest a preoccupation with claiming a specific place. Jerusalem resonates deeply in the group's communal memory as this particular place. The edict introduces a proposition resonant throughout Ezra–Nehemiah, where restoration of the religious and physical infrastructure (e.g., temple, city walls) is the sole responsibility of the repatriates, a group divinely chosen for this task. Although there were individuals who remained in the land throughout the exilic period (cf. 2 Kgs 24:14) and possibly persisted in observing the traditions of ancient Israel, their stories go primarily untold except through the narration of the conflicts that emerge once the returnees resettle in Judah and surrounding territories.

Where the Spirit Leads, Women Follow (1:5-11)

"The heads of the families of Judah and Benjamin, and the priests and the Levites—everyone whose spirit God had stirred"—made ready to return to Jerusalem to participate in the rebuilding of the house of God. The same spirit that stirred Cyrus in Ezra 1:1 now stirs some diaspora residents in Ezra 1:5. Once again, the return appears initiated by divine rather than imperial interests. The inclusion of priests and Levites among the repatriates establishes that the exiled Judean community sustains some form of Yahwistic worship that allows them to remain connected

Image from https://pixabay.com/photos/refugee-refugees-integration-light-1902581/.

Ezra 1:5-11

[5]Then the heads of the families of Judah and Benjamin and the priests and the Levites—everyone whose spirit God had stirred—got ready to go up and rebuild the house of the LORD in Jerusalem. [6]All their neighbors aided them with silver vessels, with gold, with goods, with livestock, and with valuable gifts, besides all that was freely offered. [7]King Cyrus himself brought out the vessels of the house of the LORD that Nebuchadnezzar had carried away from Jerusalem and placed in the house of his gods. [8]King Cyrus of Persia had them released into the charge of Mithredath the treasurer, who counted them out to Sheshbazzar the prince of Judah. [9]And this was the inventory: gold basins, thirty; silver basins, one thousand; knives, twenty-nine; [10]gold bowls, thirty; other silver bowls, four hundred ten; other vessels, one thousand; [11]the total of the gold and silver vessels was five thousand four hundred. All these Sheshbazzar brought up when the exiles were brought up from Babylonia to Jerusalem.

to the faith and traditions of the ancestral homeland in Judah. Biblical references to migration, either voluntary or forced, often include entire families (Gen 12:5; 31:17; 46:5; Ruth 1:1; Jer 43:5-7). Other accounts describe women migrating alone as heads of households or displaced by war. For instance, in the book of Ruth, Naomi appears as a long-time immigrant to Moab before returning to her homeland in Bethlehem following the deaths of her male kin (Ruth 1:6). When Naomi leaves Moab, her daughter-in-law Ruth, a Moabite immigrant, accompanies her (Ruth 1:16). Accounts of women displaced by war appear in Numbers, Judges, and 1 Samuel (Num 31:9; Judg 21:19-23; 1 Sam 30:1-2). Judges 21:19-23 describes the forcible removal of the women of Shiloh to the territory of the Benjaminites. Although few, these brief references suggest that women were just as likely to engage in migratory activity, whether voluntarily or involuntarily. Given this tendency, the reference to male heads of households in Ezra 1:5 should not be read exclusively as indicative of the absence of women in this call of return and reconstruction. In Haggai 1:14, "the LORD stirred up the spirit . . . and the spirit of all the remnant of the people, and they came and worked on the house of the LORD of hosts, their God." When read inclusively, the reference to "all the remnant" most likely includes women. In Ezra 1:5, God stirs everyone's spirit, including the women who will return.

It is unclear why those who remained in Judah and Jerusalem did not rebuild the temple or city walls. The reasons can vary, including no interest in rebuilding, no funds or materials to rebuild, or lack of support from imperial or other sources. Judeans in the homeland may have been ill-equipped to embark on a building campaign as massive as the reconstruction of the house of God, which, by all accounts, required a substantial labor force.[4] First Kings describes the labor-intensive work associated with building the first temple (i.e., more than thirty thousand laborers and stonecutters), an endeavor that took seven years to complete (1 Kgs 5:1–6:38). In Nehemiah 3, construction activities in Jerusalem require a workforce composed of persons residing in several towns neighboring Jerusalem. In addition to a work crew, a need for wood and other building materials would exist. Importing some of these materials would make the reconstruction of God's house a costly endeavor (2 Sam 5:11; 1 Kgs 5:8; Ezra 3:7). Unlike the repatriates who bring thousands of people with them (Ezra 2), for those in the homeland, the need for labor would divert men and possibly women away from their families and the care of their households (e.g., fields, animals, etc.) in favor of caring for the house of God.

Lisbeth Fried provides a persuasive and thought-provoking theological explanation for the homeland's lack of attention to reconstructing the temple. She proposes, "The impetus to build could not come from the local Judean populace who did not control the tangible proof of YHWH's presence," which would have been the sacred vessels used in the rituals of the temple.[5] Similar to other religious groups of the ancient Near East, where the deity was thought to reside in his or her temple, the Judeans viewed the Jerusalem temple as God's abode. The decimation of the temple and the removal of its sacred vessels by imperial forces was an egregious religious offense and viewed by some biblical prophets (i.e., Jeremiah, Ezekiel, Micah, Zephaniah) as justification for the deity's

4. See Israel Finkelstein, "Jerusalem in the Persian (and Early Hellenistic) Period and the Wall of Nehemiah," *JSOT* 32 (2008): 501–20. Archaeologists dispute the size and population of Jerusalem and Judah during the Persian period, arguing that the lack of material culture from that period complicates the matter. They suggest that the numbers of those living in Jerusalem range anywhere from 400 to 1500 (Philip King and Lawrence E. Stager, *Life in Biblical Israel*, LAI [Louisville: Westminster John Knox, 2002], 389); Carter and Lipschits are among those who estimate the population throughout Judah at twenty thousand to thirty thousand (Finkelstein, "Jerusalem," 502–3). These numbers depend greatly on the biblical narrative, particularly Nehemiah 3 and the building of the wall.

5. Lisbeth Fried, "The Land Lay Desolate: Conquest and Restoration in the Ancient Near East," in *Judah and the Judeans in the Neo-Babylonian Period*, ed. Oded Lipschits and Joseph Blenkinsopp (Winona Lake, IN: Eisenbrauns, 2003), 51. See also Lisbeth S. Fried, *Ezra: A Commentary*, Critical Commentaries (Sheffield: Sheffield Phoenix, 2015). Those remaining in the land following the exile no longer have the temple or the sacred vessels symbolizing God's presence. The people returning to Judah and Jerusalem are given the sacred vessels with the instruction to rebuild the temple.

anger. The return of the sacred vessels and the reconstruction of a place of worship in Jerusalem would prove that the divinity's anger had abated. Here, possession of the sacred vessels, like David's possession of the ark (2 Sam 6:15-21), positions the repatriates and those remaining in Babylon as the authentic inheritors of the faith and traditions of Israel (cf. Ezra 4:2). Still, possession of these objects alone might not have been enough to indicate God's return to Jerusalem. While the returned objects retain their value as instruments to be used in worship, the Torah, its teaching together with communal observances, will represent God's presence among these people going forward (Neh 8:8).

For Ezra's audience, the return of the temple vessels has theological implications. Yet, the motivation undergirding Cyrus's actions was most likely political and economic rather than spiritual. Jerusalem, as another revenue stream for the Persian Empire, would be unobtainable without the presence of stable commerce. The repopulation of the city by Jews migrating from Babylon and other territories would provide a surge of social and economic growth to the area.[6] From an imperial perspective, allowing the reconstruction of the temple was a strategic necessity. Lester Grabbe suggests, "It is only common sense that uncultivated land and areas without a sufficient population to work it were detrimental to the royal purse."[7] In essence, a city without a reputation is one to which no one will flock, and a city without a temple is one that in all likelihood will not establish a meaningful reputation. You must (re)build it for them to come.

King Cyrus's personal involvement reads as benevolent or extreme imperial oversight at best, as only he has the authority to release the sacred objects under consideration (Ezra 1:7). He entrusts these sacred objects to his treasurer, Mithredath, who in turn hands them over to Sheshbazzar, the "prince" or "chief" of Judah (Ezra 1:8). The title for Sheshbazzar as נשׂיא, "prince" or "chief" of Judah, appears only in Ezra 1:8. Elsewhere, he is referred to as the פחה, "governor" (Ezra 5:14). It is not likely that the writer intends to situate Sheshbazzar as an heir of the last monarch of the Southern Kingdom (the territories of Judah and Benjamin). Some

6. John J. Ahn, *Exile as Forced Migrations: A Sociological, Literary, and Theological Approach on the Displacement and Resettlement of the Southern Kingdom of Judah* (Göttingen: de Gruyter, 2011), 37.

7. Lester L. Grabbe, *A History of the Jews and Judaism in the Second Temple Period*, vol. 1: *Yehud: A History of the Persian Province of Judah*, LSTS 47 (London: T&T Clark, 2004), 197.

commentators suggest that the labeling conventions vary based on where the title originates, either with the Judeans themselves (נשׂיא) or a foreign king (פחה).[8] In the text, the title נשׂיא establishes the role of those dealing with the temple vessels. This title applies to the function that Sheshbazzar performs as the one entrusted with the sacred objects (cf. 1 Kg 8:1-4; Num 7) and accounts for its limited application in these verses.[9] Sheshbazzar handles the sacred vessels, a task singularly delegated to the priests and Levites (1 Kgs 8:1-4; 2 Chr 5:2-7). Here, the writer is careful to give Sheshbazzar a title that does not specifically identify him as a member of the priesthood (כהן) but one whose position would authorize his handling of the sacred instruments (נשׂיא). Sheshbazzar's title blurs the distinction between governmental and religious roles.[10] In a contemporary sense, the United States clearly distinguishes between religion and government. Government titles (senator, councilperson, etc.), irrespective of gender, carry no religious import, and these officials cannot perform religious rituals based solely on their governmental roles. Similarly, ecclesial titles are authoritative only within the religious bodies that recognize them as such. The governor does not enter a Baptist or United Methodist church and serve the Lord's Supper without ecclesial authority, nor does the county clerk raise the Torah scrolls unless a member of the congregation.

In Ezra and elsewhere in biblical narratives, women do not hold priestly offices, titles, or roles reserved for males in this ancient world. One becomes a priest through succession (e.g., Exod 28:1; Num 3:10; 18:7), a position unattainable by women given these prerequisites. Modern times, however, have seen more women in governmental roles while others hold ecclesial titles and positions, sometimes simultaneously. Historically women have gained quicker access to governmental roles and the titles that come with them than in the religious realm.

In Ezra 1:9-11, we find a detailed account of the temple articles the Persians confiscated from the Babylonians and returned to Sheshbazzar. In ancient Mesopotamia, the treasure houses or temples of the reigning ruler served as the repository of the spoils taken from the conquered, symbolizing their defeat and the vanquishing of their God. Second Kings 24:13 reports that King Nebuchadnezzar looted the Jerusalem temple, emptied it of its most valuable articles, and "cut in pieces all the vessels

8. Fried, *Ezra*, 83.

9. Fried, *Ezra*, 83.

10. Numbers 18:3 proscribes death for any persons other than the priest who touches the utensils (vessels) of the sanctuary or the altar.

of gold." This report differs from 2 Kings 25:13-17, which reports that some of the confiscated objects were destroyed, while other articles were removed to Babylon. These texts introduce a discrepancy between the quantities listed in Ezra 1:9-10 (2499) and the tally recorded in 1:11 (5400). Various solutions have been proposed to account for the inconsistency. For example, solutions that focus on the numerical discrepancies in verses 9 and 10 point to the ambiguity of the terms מִשְׁנִים (a double, copy, or second) and מחלפים (knives) and possibly represent a scribal error where מִשְׁנִים was translated as the number 2000 and מחלפים was originally 920.[11] Nonnumerical solutions entail envisioning the list as a partial inventory based on lost or omitted items. The discrepancy exposes the contradiction between what the Babylonians took and what the Persians returned. In essence, not all the confiscated treasures came back with the repatriates.

Confiscation of Torah Scrolls and Religious Artifacts

In Germany and within other occupied countries during the 1930s and 1940s the Nazis confiscated items of value from Jewish communities. Included in these stolen or desecrated objects were Torah scrolls that were erased, sold, and repurposed as wallets, shoes, and other leather goods.[12] Other Judaica, like skull caps, prayer shawls, wine chalices, and rare books were collected and put on display in Prague for what the Nazis called their "museum of an extinct race."[13] The items in this museum were eventually returned to the Jewish community, but many were lost or intentionally destroyed over the years.

The emphasis on the returned vessels pays little attention to what is possibly held back, which as a larger reflection of the exilic experience itself is an irrecoverable loss. The narrator lifts up the benevolence of Cyrus

11. Michael Segal, "Numerical Discrepancies in the List of Vessels in Ezra I 9-11," *VT* 52 (January 2002): 123.

12. "Humiliation and Abuse: Artifacts Made from Desecrated Torah Scrolls," Yad Vashem, https://www.yadvashem.org/artifacts/museum/desecrated-torah-scrolls.html.

13. Bernard Weinraub, "Trove of Judaica Preserved by Nazis to Tour U.S.," *New York Times*, September 20, 1983, sec. U.S., https://www.nytimes.com/1983/09/20/us/trove-of-judaica-preserved-by-nazis-to-tour-us.html.

but does not capture whether the returned vessels include the sacred items like the כפרת (the sacred cover on which sat the two cherubim, Num 7:89) or the ark of the covenant, items that may have been particularly meaningful to Judean liturgical practices. There remains a possible, albeit unsubstantiated, theory that some of the sacred vessels may have stayed in Babylon as evidence of the deity's presence among the Judeans remaining there. The chapter concludes by reaffirming the articles entrusted to Sheshbazzar (Ezra 1:8) and describes the migrating group collectively as the גלה (*gōlāh*), "exiles" or "diaspora group" (Ezra 1:11).

TRANSLATION MATTERS

The Hebrew term גלה, meaning exile or captivity, differs from the Septuagint's ἀποικίας, translated as "the place of transportation." The Hebrew term denotes the people as a particular community, while the Septuagint's translation focuses on the transporting of objects. *HALOT* (*Hebrew and Aramaic Lexicon of the Old Testament*) translates גלה as "deportation" and "exile."[14] While modern interpreters have used these terms to identify the גלה, the term "deportation" (and "deportees") is problematic since it implies that Judeans forcibly displaced by the Babylonians were not indigenous to the land.

The term גלה appears in the Hebrew portions of Ezra (Ezra 1:11; 2:1; 4:1; 6:20; 8:35; 9:4; 10:6-8, 16) and once in Nehemiah (Neh 7:6). We find similar designations in Jeremiah (Jer 28:6; 29:1, 4, 20, and 31), Ezekiel (Ezek 1:1; 3:11, 15; 11:24-25), and Zechariah (Zech 6:10). The term serves as the common designation for those returning from Babylon. Like the symbolic meaning attached to the returned vessels, the descriptor גלה informs the group's sense of self and influences its construction, justification, and maintenance of its boundaries. The term גלה also includes the women who return. These women must establish new support systems that are independent of their husbands. As their husbands return to build an edifice to their God, they too must build—creating ways to connect with other women who also find themselves in a new and different place.

14. *HALOT*, 183.

The poem "What We Build" captures the loss, hopes, and resolve when women must leave behind their familiar communities and relationships to begin anew in unfamiliar places.

What We Build

Our men went to build a house
for the Lord and contemplated
God's word
While they built, contemplated,
argued, decided, and imposed
We too were building
A home for our men, our
children, our neighbors,
ourselves
A community of silenced, but
not silent women
Passing gracefully yet forcefully
(mostly unseen)
through times of loss, times of
rejoicing and affirmation
Establishing and keeping home
fires burning for others
While our own spirits glowed
and flamed in deep relationship
with God, with one another
Womanly spirit at one with the
Creator

Forced to uproot from the
community what we had created
and nurtured in a foreign land
So that our men could rebuild
once again . . . how many times
has it been?
How many more times will
there be?
From the beauty and comforts
that we created out of our
Babylonian exile
We pulled up stakes, accepted
gifts from our tearful sisters who
remained behind
Torn between safe knowledge of
what we had (God forgive us)
And our destiny to return to
ancestral lands (we give thanks,
O Lord)
To build once again
So that our men could build the
house of the Lord.

Leslie Maro

Ezra 2

Lists, Lists, and More Lists

Ezra 1 provides an account of the occasion and rationale for repatriation (royal decree and restoration of the Lord's house). Ezra 2 follows this report with an extensive list of names, hometowns, and numbers of those returning. Lists, as written repositories for collecting, organizing, and categorizing dates, places, people, and things, are instrumental in the cultural production of memory. Historically, lists appear in the earliest writings known to humanity (e.g., Sumerian Kings List and the God and Sacrifice lists of Ugarit).[1] As cultural artifacts, lists provide insight into how people lived, what they valued, and their social networks. Lists also serve as biographies of identity, cataloging relationships as they change even long after they cease to exist, thus bridging the gap between the living and the dead.

The list in Ezra 2 mirrors the ones found in Nehemiah 7:6-69 and 1 Esdras 5, albeit the account in 1 Esdras 5 contains noticeable deviations and depicts the group returning under Darius rather than Cyrus. According to Tamara Cohn Eskenazi, the lists in Ezra and Nehemiah are central to understanding the structure of both writings and function

1. The oral transmission of noteworthy information most likely preceded the formal written process of record keeping and list making.

repetitively to link the גלה community and their activities.[2] The structure of the list in Ezra 2 is as follows:

- Group leaders (Ezra 2:2)
- General populace (Ezra 2:3-35)
- Priests (Ezra 2:36-39)
- Levites (Ezra 2:40-42)
- Servants (Ezra 2:43-58)
- Groups with questionable lineage (Ezra 2:59-61)

Memories

Contemporary archivists dedicated to keeping memories alive of those who died in the Holocaust/Shoah or who survived Nazi captivity remind us that physical record keeping of names enables those in the present and future generations to locate their ancestors and thereby construct their present identity in relation to their family's past. While the present list in Ezra 2 may be a snapshot of individuals in the immediate context of temple reconstruction, it also provides a means for the next generation to link their lives to a captive past whose family members survived and found their way back to the ancestral home or some other future yet to be told.

The practice of reading the names of those who survived as well as those who did not is a means of restoring dignity to human beings who suffered in captivity. The reading of names enables them to be seen and to ask questions about their stories. In his essay "How to Tell a True War Story," Tim O'Brien reminds us that there is no one way to relate the stories of those who have experienced war, captivity, trauma, or suffering other than to hear and tell their stories repeatedly—and it will be different each time.[3] With each name on Ezra's list there are myriad stories. How are their stories to be heard? Is it possible to bear witness to their experience?

The Holocaust memorial at Judenplatz in Vienna commemorates the sixty-four thousand Austrian Jews who were deported, held captive, and died in forty-two concentration camps (including the six killing centers of Auschwitz, Chemno,

2. Tamara Cohn Eskenazi, *In An Age of Prose: A Literary Approach to Ezra–Nehemiah*, SBLMS 36 (Atlanta: SBL, 1988), 40.

3. Tim O'Brien, *The Things They Carried* (Boston: Mariner Books Classics, 2009).

Sobibor, Treblinka, Madjanek, and Belzec). The memorial is in the shape of a library where the binding of the books faces inward so that we cannot see the title. As one looks at each book, one bears witness to someone whose past, present, and future will not be known. The memorial reminds the living of the principle of Tikkun Olam, or "repair of the world": the responsibility of the living to make the future world a better place through recognizing the dignity and worth of every human being, especially those whose names—whose very lives—have been erased or not recorded.

Considering the Shoah, the book of Ezra's list of returning exiles from Babylon calls us to remember the lives of those named in the book—and the lives of those not named in the book—thus bearing witness to their individual and collective humanity and stories. In the act of reading their names, their memory transcends the historical act of rebuilding the temple. Their memory and their legacies outlast whatever freewill offerings of gold, silver, and priestly robes they may have given to the temple building fund.

Charles Rix

There is no shortage of lists in the Scriptures of ancient Israel. There are lists of names and genealogies (Gen 9:10-32; 36:1-43; Num 1:5-15; Ruth 4:18-22; 1 Chr 2:5-15; Ezra 7:1-5; 8:1-14; Neh 7:8-57), places (Josh 18:21-28; Judg 1:27-34; Jer 25:20, 23; Neh 11:25-30), nations (Gen 10:1-32), kings (Josh 12:9-24), sundry items (Exod 30:23-25, 34), offerings, temple furnishings, and objects (Exod 25:3-7), and other enumerations that connect the social and religious conditions of different historical periods. Contrasting the literary significance and variation of lists in biblical narrative for ancient and modern audiences, Elchanan Samet theorizes there is a lack of interest in biblical lists from modern readers as a matter of literary taste, in contrast to ancient audiences who, he suggests, valued lists for their "celebratory and elevated note" as poetry and prose.[4] While contemporary audiences may gloss over biblical lists due to lack of interest or concerns regarding the pronunciation of names, the creation and preservation of lists informed the cultural and social memory of early Israelite and later Jewish societies.

4. Hayyim Angel refers to Elchanan Samet and his observations about the use of lists by ancient and contemporary audiences in "The Literary Significance of the Name Lists in Ezra–Nehemiah," *JBQ* 35 (2007): 143–44.

Genealogies

Genealogies and bloodlines as "embodied stories . . . include what we are born into (place; racial, ethnic, and gender formation; social status; cultural traditions); how we were taught to be part of a family and community; the stories we were told (and retell) about who our people were and are; and legacies we have inherited, both painful and proud."[5]

Lists as Repositories for Collecting Memories (2:1-35)

The lists in Ezra 2 begin with an introduction to those leading the return to Jerusalem and Judah: Zerubbabel, Jeshua, Nehemiah, Seraiah, Reelaiah, Mordecai, Bilshan, Mispar, Bigvai, Rehum, and Baanah (Ezra 2:2). The writer makes no hierarchical distinctions among these men. The ordering of names in the list, even if not obvious, is significant to the overall narration of events as they implicitly communicate the power dynamics between the leaders who are listed first and the general populace who are listed second.[6]

The report of the resettlement of the גלה into "Jerusalem and Judah, all to their own towns" (Ezra 2:1) leads the reader to conclude that the repatriates have successfully returned to the places where they have ancestral connections. Their resettlement presents a somewhat paradoxical situation with a need to establish common ancestry and continuity while simultaneously asserting the validity of their belongingness. The depiction of a common ancestry links the promises of the Abrahamic covenant (land and descendants) to the promise of restoration (return to the land of their ancestors). The common ancestry is not established just through the patriarchs (Abraham, Isaac, and Jacob), however, but through the matriarchs as well (Sarah, Rebekah, Rachel, and Leah). One might imagine that returning to *our* towns includes the ancestral houses of fathers and mothers (cf. Ruth 1:8 and Song 3:4). In Ruth, Naomi tells her daughters-in-law to return to their mother's house. In the Song of Songs, the mother's house is the place of conception. Common ancestry and continuity cannot be achieved without the wombs of the women who return with the men or the women some גלה men will marry who already reside in the land.

5. Elaine Enns and Ched Meyers, *Healing Haunted Histories: A Settler Discipleship of Decolonization* (Eugene, OR: Cascade, 2021), 87.

6. Eskenazi, *In the Age of Prose*, 50.

Ezra 2:1-35

[1]Now these are the people of the province who came from those captive
exiles whom King Nebuchadnezzar of
Babylon had carried captive to Babylon;
they returned to Jerusalem and Judah,
all to their own towns. [2]They came
with Zerubbabel, Jeshua, Nehemiah,
Seraiah, Reelaiah, Mordecai, Bilshan,
Mispar, Bigvai, Rehum, and Baanah.

The number of the Israelite people:
[3]the descendants of Parosh, two thousand one hundred seventy-two. [4]Of
Shephatiah, three hundred seventy-
two. [5]Of Arah, seven hundred seventy-
five. [6]Of Pahath-moab, namely, the
descendants of Jeshua and Joab, two
thousand eight hundred twelve. [7]Of
Elam, one thousand two hundred fifty-
four. [8]Of Zattu, nine hundred forty-five.
[9]Of Zaccai, seven hundred sixty. [10]Of
Bani, six hundred forty-two. [11]Of Bebai,
six hundred twenty-three. [12]Of Azgad,
one thousand two hundred twenty-two.
[13]Of Adonikam, six hundred sixty-six.
[14]Of Bigvai, two thousand fifty-six. [15]Of
Adin, four hundred fifty-four. [16]Of Ater,
namely, of Hezekiah, ninety-eight. [17]Of
Bezai, three hundred twenty-three.

Particular places, similar to our interactions with family, can be repositories for collecting memories. In the catalog of returnees in Ezra 2:2-35, twenty-three of the thirty-nine names listed refer to towns located in Jerusalem and territories, while the other sixteen names refer to the ancestral houses of those returning. The names of towns and ancestral houses are intertwined as descendants of Israel without explanation. In general, our identities are shaped by various cultural factors (family, religion, geographic location, etc.), including various places we call home and the various interactions that occur in each of them. For example, in introducing ourselves to others, we often share our name and hometown even if we have not lived in that particular place for years.

Most genealogies in the Scriptures of ancient Israel trace familial connections through the house of the patriarch rather than the matriarch, with a few exceptions (e.g., Gen 35:23-26; 36:2-14). Even if we account for when women interrupt a patriline (Jacob's wives), the interruption is to preserve the patriline. Rachel and Leah create their own houses (Gen 35:23-26), but their houses are subsumed under the house of the patriarch, Jacob.[7] Today, tracing lineage through the father's surname is more complex when children can carry the surname of the mother regardless of her marital status.

7. For more information on this topic, see Cynthia Chapman, *The House of the Mother: The Social Roles of Maternal Kin in Biblical Hebrew Narrative and Poetry*, AYBRL (New Haven: Yale University Press, 2016).

Ezra 2:1-35 (cont.)

18Of Jorah, one hundred twelve. 19Of Hashum, two hundred twenty-three. 20Of Gibbar, ninety-five. 21Of Bethlehem, one hundred twenty-three. 22The people of Netophah, fifty-six. 23Of Anathoth, one hundred twenty-eight. 24The descendants of Azmaveth, forty-two. 25Of Kiriatharim, Chephirah, and Beeroth, seven hundred forty-three. 26Of Ramah and Geba, six hundred twenty-one. 27The people of Michmas, one hundred twenty-two. 28Of Bethel and Ai, two hundred twenty-three. 29The descendants of Nebo, fifty-two. 30Of Magbish, one hundred fifty-six. 31Of the other Elam, one thousand two hundred fifty-four. 32Of Harim, three hundred twenty. 33Of Lod, Hadid, and Ono, seven hundred twenty-five. 34Of Jericho, three hundred forty-five. 35Of Senaah, three thousand six hundred thirty.

DNA and Women Genealogies

Many of the lists in Ezra–Nehemiah pay sole attention to the male lineage of the Judean community, often tracing these lines back to Aaron, Levi, or other great male leaders of Israel. The absence of women's names and genealogy may imply that women are essential to maintaining the family line, but there are other ways to trace lineage. For example, biologists exploring ancestry discovered that human lineage can be traced back thousands of years only through the mitochondrial DNA (mtDNA) of the mother. Their hope is to find "mitochondrial Eve" or a woman through whom all families descend.[8]

When we consider familial connections, we typically construct and communicate genealogies in this context. Genealogies capture legacies, however, and therefore can be conceived more broadly. For example, it is possible to think of genealogies based on persons who have influenced us in various areas of our lives (business, education, mentors, and even scholarship). Like familial genealogies that do not trace all family linkages, we construct other types of genealogies similarly. That is, we make choices of which lines to trace, which persons are most influential, and

8. Carol P. Christ, "A Clash of Cultures," *Feminism and Religion* (blog), February 27, 2012, https://feminismandreligion.com/2012/02/27/a-clash-of-cultures-in-our-genes-by-carol-p-christ/. For more on this subject, see Michael Slezak, "Eve's Closest Relative Found," *New Scientist* 224 (October 11, 2014): 8–9.

whose voices should be preserved. In making these choices, we too suppress or leave out others whose contributions tend to remain invisible, yet their wisdom and guidance have left their wounds on us.

The Ties That Bind (2:36-58)

In Ezra 2:36-58 we find a second list that includes categories and genealogies of the temple community. The priests, Levites, singers, gatekeepers, and temple servants (including the descendants of Solomon's servants) account for over half of the listing in Ezra 2. These temple personnel were the caretakers for the community's religious practices (sacrificial system) and maintained the connection between the people and the deity. Women could not serve as priests in this community, positions reserved for specific males (descendants of Aaron) who oversaw the ritualistic elements of the community's worship practices. It is likely, however, that women participated in various capacities in the temple community. In Exodus 15:20-21, Miriam's chorus of female dancers celebrates liberation from Egyptian bondage with tambourines. Jephthah's daughter greets him with dancing in Judges 11:34, while David is met in 1 Samuel 18:6-7 by women singing, dancing, and playing musical accompaniments. These texts point to the skills and talents used by women in a celebratory fashion and possibly extend to their worship practices as well (Ps 68:24-25). Here too, we can include the wives of priests who were most likely responsible for making vestments, food preparation (baking), preparation of meals consumed in various ritual offerings, and temple housekeeping (cleaning).[9]

The narrator makes a distinction between temple servants (Ezra 2:43-54) and those descended from Solomon's servants (Ezra 2:55-57). The translation of the Hebrew term עבד as "servants" rather than "slaves" obscures Solomon's use of captured peoples as corvée (forced) laborers (1 Kgs 9:20-22; 2 Chr 8:7-8). The distinction is significant if we consider that descendants of the priests, Levites, and possibly temple servants were those born into a profession, whereas the descendants of Solomon's servants were those whose forefathers and foremothers were most likely born into servitude (i.e., slavery). According to Leviticus 25:35-46, conquered peoples (excluding the Israelites) could be enslaved in perpetuity—property to be inherited. In contrast, Deuteronomy 15:12-18 calls for the release of the slaves in the sixth year.

9. Phyllis A. Bird, *Missing Persons and Mistaken Identities: Women and Gender in Ancient Israel*, OBT (Minneapolis: Fortress, 1997), 95.

Ezra 2:36-58

[36]The priests: the descendants of
Jedaiah, of the house of Jeshua, nine
hundred seventy-three. [37]Of Immer,
one thousand fifty-two. [38]Of Pashhur,
one thousand two hundred forty-seven.
[39]Of Harim, one thousand seventeen.

[40]The Levites: the descendants of
Jeshua and Kadmiel, of the descendants of Hodaviah, seventy-four. [41]The
singers: the descendants of Asaph,
one hundred twenty-eight. [42]The descendants of the gatekeepers: of Shallum, of Ater, of Talmon, of Akkub, of
Hatita, and of Shobai, in all one hundred thirty-nine.

[43]The temple servants: the descendants of Ziha, Hasupha, Tabbaoth,
[44]Keros, Siaha, Padon, [45]Lebanah,
Hagabah, Akkub, [46]Hagab, Sham-
lai, Hanan, [47]Giddel, Gahar, Reaiah,
[48]Rezin, Nekoda, Gazzam, [49]Uzza,
Paseah, Besai, [50]Asnah, Meunim, Ne-
phisim, [51]Bakbuk, Hakupha, Harhur,
[52]Bazluth, Mehida, Harsha, [53]Barkos,
Sisera, Temah, [54]Neziah, and Hatipha.

[55]The descendants of Solomon's
servants: Sotai, Hassophereth, Peruda,
[56]Jaalah, Darkon, Giddel, [57]Shephatiah,
Hattil, Pochereth-hazzebaim, and Ami.

[58]All the temple servants and the
descendants of Solomon's servants
were three hundred ninety-two.

As for the male and female slaves whom you may have, it is from the nations around you that you may acquire male and female slaves. You may also acquire them from among the aliens residing with you and from their families who are with you who have been born in your land; they may be your property. You may keep them as a possession for your children after you, for them to inherit as property (Lev 25:44-46).

TRANSLATION MATTERS

The Hebrew term עבד is translated interchangeably "slave" or "servant." Wilda Gafney points out, however, that the synonymous usage is often incorrect. She offers, "Whereas the term 'servant' may be intended to focus on the nature of their duties, the translation 'slave' addresses their estate—bought, sold, and captured, many held in perpetuity, with their children born into their estate; limited opportunities for manumission; bereft of autonomy, particularly with regard to their persons, sexuality, and reproduction."[10] The selection of "servant," "slave," or "enslaved person" is contextually driven and a matter of the translator's interpretative choice.

10. Wilda Gafney, *Womanist Midrash: A Reintroduction to the Women of the Torah and the Throne* (Louisville: Westminster John Knox, 2017), 75.

Unlike their forebears, who were forced to construct Solomon's temple, the descendants of Solomon's servants voluntarily return to build the house of God. Rather than being exploited, this group is among those who accept Cyrus's invitation (Ezra 1:1) and travel with the caravan as contributing members of this newly formed community. While they are excluded from the signatory list in Nehemiah 10:28-29 and its oath-taking, they are portrayed as freed and assimilated landowners (Neh 11:3), which suggests a shift in their social status over time.

Slavery and Its Descendants

Chattel slavery in the United States (fifteenth to nineteenth centuries) created a system of racial hierarchy and oppression that has persisted, despite its abolition by the Thirteenth Amendment in 1865. The socioeconomic disparities, racial discrimination, and intergenerational transmission of trauma has left its impact on numerous generations of Africans and African Americans. Despite these challenges, their descendants have made significant contributions in various fields, including music, cuisine, literature, sports, politics, and science. These contributions demonstrate the resilience, talent, and ongoing impact of their descendants. Yet, despite these numerous achievements by African Americans and other people of color, racial iniquities and economic disparities continue to exist and as a matter of justice require serious attention if a more equitable society is to be achieved.

Missing Links (2:59-70)

The register continues with two groups having questionable or objectionable lineages. The first group represents persons who "could not prove their families or their descent, whether they belonged to Israel" (Ezra 2:59), while the second group is unable to validate their familial connections to the priesthood (Ezra 2:60-62). The inability of the first group to validate their ancestral connections foreshadows later concerns with those considered outsiders (Ezra 9:1-3). The concern for priestly genealogical purity serves as the foundation for the rejection of the second group. There is a possibility that the questionable status of Barzillai's lineage, as reported in Ezra 2:61, poses a threat to the purity of the priestly line because he marries a Gileadite. This does not, however,

Ezra 2:59-70

59The following were those who came up from Tel-melah, Tel-harsha, Cherub, Addan, and Immer, though they could not prove their families or their descent, whether they belonged to Israel: 60the descendants of Delaiah, Tobiah, and Nekoda, six hundred fifty-two. 61Also, of the descendants of the priests: the descendants of Habaiah, Hakkoz, and Barzillai (who had married one of the daughters of Barzillai the Gileadite and was called by their name). 62These looked for their entries in the genealogical records, but they were not found there, so they were excluded from the priesthood as unclean; 63the governor told them that they were not to partake of the most holy food until there should be a priest to consult Urim and Thummim.

64The whole assembly together was forty-two thousand three hundred sixty, 65besides their male and female servants, of whom there were seven thousand three hundred thirty-seven, and they had two hundred male and female singers. 66They had seven hundred thirty-six horses, two hundred forty-five mules, 67four hundred thirty-five camels, and six thousand seven hundred twenty donkeys.

68As soon as they came to the house of the Lord in Jerusalem, some of the heads of families made freewill offerings for the house of God, to erect it on its site. 69According to their resources they gave to the building fund sixty-one thousand darics of gold, five thousand minas of silver, and one hundred priestly robes.

70The priests, the Levites, and some of the people, as well as the singers, the gatekeepers, and the temple servants, lived in their towns and all Israel in their towns.

prevent him from inheriting from his wife's estate.[11] In an ancient context, genealogical purity for priests and laity serves as a marker of Judean identity, establishes boundaries, and allows for the reorganizing of the returning community. In a modern context, genealogical purity has been used to support genocidal attempts to eradicate particular ethnic groups (e.g., Jews, Native Americans, Armenians).

11. Ingeborg Löwsch notes that listing the daughter of Barzillai within the priestly lineage is interesting because a Gileadite marries into the line, and her husband takes her name. See "Miriam Ben Amram, or, How to Make Sense of the Absence of Women in the Genealogies of Levi (1 Chronicles 5:27–6:66)," in *The Bible and Feminism: Remapping the Field*, ed. Yvonne Sherwood (Oxford: Oxford University Press, 2017), 366n57. Löwsch appeals to Tamara Cohn Eskenazi's assumption that taking his wife's name placed this man in her family with a share of the inheritance (Eskenazi, "Out from the Shadows: Biblical Women in the Postexilic Era," *JSOT* 17 [1992]: 25–43).

The assembly count concludes in Ezra 2:64-65 for a total of 49,897 persons and is followed by a count of livestock (horses, camels, mules, and donkeys). The writer clearly distinguishes between those persons included in the assembly (42,360) and the servants (7,337) and their singers (200) who do not appear as part of the assembly. In Ezra 2:65, rather than the Hebrew עבד (enslaved person/servant), we find the term אמה (maid, handmaid, enslaved person). The term's usage can be associated with women's reproductive capability. For example, Ruth and Abigail self-identify as אמה (Ruth 3:9 and 1 Sam 25:24). In both instances, their self-identifications lead to sexual liaisons with Boaz and David, respectively. Hagar is labeled an אמה in Genesis 21:12; her womb will be used to bear an heir for Abraham. Wilda Gafney observes, "It is a morbid commentary that the new community could not function without enslaved humans, including enslaved women and girls available for sexual and reproductive use."[12] This enslaved community may operate independent of the larger assembly given that it has its own cadre of female and male singers (cf. 2 Sam 19:36; Eccl 2:8; 2 Chr 35:25), which does not appear to be the case in Ezra 2:41, where the singers appear to be only men. This diverse group travels with a total of 8,136 animals. While this number does not suggest that the returning caravan is wealthy, it does indicate that they have means.

The pilgrimage to the house of the Lord is given primacy over settling into their new homes. The first stop is Jerusalem (Ezra 2:68), where some heads of households freely contribute to the building fund and the vestments of priests (Ezra 2:69). This gesture underscores their commitment to reestablishing Jerusalem as the place for the worship practices of a newly reconstituted community. In Ezra 2:70, the conclusion that "all Israel [returned to] their towns" attempts to include questionable groups that lack ancestral and priestly connections (Ezra 2:59, 61). Therefore, they count among those mentioned in 1:3 as "any of those among you who are of his people" or those opting to join "his people" (cf. Exod 12:38).

We began our inspection of Ezra 2 with some reservations about what to do with these lists. We asked ourselves who cares about long genealogical lists that go on and on. We were equally perplexed about how these lists relate to our contemporary audiences. We discovered, however, that these lists helped this group connect their past, present, and future

12. Gafney, *Womanist Midrash*, 80.

Sankofa—Looking Back to Learn and Launch

Sankofa is a word in the Twi language from the Akan tribe in Ghana. Sankofa translates to "go back and get it" (*san*, to return; *ko*, to go; *fa*, to fetch, to seek and take). Sankofa is often associated with the proverb, "*Se wo were fi na wosankofa a yenkyi*," which translates as, "It is not taboo to fetch what is at risk of being left behind."[13]

in a similar way that both of us connected our histories when sharing our stories about our familial roots. The lists say a lot about identity and sense of belonging, which makes them important contributions to how we capture and document for posterity the stories within stories that reflect our commitment to family, community, and God. In a way, these lists embody the African concept of "Sankofa" where knowing and honoring the past serve as a guide for launching the future.

13. "The Power of Sankofa: Know History," Berea College, https://www.berea.edu/centers/carter-g-woodson-center-for-interracial-education/the-power-of-sankofa/.

Ezra 3

Feasts and Festivals

Two distinct yet collaborative units appear in Ezra 3. In the first unit (Ezra 3:1-6), the institution and participation in the religious rituals of their forebears capture the group's sense of impermanence and inform and form their identity as God's people. This sense of impermanence appears resolved once the group begins the erection of a permanent place for worship (Ezra 3:10). The second unit (Ezra 3:7-13) details the economies of temple building, the specific Levites tasked with its construction, and the diverse views the returnees have regarding the new edifice upon its completion.

Rituals perform a significant function in every society. As a supportive mechanism by which individuals and communities keep traditions alive, rituals give meaning to our lived experiences. Similarly, the establishment of calendars (linear or cyclical) and the practice of dating events (birthdates, holidays, anniversaries, etc.) allow us to commemorate and anchor significant incidents in time and thus provide a way for us to order the world, its activities, and our place within it (past, present, and future). In a religious context, calendars and dating become a way for the past to influence the present concerning communal formation and solidarity. For example, the Christian ritual of baptism brings the one baptized into the community while simultaneously reinforcing for other participants their baptism and identity as members of the Christian community.

In Ezra 2, the repatriates began to settle in Judah and its vicinity (Ezra 2:70). Here in Ezra 3, this group must now start reconstructing their communal and religious identity in what will be a new place for some. Rituals rooted in the Mosaic tradition serve as markers of a collective religious identity that specifically situates the newly formed *golah* community within the beliefs of ancient Israel. Still, when addressing the salient issues of sexism, classism, and religious hegemony, one cannot help but notice how Ezra 3 reinforces, as much by what is not said as by what is said, the patriarchal, hierarchical, and stratified structure of Judean society.

New Moon, New Beginnings (3:1-7)

The opening language in Ezra 3:1 mirrors the concluding language of Ezra 2:70, which effectively shifts the audience's attention in both space and time from the group's journey from Babylon to their settling throughout Judah to their first worship gathering in the city of Jerusalem. This gathering occurs in the seventh month, which traditionally links to the Jewish Festival of Sukkot (the Feast of Tabernacles or Festival of Booths). The group's observance of this important religious festival mirrors Israel's earlier wilderness experience and its impermanence (Lev 23:34, 42-43; Deut 16:13, 16; 31:10).[1]

Celebrating in the Midst of a Pandemic[1]

The Jewish festival Sukkot (Festival of Booths) is sometimes referred to as the *Time of Rejoicing*. The week-long festival that occurs five days after Yom Kippur (Day of Atonement) is a celebration of the harvest while also commemorating God's protection of the Israelites following their exodus from Egypt. Is it possible to rejoice during a global pandemic? The restrictions of COVID-19 brought about a change in our behaviors and activities. While some of us did not leave our homes to live temporarily in booths, we learned to live without some modern comforts, which brought us nearer (in a nonphysical way) to our neighbors and those who had no homes or booths. Confined to our homes, we drew closer to our families, reevaluated what was most important in life, reconnected to one another in ways that produced new stories and shared memories. With most of our churches, mosques, and synagogues closed, we even learned how to worship God in virtual environments and where technology and social media (Zoom, WebEx, FaceTime, Facebook, and others) became the impermanent booths that connected congregations and expanded our concept of community.

1. This is an adaptation from Dov Lipman, "Time to Rejoice on Sukkot, despite Coronavirus," *Jerusalem Post* (October 1, 2020), https://www.jpost.com/opinion/time-to-rejoice-on-sukkot-despite-corona-644206.

Ezra 3:1-7

1When the seventh month came and the
Israelites were in their towns, the people
gathered together as one in Jerusalem.
2Then Jeshua son of Jozadak with his
fellow priests and Zerubbabel son of
Shealtiel with his kin set out to build the
altar of the God of Israel, to offer burnt
offerings on it, as prescribed in the law
of Moses the man of God. 3They set
up the altar on its foundation because
they were in dread of the people of
the lands, and they offered burnt offerings upon it to the Lord, morning and
evening. 4And they kept the Festival
of Booths, as prescribed, and offered
the daily burnt offerings by number according to the ordinance, as required
for each day, 5and after that the regular
burnt offerings, the offerings at the new
moon and at all the sacred festivals of
the Lord, and the offerings of everyone
who made a freewill offering to the Lord.
6From the first day of the seventh month
they began to offer burnt offerings to the
Lord. But the foundation of the temple
of the Lord was not yet laid. 7So they
gave money to the masons and the
carpenters, and food, drink, and oil to
the Sidonians and the Tyrians to bring
cedar trees from Lebanon to the sea, to
Joppa, according to the grant that they
had from King Cyrus of Persia.

Throughout the Scriptures of ancient Israel, the erection of altars as places to seek God's approval is commonplace. Noah, Abraham, Jacob, Moses, Gideon, Elijah, Saul, and David all built altars to God for various reasons. Thus, altars appear as sites where reverence and worship of God take place. During the period in which Ezra is written, it is the priest who officiates and offers burnt offerings. This officiation is inherently a male exercise. The writer places Jeshua and his fellow priests ahead of Zerubbabel and his kin when listing those who set out to construct the altar (Ezra 3:1, 2). The mention of their fathers (Jozadak and Shealtiel) provides the continuity that links these families (pre- and postexilically) to prominent priestly and Davidic houses. Jozadak is the son of the chief priest Seraiah, executed by Nebuchadnezzar (2 Kgs 25:18-20; 1 Chr 6:14, 15). Shealtiel is the son of Jehoiachin, the only surviving king of the Davidic monarchy, who surrendered during one of the Babylonian invasions (2 Kgs 24:12). While the listing presents a collaboration between the priesthood and government (i.e., the Davidic lineage), the ordering and distinction between "priests" and "king" suggest an institutional structure where the priesthood has gained greater authority. The collaboration between the priests and the ruling elders (i.e., religion and government, respectively) appears as a welcomed working arrangement. Yet, in a contemporary sense, would we want the US government building altars? The issue is one of control and neutrality. Government involvement complicates stakeholder interests when determining who or what an altar represents (which religion? which deity?) and potentially opens the door for unethical and illegal practices by government and religious officials. While the officiation of burnt offerings is exclusively male, the same may not be true of the altar's construction. Mud bricks, as the primary building material used in the construction of ancient Israelite homes in general and altars in particular, required the gathering and mixing of straw, reeds, water, and sand. Given the labor required to produce mud bricks for construction projects, it is feasible that all family members had a hand in the altar's construction.[2]

Altar Building in Ancient Israel

Early Israelite altars were made of stone and devoid of stairs. Priests performing their official duties wore loincloths (and no undergarments). The absence of stairs ensured that the priests did not expose their genitals unintentionally (Exod 20:26).

Israelite altar at Beer-Sheva, https://en.wikipedia.org/wiki/Tel_Be%27er_Sheva#/media/File:Tel_Be'er_Sheva_Altar_2007041.JPG.

The construction of the altar proceeds despite the group's "dread of the people of the lands" (Ezra 3:3). The Hebrew phrase מעמי הארצית ("from the peoples of the lands") suggests interaction with multiple groups. While the identification of the neighboring peoples is unknown at this point, the mention of them here foreshadows the conflict and competition that will arise between them and the repatriates (Ezra 4). The repatriates' fear raises questions of their receptivity by those already living in the land. Arguably, they may know that their presence will be met with resistance or, at best, be problematic. Constructing an altar in Jerusalem potentially represents an intrusion to the practices and beliefs of those who remained in the land following the exile. Still, the fear of the neighboring peoples does not halt the construction of the altar, an activity that, according to Ezra, is divinely sanctioned (by God) and politically supported (by Cyrus).

2. Robert S. Homsher, "Mud Bricks and the Process of Construction in the Middle Bronze Age Southern Levant," *BASOR* 368 (November 2012): 22.

The sense of impermanence that comes with celebrating the Festival of Booths (Sukkot) in Ezra 3:4 reflects a people who appear uncertain about both their identity and their acceptance in a new place. This uncertainty mirrors that of their forebears following their exodus from Egypt and subsequent wilderness wanderings. Who are the returnees in this space: God's people, citizens of the Persian Empire? By situating themselves within the religious festivals "according to the law of Moses," the people ground themselves in the traditions of their ancestors where Torah, land, ancestry, and temple constitute what it means to be God's people. The festivals unify the group by providing a shared sense of purpose where the companion aspects of their common goal and future as a religious community coalesce.

The sacrificial offerings continue in Ezra 3:5 with the inclusion of two additional offerings, the new moon offering (Rosh Chodesh) and the freewill offering. Using a lunar calendar, Rosh Chodesh is the first day of the Jewish/Israelite month, representing the "first sighting" (מולד) of the new moon and indicating new beginnings. The sighting of the new moon signals the moon's transition from ominous darkness to a hopeful renewal represented by the moon's light.[3] This transition becomes ritualized in celebrations of the new moon festival by various ancient (e.g., Babylonian, Egyptian, Mesopotamian) and contemporary (e.g., Wicca, Navajo) cultures. References to new moon festivals frequently appear in biblical narratives (e.g., Num 10:10; 1 Sam 20; Ps 81:3; Hos 2:11; Amos 8:5). According to the Talmud (b. Ḥullin 60b), the moon, personified as a woman, was created equal to the sun, her male counterpart.[4] God diminishes the moon's size when she questions the rationale of co-regency among celestial bodies.

Women's participation in new moon festivals has a long history. Initially celebrated by both men and women, the festival became less prominent as the Sabbath became more significant (i.e., Neh 9 and 10).[5] Today, Jewish women have reclaimed the Festival of Rosh Chodesh as a way to envision and create possibilities for "women-centered ceremonies" that empower and promote the equality of women.[6] Interestingly, Yom Kippur (Day of Atonement) and Rosh Hashanah (Jewish New Year) are not mentioned here or elsewhere in Ezra or Nehemiah and only briefly

3. Steven Holloway, "New Moon," in *Eerdmans Dictionary of the Bible*, ed. David Noel Freedman (Grand Rapids: Eerdmans, 2000), 962.

4. Marcia Falk, *The Book of Blessings: New Jewish Prayers for Daily Life, the Sabbath, and the New Moon Festival* (New York: Reform Judaism Publishing, 2017), 329.

5. In the scriptures of ancient Israel there are festivals at the beginnings of the month (e.g., Num 10:10; 28:11; 1 Chr 23:31).

6. Falk, *The Book of Blessings*, 329–30.

appear in Leviticus 23:27-28 and 25:9. The absence of these two significant festivals in Ezra and Nehemiah suggests holidays can change in importance over time.

The Crescent Moon

The Jewish calendar is lunar based. This lunar cycle means that the moon's rotation rather than the sun's rotation serves as a predominant way of measuring time. In Exodus 12, when Moses and Aaron are in Egypt, God says, "This month shall mark for you the beginning of months; it shall be the first month of the year for you" (Exod 12:1-2). How do Moses and Aaron understand the reference to "this month"? In the Mishnah (m. Rosh Hashanah 2:8), rabbis debate this same question to determine how to mark the start of a month by observing the moon's phases. The מולד, plural מולדות, is a Hebrew word meaning "birth." Theoretically, the מולד represents the time of the moon's birth (sighting) when the crescent first appears after its lunar cycle's completion. For Jews of the Second Temple period, the crescent moon marked the start of a new month.

Image from https://www.pexels.com/photo/crescent-moon-in-the-night-sky-16949370/.

References to the grain offering (מנחה) and the drink offering (נסך), offerings given during Sukkot (Lev 23:34-44), are also absent from Ezra 3:1-7. The freewill offering, however, as a voluntary offering of all the people, points to the communal nature of the gathering as both men and women present their gifts to God (Ezra 3:5). Freewill contributions go above and beyond the offerings and sacrifices prescribed by Levitical law. The voluntary nature of the offering suggests that persons were willing to commit even more of their resources to benefit the entire community. We find contemporary examples when churches, synagogues, and mosques build new or renovate existing houses of worship. In these instances, members of the congregation donate money specifically to fund these types of endeavors. While these monetary contributions may vary in size, member participation adds to the collective sense of identity, solidarity, and belonging. In Ezra 3:1-7 the impetus for building the Lord's house appears closer to the time of Cyrus. This timing suggests that the work begins almost immediately and counters the portrait in Ezra 3:8-13, which situates the work much later, in the time of Darius I (522–486 BCE).

It's a Celebration (3:8-13)

In Ezra 3:8-13, a second dating appears for the erection of the Lord's house as well as a reversal in who initiates the work. In Ezra 3:1, the project begins seven months after the group arrives in Judah, with Jeshua and Zerubbabel leading the people's efforts. Here in Ezra 3:8, however, the dating places the start of the project a year and a half later (second year, second month) and switches the order of the leaders' names, placing Zerubbabel first and then Jeshua. This ordering matches the arrangement of names provided in a similar account in Haggai 2:1-3:

> In the seventh month, on the twenty-first day of the month, the word of the Lord came by the prophet Haggai, saying: "Speak now to Zerubbabel son of Shealtiel, governor of Judah, and to Joshua son of Jehozadak, the high priest, and to the remnant of the people, and say, Who is left among you that saw this house in its former glory? How does it look to you now? Is it not in your sight as nothing?"

Haggai chastises the repatriates for their failure upon their return to address the dilapidated conditions of the Lord's house. Biblical scholars suggest that the temple's reconstruction took place during the time of Darius I.[7] It is possible that the practical needs of this newly formed community (permanence, housing) diverted them from their original mission to rebuild "a house at Jerusalem" (Ezra 1:2; Hag 1:2). The subtle compression of the timeline together with reordering the names of the community's leaders in Ezra 3:1-7 points to a social structure in which the priests are given greater prominence and authority than governmental leaders. This portrait of authority is undermined in Ezra 3:8, however,

7. Lisbeth S. Fried (*Ezra: A Commentary*, Critical Commentaries [Sheffield: Sheffield Phoenix, 2015], 199) and Carol L. Meyers and Eric M. Meyers (*Haggai, Zechariah 1–8: A New Translation and Commentary*, AB 25B [Garden City, NY: Doubleday, 1987], introduction) are among those who credit the reconstruction of the temple to the time of Darius I. Diana Edelman places the reconstruction to the time of Artaxerxes I (465–424 BCE) (*The Origins of the "Second" Temple: Persian Imperial Policy and the Rebuilding of Jerusalem*, rev. ed. [Hoboken, NJ: Taylor and Francis, 2014]). For a history of interpretation of this scholarship, see Edelman, *The Origins of the "Second" Temple*, 3–9.

Ezra 3:8-13

[8]In the second year after their arrival at the house of God at Jerusalem, in the second month, Zerubbabel son of Shealtiel and Jeshua son of Jozadak made a beginning, together with the rest of their people, the priests and the Levites and all who had come to Jerusalem from the captivity. They appointed the Levites from twenty years old and up to have the oversight of the work on the house of the LORD. [9]And Jeshua with his sons and his kin, and Kadmiel and his sons, Binnui and Hodaviah, along with the sons of Henadad, the Levites, their sons and kin, together took charge of the workers in the house of God.

[10]When the builders laid the foundation of the temple of the LORD, the priests in their vestments were stationed to praise the LORD with trumpets, and the Levites, the sons of Asaph, with cymbals, according to the direc-

and indicates that perhaps the priesthood had not solidified its dominant position in the community at this time.

Here, the narrator makes a point of naming the male ancestral houses to which Zerubbabel and Jeshua belong ("son of Shealtiel," "son of Jozadak"). This naming differs in 1 Kings 24, which includes female members of Zerubbabel's genealogy (mothers and wives). Overall, the term "house" can have various meanings in biblical narrative, either as a reference to one's lineage (father or mother), as one's physical dwelling, or symbolically as a place where the deity resides (religious edifice). With the resettlement recounted in Ezra, the continuity and permanence of the repatriates' houses (ancestral and physical) have been established and are now juxtaposed with God's house, which remains incomplete. The oversight for the work belongs to the Levites (Ezra 3:8), while the liturgical elements of worship reside with the priests (Ezra 3:9). This distinction is important because it speaks to the division of labor among temple personnel. The division also reflects the expanded role of the Levites in the postexilic period. The presence of priests would be premature absent a physical temple to carry out their duties.[8]

The construction of the temple's foundation possibly required considerably more resources than those needed to construct the altar. Therefore, while the gifts and contributions of women go unmentioned in this chapter, there is reason to believe that women too contributed resources to this project as part of the community. We see this earlier in the book

8. Fried, *Ezra*, 175.

tions of King David of Israel; [11]and they sang responsively, praising and giving thanks to the LORD,

"For he is good,
for his steadfast love endures
forever toward Israel."

And all the people responded with a great shout when they praised the LORD because the foundation of the house of the LORD had been laid. [12]But many of the priests and Levites and heads of families, old people who had seen the first house on its foundations, wept with a loud voice when they saw this house, though many shouted aloud for joy, [13]so that the people could not distinguish the sound of the joyful shout from the sound of the people's weeping, for the people shouted so loudly that the sound was heard far away.

of Exodus when both men and women donate to the building of the tabernacle: "So they came, both men and women; all who were of a willing heart brought brooches and earrings and signet rings and pendants, all sorts of gold objects, everyone bringing an offering of gold to the LORD" (Exod 35:22). Whereas the specific economies involving the altar's construction are absent from Ezra 3:1-6, here preparation for the project reads like an abridged version of 1 Kings 5:1-11 and the arrangements made for the erection of Solomon's temple (cf. 1 Chr 22:4). By paralleling Zerubbabel's and Jeshua's actions to those associated with constructing Solomon's temple, the writer strengthens this group's ties to the land, traditions of ancient Israel, and the Davidic line.

The completion of the foundation in Ezra 3:10 ushers in a liturgical moment of celebration where only the priests wear vestments. The vestments as ritual attire worn by male priests are described in Exodus 28–29 as well as in Leviticus 1–8. The vestments mark the priest as one set aside for service to the deity; more important, they distinguish the priest from the rest of the congregation. Deborah Rooke examines the gendered nature of priestly attire as clothing that designates the status and condition of the priest (i.e., ritually pure and holy). Rooke observes, "This is not an issue of sex, but of gender; what it means to be a man in the presence of God is very different from what it means to be a man in everyday society."[9] The vestments, although associated with the rituals

9. Deborah W. Rooke, *Embroidered Garments: Priests and Gender in Biblical Israel*, King's College London Studies in the Bible and Gender 2 (Sheffield: Sheffield Phoenix, 2009), 30.

and functions of the priestly office, also function as symbols of male perfection (physically and ritually) and are worn only by those who are Aaron's descendants and only those who fit the physical criteria of an unblemished body (Lev 21:16-24). The vestments may be clothing worn by men, but those who made them were most likely women.[10] Susan Ackerman notes that many of the ancient Near Eastern goddesses were spinners and weavers and that the biblical text most likely connects the Canaanite goddess Asherah to this art as well.[11]

Vestments: The Women Who Make Them and the Women Who Wear Them

The biblical text provides evidence that women were weavers in Israelite society. We find skilled female weavers in Exodus 25:25. The woman of Proverbs 31 "seeks wool and flax and works with willing hands" (Prov 31:13), and "she puts her hands to the distaff, and her hands hold the spindle" (Prov 31:19). In addition, this woman sews clothing of "fine linen and purple" (Prov 31:22) and sells linen garments and sashes for market (Prov 31:24). The biblical record corresponds to the archeological evidence where weaving is often found in the domestic spaces that women inhabited.

There is a prohibition against mixing wool and flax except when making priestly garments (Exod 39:22-24, 27; Deut 22:11). Historically, Christian vestments were seen as the attire of male clergy, and, early on, Christian clergywomen shunned them because of their gendered association. Today, female clergy, similar to their male counterparts, wear vestments as part of their offices' ritualistic and symbolic function. By donning vestments, women reinforce their roles as clergy without drawing attention to their gender. The gendered nature of vestments for at least some Christian denominations has been removed. This may not be the case in other Christian denominations.

The completion of the foundation brings about a joyous celebration featuring an antiphonal choral liturgy in Ezra 3:11, "and they sang responsively, praising and giving thanks to the Lord, 'For he is good,

10. Jennie Ebeling, *Women's Lives in Biblical Times* (London: T&T Clark, 2010), 56–57.

11. Susan Ackerman, "Asherah, the West Semitic Goddess of Spinning and Weaving?," *JNES* 67 (January 2008): 7.

for his steadfast love endures forever toward Israel.'" An antiphony is a musical dialogue between members within a worship setting. The antiphony in Ezra 3:11 is offered in two parts—the praise of the priests and the thanksgiving of the Levites. The praise acknowledges a characteristic feature of God as good, while thanksgiving affirms God's actions, specifically toward this group, Israel. The phrase "his steadfast love endures forever" is a frequent refrain found in the Psalms, Chronicles, and Jeremiah (e.g., Ps 100:5; 106:1; 136; 1 Chr 16:34, 41; Jer 33:11) occurring over thirty-seven times in these books. Only in Ezra 3:11, however, do we find the additional emphasis on the גלה as the people of Israel. Here, the writer of Ezra uses the antiphon to introduce the first appearance of public worship by this group. The recitation from the Psalms serves to reinforce their identity as a people and distinguishes them from other groups that may have also worshiped Yahweh.

The Power of Liturgy to Construct Community Identity

Feminists and womanists remind us that the words and symbols that we use in worship define our foci and values as a community. For example, when our God language in worship is masculine, it perpetuates a community ethic that values masculinity over femininity since males alone are considered to be created in God's image.[12] Further, womanist theologians point out that symbols and rituals can harm minority communities and function to reinforce oppressive power structures when God is imaged predominantly as white and Western.[13]

The antiphonal singing of the priests and Levites brings a great shout from everyone. It is unclear whether this great shout refers to the people singing along with the priests and Levites or represents their affirmation

12. Some examples: Carol P. Christ and Judith Plaskow, *Goddess and God in the World: Conversations in Embodied Theology* (Minneapolis: Fortress, 2016); Rebecca S. Chopp, *The Power to Speak: Feminism, Language, God* (New York: Crossroad, 1989); Rosemary Radford Ruether, *Sexism and God-Talk: Toward a Feminist Theology* (Boston: Beacon, 1983).

13. Jacquelyn Grant, *White Women's Christ and Black Women's Jesus: Feminist Christology and Womanist Response*, AARAS 64 (Atlanta: Scholars Press, 1989); Delores S. Williams, *Sisters in the Wilderness: The Challenge of Womanist God-Talk* (Maryknoll, NY: Orbis Books, 1993).

of what they hear and see, "the foundation of the house of the Lord had been laid" (Ezra 3:11). Whether the phrase כל־העם, "all the people," in Ezra 3:11 includes women and children is debatable. The participation of women and children at the dedication of the walls, another momentous occasion for this group, is explicit in Nehemiah 12:43: "They offered great sacrifices that day and rejoiced, for God had made them rejoice with great joy; the women and children also rejoiced." The laying of the foundation can be read both literally and symbolically. The physical foundation establishes the permanency of their worship place in Jerusalem. Symbolically, the foundation establishes this group as a newly formed worshiping community.

TRANSLATION MATTERS

The Hebrew word for foundation הוסד (*husad*) has a dual meaning: "to lay a foundation" and "establish" or "found" something. The form of this word in Ezra 3:11 is the *hof'al* meaning "to be founded." Thus, it carries literal and symbolic meanings.

The concluding verses, Ezra 3:12-13, depict the dissonance when a nostalgic past collides with an inspired present. The dissonance results from a generational gap whereby the "old people who had seen the first house on its foundations, wept with a loud voice when they saw this house" while those who had possibly never seen the first temple (because they grew up in exile) "shouted aloud for joy." The older priests, Levites, and familial heads cannot forget the past, and a younger group, those most likely mentioned in Ezra 3:8, are excited about new beginnings. The older group's perception of the new foundation was expressed in terms that something lost was not recovered. This group holds a memory that nothing new can be as good as what was, in this case, the grandeur of Solomon's temple (see excursus, "Did Solomon's Temple Really Exist?"). A nostalgic look back provides a sanitized impression of events and does not take into account the historical realities of the time, which were anything but perfect. Perhaps the elders held on to a glorified version of the first temple because the circumstances surrounding its destruction and the forced removal from their homeland are wounds not easily forgotten. Building the second house of the Lord triggers these memories and reintroduces the trauma of exile. Contemporarily, to hark back to the "good old days," as in the call to "make America great again," omits the reality of gender, racial, ethnic, sexual, and economic oppression and marginalization that existed and continues to exist for some groups. This sanitization of America's past by various persons invested in this portrait of the United States continues to plague all sectors of American society (government, education, economics, race relations, and religion).

Did Solomon's Temple Really Exist?

Solomon's temple continues to draw interest as a matter of controversy. Some scholars suggest that outside the biblical material, there is a lack of direct archaeological evidence to support its existence.[14] The absence of a temple would support the need for Ezra's group to build a new foundation for the new temple structure. Modern excavations, however, have uncovered the remains of temples that potentially share cultural similarities with the Jerusalem temple described in the biblical text (e.g., the Motza temple in Jerusalem, and Ain Dara in northwest Syria). This raises the question of why a foundation needs to be built if it already exists.

The biblical portrait of a cacophony of voices (some weeping and others shouting with joy) at the laying of the temple's foundation depicts contrasting perspectives of what it means to return. For some, returning to the land recognizes that things have changed. The elders and religious elite are not returning to Jerusalem and its former glory as a religious center. For others, it offers the possibility of a new and different religious community in ancestral lands. In part celebration and in part grief, the sound is loud enough to be heard beyond the immediate vicinity of

14. For those who hold this view, see Mark S. Smith, "In Solomon's Temple (1 Kings 6–7): Between Text and Archaeology," in *Confronting the Past: Archaeological and Historical Essays on Ancient Israel in Honor of William G. Dever*, ed. Seymour Gitin, J. Edward Wright, and J. P. Dessel (Winona Lake, IN: Eisenbrauns, 2006), 275–82; Diana Edelman, "What Can We Know About the Persian-Era Temple in Jerusalem?," in *Temple Building and Temple Cult: Architecture and Cultic Paraphernalia of Temples in the Levant (2.-1. Mill. B.C.E.)*, ed. Jens Kamlah, Abhandlungen des Deutschen Palästina-Vereins 41. (Wiesbaden: Harrassowitz, 2012), 343–68.

Jerusalem: "for the people shouted so loudly that the sound was heard far away" (Ezra 3:13). As the chapter concludes, this intermingling of grief and joy creates a liminal space that holds in tension who they were and who they are to become.

Ezra 4–6

Power, Politics, and Policies

Ezra 4–6 incorporates several Aramaic sources to depict the conflict brewing between the people in the land and the returnees.[1] Ezra 4 sets the stage for the impending rivalry between these groups, beginning with a series of correspondence (three letters) between them and Persian kings. Ezra 5 and 6 amplify the tension by naming specific antagonists. Ambiguities abound in these chapters pertaining to (1) the precise identity of those framed as outsiders, (2) the concerns that prompt the conflict between local inhabitants and the exilic returnees, and (3) the chronological sequencing of writing campaigns involving Persian rulers. Overall, these chapters depict the shifting power dynamics, political loyalties, and ideologies that attend to the exchanges between ethnic-religious groups living in close proximity to a contested urban space, Jerusalem.

Standoff and Subterfuge (4:1-5)

The juxtaposition of the descendants of those brought to the land under Assyrian King Esar-haddon, ca. 681–669 BCE (and therefore foreigners), with those removed from the land (exiles with ancestral connections to Judah, Benjamin, and the Davidic monarchy) sets up outsider-insider polarization and the subsequent conflict that follows. In Ezra 4:1, those outside the community receive the label "adversaries of Judah and Benjamin" and self-identify with a group displaced by King Esar-haddon

1. Ezra 4:8–6:18 is written entirely in Aramaic, the common language used during the time of Ezra and Nehemiah's composition.

Ezra 4:1-5

[1]When the adversaries of Judah and
Benjamin heard that the returned exiles
were building a temple to the Lord, the
God of Israel, [2]they approached Zerubbabel and the heads of families and
said to them, "Let us build with you, for
we worship your God as you do, and
we have been sacrificing to him ever
since the days of King Esar-haddon
of Assyria, who brought us here." [3]But
Zerubbabel, Jeshua, and the rest of
the heads of families in Israel said to
them, "You shall have no part with us
in building a house for our God, but we
alone will build for the Lord, the God
of Israel, as King Cyrus of Persia has
commanded us."

[4]Then the people of the land discouraged the people of Judah and
made them afraid to build, [5]and they
bribed officials to frustrate their plan
throughout the reign of King Cyrus
of Persia and until the reign of King
Darius of Persia.

(Ezra 4:2). Esar-haddon employed a policy of displacing conquered peoples into other imperial-controlled territories, continuing a policy put in place by the previous Assyrian king, Sennacherib.[2]

These adversaries *hear* about the building project. This *hearing* follows the "sound that was heard far away" reported in Ezra 3:13. As a continuation of the activities in Ezra 3:13, this *sound* draws the attention of those living in the land. The adversaries seek to participate in the building endeavor based on the perceived notion of mutual religious affiliation, namely, their worship of the same deity: "Let us build with you, for we worship your God as you do, and we have been sacrificing to him since the days of King Esar-haddon" (Ezra 4:2). Remarkably, the group's claim of religious affiliation is not contested but instead is tacitly acknowledged. Here, the nonresponsiveness of Jewish leadership heightens the negotiating of identity taking place based on the group's claims of a shared religious heritage.

It is unclear where these sacrifices and worship take place. Given this group's long-standing history in the land prior to and following the destruction of the Jerusalem temple in 587/586 BCE, there is a possibility they did not perform rituals in Jerusalem. Curiously, one wonders why this group seeks to join the repatriates' building campaign if they already have a place to worship and sacrifice (i.e., a temple).

2. Israel Eph'al, "Esarhaddon, Egypt, and Shubria: Politics and Propaganda," *JCS* 57 (2005): 100; Avraham Faust, "Settlement and Demography in Seventh-Century Judah and the Extent and Intensity of Sennacherib's Campaign," *PEQ* 140 (2008): 170.

Zerubbabel, Jeshua, and familial heads deny their request on religious and political grounds; they insist, "You shall have no part with us in building a house for our God, but we alone will build for the LORD, the God of Israel, as King Cyrus of Persia has commanded us" (Ezra 4:3).

Monarch Name	**Nation**	**Date of Reign**	**Noted For**
Esar-Haddon	Assyria	681–669 BCE	Displacement and resettling of conquered groups to imperial provinces
Osnappar (Ashurbanipal)	Assyria	668–629 BCE	Displacement and resettling of conquered groups to imperial provinces at the Fall of the Northern Kingdom (722/721 BCE)
Cyrus	Persia	559–530 BCE	Allowing exiled Jews to return to Judah and Jerusalem
Darius (I–III)	Persia	522–486 BCE	Allowing the returnees to resume construction of the Jerusalem temple. Setting up the administrative structure for Persian controlled provinces (Satraps)
Ahasuerus/ Xerxes	Persia	486–465 BCE	Stopping the returnees from rebuilding the temple upon their return to Judah and Jerusalem
Artaxerxes I	Persia	465–424 BCE	Financing Ezra and Nehemiah's mission in Jerusalem
Darius II	Persia	423–405 BCE	Regaining Greek cities during Peloponnesian war 431–404 BCE
Artaxerxes II	Persia	404–359 BCE	
Artaxerxes III	Persia	359–338 BCE	
Artaxerxes IV	Persia	338–336 BCE	
Darius III	Persia	336–330 BCE	Last of the Persian Kings—defeated by Alexander the Great

We discussed the difficulty of dating in our introduction. While we are not particularly concerned about dating, we do want to provide a sense of the text's complicated chronology. The naming of the kings in Ezra does not reflect that several Persian kings were referred to by the same name and reigned during different periods of Persian rule. For example, three kings named Darius reigned over Persia (Darius I, 522–486 BCE; Darius II, 423–405 BCE; and Darius III, 336–330 BCE). Similarly, Artaxerxes shares his name with four kings (Artaxerxes I, 464–423 BCE; Artaxerxes II, 404–359 BCE; Artaxerxes III, 359–338 BCE; Artaxerxes IV, 338–336 BCE). The text of Ezra–Nehemiah does not distinguish among the kings who share the same name, making it difficult to date the narrated events and the specific actions attributed to them.[3] The list of Persian kings also does not include all the rulers but only those who appear in and impact the narrative in Ezra and Nehemiah. For example, Persian history records two kings, Cambyses (530–522 BCE) and Bardiya (522 BCE), between the reigns of Cyrus the Great (Cyrus II) and Darius I. The absence of these kings in Ezra–Nehemiah may reflect the rapidly shifting political climate occurring within the Persian Empire.

The repatriates' possessive claim of "our God" and their insistence that "we alone will build" a house as commanded by King Cyrus (Ezra 4:2) makes their concern both religious and political. According to 2 Kings 21:7 and 2 Chronicles 6:6-9, God establishes Jerusalem as God's abode and place of worship. Politically, the repatriates' appeal to their connections to King Cyrus reads alternatively as a statement of loyalty to the Persian Empire. Cyrus's edict in Ezra 1:2-3, however, makes no such claim to exclude the local inhabitants or anyone else in this endeavor.

Interestingly, both groups are survivors of colonial expansionist practices who identify with their oppressors. It seems ironic that those who are designated the "people of the land" (עם־הארץ) are not indigenous to the land (Ezra 4:2, 4). The political undertones are apparent as those in the land have lived there long enough to establish a political foothold under previous regimes (e.g., Assyria and Babylon). The repatriates challenge this foothold when they state they are following the orders of King Cyrus, who now rules over both groups (Ezra 4:4). Politics and power converge such that the adversaries have enough political influence to bring the entire building project to a standstill, "and they bribed officials

3. For more information on the dating of the kings, see Lisbeth S. Fried, *Ezra: A Commentary*, Critical Commentaries (Sheffield: Sheffield Phoenix, 2015).

to frustrate their plan throughout the reign of King Cyrus of Persia and until the reign of King Darius of Persia" (Ezra 4:5).

Where Are You From?

The proverbial question "Where are you from?" is a way of possessing spaces and creating boundaries of who can also inhabit those spaces. This sense of spatial ownership comes about when these spaces become "my neighborhood" and not "our neighborhood." Moreover, we make these claims of spatial retention even if we are not indigenous to the spaces in question.

In Ezra 4:4-5, the narrator frames the group's response to this rejection as one of retaliation as their obstruction of the building efforts makes the repatriates "afraid to build" (the literal translation of the Hebrew says, "weakening the hands of"). The exact nature of the returnees' fear is, however, left unexplored. The narrator characterizes the people in the land as politically connected and corrupt, using bribery to attain their ends. We can draw contemporary parallels when local inhabitants use their political clout to stymie projects they do not want in their communities. The identity of the bribed officials is ambiguous. These persons could be the same Persian overlords to whom the repatriates make their appeal or Judean officials. Realistically, no government is immune from unethical acts by employees. Recent attempts to hold accountable several presidents of the United States (e.g., Richard Nixon, Bill Clinton, Donald J. Trump) for unscrupulous behavior and the prosecution of local government officials for unethical conduct attest that persons at every level of government can abuse their positions.

The writer does not explain what the bribery entailed or what actions the officials took to cause the stoppage of the building activities directly. We find an alternative view for the delay in the book of Haggai. In Haggai, the prophet accuses the Jews and their leadership (Zerubbabel and Joshua/Jeshua) rather than the bribery of unnamed officials for the people's failure to construct the temple, specifically Haggai 1:1-4 states,

> In the second year of King Darius, in the sixth month, on the first day of the month, the word of the Lord came by the prophet Haggai to Zerubbabel son of Shealtiel, governor of Judah, and to Joshua son of Jehozadak, the high priest: "Thus says the Lord of hosts: These people

> say the time has not yet come to rebuild the LORD's house." Then the word of the LORD came by the prophet Haggai, saying: "Is it a time for you yourselves to live in your paneled houses, while this house lies in ruins?"

Haggai's account adds complexity to the accusation in Ezra 4:4-5. The account questions the authenticity of the repatriates' claim that their fear of the people halts the temple's construction for decades. Their fear and the accusation of bribery produce a portrait in which the adversaries and/or the people in the land seem like a seedy, immoral, and unethical group, thus justifying their rejection in Ezra 4:2-3.

Given our context, we considered where to put our textual loyalties—to align them with the outsiders who want to assist in the construction or to side with the repatriates who seemingly have a healthy suspicion of outsiders and want to maintain their religious boundaries. We conclude that when those who are not a part of our religious communities offer to participate in projects that may or may not benefit them, they model for us what it means to be neighborly. It is a model of inclusivity that offers a vision of hope in times of xenophobia and cultural divisiveness.

Royal Correspondence (4:6-24)

Ezra 4:1-5 sets the stage for the subsequent conflict between the repatriates and other groups in the territory of Judah. In Ezra 4:6-24, the writer parenthetically inserts the opponents' correspondence to Persian kings protesting the repatriates' activity in Jerusalem and explains the varied imperial responses that address the matter. The first letter-writing campaign presumably occurs during the Persian king Ahasuerus's (or Xerxes's, 486–465 BCE) reign. The book of Esther also mentions Ahasuerus. Both texts most likely refer to Xerxes I, who ruled Persia in the early to mid-fifth century. Although the contingent in Ezra 4:5 lodges an accusation to the king, the text contains no record of the charges or his reply (Ezra 4:6). The lack of an imperial response counters other depictions of royal correspondence between the Persian Empire and its subjects.[4] For example, in the book of Esther, we find King Ahasuerus responding to various concerns within the 127 provinces under his control

4. Amélie Kuhrt, "State Communications in the Persian Empire," in *State Correspondence in the Ancient World: From New Kingdom Egypt to the Roman Empire*, ed. Karen Radner, Oxford Studies in Early Empires (Oxford: Oxford University Press, 2014), 112–40.

Ezra 4:6-24

6In the reign of Ahasuerus, in his ac-
cession year, they wrote an accusation
against the inhabitants of Judah and
Jerusalem.

7And in the days of Artaxerxes,
Bishlam and Mithredath and Tabeel
and the rest of their associates wrote
to King Artaxerxes of Persia; the letter
was written in Aramaic and translated.
8Rehum the royal deputy and Shimshai the scribe wrote a letter against
Jerusalem to King Artaxerxes as follows 9(then Rehum the royal deputy,
Shimshai the scribe, and the rest of
their associates, the judges, the envoys, the officials, the Persians, the
people of Erech, the Babylonians, the
people of Susa, that is, the Elamites,
10and the rest of the nations whom the
great and noble Osnappar deported
and settled in the cities of Samaria and
in the rest of the province Beyond the
River wrote—and now 11this is a copy
of the letter that they sent):

"To King Artaxerxes: Your servants,
the people of the province Beyond the
River, send greeting. And now 12may
it be known to the king that the Jews

(e.g., Esth 6:1; 8:10; 9:20, 30). The communications between the king and his provinces suggest royal involvement in local affairs that threatened imperial rule. Haman's letter brings to the king's attention that a certain group (i.e., Jews) does not adhere to the king's law, which elicits the king's decree to exterminate this group (Esth 3:8-10). Speculatively, the absence of an imperial response in 4:6 could be that the conflict between local groups is insufficient to warrant the king's reply since it does not threaten imperial rule. Or, the author does not want to record what the king said since the response does not fit the history the author wants to present. Another reason might be that the author wants to portray the king negatively.

Against the disparaging portrait of unethical, unscrupulous officials and a discouraging local populace (Ezra 4:4), a writing campaign initiated by Bishlam, Mithredath, Tabeel, and their associates during the reign of Artaxerxes I occurs in Ezra 4:7.[5] This letter also appears to go unacknowledged by the king. A much larger group submits a second letter to Artaxerxes (Ezra 4:8-10). This group's complaint, recorded in Ezra 4:11-16, presents an equally unflattering depiction of the repatriates as seditious tax evaders. Like Haman, who asks for letters to exterminate

5. The account places the appearance of Artaxerxes I (465–424 BCE) before that of Darius I (522–486 BCE), which again highlights the problem of a chronological reading of the text.

Ezra 4:6-24 (cont.)

who came up from you to us have gone to Jerusalem. They are rebuilding that rebellious and wicked city; they are finishing the walls and repairing the foundations. 13Now may it be known to the king that, if this city is rebuilt and the walls finished, they will not pay tribute, custom, or toll, and the royal revenue will be reduced. 14Now because we share the salt of the palace and it is not fitting for us to witness the king's dishonor, therefore we send and inform the king, 15so that a search may be made in the annals of your ancestors. You will discover in the annals that this is a rebellious city, hurtful to kings and provinces, and that sedition was stirred up in it from long ago. On that account this city was laid waste. 16We make known to the king that, if this city is rebuilt and its walls finished, you will then have no possession in the province Beyond the River."

17The king sent an answer: "To Rehum the royal deputy and Shimshai the scribe and the rest of their associates who live in Samaria and in the rest of the province Beyond the River,

the Jews, this group writes the king to remind him of Jerusalem's previous downfall and destruction as divine punishment for the Jews' acts of sedition (Ezra 4:15-16). The letter shifts the focus from concerns about the repatriates' construction activities in the city (i.e., temple building) to the city itself and finally to the entire province.

The complaint casts Jerusalem as the object of concern, a "rebellious" and "wicked" city (Ezra 4:12). When cities are recast as places of evil, suffering, and violence, they become marked as targets of persecution deserving of reciprocal treatment. For example, in the book of Jonah, Nineveh represents "a wicked city" and, according to Jonah, deserving of God's judgment (Jonah 1:1; 3:10–4:5). Other biblical books in the Scriptures of ancient Israel emphasize the wickedness of the people rather than characterize cities as a whole as wicked (e.g., Gen 18; Ezek 16:23). Once labeled, the bad or wicked city becomes deserving of whatever negativity befalls it, the just consequences of the people's (collective) egregious actions.

However, not all biblical texts characterize cities as destructive and inhumane. For example, some biblical cities are potent symbols that inspire hope and justice (Isa 2:2-4; Mic 4:1-4). Today, some cities carry the stigma of injustice that accompanies the social stratification, regentrification, and exploitation that often affects the city's most vulnerable, thus remaining places of concern. Rural towns are not immune from these concerns as some have similar issues that go unaddressed.

greeting. And now [18]the letter that you sent to us has been read in translation before me. [19]So I made a decree, and someone searched and discovered that this city has risen against kings from long ago and that rebellion and sedition have been made in it. [20]Jerusalem has had mighty kings who ruled over the whole province Beyond the River, to whom tribute, custom, and toll were paid. [21]Therefore issue an order that these people be made to cease and that this city not be rebuilt, until I make a decree. [22]Moreover, take care not to be slack in this matter; why should damage grow to the hurt of the king?"

[23]Then when the copy of King Artaxerxes's letter was read before Rehum and the scribe Shimshai and their associates, they hurried to the Jews in Jerusalem and by force and power made them cease. [24]At that time the work on the house of God in Jerusalem stopped and was discontinued until the second year of the reign of King Darius of Persia.

Ezra 4:12-13 does not frame the complaint in moral or ethical terms but rather as an issue of economics. The opponents charge that "the Jews" (Aramaic, יהודיא) will withhold the tribute, customs, and tolls due to the empire once they rebuild Jerusalem's walls. The claim of decreased revenues highlights the potential effects on the Persian Empire, more specifically, King Artaxerxes. The objectors depict themselves as sharing "the salt of the palace" (Ezra 4:14), aligning their interests with the Persian king and his agenda. The first claim (Ezra 4:12), directed at the opposition's ethnicity, continues the in-group/out-group rhetoric, while the second claim (Ezra 4:13), directed at gaining the king's favor, is political opportunism.

In Ezra 4:15, the opponents advise the king to search "in the annals of your ancestors" to discover the truth of their claims. The suggestion that the king should search the annals ironically matches a similar scene in the book of Esther (Esth 6:1). King Ahasuerus, unable to sleep, asks that the royal annals be brought to him, perhaps as a soporific. He learns from these records that he has failed to honor the Jew, Mordecai, for protecting him. We find missing from the report in Ezra 4:15 the uprising of leaders in the Northern Kingdom that led to its destruction by the Assyrians. Given that the opponents associate themselves with the Assyrian king Esar-haddon prior to the fall of the Northern Kingdom, they too belong to a group that rebelled against an imperial power and are thus themselves people with a rebellious history. The phrase "the pot calling the kettle black" best describes the duplicity of their claims.

While the complaint voices and outlines the ensuing detriment to imperial interests if the project continues, it simultaneously strengthens the argument for Jerusalem's restoration—namely, the potential increase to imperial coffers as the city and temple can provide additional revenue streams to fund the king's military or other agendas.

The letter concludes with the Aramaic phrase עבר־נהרה, "the province Beyond the River," and refers to a region west of the Euphrates.[6] The amalgamation of territories under this labeling points to a loss of autonomy as various peoples, cultures, traditions, and identities are consolidated as if they were one homogeneous group (Samaria, Judah, Gaza, Ashdod, and other territories west of the Euphrates River). A historical example of this amalgamation of cultures in Western society is Andrew Jackson's Removal Act of 1830, which forcibly relocated and combined on the same reservation several indigenous nations with different beliefs, practices, and traditions. In Ezra, the labeling suggests Judah's status as an imperial colony and, as noted above, a threat to imperial interest in the entire area if the claim of sedition is not addressed.

A View from the River

The phrase "province Beyond [or Across] the River" is translated variably in different languages: in Hebrew as Avar-Ha-Nāhār, in Akkadian as Ebir-Nari, and in Syriac as Ābēr Nahrā. In the context of Persian rule, it denotes the region situated west of the Euphrates River, which was known as the province of Judah. As the Persian capital, Susa held the central seat of power during the period captured in Ezra–Nehemiah; being farther from this center implies a diminishing level of authority. As such, inhabitants of the "province Beyond the River" would likely be groups residing at the margins, with significantly less influence or power than those closer to the Persian center. The book of Ezra captures how various groups living on the margins of Persian-controlled territories vie with one another for the limited authority bestowed by the king in this region.

6. Scholars acknowledge the difficulty in precisely capturing the provincial divisions of Judah during Persian rule (see Lester L. Grabbe, *A History of the Jews and Judaism in the Second Temple Period*, vol. 1: *Yehud: A History of the Persian Province of Judah*, LSTS 47 (London: T&T Clark, 2004). The issue has to do with determining the extent and structure of its borders. Further information on the structure of the Persian administration can be found in the introduction.

The adversaries represent themselves as loyal subjects of the empire (Ezra 4:11). Their complaint shifts from the temple's construction to the city's history. The complainants' rhetoric depicts the city of Jerusalem and the Jews working in it to restore the temple as evil. Notably, throughout the Scriptures of ancient Israel, the rhetoric attending cities depicts them as places of depravity, sin, chaos, and desolation. For the most part, biblical texts, particularly the biblical prophets, target cities as objects destined for divine wrath and destruction when the inhabitants fail to act justly toward their citizens (e.g., Gen 19:12-14; Lev 26:31; Num 21:2-3; Isa 26:5; Ezek 6:6; 35:4; Jer 48:8). The prophetic critique against the religious elite also includes imperial rulers who appropriate the resources of city (and rural) inhabitants for their own ends. The conflict between Russia and Ukraine provides a contemporary example of what happens when the rhetoric of those in power label Ukrainian cities such as Kyiv as evil places of deceit and insurgency. The ultimate goal of this highly persuasive propaganda is to stigmatize and delegitimize the city and its occupants, therefore justifying invasion and the use of military force to subjugate them.[7] The rhetoric of powerful Russian officials is enough to persuade some Russian citizens of the evilness of Ukrainian cities and, by extension, the evilness of its leaders. Likewise, the adversaries' rhetoric in Ezra is powerful enough to sway the king to intervene, who issues a cease-and-desist order that halts the work (Ezra 4:17-24).

One final observation is that self-interest and self-preservation attend these letters with minimal regard for the implications of drawing imperial involvement into local conflicts. These letters expose the adversarial relationship between the *golah* and the people of the land and demonstrate how an imperial presence triggers conflict as groups vie for power and recognition. The opposition presents the repatriates as a threat to imperial rule and economic stability in the region. Yet, the depiction of instability invites imperial intervention through either the replacement of local leadership with imperial appointees or the establishment of a military presence (in the city) to ensure that the empire's interests are served and preserved (e.g., 2 Kgs 25:22; Jer 39:9). Neither group benefits from these options as local leadership is replaced and the city becomes a military garrison. Typically, acts of sedition or threats of sedition arouse imperial ire and result in violent retaliation (e.g., Exod 1:8-14; 2 Kgs

7. Andrew Srulevitch, "Why Is Putin Calling the Ukrainian Government a Bunch of Nazis?," ADL (March 4, 2022), https://www.adl.org/blog/why-is-putin-calling-the-ukrainian-government-a-bunch-of-nazis.

18:1-8; Dan 1:1-6). We encounter no such response by Artaxerxes other than a written order to cease and desist. Given this, these letters simultaneously undermine the king's authority. We find a similar portrait of this subversion in the book of Esther whereby the king's advisors, Haman, and Esther are able to influence the decisions of Ahasuerus. Like the book of Esther, Ezra 4 mocks imperial rule. While the focus of these books differ, both depict how the king's leadership determines the king's priorities and, subsequently, his actions. These books offer a counter-narrative that recognizes the power and influence of an imperial presence yet simultaneously acknowledges how this presence fails to address concerns at the local level.

If You Build It They Will Come (5:1-5)

Ezra 5 resumes the reconstruction account begun in Ezra 4. This continuance, however, now includes the prophets Haggai and Zechariah. Ezra, Haggai, and Zechariah offer contrasting reasons for the delay in the temple's reconstruction. The inclusion of Haggai and Zechariah attests to some form of the prophetic tradition in the postexilic period. The books bearing their names, specifically Haggai and Zechariah 1–8, predate the rededication of the temple in 515 BCE under the reign of Darius I.[8] Although serving as a source of inspiration for moving the work forward, the prophets themselves do not speak in Ezra's account. The book of Zechariah emphasizes Jerusalem and the temple; however, actual references to the construction activity appear only in Ezra 8:9.[9] Conspicuously, there is no direct condemnation against the repatriates for the delay in rebuilding God's house. In contrast, the book of Haggai provides a staunch critique of the people's neglect, citing their own self-interest as the major inhibitor to completing the work (Hag 1:4). The letter to Ahasuerus (Ezra 4:4-6) could be responding to Haggai's critique that the temple remained in ruins despite the repatriates' resettlement in the land for numerous years following Cyrus's decree that released the people to return and build God's house.

8. Elsewhere we note the problem of chronology in Ezra–Nehemiah (see commentary on Ezra 4:5). While there are several Dariuses and Artaxerxes named in these works, all those named Artaxerxes reign after Darius I. The chronology of the text is problematic because the writer places the halting of the temple's construction under a king who rules after the temple is already complete. See Lisbeth S. Fried, *Ezra: A Commentary*, Critical Commentaries (Sheffield: Sheffield Phoenix, 2015), 280; and Bob Becking, *Ezra–Nehemiah*, HCOT (Leuven: Peeters, 2018), 149.

9. Zechariah 8:9 does mention a foundation ceremony in which the prophets participated in the celebration.

Ezra 5:1-5

[1]Now Haggai the prophet and Zechariah son of Iddo prophesied to the Jews who were in Judah and Jerusalem in the name of the God of Israel who was over them. [2]Then Zerubbabel son of Shealtiel and Jeshua son of Jozadak set out to rebuild the house of God in Jerusalem, and with them were the prophets of God, helping them.

[3]At the same time Tattenai the governor of the province Beyond the River and Shethar-bozenai and their associates came to them and spoke to them thus, "Who gave you a decree to build this house and to finish this structure?" [4]They also asked them this, "What are the names of the men who are building this building?" [5]But the eye of their God was upon the elders of the Jews, and they did not stop them until a report reached Darius and then answer was returned by letter in reply to it.

In other words, the narrator reframes the events by switching the blame for the delay to outsiders (whom the repatriates say they fear) rather than holding the returnees accountable for the postponement of the temple's construction (see commentary on Ezra 4).

The governor Tattenai, Shethar-bozenai, and their associates travel to Jerusalem. As a Persian official charged with overseeing Persian interests in the area, Tattenai's question—"Who gave you a decree to build this house and to finish this structure?" (Ezra 5:3 and 5:9)—reads as though he has no knowledge of Cyrus's decree. His seeming unfamiliarity with the edict suggests a time differential between the issuance of the decree and Tattenai's assumption of his role as governor. Following the lengthy absence of any building activity in the area of Jerusalem and the claims of sedition in Ezra 4:12, 13, and 16, Tattenai's question also reads as a request for information by someone who has no intimate knowledge of what is occurring in the territory he governs. The Persian penchant for using indigenous people as its eyes to manage its vast empire makes it ironic that Tattenai is oblivious to the situation in Jerusalem. The Jews do not recognize him as an authoritative extension of the Persian Empire even though he carries the title "governor of the province Beyond the River." They do not respond to his inquiry about a decree, and his request for the names of those participating in the building project goes unanswered. Despite the Jews' lack of response to the governor's inquiries, neither he nor those with him halt work on the temple. While Tattenai may represent the eyes of the empire, the writer juxtaposes his authority (i.e., eyes) with the authority of the Jewish deity whose eyes are "upon the elders of the Jews" (Ezra 5:5).

The Eyes of the Empire

The Greek historian Xenophon in his book *Cyropaedia*, discusses how Cyrus extracts information about the various provinces under his control: "The king will listen to any man who asserts that he has heard or seen anything that needs attention . . . the saying that the king has 1,000 eyes and 1,000 ears; and hence the fear of uttering anything against his interest since 'he is sure to hear', or doing anything that might injure him 'since he may be there to see.'"[10]

The text shifts from naming Zerubbabel and Jeshua as persons leading the reconstruction efforts (Ezra 5:2) to subsuming their names under the singular designation "the elders of the Jews" (Ezra 5:5). On the one hand, removing a group's leadership disempowers them. The Babylonians used this strategy to diminish the power and control of the religious and political elite in Judah and Jerusalem (during and after the exile). For the Jews, perhaps the exilic experience has taught them that naming names comes with a price, the removal of its leadership, and the group's autonomy. The shift from specific names to the collective could be intentional since it protects the identity of the repatriates' leadership. Zerubbabel and Jeshua are protected by this collective identity. We see the power of this unification in collective bargaining, the power of people to select and elect their leaders, and the power to effect change based on community organizing.

Restoration by Royal Decree (5:6-17)

Tattenai, having witnessed firsthand the situation in Jerusalem, outlines his findings to King Darius. Some interpret Tattenai's letter as a counter to Rehum and Shimshai's letter written on behalf of the local populace (Ezra 4:9-16). Others suggest that because Tattenai's letter displays no knowledge that the work was halted, no knowledge of intergroup conflict, nor any reference to seditious acts that would potentially affect the current king's revenue (i.e., tribute, custom, or toll; Ezra 4:13), the letter simply reflects the reporting procedures that attend the administration of Persian territories.[11] Following the letter's introduction

10. Xenophon, *Cyropaedia* 8.C.2.12, in *The Project Gutenberg Ebook of Cyropaedia*, trans. Henry Graham Dakyns, https://www.gutenberg.org/files/2085/2085-h/2085-h.htm.

11. Fried, *Ezra*, 253–55.

Ezra 5:6-17

[6]The copy of the letter that Tattenai the governor of the province Beyond the River and Shethar-bozenai and his associates the envoys who were in the province Beyond the River sent to King Darius; [7]they sent him a report in which was written as follows: "To Darius the king, all peace! [8]May it be known to the king that we went to the province of Judah, to the house of the great God. It is being built of hewn stone, and timber is laid in the walls; this work is being done diligently and prospers in their hands. [9]Then we spoke to those elders and asked them, 'Who gave you a decree to build this house and to finish this structure?' [10]We also asked them their names, for your information, so that we might write down the names of the men at their head. [11]This was their reply to us: 'We are the servants of the God of heaven and earth, and we are rebuilding the house that was built many years ago, which a great king of Israel built and finished. [12]But because our ancestors had angered the God of heaven, he gave them into the hand of King Nebuchadnezzar of

and salutation in Ezra 5:6-7, we find a report of the materials used in the temple's reconstruction: "It is being built of hewn stone, and timber is laid in the walls" (Ezra 5:8). Notwithstanding the controversies regarding the existence of Solomon's temple, the reference to hewn stones suggests the possibility of recycling building materials from the ruins of the first temple (1 Kgs 7:9-12). The repurposing of materials was a common practice in the ancient Near East.[12] For example, broken clay pots became writing material (ostraca). The Tel Dan stele was discovered in a wall in the ancient city of Dan.[13] The size and weight of ashlar stones used in temple construction in general makes recycling these stones from the previous temple a feasible option. The use of timber within the walls represents additional fortification, perhaps against natural disasters or invasion.

12. During excavation of the city of Azekah in the Elah Valley (the traditional site where David fought Goliath), archaeologists discovered that the early Canaanite inhabitants moved tons of mud from a nearby stream to the city center to form mud bricks. Though destroyed over time, these bricks were repurposed by later inhabitants to make new bricks. This practice continued through the Byzantine period. See Ariel David, "The Mud Whisperers: Israeli Archaeologists Invent Disgusting but Effective New Way to Date Ancient Ruins," *Haaretz* (September 15, 2020), https://www.haaretz.com/archaeology/.premium-israelis-invent-disgusting-but-effective-new-way-to-date-ancient-ruins-1.9157297.

13. Avraham Biran and Joseph Naveh, "An Aramaic Stele Fragment from Tel Dan," *IEJ* 43 (1993): 81–98.

Ezra 5:6-17 (cont.)

Babylon, the Chaldean, who destroyed this house and carried away the people to Babylonia. 13However, King Cyrus of Babylon, in the first year of his reign, made a decree that this house of God should be rebuilt. 14Moreover, the gold and silver vessels of the house of God, which Nebuchadnezzar had taken out of the temple in Jerusalem and had brought into the temple of Babylon, these King Cyrus took out of the temple of Babylon, and they were delivered to a man named Sheshbazzar, whom he had made governor. 15He said to him, "Take these vessels; go and put them in the temple in Jerusalem, and let the house of God be rebuilt on its site." 16Then this Sheshbazzar came and laid the foundations of the house of God in Jerusalem, and from that time until now it has been under construction, and it is not yet finished.' 17And now, if it seems good to the king, have a search made in the royal archives there in Babylon, to see whether a decree was issued by King Cyrus for the rebuilding of this house of God in Jerusalem. Let the king send us his pleasure in this matter."

Is Tattenai's Letter Authentic?

There has been some debate over the authenticity of the Aramaic portions of Ezra. Is Tattenai a historical figure? If so, what are the implications of the letters in Ezra 4? Lisbeth Fried, relying on the work of Arthur Ungnad, notes the discovery of a cuneiform tablet with the name Ta-at-tan-nu dating to about 502 BCE. The inscription and title for this person is similar to that in Ezra 5:3-5.[14] If authentic, Tattenai, as a governor of the province reporting to imperial authorities, would have investigated and witnessed the reconstruction efforts occurring in Jerusalem during the time of King Darius rather than King Artaxerxes. Fried considers the letters in Ezra 4 authentic with some editing and amending of the text.

In Ezra 5:9-10, Tattenai makes a formal report of his visit to the king. The report includes his inquiry regarding royal authorization for the work and the names of those performing it (5:3, 4). In a bureaucratic fashion, Tattenai conveys to the king what he saw and what the people said. The formality of his report displays no interpretative assessment of

14. Fried, *Ezra*, 242–43; Arthur Ungnad, "Keilinschriftliche Beiträge Zum Buch Esra Und Ester," *ZAW* 58 (1941): 240–44.

the rationale for the circumstances he investigates or the people involved. Based on accounts in the Elephantine Papyri, it is plausible that the visit reflects the actual practices of Persian officials.[15] Today, we often find that the bureaucracy of governmental structures appears ill-prepared to address the lived conditions, experiences, or needs of a diverse population. Politicians make laws that further their agendas or those of special interest groups with minimal regard for the people who elect them to office. In these verses, this governor does not know the repatriates' story, so rather than address his questions, this group educates him on the history of their ancestral roots in Judah and Jerusalem.

In retelling their history as a people of the land, the group describes themselves as servants of the "God of heaven and earth" (Ezra 5:11). The phrase sounds like a generic reference used by the Persians for the various deities worshiped throughout the Persian Empire.[16] The language aligns with an imperial religious understanding of the partnership between the deity and the Persian king as keepers of the "cosmic-moral order."[17] The language on the surface implies loyalty to God and the king. The subversiveness of this epithet would not, however, be lost on the writer's audience as it signifies loyalty solely to the deity. Although their response does not refer directly to the Jewish God, their claim of the sovereignty of their God rather than the sovereignty of the king and the Persian Empire could be understood as undermining the king's authority.

The emphasis on rebuilding the house of God rather than constructing a new one continues the group's connection and identity with its historical past, which would make them indigenous to the land as opposed to the numerous groups transplanted through imperial invasion (cf. Ezra 4:2). The reference to the "great king of Israel" rather than to King Solomon functions in a twofold manner similar to the "God of heaven and earth." History records Darius I as a usurper of the throne who experienced serious revolts before solidifying his control over the Persian Empire. In his need to validate his ascendancy and maintain his power, stability in the provinces was crucial. One way to facilitate provincial stability without the use of military force would have been for the people to view the king as a benevolent supporter of local groups. Here, the vagueness of the identity of the "great king" in verse 11 makes it possible for the writer to

15. Amélie Kuhrt, "The Problem of Achaemenid 'Religious Policy,'" in *Die Welt der Götterbilder*, ed. Brigitte Groneberg and Hermann Spieckermann (Berlin: de Gruyter, 2007), 117–42. (See TAD A4.5; Cowley 27.)

16. Kuhrt, "The Problem of Achaemenid 'Religious Policy,'" 121, and Fried, *Ezra*, 56.

17. Kuhrt, "The Problem of Achaemenid 'Religious Policy,'" 121.

draw connections between the completion of the first temple by Solomon and, perhaps, a hope that another "great king," Darius, will help rebuild and complete the temple currently under construction.

In Ezra 5:12, we find the first explanation for the group's exile: "But because our ancestors had angered the God of heaven, he gave them into the hand of King Nebuchadnezzar of Babylon, the Chaldean, who destroyed this house and carried away the people to Babylonia." This group identifies with the actions and shortcomings of their ancestors—religious idolatry and covenantal disloyalty—thus rationalizing the group's removal from their ancestral homeland.[18] The concepts of shame and blame intersect with theodicy in this verse as self-blame becomes a way to reconcile and make sense of the group's perceptions and rationale regarding God's role in the destruction of the temple and the subsequent exile of some of the populace.

We question whether groups should blame themselves when bad things happen, especially when circumstances are beyond their control. That is, neither this group nor their ancestors could have prevented the imperial invasion of Judah and Jerusalem by Babylon or Persia. Perhaps a better question is why some groups that experience traumatic events blame themselves. The cognitive dissonance that produces self-blame can lead to group preservation and resilience as the group seeks to maintain or hold on to religious beliefs.[19] For example, groups that experience a crisis of faith following horrific suffering (i.e., genocide, forced migration, religious and political persecution) will abandon their beliefs entirely or reinterpret how they understand God and God's activity in human affairs to mitigate the dissonance. Self-blame counters the questions of theodicy whereby the group assumes accountability for overwhelming situations. This sense of control can lead to positive outcomes like South Africa's Truth and Reconciliation Commission, which unearthed the inequities in the apartheid system and held responsible parties accountable. This led to demonstrable changes in the nation. Yet, we also acknowledge that sometimes groups will not assume blame for their actions or inactions, projecting the blame onto other groups, thus leaving the dissonance

18. Jer 25:1-14; 39:1-10; Ezek 12:13; 17:20; Mic 4:10.

19. Cognitive dissonance is the mental discomfort that exists when the experience of a person or group conflicts with their system of beliefs, ideology, or actions. For example, when one rationalizes using plastic bags when believing in recycling, or when one is conflicted because one believes in the protection of animals while also eating them.

unresolved; the choices these groups make ultimately go against the group's best interests.

For the repatriates, self-blame became the response that this community needed to move forward following the trauma of exile and the ensuing identity crisis of whether they were still God's people. The generic reference to *all* people in Ezra 5:12b goes against biblical accounts that report the extraction of Jerusalem's elite and religious leaders. Second Kings 25:12 and Jeremiah 52:16 indicate that Nebuchadnezzar did not displace the poor who remained to serve as "vinedressers and tillers of the soil." Archaeological evidence supports the existence of some measure of depopulation and repopulation of Jerusalem following the city's invasion and destruction.[20] It is most likely that those "carried away" represent the exilic minority, who now imagine themselves as the majority upon returning to Judah and Jerusalem. Here, the insertion of the deity's anger, the temple's destruction, and the people's displacement serve to validate this self-blame. The biblical use of the word "all" never really represents everyone, in the same way that "all Baptists" or "all Methodists" do not represent all Protestants.

The identification of Nebuchadnezzar as a Chaldean (Ezra 5:12) and Cyrus as a Babylonian (Ezra 5:13) is not mere happenstance. Both men ruled as kings over Babylon. Nebuchadnezzar succeeded his father, Nabopolassar, a Chaldean immigrant who founded the Neo-Babylonian Empire (ca. 626 BCE). As immigrants, the Chaldeans rose to power in Babylon and defeated the Assyrians. Cyrus, the Persian, proclaimed himself king of Babylon when he defeated Nabonidus, the last king of the Babylonian Empire (ca. 539 BCE).[21] He restores the people to their lands and supports rebuilding their houses of worship. Despite the portrait of imperial benevolence under Cyrus's rule, his linkage to Babylon presents another regime change in the history of regime changes in the territory. Speculatively, the writer mimics his title "King of Babylon," not as a sign of allegiance but rather as a subversive rebuke of the empire, as Cyrus is

20. See Gabriel Barkay, *Ketef Hinnon: A Treasure Facing Jerusalem's Wall* (Jerusalem: Israel Museum, 1986); Bustenay Oded, "Where Is the 'Myth of the Empty Land' to Be Found? History versus Myth," in *Judah and the Judeans in the Neo-Babylonian Period*, ed. Oded Lipschits and Joseph Blenkinsopp (Winona Lake, IN: Eisenbrauns, 2003), 55–74.

21. "I am Cyrus, king of the world, great king, mighty king, king of Babylon, king of Sumer and Akkad, king of the four quarters." Cyrus Cylinder, Fragment A, v. 20, as translated by Mordechai Cogan in *The Context of Scripture*, vol. 2: *Monumental Inscriptions from the Biblical World*, ed. William W. Hallo and K. Lawson Younger Jr. (Leiden: Brill, 2003), 315.

associated with the same empire responsible for the group's exile. The association reminds an ancient audience of imperial aggression, oppression, and loss of indigenous autonomy under imperial rule. A similar mimicking occurred during the antebellum period when slaveholders called themselves "master," which the enslaved would repeat when addressing their owners. The term implied respect for the slaveholder and reinforced the identity of the enslaved as property. Its usage was far from respectful, however, and possibly carried pejorative connotations when repeated by the enslaved.

Ezra 5:14-17 describes the return of the temple vessels, an incomplete building project, and a request for its validation. The temple vessels mentioned in Ezra 5:14-15 are possibly among those referenced in the infamous handwriting on the wall scene where King Belshazzar and his guests bring out the statues of the gods of their defeated adversaries during the king's celebratory feast (Daniel 5). Since the Jews lacked a carved or cast image of their deity (Exod 20:4, 5; Lev 26:1; Deut 5:8), the king used the sacred temple vessels instead (Dan 5:1-4). Cyrus returns these same vessels to Sheshbazzar when the repatriates return to reconstruct the temple. Like instruments used in contemporary rituals of various religions, these vessels most likely function practically during ritual sacrifices (cf. Ezra 1:9, 10; 1 Kgs 7:45-50; 2 Kgs 12:13). The delivery of these instruments to "a man named Sheshbazzar" fails to recognize his connections to the Israelite monarchy as the prince of Judah and speaks to his limited significance by the later writers of Ezra–Nehemiah (Ezra 1:8). Appointed by Cyrus as a governor, Sheshbazzar aids in the temple's reconstruction. His appearance provides continuity to support an uninterrupted period between the repatriates' arrival and the temple's completion.[22]

Overall, a visit by an imperial administrator allows the retelling of Ezra 1 to include elements previously absent. For example, Ezra 1 reports the return of the temple vessels together with the impetus to rebuild the house of God based on an imperial decree but lacks any reference to its start or completion. Ezra 5 amends this report to include when the work began, which is still incomplete, according to Ezra 5:16. The elders conclude their explanation with a diplomatic suggestion ("if it seems good to the king"!) to find evidence validating their story regarding permission to

22. See our commentary on Sheshbazzar in Ezra 1.

rebuild God's house (Ezra 5:17).[23] The search of the royal archives would reveal authorization to build and whether the king allocated imperial funds to support the project.[24] The request for the king's resolution of the matter raises the question of whether Darius will honor the decree of Cyrus, including the commitment of royal resources. The elders' persistence demonstrates how the stories and narratives of ordinary, everyday citizens have the power to influence the actions of political leaders at all levels of government. For example, the protest by the Sioux Tribe at Standing Rock, which included sharing stories of the sacredness of their lands and water, led the courts to temporarily suspend the Keystone XL pipeline in 2020.[25] Still, this chapter has a subversive feel as we read several double entendres that insult and flatter imperial rule to achieve the repatriates' goals while simultaneously maintaining their integrity and fidelity to their God.

Anything Cyrus Does, Darius Does Better? (6:1-5)

Up to this point, the biblical text makes casual references to King Darius as one of the Persian monarchs in a series of Persian monarchs (Ezra 4:5, 24; 5:5-7). In Ezra 6:1, King Darius emerges as an active participant in the lives of his subjects when he honors the request by the Jewish elders (Ezra 5:17) and issues a decree to search the archives in response to their petition. Royal decrees typically serve the imperial interests. Like executive orders signed by the president of the United States, royal decrees reinforced the power of the reigning ruler. Ancient government documents were preserved so that they could be referenced later if needed. As part of the public record and included in governmental archives, civic decisions were subject to appeal and arbitration with the outcome ultimately determined by the king.[26] A search of the בית ספריא (house of documents/archives) was no small feat since government records, including minor decisions, were copied and covered the reigns

23. Many scholars attribute the request to search the archives to Tattenai (e.g., Liz Fried, Lester Grabbe, Ralph Klein). We read 5:17 as a continuation of the elders' response to Tattenai—the elders are the ones who petition the king to validate their story.

24. Fried, *Ezra*, 253.

25. Lisa Friedman, "Standing Rock Sioux Tribe Wins a Victory in Dakota Access Pipeline Case," *New York Times* (March 25, 2020), https://www.nytimes.com/2020/03/25/climate/dakota-access-pipeline-sioux.html.

26. Kuhrt, "State Communications in the Persian Empire," 137.

Ezra 6:1-5

1Then King Darius made a decree, and
they searched the archives where the
documents were stored in Babylon.
2But it was in Ecbatana, the capital in
the province of Media, that a scroll was
found on which this was written: "A record. 3In the first year of his reign, King
Cyrus issued a decree: Concerning the
house of God at Jerusalem, let the house
be rebuilt, the place where sacrifices are
offered and burnt offerings are brought;
its height shall be sixty cubits and its
width sixty cubits, 4with three courses of
hewn stones and one course of timber;
let the cost be paid from the royal treasury. 5Moreover, let the gold and silver
vessels of the house of God that Nebuchadnezzar took out of the temple in
Jerusalem and brought to Babylon be
restored and brought back to the temple
in Jerusalem, each to its place; you shall
put them in the house of God."

of various Persian kings (Cyrus and Cambyses). The more recent the monarch, the more accessible his edicts. As the reign of Cyrus predates Darius's reign by at least thirty-seven years, a request to locate a single dated document is remarkable, as is Darius's intentional effort to locate it. The offsite storage of the royal archives in the summer home of the kings poses no security risk if discovered by others. The elders' request in Ezra 5:17 together with the king's inquiry and decree in Ezra 6:1 suggest that archival searches afforded the local populace opportunities to obtain justice should local elites abuse their power.

The search reveals that Cyrus's edict is located not in Babylon but in Ecbatana, the summer home of the Medes and later Persian kings.[27] Kristin Kleber offers this reflection on those who bear the costs of royal excursions and summer homes:

> When the royal court traveled in a large formation, the expenses exceeded the productive power of the royal domains. The population in the vicinity as well as the local state administrations (such as the Persepolis administration) and temples (attested in Babylonia) had to provide additional foodstuffs. They also bore the burden of grinding the grain into flour. The king's table served meals not only for the king

27. Persian (Iranian) Jews believe Ecbatana (modern name Hamadan) houses the tomb of the Jewish queen Esther and her uncle Mordecai. The *Encyclopedia Iranica* notes, "This tradition is not supported by the Jews outside of Persia and does not appear in either Babylonian or Jerusalemite Talmuds." Amnon Netzer, "Esther and Mordechai," *Encyclopaedia Iranica*, vol. 8.6, 657–58, https://www.iranicaonline.org/articles/esther-and-mordechai.

> and his family but also for numerous courtiers, officials, accountants, servants, and armed guards traveling with the king, as well as the horses and mules used during the journeys.[28]

A modern-day example is Camp David, the country retreat used by all US presidents since 1933, the forty-fifth president being the exception. The price tag to the American taxpayer for the upkeep, security, travel expenses, and invited guests is approximately $8 million annually.[29] Summer homes and country retreats are luxuries that only the wealthy can afford. The expense for these alternate residences, when used to house government officials, is borne by those who may not even own a home.

The language of the edict has been slightly altered in Ezra 6:3-5 and differs from its appearances in both Ezra 1:2-4 and Ezra 5:13-15. Cyrus's decree, as it appears in Ezra 1, is the editor's redacted version of the Cyrus Cylinder. As such, it is likely that it was copied and edited from an official government document (the Cylinder). The same holds true for the version here and the one in Ezra 5:13-15 (copied from Ezra 1:2-4). The versions in Ezra 1 and 5 do not reference the dimensions of the temple, its sacrificial system, or its funding from the royal treasury. The inclusion of all three variations of the source document may reflect the literary embedding characteristic of official government documents and adapted by the biblical writer in narrating the overall story of the start, interruption, and completion of the temple's reconstruction.[30]

Tax Rebates (6:6-13)

Darius's response to Tattenai and associates appears in Ezra 6:6-12. Restoration of the temple is to continue, and those not associated with the work are told to "keep away" (Ezra 6:6). Theologically, an ancient audience would view the reconstituted temple as divinely ordained and the deity's approval of Darius as the newly established ruler. The king makes

28. Kristin Kleber, "Taxation in the Achaemenid Empire," *Oxford Handbook Topics in Classical Studies*, online ed., Oxford Academic (April 1, 2014), 6, https://doi.org/10.1093/oxfordhb/9780199935390.013.34.

29. "Camp David Being Used Less and Less by Presidents," CBS Baltimore (February 21, 2017), https://www.cbsnews.com/baltimore/news/camp-david-being-used-less-and-less-by-presidents/.

30. Richard Steiner discusses this at length in "Bishlam's Archival Search Report in Nehemiah's Archive: Multiple Introductions and Reverse Chronological Order as Clues to the Origin of the Aramaic Letters in Ezra," *JBL* 125 (2006): 641–85.

Ezra 6:6-13

6“Now you, Tattenai, governor of the province Beyond the River, Shethar-bozenai, and you, their associates, the envoys in the province Beyond the River, keep away; 7let the work on this house of God alone; let the governor of the Jews and the elders of the Jews rebuild this house of God on its site. 8Moreover, I make a decree regarding what you shall do for these elders of the Jews for the rebuilding of this house of God: the cost is to be paid to these people, in full and without delay, from the royal revenue, the tribute of the province Beyond the River. 9Whatever is needed—young bulls, rams, or sheep for burnt offerings to the God of heaven, wheat, salt, wine, or oil, as the priests in Jerusalem require—let that be given to them day by day without fail, 10so that they may offer pleasing sacrifices to the God of heaven and pray for the life of the king and his children. 11Furthermore, I decree that, if anyone alters this edict, a beam shall be pulled out of the house of the perpetrator, who then shall be impaled on it. The house shall be made a dunghill. 12May the God who has established his name there overthrow any king or people who shall put forth a hand to alter this or to destroy this house of God in Jerusalem. I, Darius, make a decree; let it be done with all diligence.”

no specific reference to the contents outlined in Tattenai's report. Instead, he affirms the rebuilding of God's house and issues his own edict that enhances the original edict of Cyrus to include the use of royal revenue to fund the work (Ezra 6:8). As the levy was not optional, the king's decree seems generous since everyone (Judeans and non-Judeans) paid something (silver, gold, animals, grain, etc.). Satrapies paid prorated taxes according to their size and wealth. In essence, it is the inhabitants of the entire province who contribute to the royal revenue (tribute), and thus there are some groups not associated with the repatriates and the house of God in Jerusalem whose taxes went toward funding the Jerusalem temple. While Darius is known for providing resources to construct the temples of other groups, his partiality to the Jews and Jerusalem could be a source of conflict as the repatriates' tribute would represent a reinvestment in their community (a tax rebate of sorts), a rebate not afforded to their neighbors. Here, reallocating what would have been his tribute aligns Darius with Cyrus, one of the most well-known favorable figures in Persian imperial history and Jewish-imperial relations.

Taxation Versus Tribute

Taxation and tribute in the ancient world were both a means to generate imperial revenue and an instrument used for imperial domination and subordination of conquered peoples. The two differ with respect to function, purpose, and constituents. Taxes were collected from the general populace in the form of monies or other resources (i.e., agricultural produce). In addition to imperial taxes, conquered peoples paid tribute to the conquering ruler as a demonstration of submission to the ruling authority. This tribute consisted of raw materials, precious metals, enslaved people, and military service. Taxation and tribute are to be distinguished from the gifts that imperial rulers received from other rulers and given in lieu of tribute. Herodotus writes, "During all the reign of Cyrus, and afterwards when Cambyses ruled, there were no fixed tributes, but the nations severally brought gifts to the king. On account of this and other like doings, the Persians say that Darius was a huckster, Cambyses a master, and Cyrus a father; for Darius looked to making a gain in everything; Cambyses was harsh and reckless; while Cyrus was gentle, and procured them all manner of goods."[31] Overall, taxation was used to support the imperial infrastructure, while tribute was a punitive obligation that resulted in severe consequences for those conquered territories that failed to comply.

The twofold requirement that the collection for the elders and priests (including bulls, rams, sheep, wheat, salt, wine, or oil) begin immediately and be collected daily (Ezra 6:9) suggests that one collection is to complete the reconstruction and a second collection for the priests to maintain the sacrificial rituals of the house of God once completed. The decree provides the priests with whatever they need for as long as they need it and points to the dependency of the cultus on local support (voluntary and involuntary) for its sustenance. The same holds true for contemporary religious organizations in the United States that rely on tithes and offerings to support their day-to-day operations (salaries,

31. Herodotus, *Darius and the Persian Empire*, 3.80-97, https://www.thelatinlibrary.com/historians/herod/herodotus5.html

building upkeep, and programs). Moreover, it is not uncommon for taxpayers to contribute to the common good even if there is little to no benefit to the individual taxpayer. For example, families and individuals without children are not exempt from paying local taxes that support the school systems in their districts.

Darius seeks prayers for the welfare of the royal family through the religious rituals (sacrifices and offerings) of the repatriates and their God (Ezra 6:10), which suggests respect for various religious groups and the religious pluralism that characterized his reign but is also astutely political given the diverse populace across his vast empire.[32] The king's request legitimates the temple, its priests, and the repatriate community, which simultaneously aligns the repatriates' interests with imperial interest and the power that comes with imperial support. Implicit in the edict is an awareness that the work can continue if it and those performing it pose no threat to the king and those close to him. The visual and vocal prayers offered daily by the priests on behalf of the royal family would convey to others and the king that the repatriates were not a threat to him or his empire. In general, prayer is a significant aspect of all religious groups as a way to communicate with the divine. Having people pray on our behalf, regardless of their religious affiliation, can be powerful because it strengthens, encourages, and creates solidarity as people of other religions join us in a common concern, issue, or celebration.

The letter closes with the king's dire and deadly warning for any who failed to heed the contents of the decree: "Furthermore, I decree that if anyone alters this edict, a beam shall be pulled out of the house of the perpetrator, who then shall be impaled on it. The house shall be made a dunghill" (Ezra 6:11). The Hebrew word בית, translated as "house," can refer to a physical structure or a person's lineage. For example, Jephthah vows to sacrifice "whatever comes out of the door of [his] house," a vow that leads to the sacrifice of his daughter (Judg 11:31, 34). Jeremiah's prophecy against the king uses "house" metaphorically to critique the unrighteous way the king builds his kingdom (Jer 22:14). In addition, the term "house" can represent a lineage, as in the house of David (cf. 1 Sam 20:16; 2 Sam 3:1; 1 Kgs 14:8), the house of Jacob (Gen 46:27), the house of Levi (Exod 2:1), and the house of Israel (Exod 40:38). Overall, Ezra–Nehemiah refers to the house of God as a physical structure thirty-three times.

32. Jacob M. Myers, *Ezra, Nehemiah*, AB 14 (Garden City, NY: Doubleday, 1965), xxix.

The writer juxtaposes the destruction of the houses of those who alter the edict (Ezra 6:11) with any complicit actions by this group that lead to the destruction of God's house (Ezra 6:12). In essence, if God's house lies in ruins so will the houses of those who were responsible for obstructing its completion. Punitively, interference in the temple's construction now comes with an alarming penalty, impalement. This form of capital punishment seems excessive, indicating that the concern is no longer a local matter but an imperial one. Historically, the Persians' use of impalement was reserved for political or religious opponents of the king. Specifically, the Behistun Inscription (ca. 520 BCE) describes Darius's use of impalement for persons who rebelled against him.[33] The form of government necessarily determines how governmental threats are perceived, understood, and penalized by the government. In ancient and modern autocracies, some civilian actions may be received as threats to the ruler and punishable by death. In democratic societies, remedies put in place to address civilian threats simultaneously mask government threats designed to curtail or quash threatening acts that endanger government officials or the government itself. These types of threats are considered felonies punishable by a fine or imprisonment. Interestingly, the United States Constitution (article 3, section 3) still carries the death penalty or lesser consequences for treason. Capital punishment for religious affiliation, while not a phenomenon in the United States, still exists in some countries throughout the world (e.g., Afghanistan).

The king's closing statement—"May the God who has established his name there overthrow any king or people that shall put forth a hand to alter this or to destroy this house of God in Jerusalem" (Ezra 6:12)—serves a theological function that is designed to situate the work and punishment for its interference as a divine rather than a human consequence. The tables have surely turned. The work that was disrupted, presumably out of fear of the neighboring people in Ezra 4:6, will now be resumed based on a decree designed to instill fear in this same group (Ezra 6:13). The adversaries who sought to disrupt and halt the reconstruction activities are now under a death sentence if they fail to contribute to its completion and ongoing support. A chronological reading of the events thus far

33. Phraortes, who led a rebellion against Darius (522–521 BCE), was impaled on a stake in Ecbatana as were his co-conspirators. The Behistun Inscription describes his impalement in gory detail together with a pictorial representation.

suggests that King Darius either never saw the opposition's letter in Ezra 4:6 or ignored it completely. As discussed elsewhere in this commentary, however, a chronological reading of the events necessarily ignores that the adversaries write to a king whose reign historically follows rather than precedes the reign of Darius.

Darius's extreme measures for those interfering in the reconstruction of God's house raises a contemporary question as to whether such involvement constitutes a violation of the separation of church and state. Today, we cannot imagine the government penalizing congregational members and communities for failing to support the building campaigns of local churches, mosques, or synagogues. Any punitive intervention would most likely be received as government overreach or the government posing as the enforcement arm of a particular religious group or political party. Nevertheless, a case can be made for government aid in the preservation and restoration of religious buildings and monuments that represent the historical, cultural, and religious diversity that characterizes the constituents of a country. For example, the historic Cathedral of Notre Dame in Paris sustained significant damage by the fire in 2019. The French government contributed significant funds toward its restoration. Yet, even in these instances, the costs are most likely borne by individual taxpayers, who may or may not have any religious affiliations at all.

A Prophecy Fulfilled (6:14-22)

Ezra 6:14-22 concludes the chapter and captures the completion of the temple and the celebratory festivities that follow. The repatriates assemble to dedicate the new edifice, which looks much like the celebration in Ezra 3:5-13 following the completion of the temple's foundation.[34] The exact prophesies of Haggai and Zechariah are not directly specified in either Ezra 5:1 or Ezra 6:14, and one must refer to these prophetic books to access the prophetic language regarding the group's prosperity and the temple's completion. Speaking of Jerusalem and the temple, Haggai says, "[I]n this place I will give prosperity, says the LORD of hosts" (Hag 2:9b). Zechariah prophesies, "The hands of Zerubbabel have laid the foundation of this house; his hands shall also complete it. Then you will know that the LORD of hosts has sent me to you" (Zech 4:9). While Zechariah's prophesy in Zechariah 4:9 includes Zerubbabel in the project's completion, Ezra 6:14 does not. Theologically, the prophets, as spokespersons

34. Cf. the completion of Solomon's temple in 1 Kgs 8:65-66.

Ezra 6:14-22

13Then, according to the word sent by King Darius, Tattenai, the governor of the province Beyond the River, Shethar-bozenai, and their associates did with all diligence what King Darius had ordered. 14So the elders of the Jews built and prospered, through the prophesying of the prophet Haggai and Zechariah son of Iddo. They finished their building by command of the God of Israel and by decree of Cyrus, Darius, and King Artaxerxes of Persia, 15and this house was finished on the third day of the month of Adar, in the sixth year of the reign of King Darius.

16The people of Israel, the priests and the Levites, and the rest of the returned exiles celebrated the dedication of this house of God with joy. 17They offered at the dedication of this house of God one hundred bulls, two hundred rams, four hundred lambs, and as a sin offering for all Israel, twelve male goats, according to the number of the tribes of Israel. 18Then they set the priests in their divisions and the

for the deity, serve as intermediaries linking the completion of the temple to the will of the deity. Here, the writer places the sovereignty of God above the sovereignty of Persian rulers by listing the deity prior to Cyrus, Darius, and Artaxerxes.

The narrative has been somewhat insistent on the chronology that depicts the involvement of Persian kings (Cyrus starts the project, Artaxerxes stops the project, and Darius completes the project). This chronology is historically inaccurate when dating the reigns of these rulers. In 6:15, we find an accurate chronological ordering of the reigns of the kings (Cyrus, Darius, Artaxerxes), which credits all the Persian kings as instrumental in the project's initiation and completion. The impression that all the Persian kings supported the temple's reconstruction is most likely politically motivated to lend authenticity to the repatriates' presence and identity. Dating the completion of the temple in the month of Adar during the reign of Darius seeks to anchor the completion in a fixed timeframe, thereby suggesting its historical reality. Ezra 4:24 states that construction activities resumed in the second year of Darius's rule and continued uninterrupted approximately until its completion in the sixth year of his reign. The temple's swift completion implies the group's overall commitment to the project and the deity for which it is built. The portrait of a committed repatriate community, who garner resources and expeditiously complete a building project, counters the critique in the books of Haggai and Zechariah that the group's failure to build a house for God upon returning to Judah and Jerusalem was analogous to their lack of covenantal fidelity and dedication to the deity.

Ezra 6:14-22 (cont.)

Levites in their courses for the service of God at Jerusalem, as it is written in the book of Moses.

[19]On the fourteenth day of the first month the returned exiles kept the Passover. [20]For both the priests and the Levites had purified themselves; all of them were clean. So they slaughtered the Passover lamb for all the returned exiles, for their fellow priests, and for themselves. [21]It was eaten by the people of Israel who had returned from exile and also by all who had joined them and separated themselves from the pollutions of the nations of the land to seek the LORD, the God of Israel. [22]With joy they celebrated the Festival of Unleavened Bread seven days, for the LORD had made them joyful and had turned the heart of the king of Assyria to them, so that he aided them in the work on the house of God, the God of Israel.

The Month of Adar
(B. Ta'anit 29a)[35]

The reference to the month of Adar appears only once in the book of Ezra (6:15). The month contains the Jewish holiday of Purim and appears in the book of Esther nine times. Thus, the writer connects the Purim story and its festival that celebrates life and community with the completion of the temple "finished on the third day of the month of Adar, in the sixth year of the reign of King Darius," a cause for celebration. Both narratives represent stories of resilience and survival.

"The mishnah teaches that from when the month of Av begins, one decreases acts of rejoicing. Rav Yehuda, son of Rav Shmuel bar Sheilat, said in the name of Rav: Just as when Av begins one decreases rejoicing, so too when the month of Adar begins, one increases rejoicing."

In the book of Esther, the month of Adar is associated with orders to execute the Jews (Esth 3:7, 13; 8:10-14; 9). The term, possibly from the Babylonian *adâru*, meaning "be darkened" or "eclipsed," suggests a dark

35. Ta'anit 29a, *Sefaria*, https://www.sefaria.org/Taanit.29a.17?lang=bi&with=all&lang2=en.

moment in Jewish history. A reversal of fortune occurs as Esther saves her people and Adar becomes associated with joy and celebration. In Ezra, the temple's completion in the month of Adar (Ezra 6:15), followed by the joyful celebration of the people of Israel, the priests, the Levites, and the rest of the returned exiles (Ezra 6:16), continues this celebratory vein. Here, we also encounter the first usage in Ezra of the phrase בני־ישׂראל, "the people of Israel," which identifies this newly formed community and its members (priests, Levites, and the rest of the returned exiles). A contemporary example of a dark moment that is later memorialized would be the Black Wall Street Massacre (1921) in Tulsa, Oklahoma. The Greenwood District, a wealthy Black district, was destroyed by white mobs. In 2021, a festival was established to commemorate and honor the cultural legacy of this community.[36]

The repatriates' celebratory activities consist of a series of offerings, among them a "sin offering" (חטאת).[37] In this instance, the sin offering does not refer to moral failures (murder, stealing, infidelity, etc.) as understood in the Christian context but rather serves as a purification offering that preserved the holiness of the sanctuary. Conditions that impacted the holiness of the sanctuary applied to the individual and the community, as all were a reflection of a holy God. Purgation offerings for the individual included but were not limited to unusual skin diseases and bodily discharges (Lev 14:19, 22; 15:15, 30). Mothers were also required to provide a sin offering after giving birth (Lev 12:6). The entire community provided a sin offering to ensure that a purified temple and a purified people were ready to engage in the rituals of sacrifice (Lev 16).[38]

Sacrificial offerings were occasions to share in a communal meal that included the consumption of meat, a rarity for most in the community. More important, animal sacrifice was one way for the community to respectfully acknowledge that, in order for humans to live, other living creatures died. Overall, Ezra 6:13-17 provides a fitting close to the charge in Ezra 1:2 in which Cyrus is told to "build [the Lord] a house at Jerusalem," returning the audience's (and our) attention to God's house and not the skirmishes that impeded its completion. In 6:18, the reference to

36. Black Wall Street Legacy Festival, https://www.blackwallstreetlegacyfest.com/.

37. Elizabeth W. Goldstein, *Impurity and Gender in the Hebrew Bible* (Lanham, MD: Lexington Books, 2015), 35–36; Knight and Levine, *The Meaning of the Bible*, 190.

38. Fried, *Ezra*, 283–84.

"the book of Moses," a source that appears only four times in the Scriptures of ancient Israel (2 Chr 25:4; 35:12; Ezra 6:18; Neh 13:1), connects the sacrifices to the commandments given to Moses.[39] We cannot with certainty identify the contents of "the book of Moses." Still, following "the book of Moses" gives authority for their actions.

The returnees were unable to perform their religious rituals for more than seventy years. They now celebrate Passover, with its emphasis on the paschal offering and the Feast of Unleavened Bread (Ezra 6:19-20, 22) as a feast of freedom. The celebration simultaneously reminds this group of their ancestors' exodus from Egypt and now their exodus from Babylon. Just as the celebration of Passover in the first month of Nisan marked new beginnings for the Hebrews in Exodus 12:2, its celebration here on the same day marks the new beginnings for this newly formed Jewish community. Unleavened bread is the bridge between Pesach and the Festival of Unleavened Bread, which together commemorate the salvific event where God redeems and liberates God's people from their oppressors. While women participate in regular seders, some Jewish women also gather for "women seders" that provide spaces for them to recount their own experiences with the exodus story. Sharon Cohen Anisfeld, Tara Mohr, and Catherine Spector describe this ownership: "The commemoration of our Exodus from Egypt has a special resonance for contemporary Jewish women. Through this holiday, women forge a powerful connection to the Jewish people, including biblical foremothers as well as female ancestors, and to their own oppression, liberation, and journeys to the Promised Land."[40]

The book of Ezra uses several terms to distinguish between the ceremonial status of Jews and non-Jews: טהר, "make clean, purify"; טממה,

39. While some scholars suggest that "the book of Moses" refers to the entire Pentateuch (Gary Knoppers, Bernard Levinson, David Carr), others, like Gareth Wearne, argue that this book is more likely Deuteronomy because of Deuteronomic themes that are present in the context of its use. See Gareth Wearne, "What Was the Book of Moses in 4QMMT?," *CBQ* 82 (2020): 237–55. Hindy Najman argues that regardless of the content of the book, appealing to Moses provides authority for the actions of the community (in Wearne, "What Was the Book," 244).

40. Sharon Cohen Ainsfeld, Tara Mohr, and Catherine Spector, eds., *The Women's Passover Companion: Women's Reflections on the Festival of Freedom* (Woodstock, VT: Jewish Lights, 2003).

God's Bride on Pesach[41]

Kim Chernin

How strange, god's
bride lives
in a cup
of Pesach wine.
Not visible
perhaps,
in the first
sip, to be known
at the breaking
of bread
by thoughts
turning in ways you
would not
anticipate. This
bitter herb: meant
for those who seek
Him/Who
never can
be known, they
say, by sight or
sense and so they
give up on the world. This
world, where
every cry of a green
newborn asks
us urgently no
longer to seek
Her/Who
has al-
ways abundantly
here been given.

"uncleanness, polluted"; and נדה, "unclean, impure."[42] In Ezra 6:20, the verb טהר refers to the purification of the priests and Levites in preparation for sacrificing the Passover lamb. The nouns טממה and נדה in Ezra 6:21 and Ezra 9:11, respectively, refer to the "uncleanness" of the nations and foreign women. According to the rules of the Passover in Exodus 12:43-44,

41. Kim Cherin's poem "God's Bride on Pesach" first appeared in *Tikkun Magazine: A Jewish Interfaith and Secular Prophetic Voice for a World of Love, Justice, and Environmental Sanity*. Kim Chernin, "God's Bride on Pesach," *Tikkun* 18 (2003): 49–58, https://read.dukeupress.edu/tikkun/article-abstract/18/2/49/81919/God-s-Bride-on-Pesach. The poem and artwork are reprinted here with permission.

42. An Aramaic letter dated from 419/418 BCE parallels the account of the Passover and Festival of Unleavened Bread that we find in Ezra 6:19-22. The concern for purity and unleavened bread are present, but there is no account of a seder or any other ritual connected to the Passover meal. See Bezalel Porten et al., *The Elephantine Papyri in English: Three Millennia of Cross-Cultural Continuity and Change*, 2nd ed., Studies in Near Eastern Archaeology and Civilisation (Atlanta: SBL, 2011), 19.

"no foreigner shall eat of it, but any slave who has been purchased may eat of it after he has been circumcised." Further, any foreigner who wishes to join in must be circumcised along with his family (Exod 12:48). Similarly, in Ezra 6:21, the sharing of the Passover with non-Judeans "who had joined them and separated themselves from the pollutions of the nations of the land to seek the Lord, the God of Israel" suggests an openness and invitation for others to join the repatriate community. Here, the reference to all non-Judeans as contaminating and polluting denotes the cultural distinctiveness and identity marker of others (religious practices, language, traditions) and establishes boundaries for each group. The voluntary participation that leads to the inclusion of others in the repatriates' community indicates that these are permeable boundaries. While this may present a greater openness to "the other," non-Judean participants must still separate themselves from the practices that made them culturally distinct.[43] Yet, we recognize that too-fluid boundaries create confusion, and ambiguity occurs. Where boundaries are too rigid, group members become intolerant of differences.

All religious communities have boundaries for participation and inclusion. Each community establishes the language for how members within the community are to understand those outside the community (e.g., unclean, impure, polluting). The language has a direct correlation to the attributes of the deity. God is holy so the people are to be holy (Lev 11:44, 45; 19:2, 20, 26). The community may be widening its circle of participants, but it is still a circle with specific boundaries that identify this group and its members as different from surrounding cultures.

Conclusions on Ezra 4–6

Throughout the letters (Ezra 4:8–6:12), we do not find the use of the tetragrammaton, YHWH. Extrabiblical evidence attests to the use of the Aramaic phrases אלה ישראל (the God of Israel) and בית אלהא די בירושלם (the

43. See Sara Japhet, "The Expulsion of the Foreign Women (Ezra 9–10): The Legal Basis, Precedents, and Consequences for the Definition of Jewish Identity," in *"Sieben Augen auf einem Stein" (Sach 3,9), Studien zur Literatur des Zweiten Tempels: Festschrift für* Ina Willi-Plein *zum 65. Geburtstag*, ed. Friedhelm Hartenstein and Michael Pietsch (Neukirchen-Vluyn: Neukirchen Verlag, 2007), 141–61; Joseph Fleishman, "An Echo of Optimism in Ezra 6:19-22," *HUCA* 69 (1998): 15–29; Matthew Thiessen, "The Function of a Conjunction: Inclusivist or Exclusivist Strategies in Ezra 6.19-21 and Nehemiah 10.29-30?," *JSOT* 34 (2009): 63–79, https://journals.sagepub.com/doi/epdf/10.1177/0309089209346350.

house of the God in Jerusalem) to distinguish conversations occurring between Jews and non-Jews.[44] The letters are written from the perspective of non-Jews (i.e., outsiders). The letters present this distinction as ideological and political. Ideologically, the text depicts God working through the empire to complete the construction of God's house. Politically, the adversaries of Judah are excluded from participating in the construction efforts (Ezra 4:1-3). The politicization continues in Ezra 5 as a matter of government oversight (Ezra 5:1-5) but shifts to the religious with the repatriates' recitation of their history and traditions (Ezra 5:11-17). In Ezra 6, we see the permeability of boundaries between the religious and political as the king, other non-Jews, and Jews are narratively grafted together since anyone willing to separate from the "pollutions of the nations of the land" can join the repatriate community in worship once the (re)construction of God's house is complete (6:21). Overall, the initial edict to build God's house in Jerusalem finds its completion and celebration in Ezra 6:19-22.

44. Fried notices that the Aramaic parts of Ezra do not use the tetragrammaton but that the Elephantine correspondence often refers to YHWH (*Ezra*, 233–35). Examples from the Elephantine documents that refer to בית אלהא (the house of God) are in TAD A4.10 (Cowley, 33) and TAD B2.10 (Cowley, 33).

Ezra 7–10

Introducing Ezra: Priest and Scribe

Numerous difficulties exist in extracting the historical Ezra from the source material (Ezra memoirs) that comprise Ezra 7–10.[1] Ezra makes his first appearance in the book bearing his name in chapter 7. His introduction includes a lengthy patrilineal pedigree that (1) places him firmly in the lineage of Aaronide priests and (2) acknowledges him as "a scribe skilled in the law of Moses" (Ezra 7:1-5). His name is an Aramaic form of the Hebrew עזר, which can be translated "help" or "helper."[2] Thus, his name connotes his twofold task. As the bearer of Torah, his mission was to "teach the statutes and ordinances in Israel," a task that would ultimately help define the religious identity of the repatriate community

1. The Ezra memoirs consist of Ezra 7:27–9:15 and Nehemiah 8. The difficulties of determining the extent to which the historical Ezra has influenced the source materials in the Ezra memoir has been studied by numerous scholars. For examples, refer to the works of Juha Pakkala, *Ezra the Scribe: The Development of Ezra 7–10 and Nehemiah 8*, BZAW 347 (Berlin: de Gruyter, 2004); and Christiane Karrer-Grube, *Ringen um die Verfassung Judas: Eine Studie zu den theologisch-politischen Vorstellugen im Esra-Nehemia-Buch*, BZAW 308 (Berlin: de Gruyter, 2001), 227–40.

2. *HALOT* suggests that Ezra is a shortened form of עזראל or "God is my help" (p. 812). Other scholars believe that Ezra's name derives from a commonly found name in the priestly genealogy, עזריהו, "the Lord is our help" (see Lisbeth S. Fried, *Ezra: A Commentary*, Critical Commentaries [Sheffield: Sheffield Phoenix, 2015], 294).

(Ezra 7:10, 25). As an official of the king, he was to help administer imperial laws in the province and execute judgment for their transgression (Ezra 7:26). Continuing with the writer's fondness for lists, we have a list in chapter 8 of those traveling with Ezra. This caravan receives the designation as those who are "holy to the Lord" (Ezra 8:28). This perception of holiness is, however, ruptured in Ezra 9 and 10 since once in the province of Judah Ezra learns that some returnees, including the priests, have married non-Judean women. The emphasis on non-Judean women as threatening, such that they and their children must be removed from the community, exposes a vulnerability—a fear perhaps—of the power these women possess (whether knowingly or unknowingly) to impact Judean identity, culture, land distribution, and religion.

Who Is Ezra? A Postcolonial Perspective

The writer of the books of Ezra and Nehemiah presents Ezra as priest, scribe, and scholar extraordinaire of the Mosaic Law. While scholars differ on the timing of Ezra's travel to Jerusalem (either during the reign of Artaxerxes I or Artaxerxes II), most concur that his trip took place a great deal later, following the dedication of the Second Temple in 515 BCE. The reader may find that the identity of Ezra, presented in the continuation of the preexilic, Yahwistic, pro-Judean (cf. anti-Samaritan) temple leadership, in fact, reveals a postexilic, pro-Persian leader who may have worked closely with the Persian administration. Is it Ezra the Persian or Ezra the Jew, who travels to Jerusalem with a vision, a strategy, and tactics that convey a comprehensive, long-term plan for Judah as a province of Persia?

For a postcolonial reader who attempts to resist imperialistic attitudes around indigenous land, the purpose of Ezra's mission is unambiguously to solidify Yehud Medinata (Province of Judah) as a Persian province by supporting the indigenous religion of the people of Judah. Empires strategically resort to religion to sustain their expansionist visions and ideology(-ies) of domination over conquered groups. In Ezra, rather than appealing to the official religion of Persia, the reigning ruler seemingly concedes to the local provincial deity, Yahweh. By aligning himself with the local deity, the king justifies his control and dominance over the province of Judah, the territory "Beyond the River." As a Persian and a Jew, skilled in both worldviews of the colonizer and colonized, Ezra is uniquely equipped and positioned for the task of effectively teaching and governing the people of Judah according to the law of both God and king. For the colonized province of Judah, the law of the Persian Empire is to be viewed in tandem with the laws of the Jewish God, with Ezra given authority to extract strict penalties for violation of either.

It is interesting, however, that the narrator maintains that it is, in fact, the deity Yahweh, rather than the Persian king, who administrates Ezra's life and ministry in Babylon and in Jerusalem. Subsequently, Ezra speaks and praises in the first person that Yahweh indeed takes initiative to deal with the king's agendas and thus controls and dominates the greatest empire on earth: "Blessed be the LORD, the God of our ancestors, who put such a thing as this into the heart of the king to glorify the house of the LORD in Jerusalem" (Ezra 7:27). In this respect, Ezra, as both a postexilic Jew and Persian leader, mimics the imperial discourse of domination and land as divine promise and blessing.

SuJung Shin

My Mind's Made Up (7:1-10)

Ezra 6 closes the narration of the temple's construction and the ritual celebrations surrounding it. As a narrative bridge between the past and present, the adverbial "after this" in Ezra 7:1 functions transitionally, shifting the story in time and place where we are once again "in the reign of King Artaxerxes of Persia." Ancient sources indicate that the name Artaxerxes was commonly used by Persian kings, making it difficult to ascertain with certainty which Artaxerxes is referenced here.[3] Whether one ascribes the period to Artaxerxes I (465–424 BCE) or Artaxerxes II (405–359 BCE), the ambiguity of situating the reign of Artaxerxes in a particular period obscures the historical timeline between Ezra's trip and Cyrus's initial edict (approximately eighty to 150 years prior).[4]

Six of the ten verses in this section concern Ezra's genealogy and imperial connections. The lengthy pedigree validates his priestly identity, a necessary requirement already set forth in Ezra 2:62, and legitimates his capabilities as a teacher of Torah. The significance of credentialing can also be found in contemporary professions, where a medical doctor needs to have a medical degree (MD), complete residency hours, and

3. There lacks a scholarly consensus on whether this is a reference to Artaxerxes I or Artaxerxes II. The various positions are addressed in Ezra 4–6 in this commentary.

4. The text records Ezra's mission occurring during the seventh year of Artaxerxes's reign (Ezra 7:8).

Ezra 7:1-10

1After this, in the reign of King Artaxerxes of Persia, Ezra son of Seraiah,
son of Azariah, son of Hilkiah, 2son of
Shallum, son of Zadok, son of Ahitub,
3son of Amariah, son of Azariah, son of
Meraioth, 4son of Zerahiah, son of Uzzi,
son of Bukki, 5son of Abishua, son of
Phinehas, son of Eleazar, son of the
chief priest Aaron—6this Ezra went up
from Babylonia. He was a scribe skilled
in the law of Moses that the LORD the
God of Israel had given, and the king
granted him all that he asked, for the
hand of the LORD his God was upon him.

7Some of the people of Israel and
some of the priests and Levites, the
singers and gatekeepers, and the
temple servants also went up to Jerusalem in the seventh year of King
Artaxerxes. 8They came to Jerusalem
in the fifth month, which was in the
seventh year of the king. 9On the first
day of the first month the journey up
from Babylon was begun, and on the
first day of the fifth month he came to
Jerusalem, for the gracious hand of his
God was upon him. 10For Ezra had set
his heart to study the law of the LORD
and to do it and to teach the statutes
and ordinances in Israel.

pass board exams to obtain a medical license. Similarly, a lawyer must earn a degree (JD) and pass a bar exam in order to practice law in a state. Credentials serve to validate these people as qualified to perform the specific tasks of their professions. Here, Ezra's credentials as a scribe "skilled in the law of Moses" demonstrate that he is qualified to instruct others in the laws of his God (Ezra 7:6).

Which King and Why It Matters

Our histories are shaped by the stories we tell about ourselves and others. Histories play a significant role in shaping our identities by connecting us to our roots, and without them the sharing of cultural traditions and societal values is lost. So why does the identity of the king matter? If history allows us to learn valuable lessons from the past and identify significant figures or events that were instrumental in shaping our histories, what happens when we lose that sense of time? What happens when the circumstances that shaped, influenced, and informed people are lost or rewritten? Perhaps the answer lies in the sense of ambiguity that comes with the loss of time, where people and events do not neatly fit into a particular temporal space according to those who control the narrative. When history is rewritten, some experiences are marginalized or forgotten since including them may require that we look at them differently or address our own complicity in erasing or forgetting them. Misinformation presented as historical facts obscures history and serves the purposes of those who create alternative agendas through its dissemination. So, the identity of the king in this text matters. His identity situates him in a particular time and place that coincides with the thoughts, behaviors, and actions of the people subjugated during his rule. This people will link him to their history together with their perspectives of what transpired (for or against) during his reign.

Moreover, Ezra has cultivated a relationship with the king such that "the king granted him all that he asked" (Ezra 7:6). Thus, it is the favor of King Artaxerxes and the favor of Ezra's God that allow Ezra to fulfill his desire to travel to Jerusalem to "teach the statutes and ordinances in Israel" (Ezra 7:10). Born in Persia, Ezra resides in one of the flourishing Jewish diaspora communities. His dual identity as Persian and Jewish does not detract from his loyalty to his God and his people. Double identities can, however, be complicated because of competing loyalties. For example, some Americans professing a Christian identity will encounter moments when American jurisprudence conflicts with their conservative or liberal Christian values (i.e., reproductive rights and marriage equality). Somewhat related are immigrants who seek to preserve essential elements of their culture while simultaneously acculturating to American society (i.e., language, religious beliefs and practices).

Ezra assembles a group consisting of temple personnel: priests, Levites, singers, gatekeepers, and temple servants (Ezra 7:7). The list speaks to the group's mission and purpose and aligns with Ezra's desire to teach the statutes and ordinances in Israel. According to Ezra 7:8-9, the group leaves Babylonia on the first day of the first month and arrives in Jerusalem on the first day of the fifth month. These references communicate more than the passage of time; they also symbolize belonging. The first month (Aviv)[5] points to the exodus event and the first Passover meal (Deut 16:1), while the fifth month (Ab) marks a time of tragedy

5. The Babylonian name for the month Aviv is Nisan.

corresponding to the destruction of the temple in 587/586 BCE. The timing of the departure and arrival in Jerusalem frames the group's mission as they read themselves into Israel's history. This historical connection is again emphasized in Ezra 7:10, which repeats Ezra's desire in Ezra 7:6. In Ezra 7:10, he gives his personal commitment and preparation, further emphasizing his desire to "study the law of the LORD and to do it and to teach the statutes and ordinances in Israel." Yet, his desire to teach the laws and statutes of his people essentially dismisses the truth claims of those already in the land. An analogy would be Christians telling Jews what they should believe or men telling women how they should act.

Ezra—Large and in Charge (7:11-26)

Like the royal decrees in previous chapters, Artaxerxes's edict in Ezra 7:11-26 is written in Aramaic. Neither the letter nor the edict therein conforms to traditional forms of Persian correspondence; thus, they make suspect the authenticity of this report. While the vestige of an ancient source is visible based on the letter's structure, Ezra's theological thrust dominates these verses as God, God's house, and God's will have a preeminent role, thus intermingling the service one provides to the deity and the service one provides to the king. In Ezra 7:12, the reference to Artaxerxes as the "king of kings" is the formulaic self-ascribed title that captures the conquest of a king over other kings. The title first appeared during the reign of the Assyrian King Tukulti-Ninurta (1243–1207 BCE) and was later assumed by Babylonian and Persian kings, most notably King Darius I.[6] The Behistun Inscription, a rock relief dated to the Persian period, carries the following inscription, "I (am) Darius, the great king, the king of kings, the king in Persia."[7] The title also appears in Daniel 2:37 as a reference to Nebuchadnezzar and in Ezekiel 26:7 to Nebuchadrezzar. Following the period of the Maccabees and beyond, the designation "king of kings" becomes a statement of faith that envisions God as one whose reign extends beyond the rule of temporal kings (2 Macc 13:4; 3 Macc 5:35). In the New Testament, "king of kings" is the title given to Jesus (1 Tim 6:15; Rev 17:14; 19:16) and represents his perpetual triumph and reign over heaven, earth, and spiritual forces. The reference to the "God of heaven" is discussed in the commentary

6. See Lowell K. Handy, *Among the Host of Heaven* (Winona Lake, IN: Eisenbrauns, 1994), 112n96.

7. Joshua J. Mark, "Behistun Inscription," *World History Encyclopedia* (November 28, 2019), https://www.worldhistory.org/Behistun_Inscription/.

Ezra 7:11-26

11This is a copy of the letter that King
Artaxerxes gave to Ezra the priest
and scribe, a scholar of the words of
the commandments of the LORD and
his statutes for Israel: 12"Artaxerxes,
king of kings, to the priest Ezra, the
scribe of the law of the God of heaven:
Peace. And now 13I decree that any of
the people of Israel or their priests or
Levites in my kingdom who freely offers to go to Jerusalem may go with
you. 14For you are sent by the king and
his seven counselors to make inquiries
about Judah and Jerusalem according
to the law of your God, which is in your
hand, 15and also to convey the silver
and gold that the king and his counselors have freely offered to the God of
Israel, whose dwelling is in Jerusalem,
16with all the silver and gold that you
shall find in the whole province of Babylonia and with the freewill offerings of
the people and the priests, given willingly for the house of their God in Jerusalem. 17With this money, then, you
shall with all diligence buy bulls, rams,
and lambs and their grain offerings and
their drink offerings, and you shall offer

on Ezra 6. See:6-17. Rather than appearing as a generic phrase for gods worshiped in Persian-occupied territories, here the phrase specifically names the "God of heaven" as Ezra's God.

The king's decree in Ezra 7:13 appears conditional since only those who freely offer to go may return with Ezra. The conditional framing of the proposition suggests that some exiles may not share Ezra's desire or enthusiasm to return. For second- and third-generation Judeans living in exile, diaspora is home. These persons would have to weigh the consequences (financial and otherwise) of uprooting their families to establish residence in Judah and Jerusalem. The condition is twofold as the king and his counselors desire that Ezra "make inquiries" (בקרא), better stated as Ezra having eyes and ears tuned to the religious activities in Judah and Jerusalem as it pertains to Jewish law (Ezra 7:14). The language of the edict suggests that the king's agenda is God's agenda (Ezra 7:14, 15) and God's agenda is Ezra's agenda (Ezra 7:27), which makes the letter a theological treatise of sorts. In general, the alignment of government and theology opens up dangerous possibilities when politicians claim to speak for God as they make policies that impact other religious and nonreligious groups. This collaboration, observable in the current culture wars where controlling women's bodies, women's education, people's participation in sports, and their marriage partners, is predicated on the theological stance of the group in power.

Unlike the freewill offering in Ezra 1:4; 2:68; and 3:5, the freewill offering in Ezra 7:16 may not be voluntary "with all the silver and gold that

Ezra 7:11-26 (cont.)

them on the altar of the house of your God in Jerusalem. [18]Whatever seems good to you and your colleagues to do with the rest of the silver and gold, you may do, according to the will of your God. [19]The vessels that have been given you for the service of the house of your God, you shall deliver before the God of Jerusalem. [20]And whatever else is required for the house of your God that you are responsible for providing, you may provide out of the king's treasury.

[21]"I, King Artaxerxes, decree to all the treasurers in the province Beyond the River: Whatever the priest Ezra, the scribe of the law of the God of heaven, requires of you, let it be done with all diligence, [22]up to one hundred talents of silver, one hundred cors of wheat, one hundred baths of wine, one hundred baths of oil, and unlimited salt. [23]Whatever is commanded by the God of heaven, let it be done with zeal for the house of the God of heaven, or wrath will come upon the

you shall find in the whole province of Babylonia and with the freewill offerings of the people and the priests, *given willingly* for the house of their God in Jerusalem" (emphasis added). The freewill offering is a voluntary offering, which makes us wonder if the emphasis on "given willingly" depicts the actual sentiments of the giver.

A shift occurs in Ezra 7:14-17 from Ezra's focus on Torah instruction to the provisions necessary for a functional sacrificial system in Jerusalem (animals and temple vessels). The distribution of the collection appears in Ezra 7:18-23. Following the purchase of sacrificial elements, any undistributed silver and gold can be used at the discretion of Ezra and his colleagues (Ezra 7:18). The vessels are to be delivered to the house of God and the God of Jerusalem (Ezra 7:19). The king's treasury will supply what the province is unable to provide (Ezra 7:20). Finally, the treasurers in the province Beyond the River are to cover any remaining needs the house of God requires (Ezra 7:21-23). The provincial treasuries must be exhausted prior to receiving help from the king's treasury. Even today, faith-based organizations receive government funds only when those funds target communal projects and are not typically used for the maintenance of houses of worship. For example, Community Development Centers (CDCs), which are non-profit organizations, receive some government aid, but this aid is restricted for use in communal projects (i.e., after-school programs, food and clothing banks, and affordable residential housing).

While Persian rulers tolerated their subjects' indigenous religious practices to maintain stability in colonized areas, the level of economic realm of the king and his heirs. [24]We also notify you that it shall not be lawful to impose tribute, custom, or toll on any of the priests, the Levites, the singers, the doorkeepers, the temple servants, or other servants of this house of God.

[25]"And you, Ezra, according to the God-given wisdom you possess, appoint magistrates and judges who may judge all the people in the province Beyond the River who know the laws of your God, and you shall teach those who do not know them. [26]All who will not obey the law of your God and the law of the king, let judgment be strictly executed on them, whether for death or for banishment or for confiscation of their goods or for imprisonment."

and material support depicted in Ezra 7:14-23 seems overly generous by Persian standards. This generosity includes exemption from paying tribute, custom, and toll taxes (7:24). Currently, the concern about whether churches and other nonprofits should remain tax-exempt entities receives mixed reviews. Some argue that nonprofits are parasitical, consuming resources (fire, police, etc.) without monetarily contributing to their operational costs. Others argue that nonprofits serve the public good by providing much-needed services to the local community that are not provided through governmental or other service agencies. A final argument concerns whether the use of government community development grants absolves the government from providing programs that communities need (e.g., shelters, student lunch programs, after-school programs). One needs to consider which is more valuable to the community: the loss of uncollected tax revenue or the benefits numerous groups receive from these programs.

Provisions Listed in Ezra 7:22-23

Hebrew Weights & Measures	English (US) Equivalent
100 talents of silver	7,500 lbs.
100 cors of wheat	652.4 bushels
100 baths of wine	607.3 gallons
100 baths of oil and unlimited salt	607.3 gallons

The portrait of benevolent Persian rulers contributing provisions from their own royal coffers counters the imperial apparatus, which flourished from its extraction of resources from conquered peoples (cf. 2 Kgs 25:13-16; Isa 10:5-6). Still, there is precedence to support a view where temple personnel were exempt from imperial building projects and the manual labor extracted by their overlords (cf. Cyrus Cylinder, lines 25-36; Gadatas letter, lines 19-29; and Xanthus stele, line 11).[8] Given the book's aggregation as a composite work, we should not rely too heavily on its account of excessive Persian support as historical fact.

The edict authorizes Ezra, as the king's agent, to appoint magistrates and judges knowledgeable in local customs and laws in the province Beyond the River (Ezra 7:25-26). These delegates, as imperial enforcers, impose punishment for any infraction of either God's law or the laws of the king, which should be taken here as one and the same. By the king's command, Ezra is to instruct all others unfamiliar with the law of Ezra's God (Ezra 7:25), once again coalescing the power of the empire with the tenants of a specific religious group. In this capacity, Ezra appears as wielding enormous power. A closer reading yields its limitations. Conceptually, power is the ability to influence and affect humans, their circumstances, and their resources, something for which Ezra has only partial capacity in his role as administrator and Torah instructor. The nature of the punishments (i.e., banishment, confiscation of goods, imprisonment, or capital punishment) draws our attention to the socioeconomic realities of colonial rule (Ezra 7:26).

The King's Heart—The Lord's Hand (7:27-28)

In these last verses of Ezra 7, Ezra speaks for the first time as he gathers his group and prepares for a journey to Jerusalem. The text now resumes in Hebrew. Again, imperial sovereignty is subordinated by a divine blessing that attributes the journey to Jerusalem as the deity's will rather than the king's need for information. The reference to putting the matter on the heart of the king reminds us of Pharaoh's heart in Exodus 4:21: "And the Lord said to Moses, 'When you go back to Egypt, see that you perform before Pharaoh all the wonders that I have put in your power, but I will harden his heart, so that he will not let the people go.'" In both instances, the king's heart (i.e., will) is subjected to the sovereignty of God. Proverbs 21:1 echoes this sentiment, "The king's heart is a stream of water in the hand of the Lord," directing it wherever God wills. The

8. The Gadatas letter is written by King Darius to his servant, Gadatas. The Xanthus stele (4th century), found in Turkey, shed light on both exemptions of financial support and manual labor. See Fried, *Ezra*, 304–5.

Ezra 7:27-28

[27]Blessed be the LORD, the God of our ancestors, who put such a thing as this into the heart of the king to glorify the house of the LORD in Jerusalem [28]and who extended to me steadfast love before the king and his counselors and before all the king's mighty officers. I took courage, for the hand of the LORD my God was upon me, and I gathered leaders from Israel to go up with me.

king may issue edicts that display the power and presence of imperial rule; however, it is God who orders the king's steps.

What's in a Name (8:1-14)

Ezra 8:1-14 catalogs the families making the pilgrimage with Ezra from Babylonia to Jerusalem. Similar to elsewhere in the book of Ezra, the writer's presentation of the genealogy is not neutral.[9] The list contains several appreciable differences that distinguish it from the registry recorded in Ezra 2 and Nehemiah 7.[10] Of the forty-one eponyms listed here, only fourteen appear in Ezra 2 and Nehemiah 7. Apart from 8:2, which begins with the descendants of Phinehas, a priestly family, the preponderance of names aligns closely with the Davidic monarchy (cf. 1 Chr 3:22).[11] The language that excludes certain families from the priesthood until verified by the priest (Ezra 2:61-63) is absent here. The list links members of this group with the first wave of returnees in Ezra 2. These connections, together with the associations to dominant priestly and monarchial houses of the distant past, remove the need for genealogical validation found in Ezra 2 (Ezra 2:62-63) and Nehemiah 7 (Neh 7:64-65). Absent these restrictions, one gets a sense of inclusiveness that unifies the group around a single motif that emphasizes the worship of God in Jerusalem. The accentuation on male heads of households and other males traveling with the group when viewed in the broader spectrum

9. Gary N. Knoppers, "Exile, Return and Diaspora: Expatriates and Repatriates in Late Biblical Literature," in *Text, Contexts and Readings in Postexilic Literature: Explorations into Historiography and Identity Negotiation in Hebrew Bible and Related Texts*, ed. Louis Jonker, FAT 2 53 (Tübingen: Mohr Siebeck, 2011), 39.

10. A parallel version of Ezra 8 appears in 1 Esdras.

11. First Chronicles 3:22 names Hattush, whom Ezra 8 designates as a descendant of David.

Ezra 8:1-14

1These are their family heads, and this is the genealogy of those who went up with me from Babylonia, in the reign of King Artaxerxes: 2Of the descendants of Phinehas, Gershom. Of Ithamar, Daniel. Of David, Hattush, 3of the descendants of Shecaniah. Of Parosh, Zechariah, with whom were registered one hundred fifty males. 4Of the descendants of Pahath-moab, Eliehoenai son of Zerahiah, and with him two hundred males. 5Of the descendants of Zattu, Shecaniah son of Jahaziel, and with him three hundred males. 6Of the descendants of Adin, Ebed son of Jonathan, and with him fifty males. 7Of the descendants of Elam, Jeshaiah son of Athaliah, and with him seventy males. 8Of the descendants of Shephatiah, Zebadiah son of Michael, and with him eighty males. 9Of the descendants of Joab, Obadiah son of Jehiel, and with him two hundred eighteen males. 10Of the descendants of Bani, Shelomith son of Josiphiah, and with him one hundred sixty males. 11Of the descendants of Bebai, Zechariah son of Bebai, and with him twenty-eight males. 12Of the descendants of Azgad, Johanan son of Hakkatan, and with him one hundred ten males. 13Of the descendants of Adonikam, those who came later, their names being Eliphelet, Jeuel, and Shemaiah, and with them sixty males. 14Of the descendants of Bigvai, Uthai and Zaccur, and with them seventy males.

of mass movements in biblical narratives overwhelmingly depicts the migration of entire families (i.e., men, women, and children) (Gen 12:1-5; 46:1-7; Exod 12:37-38; Ruth 1:1). This second wave of migrants, now six to seven generations removed from the first group of repatriates, speaks to the attractiveness of Jerusalem and conceivably prefigures immigrating to Israel in contemporary Judaism (*aliyah*, "going up").

In Ezra 8:7 and 8:10, the names Athaliah and Shelomith call into question an ideological premise pervasive throughout biblical narrative that views patrilineality as normative.[12] Both names can refer to either a man or a woman. In 1 Chronicles 8:26, the name Athaliah refers to a son of Jeroham of Benjamin. In 2 Kings, however, Athaliah appears as a monarch who reigned in Judah for six years prior to her execution (2 Kgs 11:16).[13] As the daughter, stepdaughter, or sister-in-law of Jezebel, Athaliah's reign sets off a chain of events that furthers the continuance

12. Refer to chapter 2 for our discussion on the writer's depiction of patrilineality as an ideologically practiced reality.

13. Overall, there lacks a scholarly consensus on whether Athaliah is the daughter of Ahab or Omri. The biblical account is equally unclear on the matter (cf. 2 Kgs 8:20, 26 and 2 Chr 21:6; 22:2).

of Davidic descendants (2 Kgs 11:12). Commentators on the book of Ezra often overlook the name Athaliah, likely due to the assumption that it is masculine.[14] Alternatively, when Athaliah is read as the name of a woman, her insertion in the list represents a matrilineal rather than patrilineal connection. As a female monarch (rather than queen), she interrupts the patrilineal ideology of male Judean kings much like Sarah, Hagar, and Rebecca interrupt the patrilineal narratives of Abraham and Jacob, or Bathsheba's interruption in the succession narrative of David and Solomon.[15] Embedding Athaliah in the list of male descendants cloaks her identity as a female. Communal memory would identify the name with one of Judah's most powerful, albeit infamous, kings/queen mothers. As such, the name retains some social (and perhaps political) capital while simultaneously linking it geographically and ethnically with persons descended from Elam, which is geographically in Persia (Ezra 8:7). The overall effect situates her and her descendants among those considered outsiders or foreigners.[16]

There are two biblical occurrences in which Shelomith is identified as a woman. In Leviticus 24:11 she is the daughter of Dibri of the tribe of Dan. This Shelomith, although an Israelite, married an unnamed Egyptian (Lev 24:10). In 1 Chronicles 3:19 Shelomith is the daughter of Zerubbabel. A seal from about 510–490 BCE containing the contested inscription "Belonging to Shelomith, maidservant of Elnathan the governor" was excavated in Jerusalem in 2008.[17] The seal suggests that some Jewish women in the Persian period have status. This archaeological evidence, although illuminating, does not, however, resolve the

Athaliah, from Guillaume Rouillé's *Promptuarii Iconum Insigniorum*, 1553, https://en.wikipedia.org/wiki/Athaliah.

14. For example, see Mark A. Throntveit, *Ezra–Nehemiah*, IBC (Louisville: Westminster John Knox, 2012); Lester L. Grabbe, *Ezra–Nehemiah*, OTR (London: Routledge, 1998); Frank Charles Fensham, *The Books of Ezra and Nehemiah*, NICOT (Grand Rapids: Eerdmans, 1982).

15. Cynthia R. Chapman, *The House of the Mother: The Social Roles of Maternal Kin in Biblical Hebrew Narrative and Poetry*, AYBRL (New Haven: Yale University Press, 2016). Chapman has observed the ways in which maternally related kin in biblical narrative are used to "introduce social and political divisions and hierarchies among men" (9).

16. The list includes names that are both people and places. We have chosen to read Elam as a place.

17. Nahman Avigad, *Bullae and Seals from a Post-Exilic Judean Archive* (Jerusalem: Institute of Archaeology, Hebrew University, 1976), 11.

question of Shelomith's gender in Ezra 8:10 where Shelomith is listed as the male descendant of Bani. Tamara Cohn Eskenazi offers a translation that removes the uncertainty, preferring to render the verse "From the descendants of Shelomith: the son of Josiphiah, and with him 160 men."[18] With this translation, the insertion of a matrilineal rather than patrilineal linkage is again observable. By choosing the gender of the name, interpreters deny these women their place in the genealogy of those persons instrumental in creating a restored Judean community.

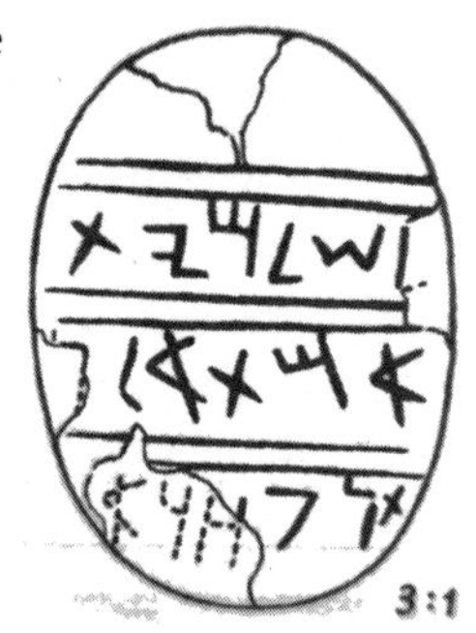

Nahman Avigad, QEDEM 4 Monographs, 1976, p. 11 (Shelomith's Seal Illustration Fig. 14). Photographer, Zev Radovan. Reproduced with permission of the Institute of Archaeology, The Hebrew University of Jerusalem.

The ambiguity concerning the gendered aspects of these names brings to the forefront contemporary naming conventions that are multigendered and, in some cases, identifiable with particular ethnic groups. We should not assume that names like Michael, Owen, and Shawn refer to white males. Nor should we assume that names like Gale, Leslie, Lindsey, and Dana are female. Yet, despite these distinctions, there remain implicit (and explicit) biases in educational, health-care, and employment opportunities when distinguishing Eurocentric names (like those mentioned above) from non-Eurocentric names (Lakeisha, Jamal, etc.). An examination of the way in which names communicate something about one's identity (gender, ethnicity, social status, etc.) points to a need for readers and interpreters to be sensitive to any implicit biases when interpreting biblical names.

Down by the Riverside (8:15-20)

Reminiscent of the Israelites' encampment by the river Jordan before entering the land of promise (Josh 3:1-3), Ezra, the priests, and the people set up a three-day hiatus by the river Ahava. The exact location of Ahava remains elusive; it has been predominantly associated with one of the

18. Tamara Cohn Eskenazi, "Ezra–Nehemiah," in *Women's Bible Commentary*, ed. Carol A. Newsom, Sharon H. Ringe, and Jaqueline Lapsley, 3rd ed. (Louisville: Westminster John Knox, 2012), 197; Eskenazi, "Shelomith in (Ezra 8:10)," in *Women in Scripture: A Dictionary of Named and Unnamed Women in the Hebrew Bible, the Apocryphal/Deuterocanonical Books, and the New Testament*, ed. Carol Meyers, Toni Craven, and Ross Shepard Kraemer (Boston: Houghton Mifflin, 2000), 155.

Ezra 8:15-20

[15]I gathered them by the river that runs
to Ahava, and there we camped three
days. As I reviewed the people and
the priests, I found there none of the
descendants of Levi. [16]Then I sent for
Eliezer, Ariel, Shemaiah, Elnathan,
Jarib, Elnathan, Nathan, Zechariah, and
Meshullam, who were leaders, and for
Joiarib and Elnathan, who were wise,
[17]and sent them to Iddo, the leader at
the place called Casiphia, telling them
what to say to Iddo and his colleagues
the temple servants at Casiphia, namely,
to send us ministers for the house of our
God. [18]Since the gracious hand of our
God was upon us, they brought us a
man of discretion, of the descendants of
Mahli son of Levi son of Israel, namely,
Sherebiah, with his sons and kin, eighteen; [19]also Hashabiah and with him
Jeshaiah of the descendants of Merari,
with his kin and their sons, twenty; [20]be-
sides two hundred twenty of the temple
servants, whom David and his officials
had set apart to attend the Levites.
These were all mentioned by name.

streams or canals in Mesopotamia, possibly near Babylonia or the Euphrates River. Despite the extensive infrastructure of the Persian Empire, the migration of so large a group would necessitate a route that offered access to water, a necessity that most likely took into account the river Ahava and other nearby streams. Perched by the river Ahava, they are about to enter a land they have possibly never seen. For them, land and home become synonymous as they migrate from the past and present to a new and different future. This group, standing at the precipice of new beginnings, represents a refreshing contrast to the biblical depiction of a people broken and defeated, living in Babylonian exile, captured by the psalmist in Psalm 137:1: "By the rivers of Babylon—there we sat down, and there we wept when we remembered Zion."

The focus shifts from Ezra's mission "to teach the statutes and ordinances in Israel" (Ezra 7:10) to his realization that the Levites are absent (Ezra 8:15). The noticeable absence of the Levites perhaps reflects the diaspora condition of a group who were once a part of a flourishing temple community that no longer exists or remains in Babylon. For Ezra, the Levites are just as necessary to his mission as the priests who accompany him. While the text does not mention the role of the Levites in this instance, elsewhere the biblical material describes them as an administrative arm of the temple (Num 3–4; 1 Chr 23:28-32).[19]

19. Fried, *Ezra*, 110–12.

The inclusion of the priests and Levites demonstrates a concern for the function and maintenance of the temple. Like so many other organizations or institutions that gather and rely on a variety of skill sets, Ezra's recognition suggests that religious institutions must do the same. Nevertheless, the inclusion of priests and Levites reads as a later insertion. The insertion ensures this group's place in the historical witness of this people with genealogical connections to Moses, Aaron, and the worshiping community.

To address his concern regarding the absence of the Levites, Ezra sends a group consisting of eleven heads of household (leaders), of which two were considered men of understanding (wise), to Casiphia (Ezra 8:16). Geographically, Casiphia may represent the presence of a religious or administrative center known to the diaspora community living outside of Babylon. Mark Leuchter suggests that the city served as "a locus of scribal activity and teaching."[20] Second Chronicles 34:13 indicates that the Levites also functioned as "officials, scribes, and gatekeepers," thus making Casiphia an ideal place for Ezra to recruit and invite them to join his caravan. There is no temple in Casiphia, which would certainly heighten the appeal for the Levites to perform their services in the Jerusalem temple. The text does not provide an explanation of why Ezra, as the group's leader, did not join the delegation to "Iddo and his colleagues the temple servants" (Ezra 8:17). On the one hand, Ezra may not have had the kind of name recognition or familiarity among the religious leaders in Casiphia as those he sent, despite his origins from a prestigious priestly family. On the other hand, he demonstrates the characteristics of a good leader and administrator who has no problem delegating a significant task to those he leads.

His request to send help for the house of God is honored, which he attributes to the gracious hand of his God (Ezra 8:18-20). Overall, Ezra's delegation collected thirty-eight Levites together with 220 temple servants whose lineage could be traced to families set aside by David to attend to the Levites in former times.[21] Seven of the nine leaders joining the group from Casiphia will be among those named later in Ezra 9 and 10 who must divorce their foreign wives or have their property confiscated.

20. Mark Leuchter, "Ezra's Mission and the Levites of Casiphia," in *Community Identity in Judean Historiography: Biblical and Comparative Perspectives*, ed. Gary N. Knoppers and Kenneth A. Ristau (Winona Lake, IN: Eisenbrauns, 2009), 182.

21. Fried, *Ezra*, 119–20.

Making Space for the Sacred (8:21-30)

Concern for the safety of the group results in the proclamation of a fast in Ezra 8:21, which is reiterated in Ezra 8:23-24. Typically, fasting in the Scriptures of ancient Israel is associated with mourning (1 Sam 31:13; 2 Sam 1:12; Zech 7:5; 1 Chr 10:12), repentance and restoration (Jonah 3:5; Jer 36:6; Neh 9:1), seeking direction (Dan 9:3), acts of humility (Isa 58:3, 5; 1 Kgs 21:37; Pss 35:13; 69:11), and for protection (Esth 4:15-16).[22] The practice is frequently done in tandem with prayer (2 Sam 12:16; Neh 1:4). The only required fast found in the Scriptures of ancient Israel is associated with Yom Kippur, the Day of Atonement (Lev 16:29, 31; 23:27, 32; and Num 29:7). Many religious traditions view fasting as a way to open channels to the divine. Thus, the practice serves as a means of spiritual growth or to seek guidance in difficult or dangerous circumstances. While still a practice of one's spirituality, fasting, as a way of discipling oneself, occurs in many forms today, as one may abstain from food or certain foods, technology, and spending money. The practice also occurs as an act of protest to seek change (i.e., suffragettes in Britain, prisoner hunger strikes). These examples present fasting as a choice, where someone chooses to abstain from something. At the same time, fasting is not a choice for some, particularly when food insecurity (i.e., starvation) and economic disparities exist. In Ezra 8:21-22, the group embarks on a fast to solicit the protection of God for their journey since traveling an alternate route may have been more rugged, unprotected (i.e., from bandits), and potentially harsh due to seasonal conditions making the journey perilous.

The textual reference to protecting children in Ezra 8:21 without a corresponding reference to maternal or female associations (i.e., wives, women, or mothers) could be of concern for those who view this absence as a slight to womanhood in general. Grammatically, the Hebrew uses the common plural, which yields an inclusive reference to men and women Given this, the makeup of the caravan can be stated differently as consisting of husbands and wives, their children, and all their possessions. Thus, we need not understand the lack of specific references to wives or women as an omission by the writer or that women are property lumped together in the phrase "all our possessions."

22. In Exodus 34 Moses performs a fast prior to receiving the second decalogue after he destroys the first one. The food that the angels provide Elijah sustains him for forty days and nights prior to entering a cave where he encounters God (1 Kgs 19:4-18).

Ezra 8:21-30

21 Then I proclaimed a fast there, at the
River Ahava, that we might humble
ourselves before our God, to seek
from him a safe journey for ourselves,
our children, and all our possessions.
22 For I was ashamed to ask the king
for a band of soldiers and cavalry to
protect us against the enemy on our
way, since we had told the king that
the hand of our God is gracious to all
who seek him, but his power and his
wrath are against all who forsake him.
23 So we fasted and petitioned our God
for this, and he listened to our entreaty.
24 Then I set apart twelve of the leading priests: Sherebiah, Hashabiah,
and ten of their kin with them. 25 And
I weighed out to them the silver and
the gold and the vessels, the offering
for the house of our God that the king,
his counselors, his lords, and all Israel
there present had offered; 26 I weighed

Unlike Nehemiah 2:7-8, where imperial military support is solicited and received, the writer makes it clear that the group's migration to Jerusalem is not predicated on military support despite the potential risk to the group's safety (cf. Ezra 8:31). Other biblical passages indicate that caravans did not travel unprotected. The Israelites' migratory move into the land of Canaan includes armed "warriors" (Josh 1:14). Armed men are strategically stationed and assist in building the Jerusalem wall (Neh 4:13 and 4:18). As a practical matter, the substantial number of men accompanying Ezra's group may make an imperial escort unnecessary as some (even all) may have been armed. His reluctance to seek a military escort is voiced in psychological and religious terms. In Ezra 8:22-24, Ezra avoids seeming faithless, which an appeal for a military escort might imply: "For I was ashamed to ask the king for a band of soldiers and cavalry to protect us against the enemy on our way, since we had told the king that the hand of our God is gracious to all who seek him." In this context, the avoidance of shame suggests that one must choose in whom one is willing to trust—God or the king.

The remainder of this section takes on a practical tone as the need for safety is further clarified given the valuable possessions the caravan carries, including donations from the king. With the potential threat of ambush to this group and lacking a military escort, Ezra divides the provisions among twelve leading priests, sets them apart, and proceeds to pronounce them and the vessels they carry "holy." Although referred to as priests, their function is to guard the valuables designated for the temple until they are delivered to the priests and Levites in Jerusalem

out into their hand six hundred fifty talents of silver, and one hundred silver vessels worth . . . talents, and one hundred talents of gold, [27]twenty gold bowls worth a thousand darics, and two vessels of fine polished bronze as precious as gold. [28]And I said to them, "You are holy to the LORD, and the vessels are holy, and the silver and the gold are a freewill offering to the LORD, the God of your ancestors. [29]Guard them and keep them until you weigh them before the chief priests and the Levites and the heads of families in Israel at Jerusalem, within the chambers of the house of the LORD." [30]So the priests and the Levites took over the silver, the gold, and the vessels as they were weighed out, to bring them to Jerusalem, to the house of our God.

(Ezra 8:29, 33). The language of purity ("You are holy to the LORD, and the vessels are holy"; Ezra 8:28) is juxtaposed with the language of protection ("Guard them and keep them"; Ezra 8:29) and speaks to the importance of the cargo and its intended use for religious purposes, thus moving both from the profane to the sacred. Today, many religions still set aside persons and objects for ritual use. An example would be sacristans who are set aside and charged with preparing the sacred elements for communion or the baptismal font. Women are well represented in this role in Roman Catholic and other traditions.

Safe Travels (8:31-36)

The fast is now complete, and Ezra and his group resume their travels to Jerusalem (Ezra 8:31). The group's movement toward Jerusalem occurs on the twelfth day of the first month (Nisan). Absent specific details of their travels, the group's safe arrival in Jerusalem serves as the direct response to the group's fast (God's hand of protection) amid concerns for the perilous nature of their journey (hand of the enemy/ambushes) (Ezra 8:32-34). The king's business is not the priority since the group cares for the needs of the temple and its administration (silver, gold, vessels, etc.), followed by the affirmation of their collective identity as a united people (twelve tribes of Israel) through the tangible and visible participation in the sacrificial offerings (Ezra 8:35-36). While the king's business does not appear as the group's first concern, the deliverance of the king's commissions to the satraps and governors weds the group's goals with those of the empire and suggests the inseparable nature of the two.

Ezra 8:31-36

31Then we left the River Ahava on the
twelfth day of the first month to go to
Jerusalem; the hand of our God was
upon us, and he delivered us from the
hand of the enemy and from ambushes
along the way. 32We came to Jerusalem
and remained there three days. 33On the
fourth day, within the house of our God,
the silver, the gold, and the vessels were
weighed into the hands of the priest Meremoth son of Uriah, and with him was
Eleazar son of Phinehas, and with them
were the Levites, Jozabad son of Jeshua and Noadiah son of Binnui. 34The
total was counted and weighed, and the
weight of everything was recorded.

35At that time those who had come
from captivity, the returned exiles,
offered burnt offerings to the God of
Israel: twelve bulls for all Israel, ninety-
six rams, seventy-seven lambs, and as
a sin offering twelve male goats; all this
was a burnt offering to the LORD. 36They
also delivered the king's commissions
to the king's satraps and to the governors of the province Beyond the River,
and they supported the people and the
house of God.

Trouble on the Home Front (9:1-4)

The business of the temple and the delivery of the king's commission marks the conclusion of Ezra 8 and the beginning of Ezra 9, which states, "After these things had been done." A group identified only as "the officials" in Ezra 9:1 approaches Ezra regarding the failure of the people of Israel, priests, and Levites to separate themselves from their non-Judean neighbors and their religious practices. While the language of abominations characterizes their interactions and serves as the justification for this critique, this critique appears as the symptom rather than the root of the writer's concern. These obscure officials claim, "[T]hey have taken some of their daughters as wives for themselves and for their sons. Thus the holy seed has mixed itself with the peoples of the lands, and in this faithlessness the officials and leaders have led the way" (Ezra 9:2). The text links the seed (i.e., sperm of Judean males) with the holiness of the people referenced in Ezra 8:28, "And I said to them, 'You are holy to the LORD.'" The juxtaposition of the holy seed with those in the land (the Canaanites, the Hittites, the Perizzites, the Jebusites, the Ammonites, the Moabites, the Egyptians, and the Amorites) has the effect of making not only their marriages unholy but also the repatriates, as God's people, unholy as well.

Ezra 9:1-4

[1]After these things had been done, the officials approached me and said, "The people of Israel, the priests, and the Levites have not separated themselves from the peoples of the lands with their abominations, from the Canaanites, the Hittites, the Perizzites, the Jebusites, the Ammonites, the Moabites, the Egyptians, and the Amorites. [2]For they have taken some of their daughters as wives for themselves and for their sons. Thus the holy seed has mixed itself with the peoples of the lands, and in this faithlessness the officials and leaders have led the way." [3]When I heard this, I tore my garment and my mantle and pulled hair from my head and beard and sat appalled. [4]Then all who trembled at the words of the God of Israel because of the faithlessness of the returned exiles gathered around me while I sat appalled until the evening sacrifice.

Anti-Miscegenation Laws

Segregationist policies that resulted in the separation of groups by race existed either by law or by custom for most of this country's history and were challenged broadly during the civil rights era of the 1960s. As part of that earlier history, anti-miscegenation laws were geared to prevent certain kinds of sexual mixing across racial lines and prohibited, among other things, a marriage between a white person and a Black person, as those categories were defined by statutes. Such laws were in effect for nearly three hundred years (1691–1967), and Alabama, the last state to remove a provision banning interracial marriages from its state constitution, did so only in the year 2000 (Wallenstein 2002, 247).[23] In the 1960s, the US Supreme Court held in *Loving v. Virginia* (388 U.S. 1 [1967]) that such laws were unconstitutional. At an earlier stage of that legal process, a judge in Virginia had upheld the state's intermarriage ban, writing the following statement in his conclusions: "Almighty God created the races white, black, yellow, malay and red, and he placed them on separate continents. And but for the interference with his arrangement there would be no cause for such marriages. The fact that he separated the races shows that he did not intend for the races to mix" (Wallenstein 2002, 219). . . . To take into account

23. Peter Wallenstein, *Tell the Court I Love My Wife: Race, Marriage, and Law—An American History* (New York: Palgrave Macmillan, 2002), 219.

the history of segregation and its continuing legacy when reading biblical texts such as Ezra, African American people of faith must have a different reading strategy—a hermeneutic of resistance. Resistance is appropriate because the dominant culture's interpretation of texts often erases that history and avoids dealing with the impact such texts have on people of color.[24]

Cheryl Anderson

The seriousness of this transgression prompts Ezra's visceral and reflective response, "I tore my garment and my mantle and pulled hair from my head and beard and sat appalled" (Ezra 9:3). Ezra's actions are those of repentance (Lev 19:27-28; Deut 14:1). Leviticus and Deuteronomy do not require shaving the entire head (e.g., Isa 22:12; Job 1:20) but rather the removal of some hair. Here, Ezra returns expecting to find a holy community, his idealized perception of the homeland. This idealized vision is shattered by the news that those who came before him have assimilated with their neighbors. His vision of home and the reality of home when he gets there are quite different.

TRANSLATION MATTERS

The term translated "appalled" (משומם) in Ezra 9:3 is the poel form of the verb שמם, meaning "appalled," "devastated," or "overcome with horror." The poel form can be translated as "inwardly shattered," "numb," or "be put to shame," which emphasizes the extent of Ezra's dismay.[25] Lancelot Brenton's translation of the Septuagint translates the corresponding Greek word ἠρεμάζων as "mourning." "And when I heard this thing, I rent my garments, and trembled, and plucked some of the hairs of my head and of my beard and sat down mourning" (Ezra 9:3). Both translations capture Ezra's outward reaction to the people's transgression (rent garments, plucking of hair, etc.). Whereas the term "appalled" implies a sense of shock or perhaps outrage, the term "mourning" (and the actions that accompany it) implies a sense of deep loss.

24. Excerpt from Cheryl Anderson's "Reflections in an Interethnic/Racial Era on Interethnic/Racial Marriage in Ezra," in *They Were All Together in One Place? Toward Minority Biblical Criticism*, ed. Randall C. Bailey, Tat-Siong Benny Liew, and Fernando F. Segovia, SemeiaSt 57 (Atlanta: SBL, 2009), 50.

25. "שמם" *HALOT*, 1563–64.

The Power of Prayer (9:5-15)

There is no mention of prayer in Ezra 1–6, which makes Ezra's expressive supplication stand out in Ezra 9:5-15.[26] The prayer's trifold elements of confession, protest, and complaint convey his extreme displeasure at the state of affairs that confronts him and those responsible for it. Confessionally, the prayer is personal and communal as he declares his remorse and humiliation at the past transgressions of his ancestors and the present behavior of the repatriates (Ezra 9:5-7). He acknowledges that, despite their disobedience, God had been faithful and benevolent toward them (Ezra 9:8-9). Still, this benevolence is juxtaposed with the benevolence of Persian kings who were instrumental in the repatriates' return to Judea and Jerusalem. Thus, a subtle protest is detectable in the references to "servitude," "slaves," and "slavery" in Ezra 9:8-9, suggesting a paradoxical state where freedom and constraint coexist. In other words, the people have a semblance of freedom, but since the group's actions are monitored (and possibly restricted) by the Persians, complete autonomy is nonexistent (cf. Ezra 5:3-5). Today, this paradox is observable when persons living under authoritarian regimes are allowed some freedoms (i.e., food or clothing choices) while these same regimes restrict other freedoms (i.e., public gatherings and free speech). Similarly, one could have autonomy in some areas of one's personal life (i.e., choice of profession, religion, etc.) but not in others (i.e., economic constraints, health considerations, legal restrictions).

The severity of their transgressions in Ezra 9:2 registers as Ezra's complaint for the group violation of Torah through intermarriage with their foreign neighbors (Deut 7:3-4). Yet, the problem is clearly not with intermarriage to foreign women since Abraham marries Hagar, an Egyptian (Gen 16:3), Joseph marries the daughter of the priest of On (Gen 41:45), Moses marries a Midianite and Cushite woman (Exod 2:21; Num 12:1), and Boaz marries Ruth, a Moabite (Ruth 4:13). David's lineage is filled with intermarriages to non-Israelites (e.g., Tamar, Rahab, Ruth).[27] The crux of the issue appears in 9:10-12, "And now, our God, what shall we say after this? For we have forsaken your commandments, which you

26. Maria Häusl notes that the absence of prayers in Ezra 1–6 suggests that these chapters were added to Ezra–Nehemiah. See "'So I Prayed to the God of Heaven' (Neh 2:4): Praying and Prayers in the Books of Ezra and Nehemiah," in *Prayers and the Construction of Israelite Identity*, ed. Susanne Gillmayr-Bucher and Maria Häusl, AIL 35 (Atlanta: SBL Press, 2019), 55.

27. The scriptures of ancient Israel do not mention Rahab in David's lineage. This association occurs in Matthew 1:5. Tamar's background as a non-Israelite is questionable.

Ezra 9:5-15

[5]At the evening sacrifice I got up from
my fasting, with my garments and my
mantle torn, and fell on my knees,
spread out my hands to the LORD my
God, [6]and said,
"O my God, I am too ashamed and
embarrassed to lift my face to you,
my God, for our iniquities have risen
higher than our heads, and our guilt
has mounted up to the heavens. [7]From
the days of our ancestors to this day
we have been deep in guilt, and for our
iniquities we, our kings, and our priests
have been handed over to the kings
of the lands, to the sword, to captivity,
to plundering, and to utter shame, as
is now the case. [8]But now for a brief
moment favor has been shown by the
LORD our God, who has left us a remnant and given us a stake in his holy
place, in order that he may brighten our
eyes and grant us a little sustenance in
our slavery. [9]For we are slaves; yet our
God has not forsaken us in our slavery
but has extended to us his steadfast
love before the kings of Persia, to give

commanded by your servants the prophets, saying, 'The land that you are entering to possess is a land unclean [נדה] with the pollutions [נדה] of the peoples of the lands, with their abominations. They have filled it from end to end with their uncleanness [טמאה]. Therefore do not give your daughters to their sons, neither take their daughters for your sons." Here, the writer narrows and reinterprets the prohibition in Leviticus 18:18-30 on Israelites adopting the aberrations of surrounding cultures and applies it to the practice of exogamy:

> And you shall not take a woman as a rival to her sister, uncovering her nakedness while her sister is still alive. You shall not approach a woman to uncover her nakedness while she is in her menstrual uncleanness. You shall not have sexual relations with your neighbor's wife and defile yourself with her. You shall not give any of your offspring to sacrifice them to Molech and so profane the name of your God: I am the LORD. You shall not lie with a male as with a woman; it is an abomination. You shall not have sexual relations with any animal and defile yourself with it, nor shall any woman give herself to an animal to have sexual relations with it; it is perversion. Do not defile yourselves in any of these ways, for by all these practices the nations I am casting out before you have defiled themselves. Thus the land became defiled, and I punished it for its iniquity, and the land vomited out its inhabitants. But you shall keep my statutes and my ordinances and commit none of these abominations, either the native-born or the alien who resides among you (for the inhabitants of the land, who were before you, committed all of these abominations, and the land became defiled); otherwise the

us new life to set up the house of our God, to repair its ruins, and to give us a wall in Judea and Jerusalem.

[10]"And now, our God, what shall we say after this? For we have forsaken your commandments, [11]which you commanded by your servants the prophets, saying, 'The land that you are entering to possess is a land unclean with the pollutions of the peoples of the lands, with their abominations. They have filled it from end to end with their uncleanness. [12]Therefore, do not give your daughters to their sons, neither take their daughters for your sons, and never seek their peace or prosperity, so that you may be strong and eat the good of the land and leave it for an inheritance to your children forever.' [13]After all that has come upon us for our evil deeds and for our great guilt, seeing that you, our God, have punished us less than our iniquities deserved and have given us such a remnant as this, [14]shall we break your commandments again and intermarry with the peoples who practice these abominations? Would you not be angry with us until you destroy us without remnant or survivor? [15]O LORD, God of Israel, you are just, but we have escaped as a remnant, as is now the case. Here we are before you in our guilt, though no one can face you because of this."

> land will vomit you out for defiling it, as it vomited out the nation that was before you. For whoever commits any of these abominations shall be cut off from their people. So keep my charge not to commit any of these abominations that were done before you and not to defile yourselves by them: I am the LORD your God. (Lev 18:18-30)

This sense of defilement (גאל) is also found in Nehemiah 13:29: "Remember them, O my God, because they have defiled the priesthood, the covenant of the priests and the Levites."

Appropriating Levitical terms such as נדה ("menstruation/impurity"), טמא ("pollution/ unclean"), חטאת ("sin"), and טהר ("purify, cleanse") displays a pernicious preoccupation with the influence of foreign women as objects of concern. Ezra (and Nehemiah) presents the זרע הקדש ("holy seed") as a major marker of Judean identity conceived wholly in terms of male identity. When translated as menstruation, נדה can be understood as defilement or making one unclean. Curiously, blood, as it appears in the Hebrew Bible, is a powerful substance, invoking a liminality that is profoundly practical and symbolic in nature. For instance, Genesis 4:10 states that Abel's blood, which can be equated with his loss of life, cries out to God after he is slain by his brother Cain. In other words, Abel's death is recounted from the perspective of the loss of blood (fatal bleeding), which has been absorbed by the ground. Leviticus 17:11 states, "For the life of the flesh is in the blood." Elsewhere in Leviticus, we find the pronouncement that all creatures are animated by blood, which is its life (Lev 17:14).

In a similar vein, Numbers 35:33 asserts that the blood (of warfare) contaminates the land. Symbolically, the sprinkling of blood as an act of consecration in ancient cultic ceremonies made the person, object, or animal holy before the deity and community (Exod 29:32; Lev 8:15, 30). Circumcision, which is also bloody, symbolizes the covenantal relationship between God and God's people (Gen 17; Exod 4:24; 12:43-49; Josh 5:2-5).

While biblical writers do not capture, in the words of Kathleen Rushton, "the bloody messiness of childbirth," but rather emphasize its joys and pains, menstrual and lochia bleeding following childbirth is presented throughout the Bible as "mysterious, powerful and frightening" (cf. Gen 31:25; Ezek 36:17).[28] It is during the bloody messiness of childbirth that women linger at a threshold, conceivably occupying a liminal space as persons who bring forth life while simultaneously susceptible to the complications that can lead to death (of both mother and child). Foreign women occupy this same liminal space as they have the capacity to bring forth life through marriage to Jewish men and the subsequent birth of mixed heritage children while simultaneously being perceived as killers of Judean culture and identity. In other words, the liminality of these women exists in their ability to affect the bloodlines of Jewish men, particularly the priests and Levites (a genealogical death of sorts).

The connotation of the term נדה changes during the postexilic period and later symbolic understandings of the term that vilify menstrual blood and, by extension, women as impure and defiling (Ezek 7:19-20; Lam 1:17; 2 Chr 29:5). Rhetorically and symbolically, its usage in Ezra 9:11 serves as a commentary on the compromised state of ancient Israel and Jewish worship while at the same time emphasizing the threat that exogamy represents to Jewish culture and traditions.[29] By aligning the women of the land with menstruating women through its use of נדה, the writer links foreign women and polluted land, implying that neither of them is fit for receiving the holy seed. As these women maintain a constant state of נדה, they can never be admitted into the community because they are never viewed as clean.

28. Kathleen P. Rushton, "The Woman in Childbirth of John 16:21: A Feminist Reading in (Pro)Creative Boundary Crossing," in *Wholly Woman, Holy Blood: A Feminist Critique of Purity and Impurity*, ed. Kristin De Troyer et al., SAC (Harrisburg, VA: Trinity Press, 2003), 87.

29. Elizabeth W. Goldstein, *Impurity and Gender in the Hebrew Bible* (Lanham, MD: Lexington Books, 2015), 84.

Exploring the liminality of foreign women is to consider how the demonization of the "other" minimizes the contributions they make to their communities and the larger society. That is, to write about liminality is to ponder what it means to stand at thresholds. Liminal spaces represent the now and not yet.[30] Moreover, we do not know quite what to do when we find ourselves in liminal spaces or what to do with people who occupy them.

Power in the Blood

Menstrual blood, as a means of uncleanliness, finds resonance across cultures. Harold Washington notes, "The cross-cultural prevalence of menstrual exclusions, for example, corresponds to the subordination of the feminine in many societies."[31] There are, however, societies that celebrate menstruation as a rite of passage, as young women come into their own and learn to exercise their own agency. For example, the Moon Time Ritual in some Native traditions celebrates the sacredness and purification of the menstrual cycle. In addition, the women of the Yurok nation in the United States celebrate their menses with ritual and heightened spiritual experience. Some cultures party (Ulithi people in the South Pacific, parts of Ghana), while others approach the menstrual event as spiritual enlightenment. Still, a young woman may feel empowered by her period and ashamed should an accident expose her blood to others. Thus, women continue to find themselves negotiating the liminal space between the natural functions of their bodies and cultural perceptions about them. This has not gone unnoticed even in the media. "Discomfort about menstrual blood has deep cultural roots that have led to the use of mystery blue liquid in menstrual hygiene product commercials. The debut of liquid that bears resemblance to blood (it's still a sanitary red liquid, after all) in period product ads instead of inorganic, lab-brewed blue liquid represents a new point in a long journey of de-mystifying and re-imagining menstrual flow."[32] Even though there remain male restrictions around menstruation

30. We define liminal as being at the threshold between two spaces—physical or metaphorical.

31. Harold Washington, "Israel's Holy Seed and the Foreign Women of Ezra–Nehemiah: A Kristevan Reading," *BibInt* 11 (2003): 432.

32. J. R. Thorpe, "This Is the Actual Reason Pad Commercials Use That Weird Blue Liquid," *Bustle* (October 20, 2017), https://www.bustle.com/p/why-do-period-product-commercials-use-blue-liquid-the-practice-has-a-long-bizarre-history-2957963.

for the Beng women of the Ivory Coast, there is nonetheless a view that recognizes the close association between blood and women's power as articulated in the following quotation from an elder within this community, "Menstruation is like the flower of a tree. You need the flower before the tree can fruit," which, according to Alma Gottieb, is "a very different ideology than the ideology of sin, dirt, pollution."[33] We concur.

The People Respond (10:1-5)

Ezra's prayer, confession, and protest draw a large gathering of men, women, and children, who join him in his mourning (Ezra 10:1). His pious act of confession and protest leads to a non-pious solution to the problem of exogamy expressed in Ezra 9:2 and 9:12-14. Shecaniah, one of the members in the gathered assembly, submits that the leaders must send away their foreign wives and children (Ezra 10:3). Theologically, this repudiation of foreign women and their children is meant to restore the Judeans to a right relationship with their God. Yet, this emphasis on foreign women as dangerous, such that they and their children must be removed from the community, exposes a vulnerability—a fear perhaps—of the power these women possess (whether knowingly or unknowingly) to impact identity, culture, land distribution, and religion. Could it be that the writer finds their liminality disorienting and, thus, needs to reinterpret the Levitical material to ease the discomfort? In other words, could it be that נדה as menstrual blood potentially restores to these women the sacredness of the feminine and the power it possesses in a similar way that זרע הקדש ("holy seed," see Ezra 9:2) preserves the co-creative power of the masculine (i.e., semen) and as such must be reduced to that which is characterized as impure, defiling, or polluting?

The king grants Ezra administrative and religious authority over the province in Ezra 7:25–26. The officials and Shecaniah's demand for action seeks to use Ezra's authority for their own ends. Ezra prays, but the people want him to act: "Take action, for it is your duty, and we are with you; be strong, and do it" (Ezra 10:4). The sequence of imperatives ("take

33. Susan Brink, "Some Cultures Treat Menstruation with Respect," *NPR* (August 11, 2015), https://www.npr.org/sections/goatsandsoda/2015/08/11/431605131/attention-trump-some-cultures-treat-menstruation-with-respect. Brink quotes Alma Gottleib from *Blood Magic: The Anthropology of Menstruation*, ed. Thomas Buckley and Alma Gottlieb (Berkeley: University of California Press, 1988).

Ezra 10:1-5

1While Ezra prayed and made confession, weeping and throwing himself
down before the house of God, a very
great assembly of men, women, and
children gathered to him out of Israel;
the people also wept bitterly. 2Sheca-
niah son of Jehiel, of the descendants
of Elam, addressed Ezra, saying, "We
have broken faith with our God and
have married foreign women from the
peoples of the land, but even now there
is hope for Israel in spite of this. 3So
now let us make a covenant with our
God to send away all these wives and
their children, according to the counsel
of my lord and of those who tremble at
the commandment of our God, and let
it be done according to the law. 4Take
action, for it is your duty, and we are
with you; be strong, and do it." 5Then
Ezra stood up and made the leading priests, the Levites, and all Israel
swear that they would do as had been
said. So they swore.

action," "be strong," "do it") interrupts Ezra's piety to move him to action. We agree with the general premise that prayer is not a substitute for action when action could resolve a problem. In the words of Senator Reverend Raphael Warnock, "It is a contradiction to say that you are thinking and praying and then do nothing. It is to make a mockery of prayer. It is to trivialize faith. We pray not only with our lips, we pray with our legs. We pray by taking action."[34] In the text, Shecaniah wants Ezra to enforce what the leaders in the community have been unable to do with respect to, presumably, the laws of Deuteronomy and its prohibition against marrying non-Israelites (Deut 7:1-6; Josh 23:12). Although the specific groups listed in Deuteronomy 7:1-6 (e.g., Hittites, Girgashites, Amorites, Canaanites, Perizzites) are no longer present by the time of Ezra, intermarriage with the neighboring groups is still perceived as a serious problem. Shecaniah demands seek to correct or make right perceived transgressions of the law (Ezra 10:3): Torah has no laws that mandate Shecaniah and the community to send away foreign wives and children. Instead Torah provides clear mandates that widows, orphans, and strangers are to be cared for (Deut 10:17-18; see also Deut 27:19). In essence, by sending the children away, they become orphans without the

34. Raphael Warnock, "ICYMI: Senator Reverend Warnock Responds to Horrific Shooting in Midtown Atlanta, Calls on Congress to Turn Prayer into Action," *Reverend Raphael Warnock*, https://www.warnock.senate.gov/newsroom/press-releases/icymi-senator-reverend-warnock-responds-to-horrific-shooting-in-midtown-atlanta-calls-on-congress-to-turn-prayer-into-action/.

protection of their fathers. Ezra's action is to secure an oath from those gathered to do what Shecaniah suggests (Ezra 10:5).

Today, the highly debated issues of gun reform, prison reform, women's choices, and environmental justice highlight the need for action beyond thoughts and prayers. The officials and Shecaniah in Ezra lobby those with governmental authority to impose on others what they cannot enact or enforce.

The Rejection of Foreign Wives (Ezra 10:6-44)

The outcome remains the same no matter which group is at fault: the threat of a second exile looms large for some Jewish men together with the removal of their wives and children whom Shecaniah's groups considers non-Jewish.[35] Essentially, this threat comes not from the empire but from those within the repatriates' group.

The summons that requires every repatriate to appear in Jerusalem within three days or forfeit their property and access to the community is problematic (Ezra 10:8). There is a certain cruelty or lack of empathy in the request with the stakes so high. The hastiness of the decision and the immediacy of the repatriates' presence appears thoughtless on the part of those charged with the people's welfare. Not all returning Jewish males married foreign women. In other words, the summoning penalizes all the returnees rather than just those who intermarried. Speculatively, the occasion and the weather (heavy rain) could make traveling within the three-day timeframe difficult despite any attempts to adhere to the quest and make the journey. Nevertheless, the people appear at the appointed place "trembling" (רעד) because of the weather or the summoning itself or both (Ezra 10:9). The sense of the verb רעד in this verse suggests extreme anxiety. Ezra announces the charges against the group, "You have trespassed [מעל] and married foreign women, and so increased the guilt of Israel. Now make confession to the Lord the God of your ancestors and do his will; separate yourselves from the peoples of the land and from the foreign wives" (Ezra 10:10-11). While agreeing with Ezra in principle on the matter of intermarriage, the people lodge a complaint that standing in an open square during horrific weather conditions to address what is most likely a lengthy

35. There is some speculation on the ethnic identity of these women as non-Judeans. The writer considers them non-Jewish, but they may in fact be Jews.

Ezra 10:6-44

6Then Ezra withdrew from before the
house of God and went to the chamber
of Jehohanan son of Eliashib, where he
spent the night. He did not eat bread or
drink water, for he was mourning over
the faithlessness of the exiles. 7They
made a proclamation throughout Judah
and Jerusalem to all the returned exiles
that they should assemble at Jerusalem
8and that, if any did not come within
three days, by order of the officials and
the elders all their property should be
forfeited and they themselves banned
from the congregation of the exiles.

9Then all the people of Judah and
Benjamin assembled at Jerusalem
within the three days; it was the ninth
month, on the twentieth day of the
month. All the people sat in the open
square before the house of God, trembling because of this matter and because of the heavy rain. 10Then Ezra
the priest stood up and said to them,
"You have trespassed and married foreign women and so increased the guilt
of Israel. 11Now make confession to the
Lord the God of your ancestors and do
his will; separate yourselves from the
peoples of the land and from the foreign wives." 12Then all the assembly
answered with a loud voice, "It is so;
we must do as you have said. 13But
the people are many, and it is a time of
heavy rain; we cannot stand in the open.
Nor is this a task for one day or for two,
for many of us have transgressed in this
matter. 14Let our officials represent the
whole assembly, and let all in our towns

process (many had intermarried) might be better resolved by a few officials rather than the whole assembly (Ezra 10:12-14). This would be akin to requiring citizens to show up at the Capitol building in Washington, DC, during inclement weather to resolve matters when they have officials charged with these responsibilities. In both cases, there are financial and other costs for joining in these assemblies. For example, the loss of income, the need to provide care for those who cannot travel, and other considerations.

We found ourselves discussing how to reconcile the gathering of the people and its conclusion in Ezra 10:1-5 with what appears as a regathering of the people in Ezra 10:9-14. Ezra 10:1-5 reports that the people (men, women, and children) gather, hear the charges against them, make confessions, and agree to separate themselves from the people of the land and their foreign wives. Yet, in 10:9-14, the people reassemble, and the matter is recapitulated with the qualification that the leaders assume responsibility for ensuring the people adhere to the final resolution (removal of non-Judean wives and their children). In these verses, it appears that the people may not know the circumstances of the summons and hear the accusation

Ezra 10:6-44 (cont.)

who have taken foreign wives come at appointed times, and with them the elders and judges of every town, until the fierce wrath of our God on this account is averted from us." [15]Only Jonathan son of Asahel and Jahzeiah son of Tikvah opposed this, and Meshullam and Shabbethai the Levites supported them.

[16]Then the returned exiles did so. Ezra the priest selected men, heads of families, according to their families, each of them designated by name. On the first day of the tenth month they sat down to examine the matter. [17]By the first day of the first month they had come to the end of all the men who had married foreign women.

[18]There were found of the descendants of the priests who had married foreign women, of the descendants of Jeshua son of Jozadak and his brothers: Maaseiah, Eliezer, Jarib, and Gedaliah. [19]They pledged themselves to send away their wives, and their guilt offering was a ram of the flock for their guilt. [20]Of the descendants of Immer: Hanani and Zebadiah. [21]Of the descendants of Harim: Maaseiah, Elijah, Shemaiah, Jehiel, and Uzziah. [22]Of the descendants of Pashhur: Elioenai, Maaseiah, Ishmael, Nethanel, Jozabad, and Elasah.

[23]Of the Levites: Jozabad, Shimei, Kelaiah (that is, Kelita), Pethahiah, Judah, and Eliezer. [24]Of the singers: Eliashib. Of the gatekeepers: Shallum, Telem, and Uri.

[25]And of Israel: of the descendants of Parosh: Ramiah, Izziah, Malchijah, Mijamin, Eleazar, Hashabiah, and

for the first time. There are various explanations that seek to harmonize and explain why the two accounts coexist in this chapter. Some commentators suggest that the author draws on multiple sources and inserts additional material in the text to unify the accounts.[36] The harmonization of the two may lend additional information to the editorial activity but provides little information on the rationale for what transpires in the text.

The account in Ezra 10:1-5 possibly functions as a summary, with Ezra 10:9-14 filling in the details, thereby providing the rationale for the exchanges between Ezra and the repatriates responding to the summons. The use of the Hebrew word דבר ("thing," "word," "matter") in Ezra 10:14 objectifies the women and children as a problem to be resolved. In the biblical narrative, the fracturing of families gets particular attention with respect to fathers, brothers, and sons (Jacob and Esau, Joseph and his brothers, Saul and Jonathan, and David and his sons), with relatively few

36. Joseph Blenkinsopp, *Ezra–Nehemiah: A Commentary*, OTL (Philadelphia: Westminster, 1988), 187–89; Lisbeth Fried, citing Jehu Pakkala, in *Ezra*, 398. See Pakkala, *Ezra the Scribe*, 96.

Benaiah. 26Of the descendants of Elam:
Mattaniah, Zechariah, Jehiel, Abdi,
Jeremoth, and Elijah. 27Of the descendants of Zattu: Elioenai, Eliashib, Mattaniah, Jeremoth, Zabad, and Aziza.
28Of the descendants of Bebai: Jehohanan, Hananiah, Zabbai, and Athlai.
29Of the descendants of Bani: Meshullam, Malluch, Adaiah, Jashub, Sheal,
and Jeremoth. 30Of the descendants of
Pahath-moab: Adna, Chelal, Benaiah,
Maaseiah, Mattaniah, Bezalel, Binnui,
and Manasseh. 31Of the descendants
of Harim: Eliezer, Isshijah, Malchijah,
Shemaiah, Shimeon, 32Benjamin, Malluch, and Shemariah. 33Of the descendants of Hashum: Mattenai, Mattattah,
Zabad, Eliphelet, Jeremai, Manasseh,
and Shimei. 34Of the descendants of
Bani: Maadai, Amram, Uel, 35Benaiah,
Bedeiah, Cheluhi, 36Vaniah, Meremoth,
Eliashib, 37Mattaniah, Mattenai, and
Jaasu. 38Of the descendants of Binnui: Shimei, 39Shelemiah, Nathan,
Adaiah, 40Machnadebai, Shashai, Sha-
rai, 41Azarel, Shelemiah, Shemariah,
42Shallum, Amariah, and Joseph. 43Of
the descendants of Nebo: Jeiel, Mattithiah, Zabad, Zebina, Jaddai, Joel,
and Benaiah. 44All these had married
foreign women, and they sent them
away with their children.

exceptions where women are involved. The closest example of a woman and child ejected from the family is Hagar and Ishmael, who, for the most part, are not claimed by Abraham and Sarah as family members.[37] Still, it appears that not every Judean male present in the assembly concurs with the decision. In Ezra 10:15, "Only Jonathan son of Asahel and Jahzeiah son of Tikvah opposed this, and Meshullam and Shabbethai the Levites supported them." The verse is ambiguous in the matter of the opposition. Are these individuals opposing the ejection of the foreign women and children or are they against leaving the decision on the matter in the hands of the leaders (see Translation Matters, p. 108)? Given the textual ambiguity, we choose a liberating reading where these four stand against the draconian edict that displaces families and disrupts the community. Therefore, despite the preponderance of positive responses to the proposal, the opposition of a minute minority suggests that not all repatriates consider interethnic marriages problematic.

37. In Jewish and Islamic tradition, Abraham acknowledges Ishmael as his son after their removal from his family. The Pirkei de'Rabbi Eliezer adds an addendum to the biblical narrative where Abraham visits and acknowledges Ishmael as his son. See Reuven Firestone, "Abraham Visits Ishmael and His Wives: Between Jewish and Islamic Traditions," *TheTorah.com*, https://www.thetorah.com/article/abraham-visits-ishmael-and-his-wives-between-jewish-and-islamic-tradition.

What's in a Name? Tikvah

Tikvah (תקוה), as a feminine noun meaning "hope," appears only twice as a proper name in the Scriptures of ancient Israel. In 2 Kings 22:14, it is the name of the father-in-law of Huldah, the prophetess. In Ezra 10:15, it is the name of a male descendant of Jahzeiah. In modern usage, Tikvah is almost exclusively a name given to females.

Even though these dissenting voices have no effect on the outcome (Ezra 10:16-18), the value of including dissenting voices can lead to an exchange of ideas that causes us to question ideologies, normative policies, and rigidly held norms. Overall, the text glosses over and neglects the human suffering or trauma that results if these women and their children are torn from their families. Sadly, instances of family separations still exist today. Migrant children attempting to enter the southern border of the United States (documented or undocumented) were separated from parents and guardians due in part to punitive policies aimed at controlling entry (Zero Tolerance Policy).[38]

TRANSLATION MATTERS

While the NRSVue's translation of Ezra 10:15 suggests that only Jonathan son of Asahel, Jahzeiah son of Tikvah, Meshullam, and Shabbethai oppose the community's draconian edict to eject the foreign wives and children, other readings of the Hebrew text and rabbinical sources suggest otherwise. For example, the JPS Tanakh translation of Ezra 10:15 reads as follows: "Only Jonathan son of Asahel and Jahzeiah son of Tikvah remained for this purpose, assisted by Meshullam and Shabbethai, the Levites."[39] Hindy Najman, drawing on the Exodus Rabbah, notes that the rabbis draw on Jonathan son of Asahel as an example of one who

38. US Department of Justice, "Attorney General Announces the Zero-Tolerance Policy for Criminal Illegal Entry" (April 6, 2018), https://www.justice.gov/opa/pr/attorney-general-announces-zero-tolerance-policy-criminal-illegal-entry; Refugees International, "The Trump Zero Tolerance Policy: A Cruel Approach with Humane and Viable Alternatives" (July 31, 2018), https://www.refugeesinternational.org/reports-briefs/the-trump-zero-tolerance-policy-a-cruel-approach-with-humane-and-viable-alternatives/.

39. Hindy Najman, "Notes on Ezra," in *The Jewish Study Bible*, 2nd ed., ed. Adele Berlin and Mark Zvi Brettler (Oxford: Oxford University Press, 2014), 1679.

carries out Ezra's orders "with zeal."[40] The Septuagint's rendering of this verse echoes the JPS's: "Only Jonathan the son of Asael, and Jazias the son of Thecoe were with me concerning this; and Mesollam, and Sabbathai the Levite helped them."[41] The Hebrew in the Masoretic Text (עמדו על־זאת) can be translated "they stood up against this" or "oppose." Joseph Blenkinsopp explains that the phrase עמדו על־זאת is ambiguous and can also be translated in a way that flips the meaning to "insisted on this," although he still opts for a translation such that Jonathan opposes the proposal.[42] Lisbeth Fried also acknowledges the ambiguity of the phrase עמדו על־זאת yet turns to its use in 1 Chronicles 21:1, "Satan rose up against Israel," and 2 Chronicles 20:23, "the Ammonites and Moabites rose up against the inhabitants of Mt. Seir" to support her choice of the phrase "opposed this."[43]

In Ezra 10:19-43, we find another list of names of those who intermarried—priests, Levites, singers, gatekeepers, and members from other repatriated families. The numbers appear small when compared to the list of returnees in Ezra 2:3-61. The real problem arises in Ezra 10:44, where translations differ concerning the final status of foreign women and their children. Some translations report that these women and children were removed from the assembly (NRSVue, ESV), while other translations simply report that the men had foreign wives who bore them children (NIV, NAS, KJV, JPS). The NRSVue agrees with 1 Esdras 9:36, the Greek version of Ezra, which reads, "All these had married foreign women, and they divorced them, along with their children" (CEB). In Hebrew,

40. Najman, "Notes on Ezra," 1680. During the discussion of the hard work and zeal Bezalel put into building the ark, the rabbis turn to Jonathan the son of Asahel for another example of this type of fervor on behalf of the community. They write: "Another illustration of this is in the verse *Only Jonathan the son of Asahel and Jahzeiah the son of Tikvah stood up against this matter* (supporting Ezra's decree that the Israelites were to send away their foreign wives); *and Meshullam and Shabbethai the Levite helped them* (Ezek 10:15). Because Jonathan devoted himself zealously to this matter while the other only helped him, his name is mentioned first. Similarly in the case of Bezalel. All the wise men assisted him, but because he devoted himself most zealously to the erection of the Tabernacle, it is written: *And Bezalel made the ark.*" See Samuel A. Berman, trans., "Midrash Tanhuma-Yelammedenu," *Sefaria*, https://www.sefaria.org/Midrash_Tanchuma%2C_Vayakhel.10.4?ven=Midrash_Tanhuma-Yelammedenu,_trans._Samuel_A._Berman&lang=bi&with=all&lang2=en.

41. Brenton's translation of the LXX.

42. Blenkinsopp, *Ezra–Nehemiah*, 191–92.

43. Fried, *Ezra*, 400.

the verse is unintelligible and thus difficult to translate. In essence, the verse does not resolve the status of the foreign women and children.[44]

TRANSLATION MATTERS

We wondered why some translations of the Hebrew in Ezra 10:44 chose to render the verse as removing the foreign women and children from the community and others noted that the foreign women had children. The Hebrew word in question is וישימו, derived from the verb שׂים, meaning "to put, place, or set." The Hebrew Lexicon *BDB* notes that Ezra 10:44 is obscure and includes the well-respected German biblical scholar Hermann Guthe's substitution of וישימו with the word וישלחו from the verb שׁלח, meaning "to send."[45] It appears that others have followed him, which accounts for the different renderings of this verse.

The chapter makes a strong case for the removal of these women and their children from the community, but there is little evidence that it actually occurred.

In the Name of Religious and Ethnic Purity

Religious communities are informed and formed based on various theological beliefs, traditions, and cultural norms. How one interprets religious purity also varies from one community to another. When members of religious communities find themselves no longer welcome or the targets of ridicule and derision based on how particular religious groups view sexuality and morality, their withdrawal is a loss to the community. The ousting or rejection of certain persons from these religious spaces spills over into secular spaces that also become unwelcoming. Durrell Watkins draws parallels between the rejection of the foreign women in Ezra–Nehemiah and the contemporary actions of some toward the LGBTQ+ community. "It might not be fair to judge Ezra–Nehemiah for the harsh response to what

44. Nehemiah will wrestle with the same issue of intermarriage and the fate of the foreign wives and children, which suggests that Ezra's edict is unsuccessful.

45. BDB, 962.

was considered an urgent need, but it is fair in our own time to notice and name that families continue to be harmed and individuals continue to be spiritually and emotionally battered in the name of religious purity."[46] Religious communities will continue to grapple with the changing religious landscape and the questions of identity that impact religious adherents and their membership in these communities.

The preservation of religious identity at the expense of husbands, their wives, and their children is problematic. Numerous biblical examples call for the care of the widow, the poor, the sojourner, and the orphan (e.g., Deut 10:18; 24:17-19; Job 22:9; 24:3; Pss 58:5; 146:9; Isa 1:17). Deuteronomy 27:19 admonishes, "Cursed be anyone who deprives an alien, an orphan, or a widow of justice." All the people shall say, "Amen!" Perhaps the ambiguity of the response in Ezra 10:44 is partly due to the mandate's conflict with the ethical and moral dimensions of the people's Torah. The desire for an ethnically pure community was not a reality then nor is it a reality now. For this ancient Judean community, issues of land, inheritance, covenant fidelity, and identity are prominent concerns. Yet, an inspection of the genealogy of this group reveals multiple instances of intermarriage (see commentary on Ezra 9:5-15). While the prohibition against intermarriage may be prescriptive for Ezra's audience (although not entirely clear from the text), the creation of social, religious, and cultural hierarchies that result may not resonate with some, not all, modern audiences who do not view intermarriage based on one's ethnicity as problematic.

Those Foreign Women

Land and temple, a dream come true. For Ezra, only the divine intervention of YHWH could secure such complete reversal of international policy that would send God's people home with the grandeur and scale of Cyrus's announcement. Even the details concur. Ezra recollects "the hand of our

46. Durrell Watkins, "Ezra–Nehemiah," in *The Queer Bible Commentary*, ed. Mona West and R. E. Shore-Goss, 2nd ed. (London: SCM, 2022), 237.

God was upon us" (Ezra 8:18). YHWH's countenance bright; nothing seemed awry.

But then officials came bearing the news. "The people of Israel, the priests, and the Levites have not separated themselves from the peoples of the lands with their abominations, from the Canaanites, the Hittites, the Perizzites, the Jebusites, the Ammonites, the Moabites, the Egyptians, and the Amorites. For they have taken some of their daughters as wives for themselves and their sons. Thus the holy seed has mixed itself with the peoples of the lands" (Ezra 9:1-2).

Foreign women—forever the snare. Ezra alarmed, fearful, and angry, tore his clothes, pulled hair from his head and beard, and sat appalled. He laments before the Lord: "I am ashamed and embarrassed to lift my face to you . . . a brief moment of favor has been shown . . . we are before you in our guilt, though no one can face you before you because of this" (Ezra 9:6, 8, 15). The communal response was to "*make a covenant* with our God to send away all these wives *and* their children" (Ezra 10:3). Ezra and these officials conveniently forgot that Boaz had done some mixing and threshing himself, resulting in David and everyone's hope for the future.

YHWH knew that these men had married foreign women even while extending favor to them during the rebuilding of the temple. When Joshua and Israel were tricked into making a covenant with the Gibeonites (all within earshot of YHWH, Josh 9:23-27), they were expected to honor it. There was no putting the Gibeonites away. In fact, when the other Canaanites attacked the Gibeonites because of their covenant with Israel, YHWH obliged Joshua to go to their aid and worked mighty miracles on their behalf.

Despite Ezra repeating the same words used to blame Solomon for the decline and eventual exile of Israel (1 Kgs 11:1-13), Solomon's love of foreign women and tolerance of their gods does not bear the blame for all. Jereboam did not have to reach far to resurrect those age-old golden calves—which were all about power and not women. While idolatry and foreign enticement was no doubt a concern to more than just Ezra and Nehemiah, oppression against the poor, most especially the fatherless and the widow, seemed to rile the God of Israel even more than jealousy of other gods. How ironic, then, that in an attempt to appease YHWH, Ezra and the leaders of Judah would default to creating a community of displaced foreign women and orphans.

The tribes of Israel had acted similarly during the time of the judges, swearing not to give their daughters to Benjamin because of the rape and murder of the Levite's concubine. Their outraged posture was incoherent with their proposed solution—advocating for the mass kidnapping, rape, and commandeering of an entire community of springtime virgins. Ezra's story too ends without reporting the fallout of such "noble" initiatives. Diligent in their piety, Ezra's returnees don't seem to know what got them cast from their homeland in the first place. Rather than simply announcing the end of the exile and chronicling the practical difficulties of the return, Ezra is deceptively more complicated. Ezra appears to be embroiled in a time parallel to Judges, a period lacking judgment and discernment. The word of the Lord rare, no king in Israel, and everyone doing as they saw fit. None of it ideal, none of it to be emulated.

Sonya Cronin

The chapter puts forth the desire for ethnic purity while simultaneously acknowledging the difficulties in achieving it. The narrator's concern with instances of intermarriage causes us to reflect on issues of identity, inclusivity, and communal solidarity. While intermarriage appears to be problematic for Ezra's audience, modern perspectives may not see it as a problem. This highlights how religious communities are changing and reinterpreting tradition and morals. It urges us to think about exclusion and how marginalized groups are treated within these communities. In the end, it pushes us to consider the delicate balance between maintaining tradition and being inclusive and compassionate.

Ezra and Nehemiah: An Allegorical Love Story

Read on a non-figurative level, the books of Ezra and Nehemiah do not provide adequate theological responses to the agonizing pain of Lamentations. Their language is deprived of theological metaphor: instead, they provide summaries of the historical events in their chronological order, interwoven with Ezra's and Nehemiah's theological and political agenda. At the heart of this agenda lies their urge for purification: the purification of both the Temple Mount and the Jewish people.

While the two rulings against intermarriage and for the establishment of regular Torah readings do not seem connected at first glance, they tell, in an allegorical reading of the books, an insightful love story. Within the matrix of stories and rituals that is Judaism, already biblical literature is rich in metaphorical descriptions of the relationship between God and God's people as a relationship between a loving but jealous husband and his unfaithful wife; also, the corpus of rabbinic literature often envisions the relationship between God and God's people—often embodied by the female city of Jerusalem—as deeply gendered and often erotic. Ezra and Nehemiah (living during the shift from First to Second Temple literature, with its ongoing struggle over a Jewish identity based on the observance of religious rulings instead of political unity and independence) operate those metaphors into a program for what we may coin "biblical couples' therapy": If we read biblical theology as the story of the covenant between God and God's people, then it is Ezra who returns God's bride to her wedding chamber, reestablishes exclusivity and loyalty, and institutes a yearly cycle of festivals that ensures the regular encounter between God and God's people in Jerusalem. The story, it seems, reached a happy ending once more.

To a Jewish feminist theologian, however, even this happy ending bears great challenges. While I love to read and live along the love story outlined in our reading and ritual cycles, the gendered images of us as a faithless woman who is getting punished for her sins and of God as a jealous and almighty husband and lover are troubling to me. They enforce traditional patterns of relationships that might make us feel safe but that are not beneficial for the emotional, mental, fiscal, and sometimes physical health of the dependent partner. While the Bible and its theology read through a historical lens might provide deep insight into biblical history and theology, we cannot rely on them solely while creating the theologies of our time. While I am saying and singing my prayers as a person failing, imperfect, and liable for my mistakes, I also deliver my sermons. Over and over, I raise the questions: What kind of relationship to God are we creating with our lives? Which images of God—even if they prove to be contradictory—make us feel both safe and strong? And if we imagine God as the husband or lover of God's people, what kind of husband or lover would we want? Which theologies make space for a variety of images of God?

Rabbi Sonja K. Pilz

Nehemiah

Building Walls of Identity and Gates of Possibility

Walls that divide property, people, nations, and territories can be helpful or harmful. Robert Frost's famous poem, "Mending Wall,"[1] highlights the need for walls as two neighbors negotiate their property boundaries. The poem's speaker questions the rationale for a fence since there are no cows to encroach on the neighbor's property or trees that intermingle. Still, his neighbor insists, "Good fences make good neighbors."[2] Partitions prevent the intermingling of property. The ownership and identity of the landowner are kept intact. But the poem's speaker wisely notes:

> Before I built a wall I'd ask to know
> What I was walling in or walling out,
> And to whom I was like to give offense.

Most of us operate with the mindset of the necessity of walls and the sense of comfort and security they provide. Nehemiah 1–13 is a continuation of Ezra 1–10. Ezra conducts religious reforms in Judah and Jerusalem.

1. Thanks to Amy-Jill Levine for leading us to this poem. Robert Frost, "Mending Wall," *Poetry Foundation*, https://www.poetryfoundation.org/poems/44266/mending-wall.

2. Frost, "Mending Wall."

Nehemiah institutes the governance infrastructure. Whereas the book of Ezra ends with the expulsion of the foreign wives, the book of Nehemiah begins with his commission to rebuild the wall of Jerusalem. Portions of Nehemiah are considered parts of a court tale that recounts the faithfulness of a Jew as he finds favor and navigates a foreign court, much like Daniel, Joseph, and Esther. Nehemiah 1–7 deals with the construction of the wall. Nehemiah 8 reintroduces Ezra, who reads the Torah together with those who will help interpret it. Nehemiah 9–10, similar to Ezra 9–10, concentrates on the community's confession and covenantal obligations to God and God's house. Nehemiah 11 chronicles the repopulation of Jerusalem by the repatriates. Nehemiah recounts the priestly and Levitical genealogies as well as the dedication of the wall in Nehemiah 12. Nehemiah 13 ends the book by describing a host of transgressions committed by the repatriates. Both Ezra and Nehemiah end with a critique of intermarriage, which suggests the prevalence of this practice.

The book of Nehemiah demands that its readers examine the significance of walls, how they engender a shared sense of solidarity and communal identity but can also become barriers that limit inclusiveness and relationship building. While rebuilding the walls of Jerusalem is important to Nehemiah, it is clear that he is also preoccupied with building gates.[3] Gates can be locked to prevent access, but they also offer a means to penetrate walls. Walls and boundaries are always permeable; they shift as the dynamics and interactions with people, cultures, and traditions change. The strong emphasis on the people's commitment to rebuilding the wall in Jerusalem matches their strong commitment to observe the covenantal obligations of their faith.

3. Gates are mentioned forty-one times (שׁער, שׁערים)—even more often than walls, which appear in the text thirty times (חומה, חומות). The Hebrew text uses both the singular and plural form of the noun "wall."

Nehemiah 1–3

Nehemiah: The Man and His Mission

Nehemiah, the Jewish cupbearer to King Artaxerxes, rebuilds the wall of Jerusalem following its destruction by the Babylonians. He is a foreigner in a Persian court located in the Persian capital of Susa. He becomes governor over the land of Judah. Nehemiah 1–7, considered part of the Nehemiah Memoir, is an account of Nehemiah's challenges, opposition, and eventual success in reconstructing the walls in Jerusalem.

Nehemiah and His Memoir

The Nehemiah Memoir is his autobiographical account of rallying the *golah* to rebuild Jerusalem's walls and to support his religious reforms. Second Maccabees 2:13 recounts Nehemiah's interest in maintaining records: "The same things are reported in the records and in the memoirs of Nehemiah and also that he founded a library and collected the books about the kings and prophets and the writings of David and letters of kings about votive offerings." Nehemiah 1–7 and 10–13 make up the heart of this memoir, even though there are disagreements about which chapters should be counted in

Nehemiah's autobiography.[1] Nehemiah 1–13 presents Nehemiah as a wall builder (Neh 1–7) and governor (Neh 5:14), although Lisbeth Fried suggests that Nehemiah is the wall builder and that the governor is Yeho'ezer and that the editor interweaves these separate people's reports to attribute both roles to Nehemiah.[2] We follow the NRSVue, which identifies Nehemiah as the wall builder who becomes governor of Judah.

Rebuilding the wall of Jerusalem protects the city from invaders but also serves as a metaphor for the boundaries that the returning exiles place around themselves—boundaries that invite some but exclude others (e.g., Samarians, Ammonites [Neh 4:1-9]). As a metaphor, the wall is life-giving as the repatriate community returns to the land of Judah to reconnect with a common ancestry, a shared language, and shared cultural values and beliefs.

Upon permission from King Artaxerxes, Nehemiah journeys to Jerusalem in response to the report of the physical condition of the city's wall and gates (1:1–2:20). Once in Jerusalem, he begins the work of repairing the wall (3:1-32). His attempt to rectify the problem is met with resistance by local leaders who profit at the people's expense (4:1-23). Nehemiah's institution of economic reforms brings justice and relief to those most impacted (5:1-19). Surviving threats of bodily harm, he completes the reconstructive task of rebuilding the wall (6:1–7:5). Here, we also find a list of returnees that mirrors the list in Ezra 2 with a few minor changes (7:6-73).

Nehemiah's possible status as a eunuch allows us to explore gender and sexuality as they intersect with male infertility and legacies. In addition, Nehemiah provides models of leadership that can be instructional for churches or other religious groups seeking to address what effective

1. Katherine Southwood and others identify Nehemiah 1–7 and 10–13 as Nehemiah's personal memoir. See Katherine Southwood, "Ezra–Nehemiah," in *Fortress Commentary on the Bible: The Old Testament and the Apocrypha*, ed. Gale Yee, Hugh Page Jr., and Matthew Coomber (Minneapolis: Fortress, 2014), 475. Joseph Blenkinsopp limits this memoir to Nehemiah 1–7 and 13 (*Judaism, the First Phase: The Place of Ezra and Nehemiah in the Origins of Judaism* [Grand Rapids: Eerdmans, 2009], 100).

2. Lisbeth S. Fried, *Ezra: A Commentary*, Critical Commentaries (Sheffield: Sheffield Phoenix, 2015), 55.

leadership entails. In these chapters, the effectiveness or ineffectiveness of leadership has serious consequences for the populace, especially those most vulnerable and susceptible to policies and practices that privilege some at the expense of others.

A Person, a Problem, and a Prayer (1:1-11)

Although Artaxerxes's name does not appear in Nehemiah until the second chapter (2:1), Nehemiah 1 takes place in the Persian capital of Susa, possibly during the twentieth year of Artaxerxes's reign (ca. 445 BCE).[3] The exact month this encounter occurs is unclear since Nehemiah 1:1 names the month Chislev (November/December), while Nehemiah 2:1 identifies it as Nisan (March/April).

Partitions of Time

Nehemiah concerns himself with dates, which may help place an event in its chronological context. Yet, the dates recorded are not as much an issue of dating as what Nehemiah chooses as his frame of reference for marking time. Artaxerxes, a powerful king, becomes Nehemiah's marker for how he casts partitions of time. He tells his story in reference to a powerful Persian leader (during the twentieth year of Artaxerxes's reign), who has a significant impact on his life. We, like Nehemiah, tend to partition time based on important events or leaders we deem to be important to us. We mark ourselves by when we are born, graduate, or have our first child, milestones in the cycle of life. We also partition time according to events. For example, September 11, 2001, marks a time of extreme fear and distress in the United States with the destruction of the Twin Towers in New York City and the Pentagon near Washington, DC, or the assassination of Martin Luther King Jr. on April 4, 1968. These events in our story are important to us and help us measure time.

3. Artaxerxes I reigned in Persia from 465 to 424 BCE. For a discussion on the theories around dating Hanani's visit, see Joseph Blenkinsopp, *Ezra–Nehemiah: A Commentary*, OTL (Philadelphia: Westminster, 1988), 204–6. Blenkinsopp also notes that Nehemiah's mission took place under Artaxerxes I and that texts from Elephantine dated to the same period attest to the presence of Sanballat and Tobiah—Nehemiah's critics.

Neh 1:1-11

[1]The words of Nehemiah son of Hacaliah. In the month of Chislev, in the
twentieth year, while I was in the citadel
of Susa, [2]one of my brothers, Hanani,
came with certain men from Judah,
and I asked them about the Jews who
escaped, those who had survived the
captivity, and about Jerusalem. [3]They
replied, "The remnant there in the province who escaped captivity are in great
trouble and shame; the wall of Jerusalem is broken down, and its gates
have been destroyed by fire."

[4]When I heard these words, I sat
down and wept and mourned for days,
fasting and praying before the God of
heaven. [5]I said, "O LORD God of heaven,
the great and awesome God who keeps
covenant and steadfast love with those
who love him and keep his commandments, [6]let your ear be attentive and your
eyes open to hear the prayer of your
servant that I now pray before you day
and night for your servants, the Israelites, confessing the sins of the Israelites,
which we have sinned against you. Both

The writer traces Ezra's lineage from his father Seraiah ("prince of the Lord") back to the great priest Aaron (Ezra 7:1-5).[4] In contrast, Nehemiah's lineage reflects only his father Hacaliah (1:1), who is otherwise unknown, and his named (Hanani) and unnamed brothers (1:2). Hacaliah's name (חכליה) originates from the Hebrew, which is vague, much like his heritage.[5] It is possible that Hacaliah's name represents the uncertainty of his lineage. Today, we may want to believe that our ancestries consist of "pure bloods" or "the originals," but such is not the case if we take genetic testing seriously. It is possible, however, to create or invent new nonbiological lineages. Yet even these new lineages are not pure since they are the amalgamation of two or more existing lineages. For example, adoption creates a newly formed lineage for the adopted child, stemming from the lineages of the adoptive parents and the lineages of the child's

4. "After this, in the reign of King Artaxerxes of Persia, Ezra son of Seraiah, son of Azariah, son of Hilkiah, son of Shallum, son of Zadok, son of Ahitub, son of Amariah, son of Azariah, son of Meraioth, son of Zerahiah, son of Uzzi, son of Bukki, son of Abishua, son of Phinehas, son of Eleazar, son of the chief priest Aaron" (Ezra 7:1-5).

5. *BDB* suggests that his name might be a compilation of the Hebrew root meaning "to wait," a shortened version of the divine name *yah* and the preposition *lamed*. Together they would create the translation "wait for Yahweh" (*BDB*, 314b). *BDB* lists another root, חכל, that is not attested to in the Hebrew Bible but appears in Arabic and Akkadian cognates and translates to "be confused," "vague," "gloomy," and "dark" (*BDB*, 314a). This raises the possibility that Hacaliah's name might represent the uncertainty of this person and his offspring.

I and my family have sinned. [7]We have offended you deeply, failing to keep the commandments, the statutes, and the ordinances that you commanded Moses your servant. [8]Remember the word that you commanded Moses your servant, 'If you are unfaithful, I will scatter you among the peoples, [9]but if you return to me and keep my commandments and do them, though your outcasts are under the farthest skies, I will gather them from there and bring them to the place where I have chosen to establish my name.' [10]They are your servants and your people whom you redeemed by your great power and your strong hand. [11]O Lord, let your ear be attentive to the prayer of your servant and to the prayer of your servants who delight in revering your name. Give success to your servant today, and grant him mercy in the sight of this man!"

At the time, I was cupbearer to the king.

biological parents. In the biblical text, Nehemiah's name appears in the list in Ezra 2:2 and Nehemiah 7:7 without an ancestral line. The lack of a clear genealogy for Nehemiah's family complicates the book's focus on genealogical purity since tracing one's lineage and familial relationships is the means the biblical writers use to make connections to the homeland.

Nehemiah's inquiry to Hanani on the state of the repatriates in the province results in a troubling report: "The remnant there in the province who escaped captivity are in great trouble and shame; the wall of Jerusalem is broken down, and its gates have been destroyed by fire" (Neh 1:3). While the identity of the remnant is ambiguous, the situation they find themself in is not.[6] The Hebrew חרפה, rendered "shame" in 1:3 and "disgrace" in 2:17, appears three more times in 4:4; 5:9; and 6:13 as "taunt."[7] The writer uses the same word to express the group's self-evaluation of their shortcomings (shame, disgrace) and the external evaluation of those shortcomings by their enemies (taunts). Linguistically, biblical cities are personified as feminine based on ancient perceptions of cities as places of nurture and security and as such spaces in need of protection (cf. Ps 122:6-7; Isa 62:4-9; 66:7-13). In this shame-and-honor culture where people seek to avoid dishonor, the metaphorical representation of a conquered and feminized city brings shame on the people who failed to protect it. It is unlikely that Nehemiah laments the destruction

6. For a discussion on who constitutes the remnant, see Lisbeth S. Fried, *Nehemiah: A Commentary*, Critical Commentaries (Sheffield: Sheffield Phoenix, 2021), 23–24.

7. חרפה, *BDB*, 357d.

of Jerusalem by the Babylonians more than 150 years earlier (Neh 1:4). Rather, the devastation could be current.[8] Ezra recounts opposition to rebuilding the city by the opposing residents in Judah (Ezra 4:4-24).

Nehemiah's prayer in 1:5-11a is a response to the news he receives from his brother Hanani and his companions. After several days of mourning over Jerusalem's devastation, Nehemiah directs a prayer to the "God of heaven" (Neh 1:5), an address that frequently appears in Ezra–Nehemiah and other Persian or later texts (1 and 2 Chronicles, Jonah, Daniel, Psalms). Nehemiah stresses collective guilt as he makes confession for the community, himself, and his family (בית־אבי, "the house of my father"), which includes his father, his brothers, and possibly any other members of his father's house (wife and daughters). Although the text mentions the father's house, we hear nothing about Nehemiah having a wife or children (Nehemiah's house).

The Function of Prayer in Nehemiah

Prayers in Nehemiah demonstrate reverence for God but, as a form of speech, serve a literary function to move the narrative along, express an ideology, or provide more information for the reader about the people's concerns.[9] Mark Boda concludes that the prayer in Nehemiah 1:5-11 shapes the book of Nehemiah: "We ascertain his depth of passion, his solidarity with the people, his commitment to Torah, and his grasp of theology."[10] Maria Häusel proposes that the prayer in Nehemiah 1:5-11 theologically binds Nehemiah's mission to God's covenant with Moses and "prepares Nehemiah's next act in Neh 2."[11] As we read the many prayers in Nehemiah, we are called to be mindful of what the editors of Nehemiah hope to convey in these petitions.

8. The destruction depicted in Nehemiah 1:3 could be attributed to Babylon's ransacking of Jerusalem in 587/586 BCE or by those who objected to the Judeans' building projects and who petitioned the king and use "force and power" to make them cease (Ezra 4:23).

9. Mark Boda, "Prayer as Rhetoric in the Book of Nehemiah," in *New Perspectives on Ezra–Nehemiah: History and Historiography, Text, Literature, and Interpretation*, ed. Isaac Kalimi (Winona Lake, IN: Eisenbrauns, 2012), 267–84.

10. Boda, "Prayer as Rhetoric," 280.

11. Maria Häusl, "'So I Prayed to the God of Heaven' (Neh 2:4): Praying and Prayers in the Books of Ezra and Nehemiah," in *Prayers and the Construction of Israelite Identity*, ed. Susanne Gillmayer-Bucher and Maria Häusl, AIL 35 (Atlanta: SBL Press, 2019), 70.

Three times, Nehemiah identifies the people's behavior as "sin" (Neh 1:6, חטאה). Sin, in this context, is a communal failure to adhere to the covenant, its commandments, statutes, and ordinances—the Mosaic covenant. He fully understands the egregiousness of the group's behavior: "we have offended you deeply" (Neh 1:7). He appeals to God to remember God's words to Moses that the people's repentance would lead to their return "to the place where I have chosen to establish my name" (Neh 1:9). Here, the chosen place is Jerusalem (2 Chr 6:6; Ps 132:13). Thus, Nehemiah frames God's intervention in the affairs of the people as a past reality and present expectation (Neh 1:10-11a). He appeals to his God before he makes his appeal to the king, indicating that, although a servant in Artaxerxes's court, his true allegiance is to the God of Israel. Nehemiah's prayer seeks to restore the broken relationship between God and God's people (i.e., covenant). Whether one interprets the prayer as penitential, where Nehemiah makes a communal confession of the sins of the people for transgressing the covenant, or as a prayer of intercession for God's intervention on behalf of the people or both, Nehemiah's concern for the people and the city and the need for divine intervention suggests that human-to-human relationships (ashamed and troubled people and city) also need restoration.

Nehemiah's concern for the city and its inhabitants is the impetus for his prayer. We offer that the prayer suggests that God does not have a lone responsibility for the welfare of the city and its inhabitants. Nehemiah is not an eyewitness to the devastation of Jerusalem. Yet, upon hearing of the state of the city and its people, he becomes an advocate for both before God. In essence, all of us should be concerned about the welfare of our cities and their inhabitants. As a people of faith, even when not physically present or connected to the city, we should care when natural disasters displace city residents.[12] We should care when homes, synagogues, mosques, and churches are vandalized or terrorized because of religious, racial, or ethnic hatred or when unjust policies and practices destroy cities. Nehemiah cares and closes his prayer by asking God to make him successful when he approaches the king as his next step (Neh 1:11a).[13] The people of faith pray first, and then they act.

The chapter concludes with identifying the profession of Nehemiah as cupbearer (משקה) to the king (Neh 1:11b). As such, he is a high-ranking

12. We recognize that not everyone identifies as a theist. We are speaking as women who identify as theists.

13. In 1:11a Nehemiah prays as follows: "Give success to your servant today and grant him mercy in the sight of this man!" While the text does not name who "this man" is, we discover in Nehemiah 2:1 that he is Artaxerxes.

official with the dangerous job of tasting the king's wine.[14] Nehemiah's duties may have extended beyond mere wine tasting and wine selection.[15] He would be well educated, well versed in court etiquette, and a close confidante of the king.[16] His prominent position and unique connections to the king make him a valuable asset to those in Judah and Jerusalem as a person who can advocate on their behalf. Nehemiah holds a powerful position, but this position is always a tenuous life-or-death position.

It is possible that Nehemiah was also a eunuch (pl. סריסים; sg. סריס) since the roles of the cupbearer and eunuch can overlap.[17] In the ancient world, eunuchs were men without testicles, penis, or both due to voluntary or involuntary castration. They often served in various roles in royal courts as they were presumed to be trustworthy and posed no threats to claims of paternity since they were unable to have children. For this reason, some held positions of great authority (see also Esth 2:14; Jdt 12:11). Eunuchs defy binary categories of male and female that suggest that gender lines might not have been drawn so straight in ancient Persia. While it is not possible to prove that Nehemiah is a eunuch (the text does not label him in this fashion), considering him as such expands our understanding of the construction of gender and sexual identity in ancient Judah.

TRANSLATION MATTERS

Nehemiah refers to himself in the Masoretic Text as a cupbearer (Neh 1:11, משקה) rather than the Hebrew term סריס ("eunuch"). The Septuagint (LXX) also identifies Nehemiah as a cupbearer (οἰνοχόος). While Nehemiah can serve as cupbearer to

14. The historian Xenophon (*Cyr.* 1.3.8-10) recounts that the job of the cupbearer is to taste the wine for the king to ensure that the king is not poisoned. See Fried, *Nehemiah*, 40.

15. Tobit 1:22 notes important roles given to Sennacherib and Esar-haddon's cupbearer: "Ahikar interceded for me, and I returned to Nineveh. Now Ahikar was chief cupbearer, keeper of the signet, and in charge of administration of the accounts under King Sennacherib of Assyria; so Esar-haddon appointed him as second-in-command. He was my nephew and a close relative." For a more detailed description of how cupbearers functioned in the ancient Near East, see Edwin Yamauchi, "Was Nehemiah the Cupbearer a Eunuch?," *ZAW* 92 (1980): 132–42.

16. Yamauchi, "Was Nehemiah the Cupbearer a Eunuch?," 134–35.

17. Hermotimus, a eunuch and cupbearer, served Xerxes I and became favored in the court (A. D. Godley, trans., "Herodotus 8.105," *Herodotus: The Histories* [Cambridge: Harvard University Press, 1920], https://www.perseus.tufts.edu/hopper/text?doc=Perseus%3Atext%3A1999.01.0126%3Abook%3D8%3Achapter%3D105).

the Persian king without being a eunuch, there are textual issues and traditions that imply this connection.[18] The Codex Vaticanus, likely relying on earlier Greek translations, reads οἰνοχόος in Nehemiah 1:11 as "eunuch" (εὐνοῦχος).[19] The Greek terms for cupbearer (*oinoxoos*) and eunuch (*eunouxos*) sound similar, which may have led to different textual traditions. Further, some Greek manuscripts may reflect historical factors that link cupbearers with eunuchs. Some scholars argue that reliefs found at Persian Persepolis depict clean-shaven attendants they presume to be eunuch cupbearers.[20] Ancient sources such as Xenophon's *Cyropaedia* (7.5.60-65), Herodotus's *Histories* (8:105), Ctesias's *Persica*, and Plutarch's *Artoxerxes* (12) attest to important roles that eunuchs played in the Persian courts as loyal servants with access to the kings—access that Nehemiah shares.[21] Origen's letter to Africanus (mid-third century CE) mentions Nehemiah as "cupbearer of the king and his eunuch."[22]

The book of Nehemiah offers other clues that support Nehemiah's identity as a eunuch. He has no wife and children, and his conversation with the king takes place in the presence of the queen, suggesting that he moves in and out of private and public spaces like a eunuch (2:6). Nehemiah's unwillingness to enter the temple as "a man like me" (6:11) could be tied to Deuteronomy's prohibition: "No one whose testicles are crushed or whose penis is cut off shall come into the assembly of the Lord" (Deut 23:1).[23] Additionally, Nehemiah's prayers to

18. For a list of scholars who consider Nehemiah to be a eunuch, see Yamauchi, "Was Nehemiah the Cupbearer a Eunuch?," 135. See also Jacob Wright and Michael Chan, "King and Eunuch: Isaiah 56:1-8 in Light of Honorific Royal Burial Practices," *JBL* 131 (2012): 99–119; Ron Stanley, "Ezra–Nehemiah," in *The Queer Bible Commentary*, ed. Deryn Guest et al., vol. 1 (London: SCM, 2006), 268–77. Yamauchi ("Was Nehemiah the Cupbearer a Eunuch?") and Blenkinsopp (*Ezra–Nehemiah*, 213) are among those who do not believe Nehemiah was a eunuch. They argue that Nehemiah is often attacked by opponents who never raise this as an issue.

19. David Marcus, *Ezra and Nehemiah*, Biblia Hebraica Qinta 20 (Stuttgart: Deutsche Bibelgesellschaft, 2006), 43. The textual apparatus indicates that the Old Greek manuscripts might have taken semantic liberties as suggested by the apparatus's note "lib-semen" (liberty in respect to semantic matters). The Septuagint Alexandrinus employs οἰνοχόος (cupbearer).

20. Yamauchi challenges those who rely on the reliefs as strong evidence that cupbearers are eunuchs ("Was Nehemiah the Cupbearer a Eunuch?," 138–39).

21. For examples of influential eunuchs, see Matthew W. Waters, *Ctesias' Persica and Its Near Eastern Context*, Wisconsin Studies in Classics (Madison: University of Wisconsin Press, 2017), 29–35.

22. Jacob Myers, *Ezra, Nehemiah*, AB 14 (New York: Doubleday, 1965), 93. Here, Myers is referencing Origen's letter to Africanus, where Africanus refers to "*Neemias oinochoos Tou Basileos kai eunouchos autou*" and translates it as "Nehemiah cupbearer of the king and his eunuch" (*Library of Greek Fathers and Ecclesiastical Historians*, XVI, p. 360).

23. Armin Siedlecki notes the tradition that uses Nehemiah's refusal to enter the temple in Nehemiah 6:11 and the Greek manuscripts to build a case that Nehemiah is a eunuch. See "Ezra–Nehemiah in Reception History," in *The Oxford Handbook of the Historical Books of the Hebrew Bible*, ed. Brad Kelle and Brent Strawn (Oxford: Oxford University Press, 2020), 531.

God to remember him for the good deeds he has done (Neh 5:19; 13:14, 22, 31) calls to mind Isaiah's promise to faithful eunuchs that they will be remembered with "a monument and a name" (Isa 56:5).[24] While we will never know for certain if Nehemiah was a eunuch, considering this possibility provides space to think beyond binary gender boundaries. Eunuchs functioned in a liminal space between male and female. Matthew Waters discusses the liminal space of the eunuch: "The eunuch was not a woman but was certainly no longer considered a man."[25] For some, Nehemiah, as a queer leader, successfully follows in the vein of Moses and David and provides a model that encourages those today—those often treated as sexual outcasts—to claim their authority as leaders.[26] For others, Nehemiah's leadership is not without flaws. Still, viewing him as a eunuch allows a space to explore the separation from home that some who identify as queer experience, the coming out experience, and a call for compassion for those marginalized within and without the community.[27]

Negotiating the Walls of Privilege (2:1-10)

In 2:1-3, Nehemiah, as cupbearer, approaches the king with an uncharacteristically sad countenance to serve the king's wine (Neh 2:1).[28] Whether intentionally or not, Nehemiah draws the king's attention to himself. The king asks, "Why is your face sad, since you are not sick? This can only be sadness of the heart" (Neh 2:2). Does the king notice Nehemiah's countenance because of concern for or suspicion of his servant? The Hebrew translated "sad" (רע) can also be rendered "distressed," "in misery," or "evil,"[29] and expressing any of these in the presence of the king can be threatening if received by the king as either

24. Stanley, "Ezra–Nehemiah," 271.

25. Waters, *Ctesias' Persica and Its Near Eastern Context*, 21.

26. Stanley, "Ezra–Nehemiah," 268, 277, and Michael S. Piazza, "Nehemiah as a Queer Model for Servant Leadership," in *Take Back the Word: A Queer Reading of the Bible*, ed. Robert Goss and Mona West (Cleveland: Pilgrim Press, 2000), 115–23.

27. Durrell Watkins, "Ezra–Nehemiah," in *The Queer Bible Commentary*, ed. Mona West and Robert E. Shore-Goss, 2nd ed. (London: SCM, 2022), 235–41.

28. There are problems with dating 1:1 and 2:1 because these dates, if accurate, place Nehemiah's encounter with King Artaxerses (2:2-8) nine months prior to his meeting with Hanani (1:2-4). The twentieth year of Artaxerxes (although the king's name is absent in 1:1) is 446 BCE; Chislev is the ninth month, and Nisan is the first month (2:1). See Paul Redditt, *Ezra–Nehemiah* (Macon: Smith & Helwys, 2014), 234.

29. *BDB*, 948–49. To this point, Fried translates the king's statement in the NRSV: "This can only be sadness of the heart" as "This is nothing but an evil heart" (Fried, *Nehemiah*, 49). Fried's translation suggests Nehemiah's countenance reflects potential treachery.

Neh 2:1-10

[1]In the month of Nisan, in the twentieth year of King Artaxerxes, when wine was served him, I carried the wine and gave it to the king. Now, I had never been sad in his presence before. [2]So the king said to me, "Why is your face sad, since you are not sick? This can only be sadness of the heart." Then I was very much afraid. [3]I said to the king, "May the king live forever! Why should my face not be sad, when the city, the place of my ancestors' graves, lies waste and its gates have been destroyed by fire?" [4]Then the king said to me, "What do you request?" So I prayed to the God of heaven. [5]Then I said to the king, "If it pleases the king, and if your servant has found favor with you, I ask that you send me to Judah, to the city of my ancestors' graves, so that I may rebuild it." [6]The king said to me (the queen also was sitting beside him), "How long will you be gone, and when will you return?" So it pleased the king to send me, and I set him a date. [7]Then I said to the king, "If it pleases the king, let letters be given me to the governors of the province Beyond the

nefarious or Nehemiah's divided loyalty.[30] The stress of maintaining good spirits in the midst of his concern for the well-being of Jerusalem and his allegiance to the king, as expressed in 1:5-11, must have been difficult for Nehemiah. He may be well aware of his fragile political status as Artaxerxes is the same king who removes queen Vashti (Esth 1:19). Nehemiah, as the king's cupbearer, is less likely to fare any better (cf. Gen 40:1-3). If the king is offended by Nehemiah's distressed appearance, it explains Nehemiah's fear and use of deferential language to confirm his commitment to the king: "May the king live forever" (Neh 2:3), "if it pleases the king" (Neh 2:5, 7), and "if your servant has found favor" (Neh 2:5). We find this deferential language directed toward other imperial rulers in the biblical texts (Dan 2:4; 3:9; 5:10; Esth 1:19; 5:4).

Today, we continue to show deference to those in positions of power and leadership (i.e., leading our governmental, religious, social groups). This deference can be based on respect or fear. When deference is born of respect, leaders are considered trustworthy, open to critique, and willing to embrace those whose views differ. When deference is born out of fear,

30. Paul Redditt brings in Joseph Fleischman's suggestion ("Nehemiah's Request on Behalf of Jerusalem," in *New Perspectives on Ezra–Nehemiah*, ed. Isaac Kalimi [Winona Lake, IN: Eisenbrauns, 2012], 250–51) that Artaxerxes's devotion to Ahura Mazda requires that he be surrounded by positive energy. See Redditt, *Ezra–Nehemiah*, 235. Blenkinsopp proposes that approaching the king with a positive attitude is part of court etiquette (Blenkinsopp, *Ezra–Nehemiah*, 213).

Neh 2:1-10 (cont.)

River, that they may grant me passage until I arrive in Judah, [8]and a letter to Asaph, the keeper of the king's forest, directing him to give me timber to make beams for the gates of the temple fortress and for the wall of the city and for the house that I shall occupy." And the king granted me what I asked, for the gracious hand of my God was upon me.

[9]Then I came to the governors of the province Beyond the River and gave them the king's letters. Now the king had sent officers of the army and cavalry with me. [10]When Sanballat the Horonite and Tobiah the Ammonite official heard this, it displeased them greatly that someone had come to seek the welfare of the Israelites.

there is an awareness of the negative consequences that could result from failure to exhibit the prescribed reverential words and actions (as in the case of authoritative leaders or abusive relationships).

Nehemiah explains his downtrodden countenance to the king, "Why should my face not be sad, when the city, the place of my ancestors' graves, lies waste and its gates have been destroyed by fire?" (Neh 2:3). He carefully phrases his response and emphasizes his need to repair the place of his ancestors' graves, which happens to be in Jerusalem.[31] Nehemiah may have hesitated to broach the topic of rebuilding Jerusalem given complaints against the Jews reconstructing the city's walls and foundations (Ezra 4:7-22). The king's concern for Nehemiah is evident in his response, "What do you request?" Once again, Nehemiah prays to the "God of heaven" before answering the king (Neh 2:4). Nehemiah's appeal to return to Jerusalem to repair his ancestors' graves in 2:5 resonates with Artaxerxes's respect for his ancestors and their burials as a practitioner of Zoroastrianism and may lead the king to sympathize with him.[32]

The king's reply is interrupted by the writer's parenthetical aside, "the queen also was sitting beside him" (2:6). This insertion of the queen's appearance with the king is similar to Esther's presence with King Ahasuerus where he inquires what he can do for her (Esth 5:3). We can infer from the similarities that the queen's presence has an influential effect on the king's decision to honor Nehemiah's request. These kings, as

31. Blenkinsopp, *Ezra–Nehemiah*, 214.

32. Joseph Fleishman, "Nehemiah's Request on Behalf of Jerusalem," in Kalimi, ed., *New Perspectives on Ezra–Nehemiah*, 255. This chapter provides a helpful discussion on Artaxerxes's connections to Zoroastrianism.

powerful as they are, have women seated beside them who also hold positions of power. The biblical text contains multiple examples of women who have influence with the reigning ruler (e.g., the queen mother in Dan 5:10-12 and Prov 31:1-9; Jezebel with Ahab in 1 Kgs 21; Esther with Ahasuerus; Bathsheba with David in 2 Kgs 1:11-31).

TRANSLATION MATTERS

When Nehemiah approaches the king, we discover that the king is seated next to a woman. The NRSVue identifies this woman as: "the queen also was sitting beside him." The typical Hebrew word for queen is מלכה, however, the Hebrew rendered "queen" in Nehemiah 2:6 is שֵׁגַל, which is an Akkadian loan word that can be translated as "queen" or "consort."[33] The NRSVue translates שֵׁגַל as "queen" (Neh 2:6; Ps 45:10) and "wives" of the king (Dan 5:2, 3, 23). Other translations (e.g., JPS, New English translation) translate שֵׁגַל as "consort." The Greek in the Septuagint for שֵׁגַל is παλλακή, which means "concubine."[34] Lisbeth Fried translates this phrase as "a royal woman sat beside him" and suggests that this woman could be any royal woman, including a queen mother.[35] While the NRSVue sets the queen's presence off with parentheses because this statement interrupts the flow of the narrative, this woman, whoever she is, is important enough to be remembered in King Artaxerxes's discussion with Nehemiah.[36]

The king's follow-up inquiry into the length of Nehemiah's absence results in the king's approval with an unknown date set for his return (Neh 2:6b). Allowing Nehemiah to leave suggests that either the king has no reservations about Nehemiah's purposes in Jerusalem (i.e., trusts him) and/or that he has other cupbearers to serve him. Nevertheless, the king has expectations that Nehemiah will return. Despite his importance, Nehemiah, like Daniel (Dan 6:1-3), Mordecai (Esth 9:4), and Joseph (Gen 41:39-41), who also hold influence in foreign courts, has limited freedom. A modern example is that of enslaved persons in the houses (and fields) of plantation owners who were permitted certain freedoms but required

33. The *HALOT* only lists two occurrences of שֵׁגַל in the Hebrew Bible (Neh 2:6 and Ps 45:9; *HALOT*, 1415). The *BDB* (p. 993c) expands the meaning to include "consort."

34. Henry George Liddell and Robert Scott, *A Lexicon Abridged from Liddell and Scott's Greek English Lexicon* (Oxford: Clarendon, 1982), 515.

35. Fried, *Nehemiah*, 50.

36. For a longer discussion on who this woman might be, see Blenkinsopp, *Ezra–Nehemiah*, 215, and Fried, *Nehemiah*, 50–51.

permission to leave. While it is unclear whether Nehemiah is enslaved, as cupbearer, he is still a servant, who serves at the benevolence or malevolence of the reigning ruler.

Having secured permission to travel (Neh 2:5-6), Nehemiah makes a second request that the king put this permission in writing (Neh 2:7) and provide building materials, "timber to make beams for the gates of the temple fortress and for the wall of the city and for the house that I shall occupy" (Neh 2:8). In ancient Persia persons are required to carry travel permits for safety reasons and government monitoring.[37] The Persians provided stations throughout the empire with supplies and provisions for travelers who carried official travel documents.[38] Documents granting travel permission are as important today as they were in the Persian period. Passports and immigration cards open doors beyond the borders of one's country. Not all passports have the same power. A US passport opens doors to 183 countries, while a passport from Afghanistan is limited to twenty-five.[39]

Nehemiah expands his request beyond the initial desire to address ancestral graves in 2:3 to include resources from the king's forest to build gates, walls, and Nehemiah's personal residence (Neh 2:8). Nehemiah's confidence increases as he moves from one request to several requests that require the king to invest in Nehemiah's mission to rebuild Jerusalem. Not everyone has this kind of access to the king and the power that the king wields. He uses his access to benefit his people, his city, and himself. Sometimes we focus on a critique of government bureaucracy without a corresponding recognition of the access to necessary services and resources that it provides to its citizens. Still, Nehemiah does not credit his good fortune to his relationship with the king but rather to the intervention of his deity: "the gracious hand of my God was upon

37. Amelie Kurht, "State Communications in the Persian Empire," in *State Correspondence in the Ancient World: From New Kingdom Egypt to the Roman Empire*, Oxford Studies in Early Empires, ed. Karen Radner (Oxford: Oxford University Press, 2014), 126.

38. TAD A6.9, see Kurht, "State Communications in the Persian Empire," 112–40, for an example of a travel document. Also, Richard T. Hallock, *Persepolis Fortification Tablets*, University of Chicago Oriental Institute Publications 92 (Chicago: University of Chicago Press, 1969).

39. "Global Passport Power Rank 2023," *Passport Index*, https://www.passportindex.org/passport-power-rank-2023.php. Henley & Partners' 2023 rankings place Afghanistan's visa-free score at twenty-six and the United States' at 187 countries. See "Global Passport Ranking," *The Henley Passport Index* (2023), https://www.henleyglobal.com/passport-index/ranking, accessed April 5, 2025.

me" (Neh 2:8). Theologically, Nehemiah prays going into the situation and in the midst of it, and at the conclusion he acknowledges God as responsible for his success.

Armed with official letters and a royal military escort, Nehemiah presents himself before the "governors of the province Beyond the River" (Neh 2:9a). While Nehemiah has not asked the king for armed escorts, they are nonetheless provided: "Now the king had sent officers of the army and cavalry with me" (Neh 2:9b). The escorts and letters from the king strengthen Nehemiah's authority, ensuring his safe passage over the thousand-mile journey from Susa to Jerusalem. Ezra receives similar letters from the king when he makes his journey (Ezra 7:11-28) but a military escort is not mentioned.[40] For the king, Jerusalem with a reconstructed temple is just another religious center among others under his rule, while Jerusalem with reconstructed walls and an armed presence suggests a military stronghold, a fortified garrison.

Nehemiah's arrival with an army and building materials would certainly draw attention. When Sanballat and Tobiah, governors within the province, hear that Nehemiah enters the province Beyond the River, "it displeased them greatly that someone had come to seek the welfare of the Israelites" (Neh 2:10). Thus begins the conflict between these local leaders and Nehemiah.

TRANSLATION MATTERS

Sanballat and Tobiah are upset that Nehemiah enters Jerusalem with the task of rebuilding Jerusalem's walls. The NRSVue translates their reaction to the news as "it displeased them greatly" (2:10). The Hebrew phrase, וירע להם רעה גדלה, however, presents an even stronger reaction to Nehemiah's mission, "it was evil to them a great evil." Their objection to Nehemiah's building plans precipitates their conflict with Nehemiah as he follows through in his plans.

Sanballat and Tobiah are both governors within Persia's province Beyond the River. The Elephantine Papyri (*TAD* A4.7 and A4.8; *Cowley* 30-31) and a bulla found at Wadi Daliyeh (north of Jericho) refer to Sanballat as

40. Ezra 2:7-9; see the commentary on Ezra 3–5 for more discussion on letters.

governor over Samaria.[41] Tobiah serves as the governor of the province or region of Ammon, whose boundaries and culture were not impacted by Babylonia's invasion of Judah (587/586 BCE) and remained intact during the Persian Empire.[42] Nehemiah's memoir never refers to either man as governor. Instead, the narrative describes them as non-Judeans and associates them with their enemies.

Sanballat (whose name means "may Sin give him life"[43]) is described as a Horonite, which connects him to Mesopotamian Haran, the center of Sin worship, or to Horonanaim (meaning "the two caves") in Moab (2 Sam 13:34; Jer 48:3, 5; Isa 15:5), or, more likely, to Beth-Horon, which the Ephraimites settled and is part of Samaria (Josh 16:5).[44] Any one of these possible natal cities associates Sanballat with Israel's enemies: the Assyrians, the Moabites, and the Samarians. Yet, biblical and extrabiblical evidence suggests Sanballat worships the God of Israel. His sons, Delaiah and Shelemaiah, like their father, appear in the Elephantine Papyri (*TAD* A4.7 and A4.8; *Cowley* 30-31) in the letter Jedaniah and his priestly colleagues address to Bagavahya, the governor of Judah, seeking to reconstruct the temple of God in Elephantine.[45] The presence of "yah," the shortened form of YHWH, in Delaiah and Shelemaiah's names, together with the marriage of Sanballat's daughter to the high priest of Jerusalem (Neh 13:28), convey the possibility that Sanballat worships the God of Israel.

41. Bezalel Porten et al., "Request for Letter of Recommendation," in *The Elephantine Papyri in English: Three Millennia of Cross-Cultural Continuity and Change*, 2nd ed., Studies in Near Eastern Archaeology and Civilisation (Atlanta: SBL, 2011), 146; and Fried, *Nehemiah*, 58.

42. For a discussion on Ammon's status as a province and Tobiah's role as governor, see Larry G. Herr, "What Ever Happened to the Ammonites?," *BAR* 19 (November 1993): 26–35, 68; and Fried, *Nehemiah*, 60.

43. Here, Sin refers to the Mesopotamian moon god and is not a reference to sin as transgression.

44. Paul Redditt, "Sanballat," in *Eerdman's Dictionary of the Bible*, ed. David Noel Freedman (Grand Rapids: Eerdmans, 2000), 1165. See Josh 16:5: "The territory of the Ephraimites by their families was as follows: the boundary of their inheritance on the east was Ataroth-addar as far as Upper Beth-horon."

45. Porten et al., *The Elephantine Papyri in English*, 146. See also Ralph Klein, "The Books of Ezra and Nehemiah," in *The New Interpreter's Bible*, ed. Leander Keck, vol. 3 (Nashville: Abingdon, 1999), 757.

Sanballat Over Time

Sanballat plays a prominent role in the book of Nehemiah as Nehemiah's primary adversary who tries to prevent him and the community from rebuilding the wall and restoring Jerusalem. Sanballat may govern the territories of Samaria and Judah during the time Nehemiah enters Jerusalem.[46] Yet, after his run-in with Nehemiah, Sanballat's name disappears from both Testaments. There is a tradition that Sanballat lurks behind Zechariah's vision of the dirty clothes (Zech 3:1-10), where the high priest Joshua, wearing dirty priestly garments (Zech 3:3), stands before the angel of the Lord and the adversary (the Satan, Zech 3:1). Some early Jewish commentators (e.g., R. Papa, 300–375 CE; Rashi, 1040–1105 CE; Kimchi, 1160–1275 CE) and Christian commentators (e.g., Jerome, ca. 347–420 CE) connect these soiled garments with the pollution of the priesthood through intermarriage.[47] Ibn Ezra (ca. 1089–1164 CE) disagrees with this connection.[48] To illustrate how badly the priesthood is tarnished, these commentators draw on the book of Nehemiah where it recounts the marriage between Sanballat's daughter and one of the grandsons of the high priest: "And one of the sons of Jehoiada, son of the high priest Eliashib, was the son-in-law of Sanballat the Horonite; I chased him away from me" (Neh 13:28).[49] R. Papa holds the high priest Joshua accountable for not preventing his sons from marrying "wives not permitted by the priests" (San. 93a). Josephus (*Ant.* 11.7.2–8.4) suggests that Sanballat and Darius III Codomannus (336–331 BCE) are contemporaneous and

46. For a helpful discussion about whether Sanballat served as governor over both Judah and Samaria, see Lester Grabbe, *History of the Jews and Judaism in the Second Temple Period*, vol. 1: *Yehud: A History of the Persian Province of Judah*, LSTS 47 (London: T&T Clark, 2004), 140–42. While evidence suggests that Judah has its own Persian-appointed governor throughout Persia's rule, there may have been a time in which Judah shared governors with Samaria. Artaxerxes may have sent Nehemiah to replace Sanballat as governor over Judah though the text does not note Nehemiah's official role until 5:14: "from the time that I was appointed to be their governor in the land of Judah, from the twentieth year to the thirty-second year of King Artaxerxes."

47. For early discussions by Jewish and Christian commentators on intermarriage prohibitions, see R. P. Gordon, *Studies in the Targum to the Twelve Prophets, from Nahum to Malachi*, VTSup 51 (Leiden: Brill, 1994), 109–10. This book cites the source material used by Jewish and Christian commentators as they interpret Zechariah 3.

48. Gordon, *Studies in the Targum to the Twelve Prophets*, 110.

49. Gordon, *Studies in the Targum to the Twelve Prophets*, 110.

live during the time of Alexander the Great.[50]

Sanballat, of the Book of Nehemiah, is a Samarian—an inhabitant of this region. Over time, the people of this land would come to be known as Samaritans.[51] The Samaritans were a mixed population, formed when the Assyrian Empire resettled people from various regions into Samaria after the conquest of the Northern Kingdom of Israel in 722 BCE. Although Samaritans identify as Israelites and revere the Pentateuch, the mutual animosity between the Jewish and Samaritan communities becomes evident in New Testament narratives like the Parable of the Good Samaritan (Luke 10:25-37). Sanballat does not often appear in modern culture. Still, the Apostolic preacher and popular author Jennifer LeClair draws on the "spirit of Sanballat" that she believes promotes community opposition to her building a house of prayer in Fort Lauderdale, Florida.[52]

The text identifies Tobiah (טוביה, which means "Yah is good") as an "Ammonite official" (2:10) or, in Hebrew, a "servant/slave" (עבד) of the Ammonites, a people not allowed in the assembly of the Lord (Deut 23:3-4). According to Genesis, the Ammonites are the offspring of the incestuous relationship between Lot and one of his daughters (Gen 19:29-38). The Ammonites are perceived as a group whose religious beliefs and practices are inconsistent with those of Israel and, as such, they should be avoided. Tobiah has roots in the Judean community as a relative of the high priest Eliashib (Neh 13:4). He marries the daughter of Shecaniah who is a prominent Jewish leader who returns from exile with Zerubbabel (Ezra 2:5).[53] Tobiah's family linkages extend to the powerful

50. H. G. M. Williamson, "Sanballa (Person)," in *The Anchor Yale Bible Dictionary: O–Sh*, ed. David Noel Freedman et al. (New Haven: Yale University Press, 1992), 973–75.

51. The exact date for the shift from identifying those living in Samaria as Samaritans is challenging to pinpoint. The change to "Samaritan" gradually occurs throughout the Persian and Hellenistic periods (5th–2nd centuries BCE). Eventually, those living in Samaria build a temple near Mt. Gerizim (ca. 5th century BCE), and those living and worshiping there are called Samaritans.

52. Jennifer LeClaire, "Don't Let the Spirit of Sanballat Distract You," Jennifer LeClaire Ministries (January 4, 2013), https://jenniferleclaire.org/articles/dont-let-the-spirit-of-sanballat-distract-you/#.

53. Tamara Eskenazi, "Daughter-in-Law of Tobiah, Daughter of Meshullam, Wife of Jehohanan," in *Women in Scripture: A Dictionary of Named and Unnamed Women in*

Tobiad family, a Jewish faction in Ammon that controlled Jerusalem in the Hellenistic period.[54]

Sanballat and Tobiah are displeased that Nehemiah "had come to seek the welfare of the Israelites" (Neh 2:10b). It is unclear what seeking the welfare of the people entails. The people's welfare could be the security they receive with the wall rebuilt or it could be the protection that comes with an army stationed in Jerusalem. Tobiah does not want what Nehemiah considers to be good (טוב) for the people of Israel. Yet he and Sanballat are also people of Israel and, as appointees of the Persian king, may have their own agenda for Israel's well-being. Government and religious officials do not always agree on what is best for their constituents and congregants. Each official has territorial interests and responsibilities to the people they serve.

These competing interests lie at the root of the conflict between Nehemiah and these leaders. Nehemiah, Sanballat, and Tobiah portray the other as "other" as they seek to move their agendas forward. For Nehemiah, the agenda is to rebuild the walls and gates of the city. Sanballat and Tobiah's agenda is unknown, but their displeasure reveals that it is clearly different from Nehemiah's. When politicians have competing interests or even the same interests but disagree on how to accomplish them, the people most affected by their conflict are not the politicians but the people they serve. We see this with the political wars in Washington, DC, and state capitals, where elected officials accomplish very little while fighting among themselves.

Constructing Walls of Protection (2:11-20)

Nehemiah arrives in Jerusalem and, after spending three days in the city (Neh 2:11), he assembles a few men for a clandestine midnight expedition to survey the condition of the walls and gates (Neh 2:12). This strategy makes little sense, given that Nehemiah holds letters of approval from Artaxerxes. Nehemiah even appears to withhold information from those accompanying him: "I told no one what my God had put in my heart to do for Jerusalem" (Neh 2:12). Because he is concerned about secrecy, Nehemiah brings only the supplies and the animal he needs to move between the walls and gates. In the darkness, Nehemiah and his crew circle the perimeter of the broken wall and its gates.

---

the Hebrew Bible, the Apocryphal/Deuterocanonical Books, and the New Testament, ed. Carol Meyers, Toni Craven, and Ross Shepard Kraemer (Boston: Houghton Mifflin, 2000), 288.

54. Paul Redditt, "Tobiah," in *Eerdmans Dictionary of the Bible*, ed. David Noel Freedman (Grand Rapids: Eerdmans, 2000), 1317.

Neh 2:11-20

[11]So I came to Jerusalem and was there for three days. [12]Then I got up during the night, I and a few men with me; I told no one what my God had put into my heart to do for Jerusalem. The only animal I took was the animal I rode. [13]I went out by night by the Valley Gate past the Dragon's Spring and to the Dung Gate, and I inspected the walls of Jerusalem that had been broken down and its gates that had been destroyed by fire. [14]Then I went on to the Fountain Gate and to the King's Pool, but there was no place for the animal I was riding to continue. [15]So I went up by way of the valley by night and inspected the wall. Then I turned back and entered by the Valley Gate and so returned. [16]The officials did not know where I had gone or what I was doing; I had not yet told the Jews, the priests, the nobles, the officials, and the rest who were to do the work.

[17]Then I said to them, "You see the trouble we are in, how Jerusalem lies in

Nehemiah Views the Ruins of Jerusalem's Walls, by Gustave Doré, 1866, https://commons.wikimedia.org/wiki/File:108.Nehemiah_Views_the_Ruins_of_Jerusalem%27s_Walls.jpg.

ruins with its gates burned. Come, let us rebuild the wall of Jerusalem, so that we may no longer suffer disgrace." [18]I told them that the hand of my God had been gracious upon me and also the words that the king had spoken to me. Then they said, "Let us start building!" So they committed themselves to the common good. [19]But when Sanballat the Horonite and Tobiah the Ammonite official and Geshem the Arab heard of it, they mocked and ridiculed us, saying, "What is this that you are doing? Are you rebelling against the king?" [20]Then I replied to them, "The God of heaven is the one who will give us success, and we his servants are going to start building, but you have no share or claim or memorial in Jerusalem."

There are at least two versions of this midnight inspection. One starts at 2:13, where the tour begins at the Valley Gate, passes Dragon's Spring, and goes on to the Dung Gate. Nehemiah pays particular attention to this area's walls and gates destroyed by fire. He then continues to the Fountain Gate and on to the King's Pool, where the damage is so extensive that Nehemiah and his beast cannot continue (Neh 2:14). In 2:15 there appears to be a reintroduction of the night journey. A possible scenario is that Nehemiah made more than one nocturnal trip through the Valley Gate.[55]

Nehemiah's unwillingness to share his plan reflects a possibility that he fears or distrusts the Jerusalem administration or he has no need to inform them, given his royal support for his mission. He addresses the group that will be involved in the reconstruction. The list of those in the group is both specific and general: the "Jews, the priests, the nobles, the officials, and the rest who were to do the work" (Neh 2:16). He first appeals to their sense of honor, calling them to rebuild the walls and erase the disgrace or shame (חרפה) that results from their failure to restore Jerusalem (Neh 2:17).[56] Nehemiah's request harks back to Hanani's account of the dire situation in Jerusalem and the accompanying shame, which he shares with Nehemiah during his visit to Susa (Neh 1:3). Second, Nehemiah claims both theological and political authority for his mission: "I told them that the hand of my God had been gracious upon me and also the words that the king had spoken to me" (Neh 2:18a).

55. Jacob Wright, *Rebuilding Identity: The Nehemiah-Memoir and Its Earliest Readers*, BZAW 348 (Berlin: de Gruyter, 2004), 96–104.

56. See discussion on honor and the repeated word "shame" (חרפה) in Neh 1:3.

The group signals their support as they exclaim: "Let us start building!" (Neh 2:18b). Additionally, they "committed themselves to the common good" (Neh 2:18b). The Hebrew ויחזקו ידיהם לטובה reads, "they strengthened their hands for good." Strong hands are essential for the building that they are about to undertake. For Nehemiah and his supporters, rebuilding the walls and gates is a public good. Community pride is restored, and divine involvement in the affairs of God's people is reaffirmed.

The walls of Jerusalem have historical and theological significance. Theologically, the reconstruction of the walls signals the end of God's reproach that led to the destruction of Jerusalem and the exile of some of its populace. Rebuilding also points to the renewal and commitment of God's people to God. Historically, the walls protected the inhabitants and the temple in Jerusalem.

In his quest to rebuild the walls, Nehemiah encounters a third enemy, Geshem the Arab, who, along with Sanballat and Tobiah, mocks and accuses Nehemiah and his community of rebelling (מרד) against the Persian king (Neh 2:19).[57] Geshem's authority spans Arabia and Lower Egypt. Because of his proximity to and relationship with Sanballat and Tobiah, he shows interest in activities occurring in Judah.[58] Questioning Nehemiah's loyalty reminds the reader of Rehum and Shimshei's letter to Artaxerxes petitioning the king to close down the repatriates' building project in Ezra 4:11-16. Their letter describes the city as "rebellious and wicked" (Ezra 4:12), a site of seditious activity (Ezra 4:15).[59] Artaxerxes responds to this report by halting the work in Jerusalem. Sanballat and Tobiah's mocking and accusation are meant possibly to intimidate Nehemiah and those involved in the reconstruction into abandoning their efforts.

This strategy proves ineffective as Nehemiah declares that they "have no share or claim or memorial in Jerusalem" (Neh 2:20). The word translated "share" (חלק) can also mean "portion" or "territory."[60] The second term, "claim" (צדקה), is the same term translated as "righteousness" or "legal right,"[61] and its usage here basically communicates that Nehe-

57. "Geshem, King of Qedar" is inscribed on a Persian-period silver bowl from Tell el-Maskhuteh, and there is another inscription with a "Gsm bin Sahr." Grabbe, *A History of the Jews*, 164.

58. Grabbe, *A History of the Jews*, 162–64.

59. Both Ezra 4 and Neh 2:19 employ a form of the verb מרד, "rebel."

60. חלק, *BDB*, 324.

61. צדקה in *BDB*, 842, and *HALOT*, 1006.

miah and his group belong in Jerusalem, while Sanballat, Tobiah, and Geshem do not. The final term, "historic right" (זכרון), is translated in *BDB* as "memorial" or "remembrance" and provides the rationale for legal rights, which Sanballat and company will not have in this newly reconstituted Jerusalem.[62]

What Nehemiah, Sanballat, Tobiah, and Geshem know about each other is based on what they hear (Neh 2:10, 19).[63] While Nehemiah could have revealed the details of his mission upon his arrival to interested parties, he chooses to remain silent. His secrecy in the context of rumors (what each hears about the other) raises the question of whether or not there are times when secrecy is the best strategy. Secrecy when one is concerned for one's personal safety and the safety of others in the midst of a hostile environment is a wise decision. Information regarding the locations of safe houses, witness identities, or state secrets is withheld intentionally to protect and prevent exploitation and exposure.

Walls of Remembrance (3:1-32)

Nehemiah and his community begin rebuilding and repairing the walls and gates of Jerusalem. The shift from the first person in chapters 1 and 2 to the third person in chapter 3 suggests that this chapter is inserted. The list in Nehemiah 3:1-32 confirms a substantial number of those involved, from the priests under the leadership of Eliashib at the Sheep Gate (Neh 3:1) to the smiths working with Malchijah to connect the corner shared with Eliashib (Neh 3:31-32). The text sets up the reconstruction as a holy task with the consecration of the Sheep Gate, the Tower of the Hundred, and the Tower Hananel. Consecrating these gates signals the sanctity of these walls. The act of consecration fosters communal bonding and shared identity as communal members set themselves and the consecrated object (wall, building, temple) apart for sacred purposes. The consecration of the walls and gates, as barriers and entrances to the city of Jerusalem, also confirms the sacredness of the city and its inhabitants.

62. זכרון, *BDB*, 272. The term זכרון in 2:20 is, essentially, "proof of citizenship."

63. Wright details what he calls "שמע Schema" that run throughout Neh 1–6 (*Rebuilding Identity*, 27–29). See also Donna Laird, *Negotiating Power in Ezra–Nehemiah*, AIL 26 (Atlanta: SBL Press, 2016), 204–5.

Neh 3:1-32

1 Then the high priest Eliashib set to work with his fellow priests and rebuilt the Sheep Gate. They consecrated it and set up its doors; they consecrated it as far as the Tower of the Hundred and as far as the Tower of Hananel. 2 And the men of Jericho built next to him. And next to them Zaccur son of Imri built.

3 The sons of Hassenaah built the Fish Gate; they laid its beams and set up its doors, its bolts, and its bars. 4 Next to them Meremoth son of Uriah son of Hakkoz made repairs. Next to them Meshullam son of Berechiah son of Meshezabel made repairs. Next to them Zadok son of Baana made repairs. 5 Next to them the Tekoites made repairs, but their nobles would not put their shoulders to the work of their Lord.

6 Joiada son of Paseah and Meshullam son of Besodeiah repaired the Old Gate; they laid its beams and set up its doors, its bolts, and its bars. 7 Next to them repairs were made by Melatiah the Gibeonite and Jadon the Meronothite—the men of Gibeon and of Mizpah—who were under the jurisdiction of the governor of the province Beyond the River. 8 Next to them Uzziel son of Harhaiah, one of the goldsmiths, made repairs.

Nehemiah 3:1-32 identifies the repatriates who fund or physically repair the wall(s) around Jerusalem, which memorializes these members of the Judean community and attaches them to parts of the wall they repair. The majority of those building around the perimeter are identified as men (אנוש) three times and sons (בן) thirty-five. Wedged within this account of men hewing stones and setting wooden beams is a report that the ruler of half the district of Jerusalem, Shallum son of Hallohesh, makes repairs with his daughters (בנות, Neh 3:12) between those repairing the Tower of the Ovens (Neh 3:11) and the Valley Gate (Neh 3:13): "Next to him Shallum son of Hallohesh, ruler of half the district of Jerusalem, made repairs, he and his daughters" (Neh 3:12). Their inclusion in a list of predominantly men makes us wonder about the role that women played in construction activities involving public structures in Persian Judah.[64]

Shallum's unnamed daughters are among the few biblical women credited with construction. Yet not all translations or translators agree that these women belong in this memorial list of builders. The Syriac translation of Nehemiah 3:12 reads "and his sons" rather than "and his

64. There are some who would like to read בנותיו, "his daughters," as "its [Jerusalem's] surrounding villages." H. G. M. Williamson (*Ezra–Nehemiah*, WBC 16 [Waco: Word, 1985], 207) is among those who disagree with this rendering and translates בנותיו more literally as "his [Shallum's] daughters."

Next to him Hananiah, one of the per-
fumers, made repairs, and they restored
Jerusalem as far as the Broad Wall.
[9]Next to them Rephaiah son of Hur, ruler
of half the district of Jerusalem, made
repairs. [10]Next to them Jedaiah son of
Harumaph made repairs opposite his
house, and next to him Hattush son of
Hashabneiah made repairs. [11]Malchi-
jah son of Harim and Hasshub son of
Pahath-moab repaired another section
and the Tower of the Ovens. [12]Next to
him Shallum son of Hallohesh, ruler of
half the district of Jerusalem, made repairs, he and his daughters.

[13]Hanun and the inhabitants of Za-
noah repaired the Valley Gate; they rebuilt it and set up its doors, its bolts, and
its bars and repaired a thousand cubits
of the wall, as far as the Dung Gate.

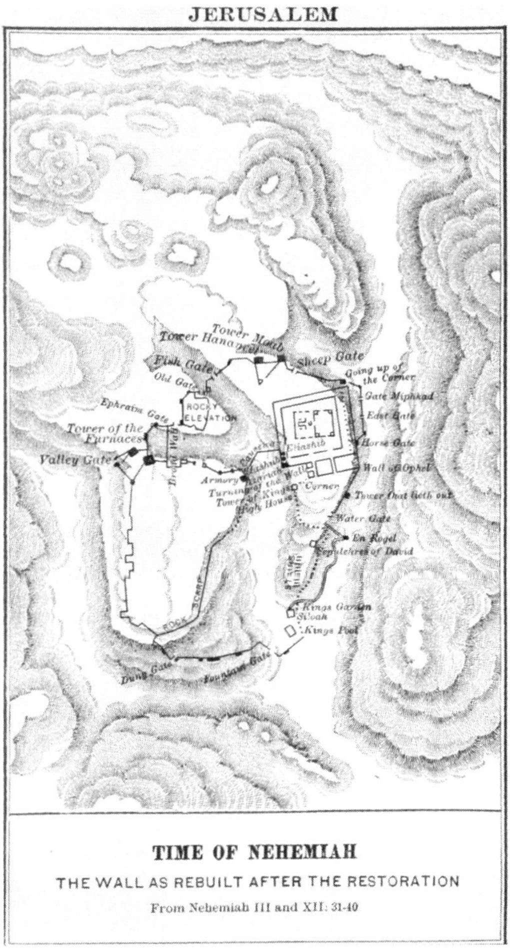

JERUSALEM

TIME OF NEHEMIAH

THE WALL AS REBUILT AFTER THE RESTORATION

From Nehemiah III and XII: 31-40

Map of Jerusalem in the Time of Nehemiah, in *The Holy Land in Geography and in History* by Townsend MacCoun, 1899, https://commons.wikimedia.org/wiki/File:MACCOUN(1899)_p133_JERUSALEM_-_TIME_OF_NEHEMIAH.jpg.

Neh 3:1-32 (cont.)

[14]Malchijah son of Rechab, ruler of the district of Beth-haccherem, repaired the Dung Gate; he rebuilt it and set up its doors, its bolts, and its bars.

[15]And Shallum son of Colhozeh, ruler of the district of Mizpah, repaired the Fountain Gate; he rebuilt it and covered it and set up its doors, its bolts, and its bars, and he built the wall of the Pool of Shelah of the King's Garden, as far as the stairs that go down from the city of David. [16]After him Nehemiah son of Azbuk, ruler of half the district of Beth-zur, repaired from a point opposite the graves of David, as far as the artificial pool and the House of the Warriors. [17]After him the Levites made repairs: Rehum son of Bani; next to him Hashabiah, ruler of half the district of Keilah, made repairs for his district. [18]After him their kin made repairs: Binnui, son of Henadad, ruler of half the district of Keilah; [19]next to him Ezer son of Jeshua, ruler of Mizpah, repaired another section opposite the ascent to the armory at the Angle. [20]After him Baruch son of Zabbai repaired another section from the Angle to the door of the house of the high priest Eliashib. [21]After him Meremoth son of Uriah son of Hakkoz repaired another section from the door of the house of Eliashib to the end of the house of Eliashib. [22]After him the priests, the men of the surrounding area, made repairs. [23]After them Benjamin and Hasshub made repairs opposite their house. After them Azariah son of Maaseiah son of Ananiah made repairs beside his own house. [24]After him Binnui son of Henadad repaired another section, from the house of Azariah to the Angle and to the corner. [25]Palal son of Uzai repaired opposite the Angle and the tower projecting

daughters" (ובנותיו), erasing these women from the list.[65] There are examples of textual tampering that replace women with men. For example, some modern English translations of Romans 16:7 interpret the name of the apostle Junia (Ἰουνία) as a masculine name, Junias, despite the lack of attestations to the masculine form of the name in the Greek.[66] The translators do not believe that a woman could be an apostle. Likewise, some translators do not consider women to be capable builders and erase them from the list. Some insist that "daughters"' in Nehemiah 3:12 is euphemistic for the *hamlets* of Jerusalem rather than a reference to actual women who repair the wall.[67] Others agree that Shallum's daughters play a role in building the wall, but only because Shallum has no sons.

65. *BHS*, 1433, textual note a.

66. For a full discussion on Junia's gender, see Jay Eldon Epps, *Junia: The First Woman Apostl*e (Minneapolis: Fortress, 2005).

67. Eskenazi refers to L. W. Batten's 1913 commentary on Ezra and Nehemiah in "Out from the Shadows: Biblical Women in the Postexilic Era," *JSOT* 54 (1992): 39–40.

from the upper house of the king at the court of the guard. After him Pedaiah son of Parosh [26]and the temple servants living on Ophel made repairs up to a point opposite the Water Gate on the east and the projecting tower. [27]After him the Tekoites repaired another section opposite the great projecting tower as far as the wall of Ophel.

[28]Above the Horse Gate the priests made repairs, each one opposite his own house. [29]After them Zadok son of Immer made repairs opposite his own house. After him Shemaiah son of Shecaniah, the keeper of the East Gate, made repairs. [30]After him Hananiah son of Shelemiah and Hanun sixth son of Zalaph repaired another section. After him Meshullam son of Berechiah made repairs opposite his living quarters. [31]After him Malchijah, one of the goldsmiths, made repairs as far as the house of the temple servants and of the merchants, opposite the Muster Gate, and to the upper room of the corner. [32]And between the upper room of the corner and the Sheep Gate the goldsmiths and the merchants made repairs.

The Erasure of Rey

When the blockbuster movie *Star Wars: The Force Awakens* hit the big screen in December 2015, many women and girls cheered because a strong, brave, and intelligent woman, Rey, a Jedi knight in training, was the main protagonist in the movie, but attempts to buy Rey action figures generally proved futile. Only male characters less important to the story were bundled for sale or placed in game sets. Incensed fans across genders launched the movement #wheresrey. Matthew Rozsa, writing for *Salon Magazine*, shared cultural journalist Michael Boehm's report of a meeting that took place with executives to plan what *Star Wars* products should be sold. He writes: "Eventually, the product vendors were specifically directed to exclude the Rey character from all 'Star Wars'-related merchandise, says the insider. 'We know what sells,' the industry insider was told. 'No boy wants to be given a product with a female character on it.'"[68] The attempt to erase Rey from products marketed to children follows a long history of writing out of the narrative women, and others less powerful in society, though their actions were essential to community well-being.

See also Fried, *Nehemiah*, 98–99. The suffix translated as "his" in the NRSVue can also be rendered the masculine "its," which refers to Jerusalem as a district (masculine).

68. Sarah Seltzer, "Did *Star Wars* Toymakers Intentionally Exclude Rey?," *Flavor Wire* (January 22, 2016), https://www.flavorwire.com/557366/did-star-wars-toymakers-intentionally-exclude-rey.

The presence of Shallum's daughters in the list of builders opens the possibility that women, often hidden behind a wall of masculinity in Ezra–Nehemiah's account of Jerusalem's reconstruction, have more agency than the text and its interpreters suggest.[69] While there are not many accounts of women builders, 1 Chronicles credits Ephraim's daughter, Sheerah, with building "both Lower and Upper Beth-horon and Uzzen-sheerah" (1 Chr 7:24). Today, women represent nearly 10 percent of the construction workers in the United States.[70] The National Association of Women in Construction (NAWIC), the National Association of Black Women in Construction (NABWIC), and Latinas in Construction provide partnerships, advocacy, and training for female construction workers in the United States.[71] Whether or not Shallum's daughters take hammer and axe to fix a broken gate or provide financial resources to make it happen, Nehemiah's list suggests that their contribution is significant enough to memorialize.

While Nehemiah's list captures those who participate in the reconstruction efforts, it also recalls the names of those who refuse to participate, namely, the nobles of Tekoa who "would not put their shoulders to the work of their Lord" (3:5).[72] The problem is political and religious. Tekoa is ten miles south of Jerusalem; perhaps these nobles are caught between supporting Geshem, who controls the southern part of Judah, and supporting Nehemiah. For Nehemiah, repairing the walls is the work of the Lord, and everyone should be involved, even those with status or a titled position. The commentary on the nobles' failure to participate insinuates that they are out of touch with the desires of the Tekoan community, who build with Nehemiah. Speculatively, the nobles' political allegiances are stronger than their religious commitment to support the work of the Lord.

Nehemiah's walls physically and metaphorically encircle the city of Jerusalem to protect Jerusalem's temple and the repatriate community from the people of the land who threaten their newly forming identity and

69. Eskenazi, "Out from the Shadows," 40.

70. Chip Mansfield, "Opportunities for Women in the Construction Industry," *American Council for Construction Education* (May 31, 2023), https://www.acce-hq.org/post/opportunities-for-women -in-the-construction-industry?gad=1&gclid=CjwKCAjww7KmBhAyEiwA5-PUSg3bWcjj2BqD_YWcLVjYjmFh9IMWWGQZjbmgnu4vIz99vqLSMTA2GRoCag8QAvD_BwE.

71. National Association of Women in Construction, https://www.nawic.org/; National Association of Black Women in Construction, https://nabwic.org/; Latinas in Construction, https://www.latinasinconstruction.net/en/.

72. The people of Tekoa build two parts of the wall on the southern side (Neh 3:5, 27).

sacred space. These walls, and Nehemiah's list of builders or patrons, memorialize these repatriates who are, for Ezra and Nehemiah, the true Israel.

The construction of walls for protection, privacy, and boundaries is often warranted. The wall signifies a renewed political, ethnic, and religious identity that will protect the center of community, Jerusalem. On the other hand, walls limit communication and cultural exchange among communities and can escalate tension between groups. A contemporary example is the tension with the construction of the border wall separating Mexico from the United States. Those who support the wall argue that it helps control the flow of migrants into the United States. For those who oppose the wall, it is a symbol of division and distrust.

The very act of building together creates community as some families work side by side and others attend to the spaces adjacent to their houses (Neh 3:10, 23, 28-30). With the availability of materials, Persian resources, and outside support, some persons can engage in home improvements (e.g., walls near them) that were not previously possible. The frequent use of the phrase "next to them they made repairs" underscores the close coordination between builders on either side to align their bricks and wooden beams.

The presence of the נתינים, "temple servants" or "the ones who are given" (Neh 3:26, 31), as participants in the wall's reconstruction complicates the portrait of voluntarism and communal solidarity. The identity of this group is ambiguous as most translations refer to them as "temple servants" (NRSVue, NIV) or choose to transliterate the Hebrew text and call them *nethinim*. The Septuagint's ναθινιμ suggests a guild of skilled servants. The Hebrew dictionary (*HALOT*) refers to them as slaves bound to the temple.[73] The book of Joshua associates the נתינים with the Gibeonites who deceive the Israelites by forcing a treaty and are cursed forever as temple servants (Josh 9:1-23). When the term is interpreted as "temple servants," it implies some sort of volunteerism on the part of the group. However, when interpreted as "temple slaves," the term suggests the absence of volunteerism, like the use of enslaved people to build the Egyptian cities of Pithom and Rameses for Pharaoh (Exod 1:11), the Colosseum in Rome, the Chateau of Versailles, and the Great Wall of China. In the United States, groups of enslaved peoples were instrumental in the construction of the US Capitol, the White House, and other major buildings. In these cases, the creation of a community is not forged but forced.

73. נתינים, *HALOT*, 732.

Nehemiah 4:1–7:73a

Triumph Amidst Challenges

Nehemiah 4–7 continues the efforts and challenges in rebuilding the walls of Jerusalem under Nehemiah's leadership. In chapter 4, Nehemiah and the repatriates face significant opposition from local adversaries like Sanballat and Tobiah, who mock and threaten them. Despite this, they persist in rebuilding the wall. In chapter 5, Nehemiah confronts these issues, advocating for economic reform and restoring properties to the poor, thus highlighting his leadership in addressing external threats and internal ethics. In chapter 6, Nehemiah deals with continued attempts by enemies to intimidate him and halt the construction. He navigates through plots and misinformation to ensure the completion of the wall without succumbing to fear or distraction. Finally, in chapter 7, the walls and gates are completed, and security protocols are established, ending with all of Israel settling in their towns.

Walls of Distrust (4:1-15)

In Nehemiah 4:1-15, the Judeans, led by Nehemiah, and the people of the land, led by Sanballat, are suspicious of one another.[1] Nehemiah's group may be a small contingent surrounded by hostile people—the Samarians, Ammonites, Ashdodites, and Arabs. Yet Nehemiah enters Jerusalem with Artaxerxes's blessing, financial support, and military escorts.

The chapter begins as an "angry and greatly enraged" Sanballat hears (שׁמע) that Nehemiah is building the wall (Neh 4:1). The Hebrew term

1. Nehemiah 4:1-15 (English Version) is 3:33–4:9 in the Hebrew text.

Neh 4:1-15

[1]Now when Sanballat heard that we were building the wall, he was angry and greatly enraged, and he mocked the Jews. [2]He said in the presence of his associates and of the army of Samaria, "What are these feeble Jews doing? Will they restore it by themselves? Will they offer sacrifice? Will they finish it in a day? Will they revive the stones out of the heaps of rubbish—burned ones at that?" [3]Tobiah the Ammonite was beside him, and he said, "That stone wall they are building—any fox going up on it would break it down!" [4]Hear, O our God, for we are despised; turn their taunt back on their own heads, and give them over as plunder in a land of captivity. [5]Do not cover their guilt, and do not let their sin be blotted out from your sight, for they have raged against the builders.

[6]So we rebuilt the wall, and all the wall was joined together to half its height, for the people had a mind to work.

[7]But when Sanballat and Tobiah and the Arabs and the Ammonites and the Ashdodites heard that the repairing of the walls of Jerusalem was going forward and the gaps were beginning to be closed, they were very angry [8]and all plotted together to come and fight against Jerusalem and to cause con-

שמע, meaning "to hear," is found several times in Nehemiah 4 and 6 (Neh 4:1, 4, 7, 15, 20; 6:1, 6, 7, 16) and reinforces the absence of in-person communication.[2] In the presence of his associates (אחיו), he mocks the Judeans and sarcastically questions the feasibility of their reconstruction efforts. The Hebrew translated "associates" is literally "brothers" (אחים) and likely refers to the Arabs, Ammonites, and Ashdodites mentioned in 4:7, which suggests a close connection between Sanballat and those with him (the army of Samaria and Tobiah the Ammonite). Behind Sanballat's taunting questions—"What are these feeble Jews doing? Will they restore it by themselves? Will they offer sacrifice? Will they finish it in a day? Will they revive the stones out of the heaps of rubbish—burned ones at that?" (Neh 4:2b)—lurks fear of these perceived outsiders' authority and strength. Tobiah adds to the mockery by doubting the wall's ability to handle the weight of a small fox (Neh 4:3). This reference highlights the dichotomy between Sanballat and his group as insiders and Nehemiah and his group as outsiders.

The insertion of an imprecatory prayer (Neh 4:4-5) abruptly interrupts their mockery. This type of prayer curses or wishes evil on an enemy. The

2. שמע appears in Neh 6:1 in the *nifal* or passive form of the verb and can be translated "reported."

fusion in it. [9]So we prayed to our God and set a guard as a protection against them day and night.

[10]But Judah said, "The strength of the burden bearers is failing, and there is too much rubbish so that we are unable to work on the wall." [11]And our enemies said, "They will not know or see anything before we come upon them and kill them and stop the work." [12]When the Jews who lived near them came, they said to us ten times, "From all the places where they live they will come up against us." [13]So in the lowest parts of the space behind the wall, in open places, I stationed the people according to their families, with their swords, their spears, and their bows. [14]After I looked these things over, I stood up and said to the nobles and the officials and the rest of the people, "Do not be afraid of them. Remember the LORD, who is great and awesome, and fight for your kin, your sons, your daughters, your wives, and your households."

[15]When our enemies heard that their plot was known to us and that God had frustrated it, we all returned to the wall, each to his work.

prayer contains no attribution. The supplicant(s) asks God to inflict great harm on their enemies as recompense for their insults (Neh 4:4-5). They desire that God "give them over as plunder in a land of captivity" (Neh 4:4) and that their sins are never forgiven (Neh 4:5). Typically, the prayers scattered throughout the book of Nehemiah identify the supplicant (see Neh 1:5-11; 2:4; 4:9; 5:19; 6:14; 11:17). The prayer's narrative placement and lack of provenance, however, offers opportunities to ascribe it to Sanballat and his allies or to Nehemiah. The narrative flow in 4:1-5 could easily move from Sanballat's questions and Tobiah's taunts to a prayer from the mouths of Sanballat and his allies. These local leaders have a stake in Jerusalem and the temple. They too are filled with apprehension that their opponents threaten their livelihood and their control in the territory.[3]

3. There is archaeological evidence that a temple dedicated to the God of Israel was built on Mt. Gerizim (in Samaria) during the mid-fifth century (see Yitzhak Magen, "The Dating of the First Phase of the Samaritan Temple on Mount Gerizim in Light of Archaeological Evidence," in *Judah and the Judeans in the Fourth Century, B.C.E.*, ed. Oded Lipschits, Gary N. Knoppers, and Rainer Albertz [Winona Lake, IN: Eisenbrauns, 2007], 176; and Magen, "Bells, Pendants, Snakes & Stones: A Samaritan Temple to the Lord on Mt. Gerizim," *BAR* 36, no. 6 [November/December 2010]: 26–35, 70). Likewise, the Jewish community in Judah rebuilt the temple in Jerusalem. Temples provide a central place to collect the monies required to support the temple structure and pay tribute to Persia. Collecting these monies could only happen when

Here Nehemiah responds to Sanballat's rage (כעס) toward the repatriates by asking that God "turn their taunt [חרפה] back on their own heads," tossing the enemy out of the land and into captivity to be dispersed as booty (Neh 4:4), that the enemy live in a perpetual state of sin (חטאת), and that God not cloak their guilt (Neh 4:5). In essence, Nehemiah prays that Sanballat and his associates experience their own exile similar to what Israel experienced with the Babylonians (2 Kgs 24:16; 25:11; 2 Chr 36:10-21). The Jews have already lived this punishment expressed by Ezra years earlier: "From the days of our ancestors to this day we have been deep in guilt, and for our iniquities we, our kings, and our priests have been handed over to the kings of the lands, to the sword, to captivity, to plundering, and to utter shame,[4] as is now the case" (Ezra 9:7). The prayer repeats themes found earlier in Nehemiah. For example, Nehemiah 4:4 employs the same term that Hanani and his companions used to describe the "shame" (חרפה) that exists in Jerusalem because of the destroyed walls (Neh 1:3). The prayer resonates with many of the imprecatory prayers in Nehemiah that promote the views of the supplicant and his character while advancing the plot.[5]

Rather than attempt to work things out through dialogue (which has yet to happen in Nehemiah) or entertain the possibility that the enemy has a relationship with, in this case, the same deity, the supplicant piously petitions God to act violently against the opposition. The prayer assumes God's exclusive support. It brings to mind Mark Twain's satirical prayer that he wrote during the Philippine-American War but that was not published until 1916 during World War I. A sample:

> O Lord our God . . .
> help us to tear their soldiers to bloody shreds with our shells;
> help us to cover their smiling fields with the pale forms of their patriot dead;
> help us to drown the thunder of the guns with the shrieks of their wounded writhing in pain;

---

citizens were committed to supporting the temple. These two temples may compete for these monies, which adds to the "inner-Yahwistic" conflict between the Samarians and the repatriates (see Altmann, *Economics in Persian-Period Biblical Texts*, 151–52).

4. The Hebrew used for "shame" in Ezra 9:7 is בשת rather than the term חרפה used by Nehemiah in his prayer.

5. Mark Boda, "Prayer as Rhetoric in the Book of Nehemiah," in *New Perspectives on Ezra–Nehemiah: History and Historiography, Text, Literature, and Interpretation*, ed. Isaac Kalimi (Winona Lake, IN: Eisenbrauns, 2012), 276–80. See excursus on "Prayer in Nehemiah" in Neh 1:5-11.

> help us to lay waste their humble homes with a hurricane of fire. . . .
> We ask it, in the spirit of love, of Him Who is the Source of Love,
> and Who is the ever-faithful refuge and friend of all that are sore beset
> and seek
> His aid with humble and contrite hearts. Amen.[6]

As Twain's prayer indicates, when supplicants presume that God is on their side, the prayer becomes a weapon rather than a petition. In Nehemiah, it seems cruel to wish the same trauma on others—to hope that they will be forcefully displaced from the land. Sanballat and his allies also have a strong relationship to Jerusalem and its surrounding territories. They have a cultural and theological investment in this space that becomes even more pronounced between the exile (587 BCE) and Nehemiah's return (ca. 450 BCE)—a period when they were stewards of the land and religion. The repatriates and the people of the land each believe that they have valid claims to the land and community identity.

Sanballat's insults and the imprecatory prayer (Neh 4:1-5) reveal an ugly reality. While Nehemiah's account of Sanballat's statements cannot be verified, if Sanballat mocks the people, it is possible that Nehemiah communicates these insults to the repatriates. Groups targeted because of race, gender, religion, sexuality, class, politics, education, and other identities often navigate a world of slurs, threats, and acts of violence directed against them. In today's global political climate, name-calling and threats are all too common. Exacerbating the situation, misinformation and alternative views of the situation create a culture of distrust. The prayer, if prayed by Nehemiah and his group, captures the mocking and threats of Sanballat, Tobiah, and Geshem. It could strengthen their resolve to build the wall and cements their relationship as a group defying a common enemy.[7] Following the conclusion of the prayer in 4:6, Nehemiah states that the people completed the wall to half of its height and that it surrounds the circumference of the city—a major feat that results from them having "a mind to work."[8]

Sanballat and his allies are enraged when they hear that, despite their threats, the gaps in the Jerusalem walls are repaired (Neh 4:7-8). Again,

6. Mark Twain, "The War Prayer," https://warprayer.org/.

7. Jacob Wright, *Rebuilding Identity: The Nehemiah-Memoir and Its Earliest Readers*, BZAW 348 (Berlin: de Gruyter, 2004), 29.

8. The Septuagint lacks 4:6 and moves directly from the prayer to Sanballat and his allies' anger that the Judeans are still rebuilding.

Sanballat and his compatriots are not physically present in Jerusalem and must rely on hearsay for their information. Moving from taunts and insults, Sanballat, Tobiah, the Arabs, the Ashdodites, and the Ammonites plan to attack Jerusalem (Neh 4:8). We are left wondering how Nehemiah learned of this plot or if it is a ploy designed to strengthen his own group's resolve.

Nehemiah and the Judeans seek divine protection with the belief that God is solely on their side, and with this protection in mind they set a guard against the enemies day and night (Neh 4:9).[9] The reconstruction efforts are taking a toll on the workers. The text describes the waning strength of the "burden bearers," which could be interpreted as physical or metaphorical (diminishing in resolve or determination) or both, given the sheer volume of the task. The people of Judah lament, expressing their frustration and exhaustion: "there is too much rubbish so that we are unable to work on the wall" (Neh 4:10). Meanwhile Nehemiah shares that their enemies plot a violent attack to halt construction (Neh 4:11). According to the text, members from the Jewish communities who live in the surrounding territories (Samaria, Geshem, Ammon, Ashdod, and Arab cities in the south) approach Nehemiah and confirm Sanballat's plot by sharing the same news, "When the Jews who lived near them came, they said to us ten times, 'From all the places where they live they will come up against us'" (Neh 4:12).[10] It is unclear if the threat is directed only to those building the wall in Jerusalem or also to the Jews in the surrounding territories.

In response, Nehemiah arms his troops (workers) and positions them in strategic parts of the wall to ambush any hostile forces (Neh 4:13). He is certain of God's support and uses this assurance to encourage his tired people: "Do not be afraid of them. Remember the Lord, who is great and awesome, and fight for your kin, your sons, your daughters, your wives, and your households" (Neh 4:14). Nehemiah underscores the significance of belonging to his group by employing familial language. His rhetoric constructs a familial identity. They belong to the family of God; Sanballat and his allies do not. This is one of the few times where Nehemiah identifies the importance of daughters and wives as family members. They belong.

In 4:15 we come full circle as Nehemiah's enemies hear that he and those building the wall have heard about a murderous plot against him

9. Nehemiah emphasizes that they pray to "our God" (Neh 4:9).

10. Nehemiah 4:12 is unclear whether the reference to ten times refers to ten individual people or the news is repeated that many times.

(Neh 4:15). Despite this account, there is no textual evidence of an actual encounter between Sanballat and Nehemiah. In essence, the problem is possibly due to either spies or hearsay predicated on the rumors that each group hears about the other. Neither side wants to work matters out diplomatically; each allows rumors to escalate to anger. The potential conflict brought about by these rumors could be detrimental for both groups. Given Nehemiah's Persian support, any violence Sanballat inflicts on Nehemiah and the Judeans could result in Sanballat's demotion if not his death. Therefore, it makes little political sense for Sanballat to goad the Samarian army into confronting the Judeans, nor is it wise for Persian-appointed governors to harm one another. Overall, in Nehemiah 4:1-15 we witness what happens when both sides consider themselves threatened and respond out of fear of the other.

Defense Walls (4:16-23)

Sanballat's impending invasion has brought about the militarization of the city where the workers must arm themselves with spears, shields, bows, and body-armor to protect their families and complete the work (Neh 4:13, 15-18).[11] Leaders are stationed behind all of the builders (Neh 4:16-17). The one with the trumpet (shofar) stands next to Nehemiah to warn the people in case of an attack (Neh 4:18). The blowing of the shofar would serve as an alarm signal to alert the workers and their families of the potential danger. In essence, Nehemiah creates an armed paramilitary group, where the laborers must now become soldiers.

Today, our communities are experiencing a growing trend of armed conflicts, where individuals feel compelled to carry firearms for various reasons, including personal protection, safeguarding their property, or ensuring the safety of their families from actual or perceived threats. It is concerning that a young person turning around in a driveway is tragically shot and that a teenager who mistakenly goes to the wrong house to pick up his brother meets a similar fate. Today, even police departments are equipped with military-grade weapons and protective gear to counterbalance the military-grade weaponry that some citizens possess. This arms escalation in both law enforcement and civilian circles raises important questions about public safety, the role of policing, and the need for constructive dialogue and policy changes to address these challenges.

11. Nehemiah 4:16-23 is 4:10-17 in the Masoretic Text.

Neh 4:16-23

[16]From that day on, half of my servants worked on construction, and half held the spears, shields, bows, and body-armor, and the leaders posted themselves behind the whole house of Judah [17]who were building the wall. The burden bearers carried their loads in such a way that each labored on the work with one hand and with the other held a weapon. [18]And each of the builders had his sword strapped at his side while he built. The man who sounded the trumpet was beside me. [19]And I said to the nobles, the officials, and the rest of the people, "The work is great and widely spread out, and we are separated far from one another on the wall. [20]Rally to us wherever you hear the sound of the trumpet. Our God will fight for us."

[21]So we labored at the work, and half of them held the spears from break of dawn until the stars came out. [22]I also said to the people at that time, "Let every man and his servant pass the night inside Jerusalem, so that they may be a guard for us by night and may labor by day." [23]So neither I nor my brothers nor my servants nor the men of the guard who followed me ever took off our clothes; each kept his weapon in his right hand.

The threat of an attack by Sanballat and his allies hovers over the builders. The builders, spread far apart, will rely on the shofar to sound if an attack occurs (Neh 4:19). With the sounding of the shofar comes the protection of God who will fight on their behalf (Neh 4:20). The physical labor and mental acuity required for those engaged in lifting, hauling, and carrying weapons while working on the Jerusalem wall seems particularly challenging, especially when carried out in scorching heat "from break of dawn until the stars came out" (Neh 4:21). Further, Nehemiah requires each builder and his servant to spend their nights in Jerusalem, away from their homes, to protect the building project and, possibly, to ensure that workers return.[12] Workers are expected to be ready to fight at all times: "neither I nor my brothers nor my servants nor the men of the guard who followed me ever took off our clothes; each kept his weapon in his right hand" (Neh 4:23). The end of verse 23 is possibly corrupt. The Masoretic Text (MT) literally says, איש שלחו המים, "a man his weapon the water," while the Septuagint (LXX) omits the phrase entirely. Whether one interprets the MT phrase as "his weapon in his right hand" or "never relieves himself," or the LXX as "there was

12. Joseph Blenkinsopp, *Ezra–Nehemiah: A Commentary*, OTL (Philadelphia: Westminster, 1988), 252.

not a man that put off his garments," it is clear that the task at hand is of a serious nature, and the individuals assigned to it are committed and focused.[13] In a sense, the builders are on call 24/7, and most people will go to great lengths when they have a vested interest in the outcome of something, be it person, place, or thing.

Yet, it is unclear whether everyone working on the wall does so willingly or benefits from the wall's completion (Neh 4:10). In times of crisis, the welfare of the entire population frequently becomes a higher priority than any personal interests of an individual. This is demonstrated during periods when it becomes necessary to institute a military draft or activate reserve forces from the National Guard to safeguard national or civic interests. These persons are "on call" and ready to serve at a moment's notice. Nehemiah 4:16-23 also raises the question for contemporary readers about private citizens arming themselves against perceived enemies. Moreover, the arming of private citizens is framed in a religious context where everything occurs under the watchful eyes and support of the deity. Today, with the formation of paramilitary and militia groups, one can speculate on whether these groups are self-serving or serve and protect the interest of the community, or both.

Economic Walls (5:1-5)

In Nehemiah 5, the narrative shifts its focus from conflicts between Nehemiah and the Samarians regarding the construction of the walls (as seen in chapter 4) to conflicts within the community concerning economic matters.[14] The portrait of solidarity in wall building breaks down in chapter 5. The intra-Jewish conflict in Nehemiah 5 describes the conditions in Persian Judah where those with capital increase their wealth at the expense of everyone else. Here, we find a world in which economic dysfunction is intensified by food shortages; families are falling into overwhelming debt.

13. Lisbeth Fried emends שְׁלְחוֹ, which she says is meaningless, to שָׁלְחוּ, which means "they sent out." Lisbeth S. Fried, *Nehemiah: A Commentary*, Critical Commentaries (Sheffield: Sheffield Phoenix, 2021), 122, 129.

14. Peter Altmann considers Nehemiah an "excursus" on economics (*Economics in Persian-Period Biblical Texts: Their Interactions with Economic Developments in the Persian Period and Earlier Biblical Traditions*, FAT 109 [Tübingen: Mohr Siebeck, 2016], 220). Jacob Wright separates chapter 5 from within the memoir and compares this chapter with the reforms in Nehemiah 13. Wright, along with other scholars, believes that chapter 5 has three distinct parts written at different periods: 5:1-13, 14-18, 19 (*Rebuilding Identity*, chap. 8).

Neh 5:1-5

[1]Now there was a great outcry of the people and of their wives against their Jewish kin. [2]For there were those who said, "With our sons and our daughters, we are many; we must get grain, so that we may eat and stay alive." [3]There were also those who said, "We are having to pledge our fields, our vineyards, and our houses in order to get grain during the famine." [4]And there were those who said, "We are having to borrow money on our fields and vineyards to pay the king's tax. [5]Now our flesh is the same as that of our kindred; our children are the same as their children; and yet we are forcing our sons and daughters to be slaves, and some of our daughters have been ravished; we are powerless, and our fields and vineyards now belong to others."

Nehemiah's Use in Community Organizing

A cursory Google search for Nehemiah yields a host of organizations bearing this biblical official's name, including faith-based development organizations, international mission groups, youth programs, women's shelters, gardening projects, and home repair organizations.[15] Nehemiah's commitment to urban renewal through repairing the walls of Jerusalem makes him an appropriate model. Andrew McLeod, a cooperative development consultant, considers the book of Nehemiah to be a "manual for grassroots community organizing" because the people, rather than the government, work together to enact political and economic change.[16]

In Nehemiah 5:1 there is an outcry of the "people" and their wives against their "Jewish kin" or "brother Jews" (JPS *Tanakh*). The inten-

15. Among the organizations influenced by Nehemiah and especially economics and redevelopment are Nehemiah Economic Development Inc. in Brooklyn, NY (http://www.nehemiahed.org/); Nehemiah Project Community Development Corporation in Camden, NJ (http://nehemiahcdc.org/); A Christian business entrepreneur organization, The Nehemiah Project (https://nehemiahproject.org/mission-vision/), in Lake Oswego, OR; The Nehemiah Project, a faith-based community development organization in Altoona, PA (https://www.tnppa.org/home/).

16. Andrew McLeod, "Why Nehemiah?," *Nehemian Organizing: How to Rebuild a City* (blog) (December 20, 2010), https://nehemian.wordpress.com/2010/12/20/why-nehemiah/. He is also the author of *Holy Cooperation! Building Graceful Economies* (Eugene, OR: Wipf & Stock, 2009).

tional distinction between the people (העם) and their wives (נשים)[17] underscores the fact that women are not counted as full members of this male-centered community. Still, these women, who most likely maintain their homes and farms while their husbands build walls and who have a stake in the community, refuse to remain silent. Also, as adult males are conscripted for military service for long periods of time, women become the heads of the households.[18]

The Hebrew noun translated as "outcry" (צעקה) is often a cry to God for justice.[19] For example, in Genesis 18:20-21 there is an outcry against the people of Sodom, which Ezekiel 16:49 explains as the mistreatment of the poor and needy. In his speech to Job, Elihu reminds him that God hears the outcry of the poor and afflicted (Job 34:28). Here, the people protest that they need grain for sustenance and in order to procure grain, the people must place their fields, vineyards, and houses as pledges (ערבים, Neh 5:2-3). These necessities include borrowing to pay the king's tax, procurements that all take place during a time of famine (Neh 5:3, 4).

The King's Tax

Families are responsible for paying the "king's tax" (מדת המלך, v. 4) or royal tribute. The book of Ezra implies that there are royal revenues that could be related to the king's tax (Ezra 4:13, 20). Peter Altmann notes that in the past the people could pay this obligatory tax with gifts, but this practice soon shifted to paying in silver, maybe coins.[20] They may have had to convert their crops into coins, participate in the commercial markets to obtain them, or borrow silver to meet the demands for payment.[21] Even if the people were able to pay the king's tax with produce, the amount owed

17. The Hebrew word נשים means both "women" and "wives."

18. Ellen F. Davis, *Scripture, Culture, and Agriculture: The Agrarian Reading of the Bible* (Cambridge: Cambridge University Press, 2009), 149–50. Leo Perdue and Warren Carter state that each satrapy needed to provide one thousand troops to Persia's army; *Israel and Empire: A Postcolonial History of Israel and Early Judaism*, ed. Coleman A. Baker (London: Bloomsbury T&T Clark, 2015), 115.

19. HALOT, paragraph 3, https://accordance.bible/link/read/HALOT#16044. For other examples of cries for justice directed to God, see Exod 3:7-9; 22:22; Ps 9:13; Job 27:9; 34:28.

20. Peter Altmann, "Tithes for the Clergy and Taxes for the King: State and Temple Contributions in Nehemiah," *CBQ* 76 (2014): 216.

21. Altmann, "Tithes for the Clergy and Taxes for the King," 216–19, and Neh 5:4.

was calculated in silver.[22] These loans increased debt and added to financial hardship. Those struggling financially expressed their sense of powerlessness (Neh 5:4) in a system that forced them to sell their fields and use their own children as debt collateral (Neh 5:5). Altmann finds that the king's tax might have taken the form of add-on payments like dues and taxes that are eventually placed in the royal treasury. While taxes provide the means to create better communities through providing public services (e.g., roads, governmental services), oppressive taxes or high interest loans can throw an individual or family into a downward spiral, as we witness both today and in what happened to families in Nehemiah's Judah (Neh 5:4-5).

The people emphasize that their tormentors are members within the community and not the Persian king. They insist, "Our flesh is the same as that of our kindred; our children are the same as their children" (Neh 5:5).[23] The situation has become so desperate that those in debt are "forcing" their sons and daughters into enslavement (עבדים, Neh 5:5). The desperation of the parents makes them complicit in the trafficking of their own children. The widow in 2 Kings 4:1-7 faces a similar threat when creditors seek to enslave her two sons to offset her debts. In Nehemiah 5:5, the subjugation of both sons and daughters points to their exploitation as child laborers. Today, one in five children from poor families is put to work in fields, households, factories, and other places of employment.[24] These children are compelled to engage in labor either to assist their families financially or are taken advantage of by individuals or businesses seeking to profit from the labor of the most vulnerable. For example, chocolate, a major commodity throughout the world, is often produced with cocoa harvested by young children.[25]

22. Altmann, "Tithes for the Clergy and Taxes for the King," 219.

23. The term "flesh" (בשׂר) often signals a familial relationship. Genesis uses this term when the man finds the woman to be a suitable partner: "This at last is bone of my bones and flesh of my flesh" (עצם מעצמי ובשׂר מבשׂרי; Gen 2:23). Likewise, Laban identifies Jacob as his flesh and offers him hospitality (Gen 29:14). The northern tribes of Israel broaden the boundaries of the family when they appeal to David, their "bone and flesh," to be king (2 Sam 5:1; 1 Chr 11:1).

24. UNICEF, "Child Labour" (June 2023), https://data.unicef.org/topic/child-protection/child-labour/.

25. Debora Patta et al., "Mars Uses Cocoa Harvested by Kids as Young as 5 in Ghana: CBS News Investigation," *CBS News* (November 29, 2023), https://www.cbsnews.com/news/children-harvesting-cocoa-used-by-major-corporations-ghana/.

The text reports that not only were the people's sons and daughters enslaved, but some of their daughters were "ravished" (כבשׁ, Neh 5:5). This verb is translated as "ravish" in the NRSVue and "bondage" in the NAS; in 2 Samuel 8:11, in the context of David's dedication of the war booty from the "nations he subdued." The word is used similarly to refer to the perceived violation of Queen Esther where the king asks, "Will he even violate [כבשׁ] the queen in my presence, in my own house?" (Esth 7:8). In Nehemiah 5:5, the added emphasis on the violation of daughters accentuates their susceptibility as targets of sexual desire. The text cannot bring itself to note that boys were also sexually exploited. The objectification of girls and women remains a concern in a patriarchal context when women have limited autonomy and decisions concerning their own bodies. Issues of bodily autonomy are still prevalent for women today.

Another accusation against their Jewish kin is that they have seized vineyards and fields, leaving the people landless and without the means to provide for their families (5:5). While these acts seem harsh and things of the past, loss of land and inheritance occurs for many people in our contemporary communities.

Responding to the "Great Cry": Nehemiah 5:1, 5, 6

God gives homeland to people as an inheritance. The land offers security and nourishment for generations. It is a cruel and hateful situation when people are stolen from their homeland or robbed of their godly inheritance. Some say oppression in the United States is in the past and that today's people of color living in America have equal opportunity. Statistics, however, do not lie. Forty percent of children of color live in poverty in the United States. Their families do not own land, and many are completely disconnected from the bounty of nourishment the land offers. Liberation theology depicts a vision of God who demands that justice and liberation prevail and extend to traditionally oppressed people of color. Isaiah writes, "For I, the Lord, love justice, I hate robbery and wrongdoing; I will faithfully give them my recompense, and I will make an everlasting covenant with them" (Isa 61:8-9).

Nehemiah 5 tells of the prophet's response after hearing the outcry of the people. He immediately experiences anger and frustration as he bears witness to oppression. The word *han* in the Korean language means righteous anger. I imagine the same *han* experienced throughout the ages when I consider people of color who have experienced a great deal of oppression through stolen lands and stolen and displaced bodies similar to Jewish oppression experienced in Nehemiah 5.

As a multiethnic woman living in America, this is personal for me. I've asked God why people of color have been destined for oppression and have endured stolen lands and stolen bodies for so long without either restitution or reparations when God loves justice. My mother grew up on her father's farm in Lisman, Alabama, during the 1960s. Her father was a sharecropper, and my mother and her siblings farmed the land for the benefit of someone else. When my grandfather tried to farm his own land, government officials prevented him. He was allowed to grow only a limited number of crops. My mom never understood why these restrictions and limitations were in place, especially in a capitalistic society where people earned a living from increased crops. My father's family were Native American; his mother was 100 percent Cherokee and his father was Blackfoot. My Cherokee ancestors experienced displacements from Ohio to Tennessee and then were forced west on a "Trail of Tears." My grandmother's homeland was stripped from her family when the government built the railroad through it and forced her family to live on an Indian reservation.

Today, although I experience *han* when I think of the continued oppression of people of color in a Democratic nation, I admire Nehemiah who, through prayer and fasting, sought counsel from God about what to do. We must note that even after the Jewish people were freed from exile, complete restoration did not come easily or naturally; it required intentionality and work. The Jewish people, in a cycle of oppression, were forced to sell their sons and daughters into slavery when they could not pay the high taxes imposed on them. Many had to mortgage their land for food. Like Native and African American oppression, their own land belonged to others. Empowered by the God of love and justice, Nehemiah did not ignore the suffering of the oppressed people. Instead, he walked in the power of God's will. He listened and responded to their cry for help by speaking directly to the oppressors and demanding that the injustice cease. The first part of Nehemiah 5 begins with a cry and a plea for justice; however, by the end of the chapter, the courage of Nehemiah gains victory for the oppressed. If more sons and daughters of the family of God would acknowledge and bear witness to the truth behind those impoverished unjustly and approach their oppression like Nehemiah with rebuke and demands for restitution, confronting the powers that continue to oppress and claim the inheritance of God's people, then Black and Brown people throughout all the land would experience a jubilee, and the people of God would rejoice in ushering in the kingdom of love, restoration, and justice.

The Reverend Crystal Paul-Watson

Economic Relief (5:6-19)

When Nehemiah hears the outcry and complaints of the people, he becomes angry (Neh 5:6). His anger is focused against those identified as "their Jewish kin" in 5:1, although the target of his anger is unclear in these opening verses. The ambiguity is resolved when the text goes on to suggest his inner turmoil in 5:7: "After thinking it over [וימלך לבי עלי], I contended with the nobles and the officials." The Hebrew word לבי can be translated as "myself," "my heart," "my inner being," or "my understanding."[26] The Hebrew literally says, "My heart took counsel within me."[27] Thus, after thinking it over, Nehemiah first turns his attention and anger to the nobles and officials by accusing them of "taking interest" from their own people (Neh 5:7). Though nobles and officials are often lumped together by the writers of Ezra and Nehemiah (Neh 2:16; 4:14, 19; 5:7; 7:5), the nobles (חרים) are internal leaders in Judah, and the officials (סגנים) are Persians who accompany Nehemiah to Jerusalem.[28] This outrage leads Nehemiah to call for a great assembly to handle the problem. In the midst of this gathering, he further clarifies his complaint, "As far as we were able, we have bought back our Jewish kindred who had been sold to other nations, but now you are selling your own kin, who must then be bought back by us!" (Neh 5:8). To make his case, Nehemiah draws on painful memories of exile and of how difficult it is to buy back those scattered.

26. See לב, *HALOT*, 515.

27. The JPS renders this "After pondering the matter carefully." Robert Alter chooses "As I reflected" (*The Hebrew Bible: The Writings* [New York: Norton, 2019], 841).

28. Daniel L. Smith-Christopher, *The Religion of the Landless: The Social Context of the Babylonian Exile*, 2nd ed. (Eugene, OR: Wipf and Stock, 2015), 113. He argues that biblical texts connect the term סגנים to foreign officials like the Assyrians and Babylonians (e.g., Jer 51:28, 57) and the חרים to the elders of Israel in preexilic times (e.g., 1 Kgs 21:8, 11). It appears that Nehemiah is criticizing both his Jewish kin and the Persian officials.

Neh 5:6-19

[6]I was very angry when I heard their outcry and these complaints. [7]After thinking it over, I contended with the nobles and the officials; I said to them, "You are all taking interest from your own people." And I called a great assembly to deal with them [8]and said to them, "As far as we were able, we have bought back our Jewish kindred who had been sold to other nations, but now you are selling your own kin, who must then be bought back by us!" They were silent and could not find a word to say. [9]So I said, "The thing that you are doing is not good. Should you not walk in the fear of our God, to prevent the taunts of the nations our enemies? [10]Moreover I and my brothers and my servants are lending them money and grain. Let us stop this taking of interest. [11]Restore to them, this very day, their fields, their vineyards, their olive orchards, and their houses, and the interest on money, grain, wine, and oil that you have been exacting from them." [12]Then they said, "We will restore everything and demand nothing more from them. We will do as you say." And I called the priests and made them take an oath to do as they had promised. [13]I also shook out the fold of my garment and said, "So may God shake out everyone from

TRANSLATION MATTERS

In Nehemiah 5:7 the word משׁא, translated by the NRSVue as "interest," may go beyond paying money. William Rudolph re-points the term as משׂא, which can be connected to giving a pledge.[29] If this is the case, then משׁא could also refer back to the money the community needs to borrow to pay the king's tax (Neh 5:4) by pledging their fields and vineyards, and placing their children into debt slavery. Peter Altmann explores other economic terms in Nehemiah 5–13 and asserts that this text presents an established economic system in Judah with terminology that is difficult for us to fully understand today.[30]

In essence, by selling their kin, the nobles and officials are returning their people to the type of bondage that preceded Cyrus's decree that allowed them to return home, requiring that the repatriates purchase

29. William Rudolph (*Esra und Nehemia, samt 3. Esra* [Tübingen: Mohr, 1949], 130) cited in Altmann, *Economics in Persian-Period Biblical Texts*, 256. For a discussion on the difficulty in translating משא and its related נשא, see Altmann, *Economics in Persian-Period Biblical Texts*, 255–60.

30. Altmann, *Economics in Persian-Period Biblical Texts*, 259.

house and from property who does not perform this promise. Thus may they be shaken out and emptied." And all the assembly said, "Amen," and praised the LORD. And the people did as they had promised.

[14]Moreover, from the time that I was appointed to be their governor in the land of Judah, from the twentieth year to the thirty-second year of King Artaxerxes, twelve years, neither I nor my brothers ate the food allowance of the governor. [15]The former governors who were before me laid heavy burdens on the people and took food and wine from them, besides forty shekels of silver. Even their servants lorded it over the people. But I did not do so because of the fear of God. [16]Indeed, I devoted myself to the work on this wall and acquired no land, and all my servants were gathered there for the work. [17]Moreover, there were at my table one hundred fifty people, Jews and officials, besides those who came to us from the nations around us. [18]Now that which was prepared for one day was one ox and six choice sheep; also fowls were prepared for me, and every ten days skins of wine in abundance, yet with all this I did not demand the food allowance of the governor, because of the heavy burden of labor on the people. [19]Remember for my good, O my God, all that I have done for this people.

them back. This accusation leaves these elite and privileged groups speechless (Neh 5:8). Nehemiah holds the accused accountable for acting badly, refusing to walk in the fear of God, and giving their enemies fodder to taunt them (Neh 5:9).[31] He insists that their acts of injustice shame them and the community before God and before other nations. Second, Nehemiah includes himself and his servants as those who are among the Jewish kin who have added to the people's suffering.[32] Using "I" language ("I and my brothers and my servants are lending them money

31. The Hebrew חרפה runs throughout the Nehemiah memoir. See commentary on Nehemiah 1.

32. Laird translates the NRSVue's "Jewish kindred" as "brothers the Yehudim" (Donna Laird, *Negotiating Power in Ezra–Nehemiah*, AIL 26 [Atlanta: SBL Press, 2016], 235). Blenkinsopp lists several possibilities and concludes that this group is most likely a wealthy part of those who returned from exile (*Ezra–Nehemiah*, 256). Roland Boer wonders whether the "Jewish kindred" represents the entire Judean community, including those who consider themselves to be part of the community (e.g., Samaritans), or if they represent a subset in an intra-Jewish conflict. ("Thus I Cleansed Them from Everything Foreign: The Search for Subjectivity in Ezra–Nehemiah," in *Postcolonialism and the Hebrew Bible: The Next Step*, ed. Roland Boer, SemeiaSt 70 [Atlanta: SBL, 2013], 225–27.)

and grain"; Neh 5:10) and "we/us" language ("let us stop this taking of interest"; Neh 5:10), he takes personal responsibility for causing the suffering and pain of his brothers and sisters, perhaps after reflecting on the people's complaint and his own complicity. Nehemiah calls for the creditors to restore the people's property and interest. Perhaps his self-acknowledgment makes it more plausible that the nobles and officials will be more inclined to hear what he has to say and act accordingly.

This abrupt return of capital may cause financial problems for the creditors, leading to a loss of income derived from confiscated fields, vineyards, olive orchards, houses, and interest from grain, wine, and oil (Neh 5:11). Nevertheless, the nobles and officials agree to restore everything extracted from those launching complaints against them (Neh 5:12a).

Nehemiah then summons the priests to administer an oath between the creditors and those whose property they have taken to ensure that the creditors fulfill their promises (Neh 5:12b). Swearing an oath in ancient Israel was serious business. An oath, especially to God, is sacred.[33] It carries with it an ethical and religious dimension beyond secular contracts. This connection between theology and economics becomes beneficial when it encourages individuals to honor their commitments, especially in terms of monetary contributions to religious causes. Nevertheless, problems can arise when people feel compelled to take oaths and make financial promises beyond their means.

Nehemiah challenges all who are gathered to choose: either honor the economic protections of members of the family or be banished from the community. In 5:13, Nehemiah shakes out the fold of his garment to make his point: "So may God shake out everyone from house and from property who does not perform this promise. Thus may they be shaken out and emptied." The verse then indicates that everyone agrees to the terms and takes the oath before God and each other. The people respond with a hearty "Amen," a round of praise, and do "as they promised" (Neh 5:13). Although the restoration looks like an application of the Jubilee (Lev 25), it is more likely a temporary fix.[34]

33. Numbers 30:2: "When a man makes a vow to the LORD or swears an oath to bind himself by a pledge, he shall not break his word; he shall do according to all that proceeds out of his mouth."

34. Blenkinsopp refers to this forgiveness of debt as "an emergency jubilee" (*Ezra–Nehemiah*, 259).

The Torah and Its Protections for the Poor and Vulnerable

The Torah provides economic safety nets for those more vulnerable: those with means are to support the poor, widows, orphans, and migrants (Deut 10:18). Employers are required to pay wages to their laborers in a timely manner (Lev 19:13; Deut 24:14-15) and leave food for the hungry (Deut 14:28-29; 24:21; Lev 19:9; 23:22; cf. Ruth 2). Members of Israel may lend money, but the loans must be interest-free for Israelites (Exod 22:25; Lev 25:37; Deut 23:19-20). Cloaks and sandals taken as collateral must be returned daily to the debtor to prevent suffering like burnt feet during the day and cold at night (Exod 22:26; Deut 24:10-13). Creditors are not allowed to enter homes to take back the collateral (Deut 24:10-11). Debt slavery is limited to six years; the slave must be treated humanely and be transitioned back into the community with resources (Exod 21:2-11; Lev 25:39-43; Deut 15:12-18). Debts are cancelled after seven years (Deut 15:1-11), and a Jubilee year, which is to take place every fiftieth year (Lev 25), requires property to be redistributed among the tribes and for debt to be forgiven. The goal is that no one amasses wealth at the expense of Israel's well-being, and that everyone has support. We do not know if these laws, especially the Jubilee, were enforced. Yet, the Scriptures of ancient Israel condemn those whose desire for wealth supersedes the needs of the community. Torah is clear that kings are to follow the law and are not allowed to extract wealth from their people (Deut 17:17-18). God, through the prophet Samuel, warns those demanding a king that kings will accumulate wealth at their expense (1 Sam 8:10-18). For example, Solomon requires each tribe to provide one month's food and other provisions for his court and his thousands of horses (1 Kgs 4:22-28), an economic system that reinforces social stratification. Likewise, Ahab and Jezebel ensure that their 850 banquet guests are properly fed during drought and famine and so deplete resources that should be shared with their hungry subjects (1 Kgs 19). The prophets (e.g., Amos, Micah, Isaiah) indict Israel's leaders for their greed. These laws provide an ethic that helps create a just and a righteous community in which all matter.

In 5:6-13, Nehemiah puts himself in a vulnerable position as he challenges the nobles, officials, and himself to act justly toward the people. Now, he emphasizes that, as governor, he did not take the food allowance

(לחם הפחה) allotted him (5:14, 15, 18).[35] Unlike former governors, he never makes the people provide him wine, grain, and forty shekels of silver, which is the governor's allowance (Neh 5:15).[36] Further, Nehemiah makes a point that, while he took interest from his people (Neh 5:10), he did not confiscate land from them, due to his "fear" of God (Neh 5:15). Instead, he claims he committed himself to work on the wall with his servants (Neh 5:16).

Bread of the Governor or Governor's Allowance

The bread of the governor in Nehemiah 5:14 (לחם הפחה) is likely a tax traditionally collected by the regional governor and consists of food and other provisions that will be given to the governor to eat and entertain friends and dignitaries.[37] Altmann points out that the translation of Nehemiah 5:14 in the Septuagint calls this requirement "the bread of extortion," which might describe how the people experienced these allowances.[38]

Nehemiah is adamant that he places no further financial hardship on his people. Yet, he holds banquets over ten days for 150 "Jews and officials, besides those who came to us from nations around us" (Neh 5:17).[39] First, these feasts require resources. Each banquet requires one ox, six choice sheep, fowls, and abundant wine (Neh 5:18). Apparently,

35. Malachi 1:8 corroborates the presence of the governor's food allowance and the importance of providing the best of food. The people offer animals inappropriate for sacrifice, and Malachi chides them for giving the governor better animals than the Lord: "When you offer blind animals in sacrifice, is that not wrong? And when you offer those that are lame or sick, is that not wrong? Try presenting that to your governor; will he be pleased with you or show you favor? says the Lord of hosts."

36. The text is unclear about who these previous governors are, if they are Jews. Nahman Avigad creates a list of governors based on coins and bullae. The two he lists before Nehemiah are Sheshbazzar and Zerubbabel, as found in Ezra 5:14 and Haggai 1:1, 14 (*Bullae and Seals from a Post-Exilic Judean Archive* [Jerusalem: Institute of Archaeology, Hebrew University, 1976], 40). See Joseph Blenkinsopp, *Judaism, the First Phase: The Place of Ezra and Nehemiah in the Origins of Judaism* (Grand Rapids: Eerdmans, 2009), 110–11.

37. Altmann, *Economics in Persian-Period Biblical Texts*, 272–73.

38. Altmann also calls our attention to the provisions required by Solomon to feed all the people at his table; see *Economics in Persian-Period Biblical Texts*, 273.

39. For a discussion on who may have received invitations to these banquets, see Fried, *Nehemiah*, 160–63.

Nehemiah has abundant resources to provide these meals, leading to questions about where he finds the resources to serve at these banquets. He refuses the food allowance allotted for the governor, resources governors often use for such occasions (Neh 5:14). Therefore, Nehemiah must have personal wealth and servants at his disposal.[40] Nehemiah, as governor, draws from large estates that provide produce as well as space to raise livestock and poultry for these meals.[41]

Nehemiah, as the governor, likely lives in the governor's house, which could be located at Ramat Rachel.[42] According to Oded Lipschits, there is "no reason to doubt that during the Persian period Ramat Rachel served as the edifice of the imperial governor in the province."[43] Ramat Rachel overlooks the southwest corner of Jerusalem and was a popular rest stop and administrative center on a major route between Susa and Egypt.[44] Excavated seals and other artifacts attest to Ramat Rachel as a center for agricultural production and the administration of taxes from the seventh century BCE through 70 CE. Archaeologists uncovered 250 seal impressions inscribed with "Yehud" that date to the Persian period that would have been affixed to containers holding agricultural goods.[45] Further, Ramat Rachel was surrounded by terraced hills suitable for grape and olive growth and fields for grain. Excavations in this city uncovered royal buildings surrounded by sophisticatedly irrigated gardens that suggest maximum crop yields. In addition to Ramat Rachel, Nehemiah could draw from several administrative centers with agricultural land to supplement the needed food supplies.[46] While financial support for these meals does not come from the bread of the governor (Neh 5:14 15), the cost of maintaining these estates and other services associated with the banquets still impacts the entire community.

40. For a discussion on similar banquets in Persia, see Fried, *Nehemiah*, 163–65.

41. Fried, *Nehemiah*, 164.

42. The book of Nehemiah waits until 5:14 to inform us of his appointment as governor (פחה). Nehemiah might not enter Judah with that title. Ramat Rachel sits south of Jerusalem, overlooking both Jerusalem and Bethlehem.

43. Oded Lipschits, "The Rural Economy of Judah During the Persian Period and Settlement History of the District System," in *The Economy of Ancient Judah in Its Historical Context*, ed. Ehud Ben Zvi, Marvin Lloyd Miller, and Gary N. Knoppers (Winona Lake, IN: Eisenbrauns, 2015), 258.

44. Ramat Rachel translates as "the heights of Rachel." The site looks down on the traditional burial site of the ancestor Rachel.

45. Lipschits, "The Rural Economy," 256–58. See also The Ramat Rachel Archaeological Project, https://www.tau.ac.il/~rmtrachl/archaeology%20of%20site.htm.

46. Fried identifies three Persian-period estates as providers of foodstuffs; *Nehemiah*, 164.

Second, those who attend Nehemiah's banquets are Jews, officials, and those from the surrounding nations (Neh 5:17). The Syriac substitutes "nobles" (חרים) for "Jews," which makes sense that the guest would be of high social status in the context of banquets and politics.[47] As governor of Judah and a Persian appointee, Nehemiah would have been required to provide hospitality to dignitaries who were gifted land by Nehemiah or the Persian king, or other nobles from the greater Persian Empire who passed through the province.[48] These banquets offered opportunities to solidify relationships of power and support. Accounts of royal Persian banquets describe them as opportunities for gift-giving, collecting tributes, and power-building.[49] In the context of Persian royal banquets, the king gifted guests precious cups based on the individual's status in the court.[50] Nehemiah, in contrast, expresses concern about the cost of these meals, especially because he does not want to burden his people (Neh 5:17-18).

The text portrays Nehemiah as a benevolent leader attuned to the suffering of those struggling financially in his community. Offering them tax relief and restoring property are compassionate and just. Perhaps Nehemiah tries to temper his privileged position by suggesting that he is partially guilty of causing the people's distress but wants them to recognize how he offered economic relief. Either way, Nehemiah addresses an inner struggle and realizes that he is part of the problem. Even though Nehemiah does not accept the food allowance, he is governor over an economic and political structure, sanctioned by Persian power, where he can demand these benefits if he so chooses. He does not create the economic system, but he benefits from it by collecting interest on loans (Neh 5:10) and accepting the perquisites of being the governor. Being confronted by the people might have given him pause. Bobbie Harro, who examines systems of oppression and privilege, suggests that "a waking up phase" can precipitate "intrapersonal change" or a "cycle of liberation" where one's self-understanding and worldview are challenged. Harro's examples include a white woman who adopts a darker-skinned child and realizes how her ingrained racism skews her expectations for the child. The mother's realization challenges

47. "Textual notes on Nehemiah 5:17," *BHS*, 1438.

48. Fried, *Nehemiah*, 161–64.

49. Altmann, *Economics in Persian-Period Biblical Texts*, 278–79.

50. Altmann, *Economics in Persian-Period Biblical Texts*, 281–82.

her and changes her attitudes and actions.[51] Nehemiah's people challenge him, and he becomes an ally who uses his place of power and privilege to confront the oppressive tax system and to enact positive change for the people. This is why many contemporary community justice organizations turn to Nehemiah as a biblical model of justice.

Intimidation and Demonization

Nehemiah 6:1-19 recounts the vitriolic attitudes and actions between Nehemiah and the leaders of the local communities. We divide this chapter into two sections that illustrate their relational dysfunction. Nehemiah 6:1-9 narrates intimidation by Sanballat and Geshem directed at Nehemiah and his community. Nehemiah 6:10-19 describes further intimidation, but this time, the sources of this activity are local prophets and officials. Despite the threats and mocking, Nehemiah stands his ground and continues his mission.

The Demonization of Sanballat and Geshem (6:1-9)

The conflict recorded in Nehemiah 4 between Nehemiah and his adversaries—Sanballat, Tobiah, and their allies—concerning the building of the walls returns in chapter 6. Nehemiah thwarts their plans to halt the construction by completing the wall except for installing the doors and gates (Neh 6:1).[52] Once again hearsay rather than face-to-face interaction marks the contention. "It was reported" to Sanballat, Tobiah, Geshem, and "the rest of our enemies" (Neh 6:1) that the wall was nearly complete.

Sanballat and Geshem ask to meet Nehemiah in a village in the plain of Ono (Neh 6:2). The plain is roughly twenty miles southwest of Jerusalem;

51. Bobbie Harro, "Updated Version of the Cycle of Socialization (2000)," in *Readings for Diversity and Social Justice*, ed. Maurianne Adams et al., 3rd ed. (New York: Routledge, 2013), 619–20.

52. Wright believes 1:1a, 11b; 2:1-6, 11, 15-18; 3:38; 6:15 to be the original wall-building account; Wright, *Rebuilding Identity*, 151. Blenkinsopp accepts the conflict accounts as part of the original version: Blenkinsopp, *Ezra–Nehemiah*, 268. The awkwardly placed material reflects future skirmishes with leaders in the provinces surrounding Judah (Samaria, Ashdod, Ashkelon, Arabia). Both 6:1a and 6:15 record that the wall is complete, so 6:1b, "Though up to that time I had not set up the doors in the gates," appears to be a gloss designed to make sense of why Sanballat and his allies still try to undermine Nehemiah's work.

Neh 6:1-9

[1]Now when it was reported to Sanballat and Tobiah and to Geshem the Arab and to the rest of our enemies that I had built the wall and that there was no gap left in it (though up to that time I had not set up the doors in the gates), [2]Sanballat and Geshem sent to me, saying, "Come and let us meet together in one of the villages in the plain of Ono." But they intended to do me harm. [3]So I sent messengers to them, saying, "I am doing a great work, and I cannot come down. Why should the work stop while I leave it to come down to you?" [4]They sent to me four times in this way, and I answered them in the same manner. [5]In the same way Sanballat for the fifth time sent his servant to me with an open letter in his hand. [6]In it was written, "It is reported among the nations—and Geshem also says it—that you and the Jews intend to rebel; that is why you are building the wall; and according to this report you wish to become their king. [7]You have also set up prophets to proclaim in Jerusalem concerning you, 'There is a king in Judah!' And now it will be reported to the king according to these words. So come, therefore, and let us confer together." [8]Then I sent to him, saying, "No such things as you say have been done; you are inventing them out of your own mind," [9]for they all wanted to frighten us, thinking, "Their hands will drop from the work, and it will not be done." But now, strengthen my hands.

to travel there would take Nehemiah away from his task for several days. Sanballat and Geshem may have chosen this location because it is near Sanballat's home in Beth-horon; it is outside the border of the province of Judah and in neutral territory between Ashdod and Samaria.[53] Alternatively, Nehemiah might find the place Ono secure because the person Ono is a valued member of the repatriates and appears on both Ezra's and Nehemiah's lists of those who returned from exile and participated in the rebuilding of Jerusalem (Ezra 2:33; Neh 7:37). Nehemiah refuses this invitation to meet with Sanballat and Geshem four times. He maintains that Sanballat is motivated by a desire to hurt him: "But they intended to do me harm" (Neh 6:2).

When Nehemiah sends his messengers to deliver his refusal, he does not accuse Sanballat, Tobiah, and Geshem of nefarious motives. Instead, he suggests that his absence will halt progress on the wall. His response is diplomatic: "I am doing a great work, and I cannot come down. Why should the work stop while I leave it to come down to you?" (Neh 6:3). The Septuagint makes Nehemiah's refusal even more gracious: "When-

53. Blenkinsopp, *Ezra–Nehemiah*, 268.

ever I finish it [a great work], I will come down to you" (6:3b).[54] In this chapter, the term שלח, "send," is reiterated seven times (in verses 2, 3, 4, 5, 8, 12, 19), underscoring the remote communication between the parties.

Sanballat and Geshem's message seems hospitable: "Come and let us meet together in one of the villages in the plain of Ono." They invite their neighboring governor to a formal meeting four times—with four replies with regrets (Neh 6:4). Nehemiah's refusal emphasizes his decision to avoid face-to-face meetings with his adversaries, as described in Nehemiah 6:3-4 and 8. Using שלח here adds a new dimension to this long-distance relationship: emissaries become the intermediaries who communicate between the opponents.

Sanballat responds to Nehemiah's refusals by sending his servant with an "open letter" (Neh 6:5). His letter, corroborated by Geshem, reports (שמע) rumors that Nehemiah sought to be king and that he and the Jews have planned a rebellion. Building a wall around Jerusalem is part of this treasonous plan (Neh 6:6-7). The papyrus is not sealed, so the messenger and anyone along the delivery route could read its contents. Sealing the papyrus would have signaled a more conciliatory approach. The unsealed letter, like social media, has the ability to communicate to a wide audience, including those engaged in the wall's construction.

Nehemiah, furious, accuses Sanballat of inventing a rebellion (Neh 6:8) and so undermining the building of the wall. Nehemiah has a point. He interprets this letter as another attempt to intimidate him and his compatriots into abandoning their building plan: "for they all wanted to frighten us, thinking, 'Their hands will drop from the work, and it will not be done'" (Neh 6:9). Ezra 4 records similar conflicts between the people of the land and Zerubbabel when he rejects their offer to help rebuild the temple. In the hopes of halting temple construction, Rehum and Shimshai send letters to Artaxerxes describing a rebellion by the repatriates. That ruse works, and the king orders all construction to cease (Ezra 4:23). Later, King Darius allowed the building to continue. Perhaps Sanballat and Geshem believed that Artaxerxes could be swayed were he to think that Nehemiah was plotting rebellion. In essence, if the contents of the letter can reach Nehemiah and those working on the wall, it could also reach the king with its fake news of sedition.

Yet, at this point in the narrative the walls around Jerusalem are almost complete, which raises questions about what Sanballat and his allies

54. *A New English Translation of the Septuagint*, ed. Albert Pietersma and Benjamin G. Wright (Oxford University Press, 2014).

gain by harassing Nehemiah. Sanballat may have found working with Nehemiah inevitable. Tipping him off about these rumors and asking to "confer together" or to "be advised" might accurately portray Sanballat's motives.[55] He might have heard rumors that Judeans hoped for a newly restored Israel with a king, and so he wanted to warn Nehemiah of accusations against him. The Persian-era prophets, Haggai and Zechariah, proclaim hope in a newly restored Israel with its monarchy. Perhaps their visions lead some Judeans to declare Nehemiah king.[56] It makes little sense for Sanballat to send a threatening letter to convince Nehemiah to accept a meeting with him if he thought Nehemiah guilty of rebellion.

In response to Sanballat's plot to make Nehemiah's hands "drop the work" (Neh 6:9a), Nehemiah petitions for God's help, "But now, strengthen my hands" (Neh 6:9b). Instead of being intimidated, Nehemiah is even more determined to complete the building. Throughout Nehemiah 6:1-9, we witness the complex power dynamics and political maneuvering of all those involved. Nehemiah has to navigate challenges and potential threats to his leadership based on the motivations and actions of his adversaries while simultaneously fulfilling his desire to be faithful to the work he is called to complete. His encounter highlights the multifaceted work of ministry and the expectations placed on individuals in positions of authority and leadership.

Shemaiah, the Prophets, and Tobiah (6:10-19)

Following his denial of Sanballat's charges, Nehemiah journeys to the house of Shemaiah (Neh 6:10). The name Shemaiah appears numerous times in Ezra–Nehemiah (Ezra 8:13, 16; 10:21, 31; Neh 3:29; 6:10; 10:8; 11:15; 12:6, 18, 34-36, 42).[57] Many of these Shemaiahs without patronyms are listed among those who participate in the building projects; therefore, they are likely trusted as part of the repatriated community.[58] Although he refuses to meet with Sanballat and Geshem, Nehemiah takes time to meet with Shemaiah, the son of Delaiah, son of Mehetabel, who is confined to his

55. The verb יעץ in the hiphil can be translated "to take advice" or "consult together"; *HALOT*, 422.

56. See Hag 2:6-9 and Zech 6:9-14, who both speak to this possibility, especially the latter with a king riding a donkey into Jerusalem—a messianic hope. Blenkinsopp makes the connection between Nehemiah and these prophecies (*Ezra–Nehemiah*, 269).

57. Blenkinsopp points out that the name Shemaiah is associated with Levitical priests (1 Chr 9:14; 15:8; Neh 11:5) and also with prophets (1 Kgs 12:22); Blenkinsopp, *Ezra–Nehemiah*, 270.

58. Ezra 8:13, 14; 10:31; Neh 3:29; 10:8; 12:6, 18, 34, 35, 36, 42.

Neh 6:10-19

[10]One day when I went into the house of Shemaiah son of Delaiah son of Mehetabel, who was confined to his house, he said, "Let us meet together in the house of God, within the temple, and let us close the doors of the temple, for they are coming to kill you; indeed, tonight they are coming to kill you." [11]But I said, "Should a man like me run away? Would a man like me go into the temple to save his life? I will not go in!" [12]Then I perceived and saw that God had not sent him at all, but he had pronounced the prophecy against me because Tobiah and Sanballat had hired him. [13]He was hired for this purpose, to intimidate me and make me sin by acting in this way, and so they could give me a bad name, in order to taunt me. [14]Remember Tobiah and Sanballat, O my God, according to these things that they did, and also Noadiah the prophetess and the rest of the prophets who wanted to make me afraid.

[15]So the wall was finished on the twenty-fifth day of the month Elul, in fifty-two days. [16]And when all our enemies heard of it, all the nations around us were afraid and fell greatly in their own esteem, for they perceived that this work had been accomplished with the help of our God. [17]Moreover, in those days the nobles of Judah sent many letters to Tobiah, and Tobiah's letters came to them. [18]For many in Judah were bound by oath to him, because he was the son-in-law of Shecaniah son of Arah, and his son Jehohanan had married the daughter of Meshullam son of Berechiah. [19]Also they spoke of his good deeds in my presence and reported my words to him. And Tobiah sent letters to intimidate me.

house. Timothy Yap notes propositions by scholars that explain why Shemaiah is confined to his house, including one that he is ritually unclean. Yap suggests that the argument that Shemaiah is unclean makes little sense when Shemaiah invites Nehemiah to meet with him in the temple. Instead, Shemaiah's confinement likely serves as a prophetic oracle where Shemaiah's confinement serves to warn Nehemiah that he should follow suit to preserve his life.[59]

Shemaiah informs Nehemiah that "they" are going to kill him that very night, so he must act quickly to save himself (Neh 6:10). The subject of the threat, "they," is not specific. We do not know if Shemaiah means Sanballat and his other enemies are coming or if the king's representatives

59. See Timothy Yap, who delves into the various reasons put forward for Shemaiah's confinement ("The House That Built Me: The 'House of God' and Its Role in the Construction of Fear in Nehemiah 6.1-15," *JSOT* 46 [2022]: 408–20, https://doi.org/10.1177/03090892211061170).

believe rumors that Nehemiah has rebelled. The accusation of treason in Sanballat's letter, a crime punishable by death, precedes this urgent cry for Nehemiah to take refuge. Nehemiah takes Shemaiah's prophetic words seriously until Shemaiah suggests that he flee to the innermost part of the temple. Nehemiah rejects this offer, making his response a matter of integrity and honor: "Should a man like me run away? Would a man like me go into the temple to save his life?" (Neh 6:11). There are several reasons that Nehemiah might refuse to flee to the interior of the temple. First, he wants to signal that he is not a coward who would run from danger. Second, to hide from those seeking to kill him is a sign of faithlessness. A third reason he might resist entering the temple is that he is not a priest and so not permitted to enter: "But you and your sons with you shall diligently perform your priestly duties in all that concerns the altar and the area behind the curtain. I give your priesthood as a gift; any outsider who approaches shall be put to death" (Num 18:7). Myers draws on Deuteronomy 23:1 and Leviticus 21:17-23 to argue that it would be offensive should Nehemiah, a eunuch (see commentary on Neh 1:14), enter the temple. Isaiah 56:1-8, which dates to the post-exilic period, clearly includes eunuchs and foreigners as part of the community. Katherine Southwood posits, "Not only are these 'outcasts of Israel' to minister in the temple, they will make 'whole burnt offerings and sacrifices' on the altar at the heart of the temple" (Isa 56:7).[60]

Nehemiah accuses Shemaiah of conspiring with Tobiah and Sanballat; he believes his opponents hired Shemaiah to entrap him (Neh 6:12). He accuses Sanballat of hiring Shemaiah "to intimidate me and make me sin by acting in this way, and so they could give me a bad name, in order to taunt me" (Neh 6:13).[61] Nehemiah seems more concerned about his reputation than his life. Rationale aside, here is a man who chooses to stand on his principles when faced with a potential threat to his life.

We have modern examples of people willing to risk their lives and stand on principles. Martin Luther King Jr. confronted racism and poverty and knew that his life was always at risk. The night before he died, he gave his "I have been to the Mountaintop" speech in Memphis, where he understood that he might not live long, but he had no choice but to

60. Jacob Myers, *Ezra, Nehemiah*, AB 14 (Garden City, NY: Doubleday, 1965), 139. Katherine Southwood, "The 'Foreigner' and the Eunuch: The Politics of Belonging in Isaiah 56:1-8," *BibInt* 30 (2020): 455.

61. The term translated here by the NRSVue as "taunt" (חרפה, v. 13) is the same word that the NRSVue translates as "shame" in Neh 1:3 with respect to Jerusalem's condition before the walls are rebuilt.

stand up for justice and for what is right. Ida B. Wells, an investigative reporter, insisted on telling the ugly truth about lynching in the United States and was forced to leave from Memphis when her newspaper, *Memphis Free Speech and Headlight*, was attacked by an angry white mob. Nadia Murad, an Iraqi Yazidi activist, was kidnapped by ISIS and sexually abused. Since escaping she continues to risk her life as she speaks out against trafficking and Yazidi genocide. Like Nehemiah, these three activists also stand their ground.

Nehemiah's complaint is not just against Shemaiah but also includes other prophets: "Remember . . . also Noadiah the prophetess and the rest of the prophets who wanted to make me afraid" (Neh 6:14). The writer draws a distinction between the prophets and Noadiah, setting her apart from the male prophets but also alongside those same prophets who oppose Nehemiah. These prophets may represent a thriving community of prophets dedicated to YHWH that continued to practice long after the exile of the priests and aristocracy.[62]

There is not consensus on whether the name Noadiah refers to a male or female. The name appears only twice, once in Ezra 8:33 and here in Nehemiah 6:14. In Ezra 8:33 Noadiah is the son of Binnui, a Levite who receives the temple vessels. While the gender of Noadiah's name may be ambiguous, the Hebrew word for "prophet" describing her in Nehemiah 6:14 (נביאה) is feminine, making Noadiah a "female prophet." The feminine form is not, however, found in the Septuagint (τῷ Νωαδια τῷ προφήτῃ, "Noadiah the prophet"), which is masculine. Other versions, like the Syriac and Arabic, follow the Septuagint's masculine designation.[63]

Few women are named as prophets in the Hebrew Bible (Deborah, Huldah, and Miriam). Tamara Cohn Eskenazi includes Noadiah in this list as the fourth named women prophet.[64] As the only female prophet

62. Harold C. Washington, "Israel's Holy Seed and the Foreign Women of Ezra–Nehemiah: A Kristevan Reading," *BibInt* 11 (2003): 427–37.

63. Esther Hamori, *Women's Divination in Biblical Literature: Prophecy, Necromancy, and Other Arts of Knowledge*, AYBRL (New Haven: Yale University Press, 2015). For more discussion on Noadiah, see Robert Carroll, "Coopting the Prophets: Nehemiah and Noadiah," in *Priests, Prophets and Scribes: Essays on the Formation and Heritage of Second Temple Judaism in Honour of Joseph Blenkinsopp*, ed. Philip R. Davies and David Clines, JSOTSup 149 (Sheffield: Sheffield Academic, 1992), 87–99; Wilda Gafney, *Daughters of Miriam: Women Prophets in Ancient Israel* (Minneapolis: Fortress, 2008), 111–14.

64. Tamara Cohn Eskenazi, "Noadiah," in *Women in Scripture: A Dictionary of Named and Unnamed Women in the Hebrew Bible, the Apocryphal/Deuterocanonical Books, and the New Testament*, ed. Carol Meyers, Toni Craven, and Ross Shepard Kraemer (Boston: Houghton Mifflin, 2000), 132.

among the group of prophets opposing Nehemiah, Noadiah is a member of the group's leadership or has an integral voice in the community. Her inclusion here, however, is probably more a result of her opposition to Nehemiah than her gender. Elsewhere, the biblical writers portray kings and prophets favorably, whether male or female, when they align with the writer's understanding of God and Torah (e.g., 1 Sam 13–14; 2 Kgs 18–20; 22–23; Isa 6; Jer 1:4-10). Conversely, those who deviate or oppose this understanding receive condemnation (e.g., Num 22–24; 1 Kgs 14:7-16; 21; Jer 28:1-17). Similarly, Noadiah and her counterparts receive Nehemiah's critique because of their intimidation ("make me afraid") and efforts to halt God's initiative for rebuilding Jerusalem's walls.

Once again, the encounter among Shemaiah, the other prophets, and Nehemiah ends with a "remember" formula that asks God to remember them "according to these things that they did" (Neh 6:14). The language of God's remembrance directed toward Nehemiah's adversaries serves as both a manifestation of his faith through prayer and a plea for justice against this group for their intimidating actions.

Noadiah, One Verse That Expresses More Than Many Prophetic Words

The book of Nehemiah dedicates only one verse to Noadiah (Neh 6:14). Nevertheless, the record of her name, title, and level of influence shows that she was a prominent figure during the Persian period and that women continued to participate in public affairs and prophetic functions in Yehud.[65] Intervention of prophets was crucial in the midst of diverse proposals for the material reconstruction of the city and the institutional reconfiguration of the nation.

Noadiah is mentioned in a short prayer attributed to Nehemiah (Neh 6:14). The prayer begins with the imperative, "Remember!" which is also found in Nehemiah 1:8; 5:19; 13:14, 22, 29, and 31. It introduces Nehemiah's plea for divine intervention against his

65. For a discussion on Yehud see the introduction.

enemies.[66] In the first phrase, God's judgment is invoked against Tobiah and Sanballat, the most active of Nehemiah's political adversaries. These leaders of Samaria and Ammon, respectively, are presented in the book as obstructing the reconstruction of Yehud. In their profile are actions like mocking Nehemiah and the Yehudites (Neh 2:19; 3:33-35), threatening Jerusalem with an attack (Neh 4:1-17), sending subterfuge letters to Nehemiah (Neh 6:2, 4 and 5), plotting to kill him (Neh 6:3), and even paying the prophet Shemaiah in order to destroy the governor (Neh 6:10-13).

The second phrase in verse 14 mentions the prophet Noadiah and an anonymous group of prophets. Noadiah, a Yahwistic name meaning "meeting with YHWH," was by all means a female prophet from Jerusalem. In the LXX, the name and title appear as a dative masculine (τῷ Νωαδίᾳ τῷ προφήτῃ). It seems that the Greek translator, influenced by the reference to Noadiah, a Levite man in Ezra 8:33, and by the usage of the name for both men and women, understood that the name and title in Nehemiah 6:14 indicated a man.[67] She is not portrayed as frightening to the whole population, only to Nehemiah. In Nehemiah 6 we find prophets who side with the governor and others who do not (Neh 6:6-7, 10-12). She is presented against Nehemiah but not connected to political leaders. Apparently, she sided with the population that was left in the land during the destruction of Jerusalem by the Babylonians (i.e., the poorest among the poor). This group survived by associating with people from the surrounding nations. Moreover, they kept the

66. According to Frederick Holmgren, Nehemiah believed in a God who cared and so he prayed for vindication and called for justice. See Frederick C. Holmgren, *Israel Alive Again: A Commentary on the Books of Ezra and Nehemiah*, ITC (Grand Rapids: Eerdmans, 1987), 106, 119. Hugh Williamson adds that, rather than taking the law into his own hands, Nehemiah invokes God, implying that vengeance is the prerogative of God alone (Deut 32:35; Ps 94:1). See H. G. M. Williamson, *Ezra–Nehemiah*, WBC 16 (Waco: Word, 1985), 260.

67. As Folker Siegert and Jürgen Kabiersch say, this case represents a deliberate avoidance of the feminine by the LXX. See Folker Siegert, *Zwischen Hebräischer Bibel und Altem Testament. Eine Einführung in die Septuaginta I*, Münsteraner Judaistische Studien 9 (Münster: LIT, 2001), 173. Jürgen Kabiersch, "Esdras II: Das Zweite Buch Esdras/Esra-Nehemiah," in *Septuaginta Deutsch. Erläuterungen und Kommentare zum griechischen Alten Testament I: Genesis bis Makkabäer*, ed. Martin Karrer and Wolfgang Kraus (Stuttgart: Deutsche Biblegesellschaft, 2011), 1237. Later manuscripts show the feminine title τη προφητιδι.

cultic practice in Jerusalem alive. They were now affected by the nationalistic and separationist perspective of the returnees from exile who took back their properties and institutional rights. Nehemiah's initiatives appear to have privileged the returnees. The standpoint of Nehemiah and of the returnees is symbolized in the reconstruction of a city wall (Neh 2:17-18; 4:1–6:16). Nehemiah "could not co-opt Noadiah, nor 'the rest of the prophets,' to support this cause."[68]

The text does not suggest that the unnamed prophets belonged to an organization for which Noadiah was a kind of "mother."[69] Two things are clear, however: that she was strong enough to frighten Nehemiah and that the governor did not consider her a "false prophetess."[70] Acts of intimidation were one thing and the theme of false prophecy was another.[71] No words of Noadiah's oracles came to us. Nevertheless, her name, title, and the place where her name appears suggest that female prophets continued to be committed to the reality of their nation and that their prophetic function was exercised in deep solidarity with the poor and the marginalized of their times.

Mila Díaz Solano

According to Nehemiah 6:15 the walls are completed in record time—on "the twenty-fifth day of the month Elul, in fifty-two days." The swiftness of the completion seems remarkable. There is evidence, however,

68. Carroll, "Coopting the Prophets," 96.

69. Gafney sees Noadiah as the mother of a Jerusalem prophetic guild that probably ranged between 100 and 450 prophets. She finds support for her proposal in 1 Kings 18 and 22. See Gafney, *Daughters of Miriam*, 113, 116.

70. These observations counter David Shepherd's proposal that Nehemiah's account both of his enemies' actions and of his own reactions may be brought into focus by viewing it through the lens of Deuteronomic Torah-instruction regarding the false prophet (Deut 18). Shepherd assumes that Nehemiah's implacable opposition to Noadiah reflects not merely his perception of her as a false prophet but also his realization that, in facing up to false prophets, the only thing to fear is fear itself. See David Shepherd, "Prophetaphobia: Fear and False Prophecy in Nehemiah VI," *VT* 55 (2005): 250.

71. Frank L. Hossfeld and Ivo Meyer, *Prophet Gegen Prophet: Eine Analyse der alttestamentlichen Texte zum Thema: Wahre und Falsche Propheten* (Zürich: Schweizerisches Katholisches Bibelwerk, 1973), 156; H. G. M. Williamson, "Prophetesses in the Hebrew Bible," in *Prophecy and Prophets in the Hebrew Bible: Proceedings of the Oxford Old Testament Seminar*, ed. John Day, LHBOTS 531 (New York: T&T Clark, 2010), 66.

that suggests the rapid completion of wall constructions by other groups. For example, during the Persian period, the walls around Athens were rebuilt in a month, and it took sixty days to restore the walls around Constantinople (447 CE).[72] Part of the reason for these endeavors was the need to uphold a defense structure in the case of Athens or to address a natural disaster in Constantinople. The speed at which Nehemiah and his compatriots complete the walls belies the level of interference from Nehemiah's opponents. The fifty-two days it takes to build or repair the walls (2,820 meters) around Jerusalem's perimeters seem possible only with the entire repatriate community engaged, including the women.[73]

Nehemiah notes that those who have tried to frighten the builders are now afraid as they hear that the wall is complete. They are now the ones frightened and acknowledge that the wall's completion is not solely the result of human efforts but also indicative of divine assistance from Nehemiah's God: "they perceived that this work had been accomplished with the help of our God" (Neh 6:16).

The completion of the wall is not celebrated in Nehemiah 6:17-19. Instead, the text reports on Tobiah's attempt to intimidate Nehemiah. Apparently, Tobiah has maintained his relationship with the nobles, who have a complicated relationship with Nehemiah. The nobles were among the group that initially supported rebuilding the wall (Neh 2:16-18) yet later are critiqued for not participating (Neh 3:5). Nehemiah also accuses them of economically oppressing their kin (Neh 5:7). Tobiah's influence with the nobles is confirmed not only by their willingness to shower him with letters and collude with him during the construction of the wall but also they are "bound by oath" to him (Neh 6:18).[74] The Hebrew of 6:18 literally reads "masters of the oath" (בעלי שבועה) and we infer from

72. Fried, *Nehemiah*, 180.

73. Fried, *Nehemiah*, 180. She draws on F. Charles Fensham, who suggests that the wall surrounds the City of David and part of western hill; F. Charles Fensham, *The Books of Ezra and Nehemiah*, NICOT (Grand Rapids: Eerdmans, 1982), 207.

74. In Hellenistic Judah (320–141 BCE) the Tobiads from Ammon, Tobiah's namesakes, and the Oniads compete for power. The Tobiads were a prominent Jerusalem family, and the Oniads descended from Zadok, the priest under David and Solomon (2 Sam 8:17; 1 Kgs 2:35), and were part of a line of high priests. For more information about the Oniads and their interactions with the Tobiads, see Alice Hunt Hudiburg, "Onias," in *Eerdmans Dictionary of the Bible*, ed. David Noel Freedman (Grand Rapids: Eerdmans, 2000), 988.

this phrase that Tobiah, as a prominent member of society, leads this group. Tobiah's familial connections link him to Nehemiah's group.[75] The nobles try to temper Nehemiah's dislike of Tobiah by sending reports of Tobiah's goodness (טובה, *tovah*), a play on Tobiah's name. Perhaps the nobles are willing to work with both Nehemiah and Tobiah.[76] Or perhaps they want Nehemiah to take another look at the good Tobiah does rather than malign him. Despite their glowing report, Tobiah's intimidating letters speak to the contrary, "And Tobiah sent letters to intimidate me" (Neh 6:19). Still, we have only Nehemiah's assessment of the letters, not a record of their content.

In Nehemiah 6, both groups encounter fear and intimidation. The term ירא, translated by the NRSVue as "frighten" (Neh 6:9), "afraid" (Neh 6:14), and "intimidate" (Neh 6:13, 19), is used to present how Nehemiah perceives the activities of his adversaries and how his adversaries perceive the actions of Nehemiah's God. Sanballat and Geshem's attempt to meet with Nehemiah and their subsequent letter (Neh 6:2-9), the prophetic attempt to destroy him (Neh 6:10-14), and Tobiah's mysterious letters lead Nehemiah to consider himself to be in extreme danger. On the one hand, the actions of Nehemiah's opponents suggest foul play. On the other hand, they can be interpreted more charitably. For example, Sanballat, Tobiah, and Geshem's initial invitation to meet could have been sincere. Similarly, Shechaniah's invitation to enter the house of God was a protective gesture.

In our society, we tend to expect that those who are not for us are against us and will hurt us in some way. These assumptions lead to further acrimony and brokenness. What possibilities might there have been had Nehemiah and his adversaries assumed the best from each other and talked? How might we do the same?

75. Nehemiah 6:18 reports Tobiah is married to the daughter of Shecaniah son of Arah, who appears in the list of returnees (Ezra 2:5; Neh 7:10). Tobiah's son Jehohanan marries the daughter of Meshullam son of Berechiah who is listed among those who rebuild the wall (Neh 3:4, 30).

76. Lester Grabbe argues that Nehemiah does not value Tobiah's community importance, and the nobles, unlike him, wish to maintain their relationship with him (*Ezra–Nehemiah*, OTR [London: Routledge, 1998], 167).

Boundaries
by Adde Gross

Walls of Community and Safety (7:1-4)

Nehemiah 7 opens with a final statement that the walls and doors have been set (Neh 7:1). With the completion, Nehemiah begins to staff the house of God and reconstitute Jerusalem's infrastructure. First, he appoints gatekeepers, Levites, and singers to keep enemies at bay (Neh 7:1-2). He then appoints his brother, Hanani, as the commander of Jerusalem and entrusts Hananiah, whom he considers to be a man who fears God "more than many" (Neh 7:2), with the citadel.[77] The NRSVue recognizes Hanani and Hananiah as two separate individuals. Some argue, however, that the name Hanani might be a variant of Hananiah, alluding to a single individual rather than two distinct persons.[78] Hanani

77. See commentary on Neh 1:2.

78. Ralph Klein, "The Books of Ezra and Nehemiah," in *The New Interpreter's Bible*, ed. Leander Keck, vol. 3 (Nashville: Abingdon, 1999), 793; Hindy Najman, "Notes

Neh 7:1-4

[1]Now when the wall had been built and I had set up the doors and the gatekeepers, the singers, and the Levites had been appointed, [2]I gave my brother Hanani charge over Jerusalem, along with Hananiah the commander of the citadel, for he was a faithful man and feared God more than many. [3]And I said to them, "The gates of Jerusalem are not to be opened while the sun is hot; while the gatekeepers are still standing guard, let them shut and bar the doors. Appoint guards from among the inhabitants of Jerusalem, some at their watch posts, and others before their own houses." [4]The city was wide and large, but the people within it were few, and no houses had been built.

makes few appearances in the text. We are introduced to him when he brings news from Jerusalem to Nehemiah that the city's walls are still in shambles (Neh 1:2). He is possibly the same Hanani listed among those who lead the procession during the dedication of the walls (Neh 12:36). Still, Hanani does not appear on the lists of those who build the wall, nor is his family named among the community members. It is, therefore, unclear why Hanani becomes commander of Jerusalem other than his familial connection as Nehemiah's brother.

On the other hand, there are several references to Hananiah. Hananiah appears as one of the builders of the wall (Neh 3:30).[79] The name Hananiah appears in the lineage of priests who participate in the dedication ceremony for the walls (Neh 12:12). Hananiah also represents his family as he places a seal on Nehemiah's covenant (Neh 10:23).

The above connections make it appear as though Nehemiah engages in nepotism. Nepotism or not, Nehemiah appoints a person or persons whom he can trust, particularly considering the intimidation he encounters from Sanballat, the prophets, and Tobiah (Neh 6).

Nehemiah's actions underscore his deep concern for security. He insists that the gates remain closed until the "sun is hot" (Neh 7:3), which suggests that the gates are open during daylight hours and closed at

---

on Nehemiah," in *The Jewish Study Bible*, ed. Adele Berlin and Marc Zvi Brettler, 2nd ed. (Oxford: Oxford University Press, 2014), 1702; Blenkinsopp, *Ezra–Nehemiah*, 276; Fried, *Nehemiah*, 184.

79. Hananiah's name is not uncommon in biblical texts (1 Chr 3:19, 21; 8:24; 25:4, 23; 2 Chr 26:11).

night to prevent attacks. In addition, he appoints community members to keep guard of the community from all points of the city (Neh 7:3). The need for this vigilance is explained, "The city was wide and large, but the people within it were few, and no houses had been built" (Neh 7:4). Nehemiah faces an existential threat that makes his fear a forgone conclusion. This fear resonates throughout Nehemiah 6 and leads to his protective measures.

Several communities today face threats and violence from those who are challenged by the presence of the "other" in their communities. Sadly, in the present political climate, synagogues, mosques, and churches have come under attack, requiring them to create a system of security (e.g., performing active shooting drills, adding police presence, screening for weapons).

Genealogical Wall (7:5-69)

Nehemiah assembles the community, including the nobles and the officials, to "be enrolled by genealogy" (Neh 7:5). The list in 7:6-73 shares affinity with the list of names in Ezra 2.[80] While the list in Ezra 2 celebrates those who return from exile, the list here memorializes those who complete the walls.[81] With few changes, Ezra 2 and Nehemiah 7 frame the accounts of Jerusalem's building projects—the temple, altar, and walls. These lists play a pivotal role in harmonizing the communal structure found in both accounts. The redundancy is intentional.[82] As Jerusalem's population is restored and the community reconstituted, the reinstatement of Torah, pilgrimage festivals, and other communal laws depict a group unified by ancestral ties and shared religious traditions.

80. Oded Lipschits explains the discrepancy of the numbers in the two lists in Nehemiah. He says that Neh 11:14-19's count of 3,044 is one-tenth of the subtotal and Neh 7:4-42 is one-tenth of those who "went up out of captivity," not counting slaves, priests, and those without lineage. See Oded Lipschits, "Literary and Ideological Aspects of Nehemiah 11," *JBL* 121 (2002): 432n38.

81. Gordon F. Davies, *Ezra and Nehemiah*, Berit Olam, ed. David W. Cotter (Collegeville, MN: Liturgical Press, 1999), 103.

82. Katherine Southwood, "Ezra–Nehemiah," in *Fortress Commentary on the Bible: The Old Testament and the Apocrypha*, ed. Gale Yee, Hugh R. Page Jr., Matthew Coomber (Minneapolis: Fortress, 2014), 479.

Neh 7:5-69

5 Then my God put it into my mind to assemble the nobles and the officials and
the people to be enrolled by genealogy.
And I found the book of the genealogy of
those who were the first to come back,
and I found the following written in it:

6 These are the people of the province
who came up out of the captivity of those
exiles whom King Nebuchadnezzar of
Babylon had carried into exile; they returned to Jerusalem and Judah, each to
his town. 7 They came with Zerubbabel,

Ezra 2 and Nehemiah 7

Family/Group	Ezra 2	Nehemiah 7
Leaders	Zerubbabel, Jeshua, Nehemiah, Azariah, Raamiah, etc.	Zerubbabel, Jeshua, Nehemiah, Seraiah, Reelaiah, etc.
Descendants (Sample)	Parosh (2,172), Shephatiah (372), Arah (775), etc.	Parosh (2,172), Shephatiah (372), Arah (652), etc.
Priests	Descendants of Jedaiah, Immer, Pashhur, Harim, etc.	Descendants of Jedaiah, Immer, Pashhur, Harim, etc.
Levites	Descendants of Jeshua, Kadmiel, Hodaviah (74), etc.	Descendants of Jeshua, Kadmiel, Hodaviah (74), etc.
Singers	Descendants of Asaph (128), descendants of Solomon's servants (392)	Descendants of Asaph (148), descendants of Solomon's servants (392)
Gatekeepers	Descendants of Shallum, Ater, Talmon, Akkub, Hatita, Shobai (139)	Descendants of Shallum, Ater, Talmon, Akkub, Hatita, Shobai (138)
Temple Servants	Descendants of Ziha, Hasupha, Tabbaoth, Keros, Siaha, etc.	Descendants of Ziha, Hasupha, Tabbaoth, Keros, Siaha, etc.
Other Descendants	Descendants of Solomon's servants (Sotai, Darkon, Giddel, etc.)	Descendants of Solomon's servants (Sotai, Darkon, Giddel, etc.)
Unverified Descendants	Descendants of Delaiah, Tobiah, Nekoda (652), etc.	Descendants of Delaiah, Tobiah, Nekoda (642), etc.
Excluded from Priesthood	Some excluded but details not provided.	Excluded due to inability to prove ancestry.

Jeshua, Nehemiah, Azariah, Raamiah,
Nahamani, Mordecai, Bilshan, Misper-
eth, Bigvai, Nehum, Baanah.

The number of the Israelite people:
8the descendants of Parosh, two thousand one hundred seventy-two. 9Of
Shephatiah, three hundred seventy-
two. 10Of Arah, six hundred fifty-two. 11Of
Pahath-moab, namely, the descendants
of Jeshua and Joab, two thousand eight
hundred eighteen. 12Of Elam, one thousand two hundred fifty-four. 13Of Zattu,
eight hundred forty-five. 14Of Zaccai,
seven hundred sixty. 15Of Binnui, six
hundred forty-eight. 16Of Bebai, six hundred twenty-eight. 17Of Azgad, two thousand three hundred twenty-two. 18Of
Adonikam, six hundred sixty-seven. 19Of
Bigvai, two thousand sixty-seven. 20Of
Adin, six hundred fifty-five. 21Of Ater,
namely, of Hezekiah, ninety-eight. 22Of
Hashum, three hundred twenty-eight.
23Of Bezai, three hundred twenty-four.
24Of Hariph, one hundred twelve. 25Of
Gibeon, ninety-five. 26The people of
Bethlehem and Netophah, one hundred
eighty-eight. 27Of Anathoth, one hundred twenty-eight. 28Of Beth-azmaveth,
forty-two. 29Of Kiriath-jearim, Chephirah,
and Beeroth, seven hundred forty-three.
30Of Ramah and Geba, six hundred
twenty-one. 31Of Michmas, one hundred
twenty-two. 32Of Bethel and Ai, one hundred twenty-three. 33Of the other Nebo,
fifty-two. 34The descendants of the other
Elam, one thousand two hundred fifty-
four. 35Of Harim, three hundred twenty.
36Of Jericho, three hundred forty-five.
37Of Lod, Hadid, and Ono, seven hundred twenty-one. 38Of Senaah, three
thousand nine hundred thirty.

39The priests: the descendants of
Jedaiah, namely, the house of Jeshua,
nine hundred seventy-three. 40Of Immer,

Given the extensive list and the multitude of descendant households, one might wonder at the availability of women to match the size of each household and over what period of time. For example, how long would it take for the family of Parosh in 7:8 to create 2,172 descendants over an unspecified number of generations? We both come from large families and find it difficult to come up with a couple hundred descendants that we could chronicle that represent three or four generations! The text underscores the variation in family sizes, with some having several hundred or more descendants while others, like the Ater family, only have ninety-eight (Neh 7:21). The differences in the number of descendants could imply that certain families possess a lengthier history within the group than others or they had multiple wives. Although the text distinguishes between those with longer and shorter genealogical histories, all are acknowledged as part of the community of Israel, even those like the descendants of Delaiah, Tobiah, Nikoda, who cannot trace their histories (Neh 7:62-63).

Neh 7:5-69 (cont.)

one thousand fifty-two. 41 Of Pashhur,
one thousand two hundred forty-seven.
42 Of Harim, one thousand seventeen.

43 The Levites: the descendants of Jeshua, namely, of Kadmiel of the descendants of Hodevah, seventy-four. 44 The
singers: the descendants of Asaph, one
hundred forty-eight. 45 The gatekeepers:
the descendants of Shallum, of Ater, of
Talmon, of Akkub, of Hatita, of Shobai,
one hundred thirty-eight.

46 The temple servants: the descendants of Ziha, of Hasupha, of Tabbaoth,
47 of Keros, of Sia, of Padon, 48 of Lebana,
of Hagaba, of Shalmai, 49 of Hanan, of
Giddel, of Gahar, 50 of Reaiah, of Rezin,
of Nekoda, 51 of Gazzam, of Uzza, of
Paseah, 52 of Besai, of Meunim, of Ne-
phushesim, 53 of Bakbuk, of Hakupha, of
Harhur, 54 of Bazlith, of Mehida, of Harsha, 55 of Barkos, of Sisera, of Temah,
56 of Neziah, of Hatipha.

57 The descendants of Solomon's
servants: of Sotai, of Sophereth, of
Perida, 58 of Jaala, of Darkon, of Giddel,
59 of Shephatiah, of Hattil, of Pochereth-
hazzebaim, of Amon.

60 All the temple servants and the
descendants of Solomon's servants
were three hundred ninety-two.

61 The following were those who
came up from Tel-melah, Tel-harsha,
Cherub, Addon, and Immer, but they
could not prove their ancestral houses
or their descent, whether they belonged
to Israel: 62 the descendants of Delaiah,
of Tobiah, of Nekoda, six hundred forty-
two. 63 Also, of the priests: the descendants of Hobaiah, of Hakkoz, of Barzillai
(who had married one of the daughters
of Barzillai the Gileadite and was called
by their name). 64 These sought their
registration among those enrolled in
the genealogies, but it was not found

Nevertheless, there exists a subset within the community, exemplified by the priests, where exclusion from this group is contingent upon their ability to trace their genealogy. This subset is "excluded from the priesthood as unclean" until a priest validates their admission through the Urim and Thummim (Neh 7:65).[83] One reason for the inability to trace one's history might occur when families lose memory of who their ancestors were. If one group fails to transmit this information through generations due to death or other factors (e.g., estrangement), these connections can be lost.

83. The Urim and Thummim are divining stones or ritual objects that are used by the priests to receive divine revelation (Num 27:21; 1 Sam 28:6). They might be part of the priestly breast plate (Exod 28:30, "In the breast piece of judgment you shall put the Urim and the Thummim"; see also Lev 8:8).

Neh 7:5-69 (cont.)

there, so they were excluded from the priesthood as unclean; [65]the governor told them that they were not to partake of the most holy food until a priest with Urim and Thummim should come.

[66]The whole assembly together was forty-two thousand three hundred sixty, [67]besides their male and female slaves, of whom there were seven thousand three hundred thirty-seven, and they had two hundred forty-five singers, male and female. [68]They had seven hundred thirty-six horses, two hundred forty-five mules, [69]four hundred thirty-five camels, and six thousand seven hundred twenty donkeys.

Even though speculative, the exile, destruction of the temple, and intermarriage may have led to the loss or destruction of genealogical records.

Services such as ancestry.com and MyHeritageDNA thrive because people seek to know more about their genetic history. Henry Louis Gates's well-received program, *Finding Your Roots*, explores the family history of celebrities, athletes, and politicians to "expand America's sense of itself" and its interconnections.[84] Nehemiah's lists function similarly to demonstrate the repatriates' relationships and so to configure this newly constituted Israel. The lists memorialize the male heads of the families who remained faithful to Nehemiah's mission and contributed time, safety, and economic resources to ensure that Jerusalem's infrastructure and its community are rebuilt.

A Reconstituted Community (7:70-73a)

After Nehemiah chronicles the names of those who return from exile in 7:6-69, he turns to financial contributions for the work by various constituencies of the community as illustrated in the chart below (Neh 7:70-72):[85]

84. PBS, *Finding Your Roots*, https://www.pbs.org/show/finding-your-roots/.

85. Ezra's parallel list of those who returned with Zerubbabel (Ezra 2:1-70) also contains a list of donations to the building fund; however, these donors specifically contribute to the building of the house of God (Ezra 2:68). Further, only the heads of the households contributed, and the monetary amount differs: "they gave to the building fund sixty-one thousand darics of gold, five thousand minas of silver, and one hundred priestly robes" (Ezra 2:69).

Ezra 7:70-73a

70 Now some of the heads of ancestral houses contributed to the work.
The governor gave to the treasury one
thousand darics of gold, fifty basins,
and five hundred thirty priestly robes.
71 And some of the heads of ancestral
houses gave into the building fund
twenty thousand darics of gold and two
thousand two hundred minas of silver.
72 And what the rest of the people gave
was twenty thousand darics of gold,
two thousand minas of silver, and sixty-
seven priestly robes.
73a So the priests, the Levites, the
gatekeepers, the singers, some of the
people, the temple servants, and all
Israel settled in their towns.

Donors	Governor (תרשתא)	Some heads of ancestral households	Rest of the people
Gold	1,000 darics[86]	20,000 darics	20,000 darics
Silver	None	2,200 minas	2,200 minas
Basins	50	None	None
Robes	530	None	None

The people's commitment to the work of rebuilding is underscored as the entire community of Judah donates, although at different levels. The contributions of the ancestral heads of the household (20,000 darics of gold and 2,200 minas of silver) equals the sum of the remainder of the people's gift, a very generous contribution. The generosity of the community's gifts demonstrates how heavily invested the entire community is in building Jerusalem's infrastructure. Those who have the financial means may recognize that collectively the amount is not enough, and they are in a position to give more. We witness in our own churches, synagogues, and mosques times when those with more resources willingly share from their bounty for the benefit of the entire community. Yet, the different levels of giving point to possible economic disparities among the people of Judah. This disproportionate giving raises ques-

86. The JPS translation of Neh 7:70 translates the NRSVue's "darics" (דרכמנים) with "drachmas." Peter Altmann notes that scholars disagree on whether the coinage in question, the Persian daric, is named after Darius I or the drachma (Altmann, *Economics in Persian-Period Biblical Texts*, 224–25). The drachma is a Greek coin equivalent to 3.64 grams of silver (Carl Bridges, "Denarius," in *Eerdmans Dictionary of the Bible*, ed. David Noel Freedman [Grand Rapids: Eerdmans, 2000], 338).

tions about the level of power and input the heads of household may hold because of their financial investment in the infrastructure. Similar questions about financial influence come into play with the governor's contribution.

In between the donations of the heads of household (Neh 7:70a, 71) and the rest of the people (Neh 7:72) lie the donations of gold, basins, and robes by the governor (התרשׁתה, the tirshatha, 7:70a). First, while the Masoretic Text (Hebrew, Neh 7:69) and the NRSVue translation do not name the governor, the Septuagint identifies him as Nehemiah and suggests that Nehemiah's role is solely to place the people's gifts into the treasury without attributing any of the donations directly to him: "And part of the heads of families gave into the treasury to Neemias for the work a thousand pieces of gold, fifty bowls, and thirty priests' garments" (Neh 7:70).[87] Second, we discovered in Nehemiah 5:14 that Nehemiah has been appointed governor (פחה) of Judah, making this insertion logical. The term used here for "governor," tirshatha, התרשׁתא is a Persian title with an ambiguous role. The NRSVue and other translations (i.e., ESV, NIV) of Nehemiah 7:70 maintain the rendition "governor." The JPS chooses to preserve the ambiguity of the title by retaining the transliteration of the Hebrew "The Tirshatha." Third, Lisbeth Fried suggests that, instead of התרשׁתה being a title, it is a corrupt spelling of an unusual personal name, Attirsata, drawn from 'Attar (the Persian fire god) or the goddess Attar with the ending (שׁתה) meaning "prosperous" or "happy."[88]

The official in 7:70, whether Nehemiah or someone else sent by the Persian king to oversee the situation in Jerusalem, provides gold, basins, and robes for the priests. This support is modest compared to that given by the heads of the ancestral households and the remainder of the people. Still, his presence suggests Persian support and interest in the rebuilding of Jerusalem and its priesthood, raising questions about how much influence and control the Persian king has over the Jerusalem temple and worship.

87. Lancelot Charles Lee Brenton, trans., *The Septuagint Version of the Old Testament: With an English Translation, and with Various Readings and Critical Notes* (Grand Rapids: Zondervan, 1970). In addition, the Septuagint credits the people only for providing all the resources and divides the heads of household into two groups. One group is credited with donating what the NRSVue attributes to the governor with thirty robes rather than 530. Codex Vaticanus and Codex Sinaiticus both insert Nehemiah into the text. See textual notes on Nehemiah 7:69, *BHS*, 1443.

88. Fried, *Nehemiah*, 188–89.

The donations in Nehemiah 7 open questions for Nehemiah's community and ours. For example, are large gifts an act of generosity or a way to control the religious community and its leaders? These questions can be asked about gifts and tithes in our own religious communities.

Verse 7:73a reports that, now the walls are complete, many temple officials (priests, Levites, gatekeepers, singers, temple servants) leave the confines of Jerusalem and settle in their own towns. Many of the people of Israel also settled outside of Jerusalem. This settling outside of Jerusalem could occur for several reasons (for example, too expensive, available space).

Nehemiah 7:73b–10:39

Building a Community Ethic

In chapters 7:73b–10:39, Ezra performs a public reading of the Torah in front of a gathered group of men, women, and all who could understand (Neh 7:73b–8:12). This significant event reaffirms the community's identity and commitment to the law of Moses and God, leading to a community prayer of confession that recounts the people's history and the shortcomings of their ancestors (Neh 9). The gathering is depicted as a transformative experience, not only in renewing the community's religious commitment but also in emphasizing social cohesion and identity around the shared sacred text, which culminates in the community taking a collective oath to follow the Torah and commit to taking care of the house of the God (Neh 10).

Torah and Community Identity (7:73b–8:12)

The Law

Many Christians believe that the "grace" of the "New Testament" replaces the "legalism" of "Old Testament" law. There are New Testament texts that can be read as promoting this belief, such Paul's letter to the Galatians, which describes the law as curse (Gal

Neh 7:73b–8:12

[73b]When the seventh month came, the Israelites being settled in their towns, [8:1]all the people gathered together into the square before the Water Gate. They told Ezra the scribe to bring the book of the law of Moses, which the LORD had given to Israel. [2]Accordingly, Ezra the priest brought the law before the assembly, both men and women and all who could hear with understanding. This was on the first day of the seventh month. [3]He read from it facing the square before the Water Gate from early morning until midday, in the presence of the men and the women and those who could understand, and the ears of all the people were attentive to the book of the law. [4]Ezra the scribe stood on a wooden platform that had been made for the purpose, and beside him stood Mattithiah, Shema, Anaiah, Uriah, Hilkiah, and Maaseiah on his right hand and Pedaiah, Mishael,

3:10-13).[1] But such readings are incorrect. Paul views adherence to distinct Jewish practice as a curse *for the Gentiles* whom he is converting. He expects his fellow Jews to follow Torah, which is not a curse but a blessing. For Paul and for Jesus, and for their fellow Jews, Torah is a gift of God's grace and not a burden.[2] It is a sign of God's gracious willingness to enter into a covenantal relationship with Israel.[3] Indeed, the term "Torah" (תורה) is better translated as "instruction" rather than "law."[4] Jon Levenson writes, "Mount Sinai is the intersection of love and law, of gift and demand, the link between a past together and a future together."[5] Those who choose to follow set themselves apart from other communities in favor of a relationship with God and with each other. The point is not that there are no connections with others; there are still friendships, businesses, political concerns, and various other occasions when members of the covenant community are together with those who are not (we might think of relationships between US citizens and Canadians on the border, or between Baptists and Methodists).

1. See Amy-Jill Levine's discussion on the law and misperceptions about it in "Bearing False Witness. Common Errors Made About Early Judaism," in *The Jewish Annotated New Testament*, ed. Amy-Jill Levine and Mark Zvi Brettler, 2nd ed. (Oxford: Oxford University Press, 2017), 759–63.

2. Levine, "Common Errors," 501. See also Jonathan Klawans's article, "The Law," in this same publication, 515–18.

3. Jon Levenson, *Sinai and Zion: An Entry into the Jewish Bible* (San Francisco: HarperOne, 1987).

4. " תורה," *HALOT*, 1711–12.

5. Levenson, *Sinai and Zion*, 104.

Malchijah, Hashum, Hash-baddanah,
Zechariah, and Meshullam on his left
hand. [5]And Ezra opened the book in the
sight of all the people, for he was standing above all the people, and when he
opened it, all the people stood up. [6]Then
Ezra blessed the LORD, the great God,
and all the people answered, "Amen,
Amen," lifting up their hands. Then they
bowed their heads and worshiped the
LORD with their faces to the ground. [7]Also
the Levites Jeshua, Bani, Sherebiah,
Jamin, Akkub, Shabbethai, Hodiah,
Maaseiah, Kelita, Azariah, Jozabad,
Hanan, Pelaiah helped the people to
understand the law, while the people
remained in their places. [8]So they read
from the book, from the law of God, with
interpretation. They gave the sense, so
that the people understood the reading.

[9]And Nehemiah, who was the governor, and Ezra the priest and scribe,
and the Levites who taught the people
said to all the people, "This day is holy
to the LORD your God; do not mourn or
weep." For all the people wept when
they heard the words of the law. [10]Then
he said to them, "Go your way, eat the
fat and drink sweet wine and send portions of them to those for whom nothing
is prepared, for this day is holy to our
LORD, and do not be grieved, for the
joy of the LORD is your strength." [11]So
the Levites stilled all the people, saying, "Be quiet, for this day is holy; do
not be grieved." [12]And all the people
went their way to eat and drink and to
send portions and to make great rejoicing, because they had understood the
words that were declared to them.

In Nehemiah 7:73b–8:8, we receive a very detailed account of when the law actually appears in the midst of the people, the person responsible for bringing it (Ezra), and the people's response to hearing it. In the seventh month the people assemble at the Water Gate, perhaps near the Gihon Springs or Pool of Siloam, to hear the reading of the Torah (Neh 7:73b–8:1).[6] The Water Gate appears three times in chapter 8 as the place where the law is read (Neh 8:1, 3) and booths are built (Neh 8:16). Given its proximity to the temple, the Water Gate as a gathering space near a water source with its capacity to sustain life symbolically serves as the nexus where the community assembles to receive the vital laws that will sustain their shared existence.[7] In 8:1, the people summon Ezra the scribe to bring the law of Moses. This is the first mention of Ezra in

6. Leen Ritmeyer, "The Water Gate of Jerusalem," Ritmeyer Archaeological Design (June 22, 2011), https://www.ritmeyer.com/2011/06/22/the-water-gate-of-jerusalem/.

7. There are questions about the location of the Water Gate. It might be near the Springs of Gihon, or on the east near the temple.

Nehemiah.[8] While the text describes Ezra as a scribe in Nehemiah 8:1, it is Ezra, the priest, who brings the law before the people (Neh 8:2). The distinction would not have been lost on an ancient audience. Ezra, the scribe, is one skilled in the law of Moses (Neh 7:6). As one skilled in the law of Moses, Ezra would be intimately acquainted with the legal, ethical, and ritualistic aspects of the Torah as well as the copying and preserving of sacred texts and traditions. Ezra, the priest, however, a descendant of the Aaronide priests, would be responsible for ensuring the religious purity of the community.

Although the book of Nehemiah rarely mentions women, the narrator asserts that the assembly at the Water Gate includes "men and women and all who could hear with understanding" (Neh 8:2).[9] This group might also include older children or foreigners (גרים, i.e., "sojourners" or "resident aliens"), two additional groups included in the hearing of the initial Torah (Deut 31:10-12). The author underscores the unity of this collective, placing emphasis on "all the people," a phrase reiterated eleven times in this chapter (Neh 8:1, 3, 5-6, 9, 11-13).[10] Essentially, we observe a zealous community, with access to and enthusiasm for the law and its interpretation.[11]

With the presence of the law and its reader in place, the scene is set for the reading. Ezra reads from early morning until midday and "the ears of all the people were attentive to the book of the law" (Neh 8:3).

8. There is a debate whether this text (Neh 8–10) is part of Nehemiah's memoir for several reasons. The first is that Nehemiah's memoir is written in the first-person voice (e.g., Neh 6) and changes to the third person (Neh 8:1–12:30). The reading of the law might belong in Ezra's account right after Ezra 8 and is later inserted into Nehemiah's narrative in Neh 8–10 to align Nehemiah with the once unnamed governor in Neh 8:9 (Joseph Blenkinsopp, *Ezra–Nehemiah: A Commentary*, OTL [Philadelphia: Westminster, 1988], 284–85). Also, Ezra 3:1 notes a gathering of the people in Jerusalem in the seventh month, the same month that he gathers the people in Neh 7:73—another clue that editors might have initially placed the law in Ezra (Hindy Najman, "Notes on Nehemiah," in *The Jewish Study Bible*, ed. Adele Berlin and Marc Zvi Brettler, 2nd ed. [Oxford: Oxford University Press, 2014], 1702).

9. When the law is read in Deuteronomy, those in the assembly include men, women, children, and sojourners (גרים, Deut 31:10-13).

10. Deut 31:12: "Assemble the people—men, women, and children, as well as the aliens residing in your towns—so that they may hear and learn to fear the LORD your God and to observe diligently all the words of this law." See Tamara C. Eskenazi, *In an Age of Prose: A Literary Approach to Ezra–Nehemiah*, SBLMS 36 (Atlanta: SBL, 1988), 97–98; Robert Alter, "Nehemiah," in *The Hebrew Bible: The Writings* (New York: Norton, 2019), 847.

11. H. G. M. Williamson, *Ezra, Nehemiah*, WBC 16 (Waco: Word, 1985), 297. See also Eskenazi, *In an Age of Prose*, 97.

Reading the law to the community in a public setting serves to equalize its access for those in the repatriate community and those who join them. Since a vast majority of people cannot read and do not have access to written copies of Torah, they can now participate in its interpretation. Here we would inquire whether hearing the text is making it accessible to everyone in the crowd, because it assumes that everyone can hear. The writer presupposes an audience unable to read but able to "listen attentively and understand." Moreover, highlighting the importance of attentive listening and understanding may stem from individuals who are not fluent in ancient Hebrew (because they are Aramaic speakers) but still come together to partake in this collective activity. Today we would make accommodations for those who are hearing impaired (e.g., signing, closed captions) and not assume that everyone can hear, read, or understand. Here too, language barriers, while significant, are not insurmountable given the multiplicity of Bible translations and available interpretive tools (websites, phone apps, Bible software).

Ezra stands on a "wooden platform" or "tower" (מגדל) that allows the crowd to see and hear him. While the law is read, another group of thirteen men stands next to Ezra, six on the right and seven on the left (Neh 8:4). The list of names appears to be a combination of priests, Levites, and other heads of families. Many of the names are recurrent throughout Ezra–Nehemiah, with the people assuming different roles at different points in the narrative. Several names also appear in the lists of priests who committed to divorcing their foreign wives, including Maaseiah, Malchijah, Hashum, Zechariah, and Meshullam (Ezra 10:18-44).[12] These individuals are on display and might symbolize those who are reinstated into the community for their willingness to comply with the requirement to send away their wives and children.

When Ezra opens the scroll the people immediately stand (Neh 8:5). The act of standing represents the reverence the people have for the law. Then Ezra blesses the Lord, the great God, and the people signal their affirmation of this blessing through their "Amen, Amen" and lifted hands (Neh 8:6). Then, they change postures and drop their bodies and faces (NRSVue) or their noses (Hebrew אפים) to the ground in obeisance. They express their reverence toward the Torah scroll, which now serves as a symbolic representation of God among the people.

12. Eskenazi notes the lack of clarity concerning these men (*In an Age of Prose*, 98). Blenkinsopp agrees with Williamson that these men are laity (*Ezra–Nehemiah*, 287).

Postures during Worship

The act of worship is an embodied act. David illustrates this when he angers Michal as he brings the ark of the covenant into Jerusalem. She looks out the window and sees David "leaping and dancing before the LORD" (2 Sam 6:16). Psalm 150 emphasizes the participation of the body in the act of worship (v. 4). Different postures accompany various styles of worship as people demonstrate reverence in different ways (arms up, bodies down, dancing, sitting still, and more). Yet these postures embody the entirety of one's self and community—head, heart, soul, body—as a gift of gratefulness to the deity.

While it is Ezra's job to read the text, it is the Levites' job to interpret it, "so they read from the book, from the law of God, with interpretation. They gave the sense, so that the people understood the reading" (Neh 8:7-8). The Levites are to assist the audience in comprehending Ezra's exposition of the law. Since Aramaic was the *lingua franca* of the territories of Judah, it is possible these interpreters needed to translate Hebrew into Aramaic. The ongoing tradition of real-time translation remains prevalent today. For example, synagogues, mosques, and churches use interpreters during worship to accommodate those who cannot hear or who do not speak the language. The United Nations uses translators in a similar way. The text makes clear that the Torah needs to be interpreted for this group—its meaning is not self-evident. In this gathering, the law is available and applicable to the men and women and, perhaps, older children who could understand.

Nehemiah and his group were responsible for building the infrastructure (i.e., walls), and now Ezra is there to restore the religious structure that unifies the people around the law. Consequently, the gathering manifests a shared faith and obedience, uniting them as a religious community with a shared ethic and identity.

Hearing the Torah causes the people to weep (Neh 8:9). The legal safeguards might evoke tears of joy for those struggling to survive and needing the law to provide them security. The tears could be tears of conviction for falling short of God's covenant. When Shaphan, the high priest Hilkiah's secretary, reads the law to Josiah, the king rends his clothes while mourning (1 Kgs 23:11). Weeping could also express the awe of receiving this gift from God.

Nehemiah, initially absent in Nehemiah 8:1-8, appears alongside Ezra and the Levites in 8:9.[13] Together Nehemiah, Ezra, and the Levites proclaim the day holy (8:9, 10, 11); the phrase "This day is holy to the Lord your God" and refraining from weeping or grieving become a responsive thread. Ezra and Nehemiah emphasize the holiness of this day and the need to celebrate it three times: first, immediately after the people hear and understand the law (Neh 8:9); second, after they are told to eat, drink, and distribute portions to those without food (Neh 8:10, 12); and third, as the community prepares to scatter and share (Neh 8:11). Its repetition helps reinforce the view that just as the day is set apart (holy), the people too are set apart: "the joy of the Lord is your strength" (Neh 8:10). The sending of portions (שלח מנות; Neh 8:12; Esth 9:22) has affinities with the book of Esther and the celebration of Purim, where portions provide the means for those who have less to celebrate the occasion. Distributing portions is a gesture of kindness and solidarity within the community, a practice that Jews still engage in today, recognizing that certain individuals may be facing food insecurity.

In Nehemiah 8:10-13, food is ritualized. The group partakes of the finest food. The Hebrew terms משמנים (oil-rich food) and ממתקים (sweet drinks) represent festival dishes of best cakes and wine.[14] Across cultures foods become embedded in the symbolism and traditions associated with various religious groups. For example, some groups may serve black-eyed peas, collard greens, and cornbread on New Year's Day. Other groups may serve jambalaya, or pork and sauerkraut. At Easter celebrations, some eat ham and deviled eggs or roast lamb and sweets. Although the dishes may differ, they symbolize and memorialize the special moments that mark the people as part of a larger community who share the same values and traditions. These moments contribute to the broader celebration that honors the designated day.

Reading the Torah together results in celebration and great rejoicing. For Ezra and the people gathered with him, the Torah provides an ethic to live by and marks them as God's own, which is a reason to celebrate. The

13. Fried is among those who suggest that Nehemiah is added to the book later (see Lisbeth S. Fried, *Nehemiah: A Commentary*, Critical Commentaries [Sheffield: Sheffield Phoenix, 2021], 210).

14. משמנים, *HALOT*, 649; ממתקים, *HALOT*, 596.

joy of the yearly celebration of Simchat Torah ("rejoicing in the Torah") that takes place at the end of Sukkot on the twenty-third of Tishri results in similar celebrations. The Jewish community celebrates reaching the end of Deuteronomy and then the return to the beginning in Genesis in the annual cycle of Torah readings by dancing, singing, and processing with the scrolls. Rabbi George Robinson explains, "To be immersed in Torah is a joyous thing for a Jew, something worthy of celebration."[15] This is the joy present among the people—men and women—gathered at the Water Gate when Ezra reads to them from "the book of the law of Moses" (Neh 8:1).

Who Gets to Interpret Sacred Scriptures Today?

The Torah is a living document, and the entire repatriate community plays a role in hearing it read by Ezra. To deepen their understanding of the text, Ezra assigns a particular group of men to interpret it, giving them power over how these texts are understood and applied to their community. Today, leaders in churches and synagogues, laity and clergy, draw on interpreters to help convey the meanings of biblical texts to their congregations. Within our respective resources are materials that rely on scholars formally trained in reading biblical texts—those who write commentaries, monographs, and articles on biblical texts. Every interpreter of the Bible brings their training and personal experiences. Any commentary or interpretation will inevitably be influenced by these factors. Today, we have access to many books, articles, blogs, and websites, some good and others not, that provide insight into understanding biblical texts. Suppose we want to have a deeper understanding of biblical texts. In that case, we should take inventory of our bookshelves and bookmarked webpages to see whom we depend on for our interpretations and whose voices are missing. How many commentaries in our repertoire are written by women, from underrepresented voices, from a global perspective, or any point of view other than our own? Those resources we integrate into our interpretations and share with our communities have authoritative status. Being mindful of our choices of resources and our own thoughts about the texts makes us better interpreters of Sacred Scriptures.

15. George Robinson, *Essential Judaism: A Complete Guide to Beliefs, Customs, and Rituals* (New York: Pocket Books, 2000), 111.

The Festival of Booths (Sukkot) (8:13-18)

The second day Ezra gathers "the heads of ancestral houses" with the priests and Levites for Torah study (Neh 8:13)—not the entire community this time. In 8:2, everyone who could understand is invited to hear the law and its interpretation. Torah study seems primarily reserved for the heads of ancestral houses, priests, and Levites, suggesting that only men participate in this activity. The ones reading and interpreting the law are men, and they decide how it should be approached.

Within this community, Torah study expands beyond the priests and Levites to include the male and female laity. In this ancient community women studied Torah, but it is unlikely that they studied alongside the priests and Levites. However, within Jesus's Jewish community, women were included in his learning circles (for example, Mary, Martha, Mary of Magdala). There is evidence that the early church admonished and discouraged women from teaching men in and out of the church (1 Cor 14:34-35; 1 Tim 2:11-12). This prohibition reflects a patriarchal structure aimed at subordinating and limiting women's religious education to the authority of their male heads of households.

Women and Torah Study

In Nehemiah 8, men, women, and children who have understanding are invited to the Water Gate to hear the Torah read by Ezra. A group of named men (Neh 8:7) and the Levites stood among the people to help people understand the reading. Ezra invites women to hear and receive insight from this group of men, suggesting that interpreting the Torah is reserved for men. Yet women have been reading and interpreting the Torah for centuries, both privately and publicly, despite restrictions placed on them by the religious community. Rachel Keren, Tamara Cohn Eskenazi, and Andrea L. Weiss explore the roles that women play in the interpretation of the Torah in Judaism through history.[16] Keren notes that because Jewish women were not obligated to study Torah, they were cut off

16. For discussion on women interpreters of Torah, see Rachel Keren, "Torah Study," *Shalvi/Hyman Encyclopedia of Jewish Women*, Jewish Women's Archive (March 20, 2009), https://jwa.org/encyclopedia/article/torah-study. See also Tamara Cohn Eskenazi and Andrea L. Weiss, "Women and Interpretation of the Torah," in *The Torah: A Women's Commentary*, ed. Eskenazi and Weiss (New York: URJ Press and Women of Reform Judaism, The Federation of Temple Sisterhoods, 2008), xxxvi–xl.

Neh 8:13-18

[13]On the second day the heads of ancestral houses of all the people, with
the priests and the Levites, came together to Ezra the scribe in order to
study the words of the law. [14]And they
found it written in the law that the LORD
had commanded by Moses that the Israelites should live in booths during the
festival of the seventh month [15]and that
they should publish and proclaim in all
their towns and in Jerusalem as follows,
"Go out to the hills and bring branches
of olive, wild olive, myrtle, palm, and
other leafy trees to make booths, as
it is written." [16]So the people went out
and brought them and made booths for
themselves, each on the roofs of their
houses, and in their courts and in the
courts of the house of God, and in the
square at the Water Gate and in the
square at the Gate of Ephraim. [17]And
all the assembly of those who had returned from the captivity made booths
and lived in them, for from the days of
Jeshua son of Nun to that day the Israelites had not done so. And there was
very great rejoicing. [18]And day by day,
from the first day to the last day, Ezra
read from the book of the law of God.
They kept the festival seven days, and
on the eighth day there was a solemn
assembly, according to the ordinance.

from studying the Torah.[17] Yet, there are women lauded for their proficiency in studying these texts. The Talmud mentions the example of Beruryah, who is noted for her knowledge of the Torah and is an early example of a woman engaged in Torah study (*Tosefta Kelim*).[18] Keren, Eskenazi, and Weiss chronicle other women involved in Torah reading and expert copiers of the texts, even if women were often discouraged or restricted from formal study.

In Christianity, many faced restrictions in studying their sacred texts. Despite women's participation in Jesus' ministry and serving the early church (e.g., Luke 8:1-3; Mark 15:40-41; Rom 16:1-16), it took until 1853 for a Protestant woman, Antoinette Brown Blackwell, to be ordained in the United States. Today, globally, women are deeply involved in the reading of the Torah and expand readings that integrate their lived experiences.

During their study, the men come across the law where "the Israelites should live in booths during the festival of the seventh month" (Neh 8:14). A public proclamation and a list of the necessary materials for the

17. Keren, "Torah Study."
18. Keren, "Torah Study."

booths' construction precedes the commemoration in which booths are erected on rooftops, in courtyards, the Water and Ephraim Gate squares, and even the courts of the house of God (Neh 8:15-16). According to Nehemiah 8:17, the tradition of celebrating the Festival of Booths (Sukkot, Neh 8:13-18; see Exod 23:14-17; Lev 23:34-43; Deut 16:14) was last celebrated in "the days of Jeshua son of Nun." Nevertheless, there are numerous biblical passages that reference this festival occurring after Joshua's time, during which the obligation to dwell in booths is not specified (Num 29:12-38; Deut 31:9-13; 2 Chr 7:8-10). The discovery of this festival calls to mind the time when the high priest Hilkiah discovers the book of the law and King Josiah reinstitutes Passover (2 Kgs 22:8-30) since "no such Passover had been kept since the days of the judges who judged Israel, even during all the days of the kings of Israel and of the kings of Judah" (2 Kgs 23:22-23).

The practice of building and living in booths (sg. סכה, *sukkah*; pl. סכות, *sukkot*), as described in Nehemiah 8:15-17, might reflect a later tradition. The people's participation in Sukkot juxtaposes the permanence with the impermanence. The repatriates, having settled in the land (permanence), are now enjoined to participate in the ritual of living in temporary shelters (impermanence). Although Sukkot is a time for joyous celebration, the festive atmosphere often overlooks the challenges women face in re-creating a sense of home in temporary spaces. Women's responsibility for the activities in the household (e.g., care of animals, children, and elderly) is essential when men are away from the home. If women do not travel to Jerusalem to participate in the festival, perhaps they celebrate Sukkot in the temporary tents on the roofs of their houses (Neh 8:16). The chapter concludes almost as it began. In Nehemiah 8:18, there is a daily reading of the book of the law and keeping of the festival for seven days. On the eighth day, the people gather together to conclude their observation of the ordinance (Neh 8:18), which underscores that the practice has become embedded in the rituals and institutionalization of the religious community.

Whether at home or in Jerusalem, the community observes Sukkot because of the collective study of the Torah by its leaders and clergy. This collective study leads to the recognition that the people are obligated to partake in this festival but may differ from Leviticus and Numbers in how and where they observe it (Lev 23:33-43; Num 29:12-38). The text does not give us a window into the process they use "to study the words of the law." Those reading these laws with Ezra live in different historical and cultural contexts than those who first received them, raising the need to fill in gaps for greater understanding of their meaning.

The need to study biblical law or the Bible has not changed. One of the meanings of Torah is "instruction," and, therefore, it is meant to be studied. Throughout history rabbis, priests, and other religious leaders interpreted the Bible to meet the needs of their communities. In the same way, we read the Bible today, recognizing that the text is multivalent and does not offer quick and clean answers to many of our theological and ethical issues. In sum, the rituals in Nehemiah 8 take place not in the temple but rather in the public space that is inclusive of community.

Cementing Community Identity: The Community Confesses and Commits (9:1–10:39)

Before taking residence in Jerusalem and dedicating the walls, the community separates from the nations surrounding them. Nehemiah 9 records the community's penitential prayer, which leads to a community pledge (Neh 10) where the repatriates affirm in writing that they freely take on the responsibilities for keeping the Torah's commandments (10:29), particularly those that require separation from foreigners (Neh 10:30), keeping the Sabbath (Neh 10:31), and maintaining the temple infrastructure (Neh 10:32-39). These acts highlight the community's desire to separate from past sins and from the people of the land before entering the "holy city" of Jerusalem (Neh 11:1). The Hebrew verb translated "separate" (בדל) forms an *inclusio* around chapters 9 and 10 (Neh 9:2; 10:28). In these next two chapters, the book of Nehemiah sets the stage for a complete separation from the people of the land—from Sanballat, Tobiah, Geshem, Noadiah, and others Nehemiah and his community label outsiders—and the community's commitment to a reconstituted Israel.

Preparation for the Prayer (9:1-5)

Nehemiah 9:1 reports that on the twenty-fourth day of "this month," after celebrating the Festival of Booths (Neh 8:13-18), the "people of Israel" gather to fast, don sackcloth, and cover themselves in dust. The act of fasting is often a response to national crises or mourning. Jehoshaphat requires Judah to fast before facing the enemy (2 Chr 20:1-4), and Esther proclaims a fast before she petitions King Ahasuerus to spare her people from annihilation (Esth 4:16). Nehemiah fasts in grief when hearing that Jerusalem's walls are still in shambles (Neh 1:1-4). In 9:1 the gathered community's joy in celebrating Sukkot soon turns to fasting and mourn-

Ezra 9:1-5

[1]Now on the twenty-fourth day of this month the Israelites were assembled with fasting and in sackcloth and with earth on their heads. [2]Then those of Israelite descent separated themselves from all foreigners and stood and confessed their sins and the iniquities of their ancestors. [3]They stood up in their place and read from the book of the law of the LORD their God for a fourth part of the day, and for another fourth they made confession and worshiped the LORD their God. [4]Then Jeshua, Bani, Kadmiel, Shebaniah, Bunni, Sherebiah, Bani, and Chenani stood on the stairs of the Levites and cried out with a loud voice to the LORD their God. [5]Then the Levites Jeshua, Kadmiel, Bani, Hashabneiah, Sherebiah, Hodiah, Shebaniah, and Pethahiah said, "Stand up and bless the LORD your God from everlasting to everlasting. Blessed be your glorious name, which is exalted above all blessing and praise."

ing. The community's collective experience of joy and sorrow (celebration followed by fasting and mourning) captures the multifaceted nature of faith. These aspects are transformative in the spiritual growth of this community and prompt the community's need for confession.

The timing of this fast and identity of this group is ambiguous when considering Nehemiah 9:1-2. It is also unclear whether the group in Nehemiah 9:2, identified as the seed of Israel (זרע ישׂראל) and those who separate themselves from "all foreigners" (בני נכר), is the same group described as the Israelites (בני־ישׂראל) in 9:1.[19] Some have taken these verses to be a reference to Yom Kippur given their emphasis on communal confession (9:2-3).[20] Just as the community that gathers is ambiguous, so are the foreigners from whom they separate.

19. Using the terms "seed" and "foreigner" calls our attention to the holy seed (Ezra 9:2). Ezra fears it will mix with the foreign women and pollute the repatriates and the land (Ezra 9:11). This imperative to separate from foreigners appears again in Neh 10:28, right before the community's voluntary acceptance of laws forbidding intermarriage with the peoples of the land (10:30), and in Neh 13:3, 23-31 after the dedication of the wall (12:27-43). Some scholars suggest Nehemiah 9 follows Ezra 9–10 or precedes Nehemiah 13:1-3 (see Blenkinsopp, *Ezra–Nehemiah*, 294).

20. Because chapter 9 continues the narrative, it is possible that this is the twenty-fourth day of the seventh month (Tishri). It is likely that when Nehemiah is written the date for Yom Kippur may not have been set.

The term "foreigners" in Nehemiah 9:2 usually refers to those from different countries or ethnicities (2 Chr 6:32; Judg 19:12; Isa 1:7; Ezek 31:12; 44:7), but here the returnees appear to expand the definition to include those among the people of the land, also Israelites.[21] There are other places in the Hebrew Bible where a member of the community feels excluded or "foreign." Job laments that because of his afflictions his friends, family, and servants disown him: "I have become an alien [נכר] in their own eyes" (Job 19:15).[22] In the eyes of the returned exiles, the people of the land are foreigners from whom they must separate in order to seal the community identity and holiness of the newly reconstituted Israel.[23] Also, separating from the other groups in the region allows the people of Israel, who share a collective history, to approach their deity in a prayer of confession for the sins of their ancestors (Neh 9:6-31) and a petition for God's help in the present day (Neh 9:32-37).

Native or Non-Native: What Makes the Foreigner Foreign? Or, From Whom Did They Separate?

At first glance, Nehemiah 9:1-5 appears to be an honest and holy attempt by the people of God to return to their origins and reaffirm their identity as a covenant people. The people of Israel engage in signs of repentance with fasting, sackcloth, and ashes. A curious turn of events occurs in verse 2, however, when "those of Israelite descent" separate themselves from "all foreigners" before confessing their sins. Only after making this identification do the true Israelites proceed to worship God by hearing the law read and engaging in confession, culminating in a doxological pronouncement.

The separation in verse two provides a means of creating a holy people devoted to God. This act implies that their ancestors failed in this endeavor, so they must first rectify the situation, and their

21. Bob Becking suggests that this includes people who disagree with the repatriates (*Ezra–Nehemiah*, HCOT [Leuven: Peeters, 2018], 256).

22. When Joseph meets his brothers in Egypt after many years, he treats them as "foreigners" (נכר, Gen 42:7). Here the NRSVue translates נכר as "stranger" (Gen 42:7).

23. See commentary on Ezra 9–10 and Nehemiah 13:23-31 on the prohibitions against foreign women.

concomitant generational sins must be confessed. Sylvester A. Johnson, in his analysis of the Ezra–Nehemiah reformation of the postexilic period, identifies similar actions throughout the Bible linked to the metanarrative of Israel, which sets the divinely identified people of God apart from those who are not.[24]

Similarly, the word "foreign" (נכר) appears to provide justification for how they will live into their identity. The word, most often translated as "foreigner" (NRSVue, NIV, NJB), can also be translated as "stranger" (NJV, FBJ) or "alien" (VUL) with Brown-Driver-Briggs going so far as to indicate the Aramaic cognate translates as "enemy."[25] Significant for the metanarrative, it often carries a negative connotation indicating that "Israel should separate itself from the nations to the extent possible."[26] In other contexts, however, נכר refers to persons who "are not necessarily non-Israelites in the ethnic sense" but "rather in their not belonging to one's own extended family or household" especially when referring to foreign women.[27] The writer of Proverbs stereotypes foreign women as promiscuous (Prov 2:16; 5:3, 17, 20; 6:24; 7:5; 22:14; 23:27).[28] In light of this, we may well ask ourselves, "Is this the case in these verses?" And if so, "Who are these foreigners? Who determines the identity of the foreigner for separation?"

Earlier chapters named the elite of Israel who were carried off into captivity, so the case has been made that the people listed in verses 4 and 5 are their descendants. Their pedigree, alongside their possession of the law and direction of the religious rituals, seems to make it clear, at least in their own minds, that they have the right to determine the identity of foreigners and take leadership over any indigenous inhabitants of the land upon their arrival.[29] But leadership is not all they have taken because chapter 7 tells us that these returnees "settled into their towns"

24. Sylvester A. Johnson, "New Israel, New Canaan: The Bible, the People of God, and the American Holocaust," *USQR* 59 (2005): 26.

25. *BDB*, 648.

26. Christopher T. Begg, "Foreigner," in *The Anchor Yale Bible Dictionary: D–G*, ed. David Noel Freedman, Gary A. Herion, David Frank Graf, J. David Pleins, and Astrid B. Beck (New Haven: Yale University Press, 1992), 829–30.

27. Begg, "Foreigner," 829–30.

28. See Begg, "Foreigner," 829–30.

29. I use the lowercase term "indigenous" to indicate those who already inhabit the land when the exiles are repatriated.

(Neh 7:73). Furthermore, as Gary Knoppers explains in his study of the ethnic diversity of Judah, the intermarriages and intermingling of various peoples within the genealogy of Judah, now identified as Israel in Nehemiah, have existed since the beginning.[30] Therefore, any attempt to identify the indigenous people of the land and set them apart as foreigners is actually a separation of the Indigenous Peoples from their own kin and confiscation of their land.[31]

One could consider the trauma affecting everyone in trying to make sense of these delineations. The voices of the repatriates are the children and grandchildren of the exiled Original Peoples. Their worldview born out of the experience of captivity comingled with an origin story dependent on their parents' and grandparents' recollections could understandably influence their behavior. As Herbert Anderson and Edward Foley, who explore the role of personal narrative in identity construction, write, "An amazing dynamic exists between our lives and our stories: each one shapes the other. Our collective life experiences are interpreted through a personal narrative framework and shaped into a master story that, in turn, influences subsequent interpretations."[32] These stories passed down would be reinterpreted and retold with changes that we may not have retained in the biblical account, but which nonetheless lived in the memories of the returning generations. These settlers calling for separation may not recognize the Indigenous Peoples who are living in the land as relatives.

As a white settler living in North America, I seek to look at this passage through a decolonizing lens with a hermeneutic of suspicion, which leads me to find a much more complicated situation than may be evident with a superficial first reading of the text. Robert Warrior's seminal work reminds us that the biblical narratives contain brutality and terror born out of conquest and have influenced the ways in which Indigenous Peoples are treated today.[33] Thus, it would be wise to exert caution and pause to consider the rhetorical narratives

30. Gary N. Knoppers, "Intermarriage, Social Complexity, and Ethnic Diversity in the Genealogy of Judah," *JBL* 120 (2001): 22.

31. I capitalize the term "Indigenous Peoples" strategically to indicate those who are not the dehumanized "other" but rather the Original Peoples of the land.

32. Herbert Anderson and Edward Foley, *Mighty Stories, Dangerous Rituals: Weaving Together the Human and the Divine* (San Francisco: Jossey-Bass, 1998), 11.

33. Robert Allen Warrior, "Canaanites, Cowboys, and Indians," *USQR* 59 (2005): 1–8.

that preclude the modern reader from seeing the ways in which a colonial worldview plays into a simplistic reading of the text, the position of the narrator, and the objectification of the Indigenous Peoples also of Israelite descent.

Suzanne Wenonah Duchesne

With a few exceptions, Nehemiah 9:3-4 resembles the public reading of Torah in 8:3 and 8:7. In chapter 9, however, Levites address the people from "stairs of the Levites" (see Neh 9:4) instead of Ezra, who is absent from this scene. There are two separate groups of eight Levites; the first group cries out to God (Neh 9:4) and the second instructs the people in worship (Neh 9:5).[34] The Levites lead the people in confession and worship but only after the community itself chooses to engage in these rituals.[35] The Levites call the people to prayer: "Stand up and bless the LORD your God from everlasting to everlasting" (Neh 9:5a). They then direct their next words and the entire prayer toward God: "Blessed be your glorious name, which is exalted above all blessing and praise" (Neh 9:5b). The prayer now becomes Israel's prayer, prayed fully by the community.

A Prayer of Confession and Petition (9:6-37)

The people's ritual actions recounted in Nehemiah 9:1-5 prepare them for the prayer they now pray in 9:6-37. This communal prayer relates Israel's history from creation (Neh 9:6) through God's promise to Abraham (Neh 9:7-8), the exodus, wilderness, and settlement (Neh 9:9-25), the period of the kings and Israel's exile (Neh 9:26-31), and their present situation (Neh 9:32-37). In between accounts of God's righteous acts on behalf of Israel, the community assumes responsibility for their ancestors' disobedience (Neh 9:16-17, 26-27, 29) and exalts God for God's mercy (רחם, Neh 9:17, 19, 27, 31), forgiveness (סליחה, Neh 9:17), graciousness (חנון, Neh 9:17, 31), and steadfast love (חסד, Neh 9:17, 32). In the community's understanding of their history, facts matter. This community, informed by their past, desires to move forward as a unified group committed to the Torah and their God.

34. Five members of each group share names, which leads some to suggest that these two groups represent different sources that were melded together. Instead, these groups might have different tasks with some overlap. Several also are named in Nehemiah 8.

35. Donna Laird, *Negotiating Power in Ezra–Nehemiah*, AIL 26 (Atlanta: SBL Press, 2016), 272.

Neh 9:6-37

6And Ezra said, "You are the LORD,
you alone; you have made heaven, the heaven of heavens, with all their host, the earth and all that is on it, the seas and all that is in them. To all of them you give life, and the host of heaven worships you.
7You are the LORD, the God who chose Abram and brought him out of Ur of the Chaldeans and gave him the name Abraham;
8and you found his heart faithful before you and made with him a covenant to give to his descendants the land of the Canaanite, the Hittite, the Amorite, the Perizzite, the Jebusite, and the Girgashite, and you have fulfilled your promise, for you are righteous.

9"And you saw the distress of our ancestors in Egypt and heard their cry at the Red Sea.
10You performed signs

Nehemiah 9 in Jewish Liturgy

Leader: Let us bless the Source of Life

Congregation: As we bless the source of life so we are blessed.

Leader: As we bless the source of life so may we be blessed.

—*Marcia Falk*[36]

The elements of reading Torah, confession, and worship in Nehemiah 9:3 remain in today's synagogue services. The rabbis credit Nehemiah 9:3 for the daily division of Torah study and prayer in Jewish practice as well as the integration of 9:6-37 in Jewish daily morning prayers.[37] The beginning of this penitential prayer is deeply embedded in the ritual of Judaism past and present. Nehemiah 9:5 might be the origin for the *bar'ku* ("the call for blessing"), the prayer that opens the morning and evening synagogue prayers and is recited before the reading of the Torah and after the *shema* (Deut 6:4-9).[38] While the words may change over time, like Marcia Falk's adaptations of the *bar'ku* for inclusive community,[39] the call to bless remains.

36. Marcia Falk, *The Book of Blessings: New Jewish Prayers for Daily Life, the Sabbath, and the New Moon Festival* (New York: Reform Judaism Publishing, 2017), 164.

37. Najman, "Notes on Nehemiah," 1702. Najman cites b. Meg.30b and b. Ta'an 12b as she notes that haftorah readings (readings from the biblical prophets) should also be studied. Nehemiah 9:6-20 also appears in the lectionary cycle for the Episcopal Church and makes up two out of three readings from Ezra–Nehemiah in this resource (http://www.textweek.com/2_chron_neh_esther.htm).

38. "Bareku," in *Oxford Dictionary of the Jewish Religion*, ed. R. J. Zwi Werblowsky and G. Wigoder (Oxford: Oxford University Press, 1997), 99.

39. Falk, *The Book of Blessings*, esp. 49, 164–65, 463–64, 479.

and wonders against Pharaoh and all his servants and all the people of his land, for you knew that they acted insolently against our ancestors. You made a name for yourself that remains to this day. [11]And you divided the sea before them, so that they passed through the sea on dry land, but you threw their pursuers into the depths like a stone into mighty waters. [12]Moreover, you led them by day with a pillar of cloud and by night with a pillar of fire, to give them light on the way in which they should go. [13]You came down also upon Mount Sinai and spoke with them from heaven and gave them right ordinances and true laws, good statutes and commandments, [14]and you made known your holy Sabbath to them and gave them commandments and statutes and a law through Moses your servant. [15]For their hunger you gave them bread from heaven, and for their thirst you brought water for them out of the rock, and you told them to go in to possess the land that you swore to give them.

[16]"But they, our ancestors, acted presumptuously and stiffened their necks and did not obey your commandments; [17]they refused to obey and were not mindful of the wonders that you performed among them, but they stiffened their necks and appointed a leader to return to their slavery in Egypt. But you are a God ready to forgive, gracious and merciful, slow to anger and abounding in steadfast love, and you did not forsake them. [18]Even when they had cast an image of a calf for themselves and said, 'This is your God who brought you up out of Egypt,' and had committed great blasphemies, [19]you in your great mercies did not forsake them in the wilderness; the pillar of cloud that

The origins of Nehemiah's prayer in 9:6 are unknown.[40] The insertion of Ezra's name as the one who recites the prayer follows the Septuagint version rather than the Masoretic Text, which omits Ezra's name. This prayer situates the identity of the people as the real Israel—the true heirs of God's promise to Abraham. The prayer's repetitive use of "our" establishes Israel's God as the deity of the repatriates ("our God," Neh 9:32) and emphasizes their claim to Israel's history and bloodline: "our ancestors" (Neh 9:9, 10, 16, 32, 34, 36), "our sins" (Neh 9:37), "our kings, our officials, our priests, our prophets" (Neh 9:32, 34).[41] Claiming the same community narrative and values based on adherence to Torah (Neh 9:14, 26, 29, 34) unifies and solidifies the community around their God.

Donna Laird's examination of the penitential prayers in Ezra–Nehemiah (Ezra 9:6-15; Neh 1:5-11; 9:6-37) reveals the important role these supplications play in alleviating community shame both past and

40. The NRSVue begins the prayer at Neh 9:6.

41. Nehemiah 9:34 eliminates "prophets."

Neh 9:6-37 (cont.)

led them in the way did not leave them by day nor the pillar of fire by night that gave them light on the way by which they should go. 20You gave your good spirit to instruct them and did not withhold your manna from their mouths and gave them water for their thirst. 21Forty years you sustained them in the wilderness so that they lacked nothing; their clothes did not wear out, and their feet did not swell. 22And you gave them kingdoms and peoples and allotted to them every corner, so they took possession of the land of King Sihon of Heshbon and the land of King Og of Bashan. 23You multiplied their descendants like the stars of heaven and brought them into the land that you had told their ancestors to enter and possess. 24So the descendants went in and possessed the land, and you subdued before them the inhabitants of the land, the Canaanites, and gave them into their hands, with their kings and the peoples of the land, to do with them as they pleased. 25And they captured fortress cities and a rich land and took possession of houses filled with all sorts of goods, hewn cisterns, vineyards, olive orchards, and fruit trees in abundance; so they ate and were filled and became fat and delighted themselves in your great goodness.

26"Nevertheless, they were disobedient and rebelled against you and cast your law behind their backs and killed your prophets, who had warned them in order to turn them back to you, and they committed great blasphemies. 27Therefore you gave them into the hands of their enemies, who made them suffer.

present.[42] These prayers recognize the community's failure to follow the commandments (מצות) (Ezra 9:10, 14; Neh 1:5, 7, 9; 9:13, 14, 16, 29, 34) and Torah (תורה) (Neh 9:13, 14, 26, 29, 34). Through the act of acknowledging the shame and guilt stemming from Israel's past and present within the prayer, the community initiates the journey toward renewing their commitment to the covenant. The people's inclination to self-reflect and confess their complicity in their fragmented relationship with God rather than lament the harshness of exile stands out and opens channels of healing as they redirect and rely on Torah to guide them. The prayer allows the community to recognize the collective responsibility it has to own its history, warts and all, and to recommit to the ideals of its covenant—in this case, the commandments in Torah that help ground it.

42. Laird, *Negotiating Power in Ezra–Nehemiah*, 247–83. Laird provides an excellent discussion of the significance of penitential prayer, specifically to this narrative, and supports her thesis of the importance for the community to confess to alleviate the community's guilt and shame so they can move forward. Ezra uses the Hebrew בוש rather than חרפה for "shame."

Then in the time of their suffering they
cried out to you, and you heard them
from heaven, and according to your
great mercies you gave them saviors
who saved them from the hands of their
enemies. 28But after they had rest, they
again did evil before you, and you abandoned them to the hands of their enemies, so that they had dominion over
them, yet when they turned and cried
to you, you heard from heaven, and
many times you rescued them according to your mercies. 29And you warned
them in order to turn them back to your
law, yet they acted presumptuously and
did not obey your commandments but
sinned against your ordinances, by the
observance of which a person shall live.
They turned a stubborn shoulder and
stiffened their neck and would not obey.
30Many years you were patient with them
and warned them by your spirit through
your prophets, yet they would not listen.
Therefore you handed them over to the
peoples of the lands. 31Nevertheless, in
your great mercies you did not make an
end of them or forsake them, for you are
a gracious and merciful God.

Community Responsibility and Reconciliation

South Africa provides an example of one government's attempt at community confession and change even though there were those who could not bring themselves to forgive and who were shunned for it. The government came to terms with the sinful nature of apartheid and set up the Truth and Reconciliation Commission "to enable South Africans to come to terms with their past on a morally accepted basis and to advance the cause of reconciliation."[43] As a result, the nation continues to provide education and financial reparations in an attempt to ensure that South Africa upholds its commitment to justice and human rights. After the Holocaust and after much controversy, West Germany's chancellors Konrad Adenauer (1949–1963) and Willy Brandt (1969–1974) called Germany to accept guilt and responsibility for their crimes against the Jewish community and to work for reconciliation and reparations. Brandt emphasized that "no German is free of history."[44] The issues presented are much more complex than presented here. As of 2025, some in Germany—and in other countries with histories of

43. Dullah Omar, former Minister of Justice, "Truth and Reconciliation Commission Website, South Africa," https://www.justice.gov.za/trc/.

44. Willy Brandt as quoted by Greg Rienzi, "Other Nations Could Learn from Germany's Efforts to Reconcile after WWII," *Johns Hopkins Magazine* (Summer 2015), https://hub.jhu.edu/magazine/2015/summer/germany-japan-reconciliation/.

Neh 9:6-37 (cont.)

32"Now therefore, our God—the
great and mighty and awesome God,
keeping covenant and steadfast love—
do not treat lightly all the hardship that
has come upon us, upon our kings, our
officials, our priests, our prophets, our
ancestors, and all your people, since
the time of the kings of Assyria until
today. 33You have been just in all that
has come upon us, for you have dealt
faithfully and we have acted wickedly;
34our kings, our officials, our priests,
and our ancestors have not kept your
law or heeded the commandments
and the warnings that you gave them.
35Even in their own kingdom, and in
the great goodness you bestowed on
them, and in the large and rich land that
you set before them, they did not serve
you and did not turn from their wicked
works. 36Here we are, slaves to this day,
slaves in the land that you gave to our
ancestors to enjoy its fruit and its good
gifts. 37Its rich yield goes to the kings
whom you have set over us because of
our sins; they have power also over our
bodies and over our livestock at their
pleasure, and we are in great distress."

violence and oppression, such as the United States—are beginning to question the emphasis on collective guilt and the extent of a country's responsibility to make amends for past injustices.

The prayer underscores God's covenant (ברית) with Abraham (Neh 9:8) that carries through to the repatriates' community (Neh 9:32). The connection between God's promises to Abraham regarding possessing the land of its former occupants ("the Canaanite, the Hittite, the Amorite, the Perizzite, the Jebusite, and the Girgashite") and the repatriates is intentional as it draws a historical trajectory of ownership that spans hundreds of years. The prayer reinforces this ideology as it frequently mentions God's call for God's people to possess the land (Neh 9:8, 15, 22, 24), which they do (Neh 9:22, 24, 25, 35). The term for land, ארץ, appears twelve times in the prayer.[45] This repetition emphasizes and establishes a strong connection between this land and its blessing with this particular community. The prayer's ideology sets up a dichotomy between those whom God chooses (Neh 9:7) and everyone else. There are those who are included in the covenant (e.g., Nehemiah, Ezra, and the repatriate community) and those who are not (e.g., Sanballat, Geshem, Tobiah, and Noadiah). Yet, those who are not included also have a strong connection to the land and its history.

45. Neh 9:8, 10, 15, 22 (2x), 23, 24 (3x), 30, 35, 36. The term יבשה (dry land, Neh 9:11) and a different word, אדמה ("ground," Neh 9:25), also appear in this text.

The prayer continues with an appeal to "God—the great and mighty and awesome God" (Neh 9:32), who honors the covenant (ברית) with Israel throughout their history and offers them steadfast love (חסד) in spite of their wickedness: "we have acted wickedly" (Neh 9:33). Once again, the people are emphatic that God's harsh punishments are just (צדיק) because of their ancestors' unfaithfulness. They hope God will take into consideration the suffering already endured "since the time of the kings of Assyria until today" (Neh 9:32). The petitioner maintains that God's faithfulness has been with this people despite the monumental failures of its priests, kings, prophets, officials, and ancestors to follow God's law and commandments during the preexilic and exilic periods (Neh 9:33-35).

The prayer acknowledges the people's shortcomings and God's faithfulness, but now the petitioner wants to voice a complaint: "Here we are, slaves to this day, slaves in the land that you gave to our ancestors to enjoy its fruit and its good gifts" (Neh 9:36). Despite arriving in Jerusalem with shekels, building materials, letters from the king, and a military escort, the repatriates still consider themselves in bondage (see Neh 2). Labeling themselves as עבדים, "slaves" or "servants" signals the perceived diminished status the repatriates occupy in the Persian Empire even when they wield more power over Jerusalem and its community than the people of the land.

The prayer protests the economic and physical toll of Persian occupation—their best products are siphoned off for Persian royalty. They grieve that their "bodies" (Neh 9:37) are not their own. The Hebrew term translated as "bodies" in 9:37, גויה, is often associated with corpses.[46] In the Samson narrative, גויה refers to the dead lion's carcass filled with honey (Judg 14:8), and to Saul's corpse that is fastened to the temple in Beth Shean at his death (1 Sam 31:10, 12). In a woe oracle concerning the fall of Nineveh, the prophet Nahum foresees "piles of dead [חלל], heaps of corpses [גויה]" (Nah 3:3). The choice of גויה for "bodies" emphasizes how they view their lack of autonomy under colonization. Despite the benevolence of the empire (Neh 2), the petitioner recognizes that governmental interests always supersede the interests of the citizens. People with power over lives and resources, even if well-intentioned, have means to take things away or exploit resources, as is the case under Persian rule and even today. Wealthy organizations, philanthropists, and governments generously donate funds to support those in need. Even though their good fortune is shared with those less fortunate, and

46. Many Hebrew words are translated as "body" in the NRSVue, including בשׂר, "flesh"; אישׁ, "man"; נפשׁ, "soul"; עצם, "bones"; פגר, "corpse"; נבלה, "carcass"; בטן, "belly." גויה is among those Hebrew terms related to body that are associated with death.

even if they are committed to the cause, these wealthy hold the purse strings and can withhold funds as they choose. A similar dynamic can occur between partners when one is financially dependent on the other.

While the petitioners express grievances about the sins of their ancestors and those of the empire, they envision and put forth a solution to the current situation that will guide the people back to God and prepare them for a collective commitment of covenant renewal (Neh 9:38).

The Community Commits: The Power of Numbers (9:38–10:29)

Nehemiah 9:38 segues from the penitential prayer (Neh 9:6-37) into a "firm agreement" that the newly constituted Israel now signs. These signatures are the people's response to God's faithfulness and mercy throughout their history.[47] The prayer reinforces the repatriates' identity as heirs to the preexilic Israelites and to Abraham's blessing of descendants and land, while suggesting that the community wants to avoid repeating mistakes from the past. The "firm commitment" (אמנה) is an early example of a binding agreement that is written, signed, sealed, and preserved. The term is related to the noun meaning "faithful," which draws us back to Abraham's faithfulness at the beginning of the prayer (Neh 9:8) and may have been chosen by the author to emphasize this connection instead of using the typical word for covenant, ברית.[48]

The list of names represents leaders and laity. Here, Nehemiah signs as the governor (תרשתא, Neh 10:1; see commentary on Neh 7:70), but Ezra does not, leading some to believe that Ezra was absent.[49] Nehemiah's signature is followed by a list of priests (Neh 10:1-8), Levites (Neh 10:9-13), and leaders of the people (Neh 10:14-27). The lists inscribe names already found among those in other lists in Ezra–Nehemiah, as well as many new names, a sign that membership in this community is fluid even though still defined by male leadership.[50] The אמנה names eighty-four prominent persons who

47. Becking, *Ezra–Nehemiah*, 282. This agreement may be a later insertion and reflects stages of development that could date to the Hasmonean or later periods (Blenkinsopp, *Ezra–Nehemiah*, 311–12).

48. The Hebrew אמנה is the hiphil participle of the verb אמן that is translated by the NRSVue as "faithful." Fredrick Carlson Holmgren, "Faithful Abraham and the 'Amānâ Covenant Nehemiah 9,6–10,1," *ZAW* 104 (1992): 249–54.

49. A person named Azariah signs the document, and some wonder if this might be another spelling of Ezra's name. Still, Azariah is not known to be substituted for Ezra.

50. For discussions on the names on the lists and their compilations, see Blenkinsopp, *Ezra–Nehemiah*, 312–13; Klein, "The Books of Ezra and Nehemiah," in *The New Interpreter's Bible*, ed. Leander Keck, vol. 3 (Nashville: Abingdon, 1999), 816; Gordon

Neh 9:38–10:29

[38]Because of all this we make a firm agreement in writing, and on that sealed document are inscribed the names of our officials, our Levites, and our priests.

[10:1]Upon the sealed document are the names of Nehemiah the governor, son of Hacaliah, and Zedekiah; [2]Seraiah, Azariah, Jeremiah, [3]Pashhur, Amariah, Malchijah, [4]Hattush, Shebaniah, Malluch, [5]Harim, Meremoth, Obadiah, [6]Daniel, Ginnethon, Baruch, [7]Meshullam, Abijah, Mijamin, [8]Maaziah, Bilgai, Shemaiah; these are the priests. [9]And the Levites: Jeshua son of Azaniah, Binnui of the sons of Henadad, Kadmiel; [10]and their associates Shebaniah, Hodiah, Kelita, Pelaiah, Hanan, [11]Mica, Rehob, Hashabiah, [12]Zaccur, Sherebiah, Shebaniah, [13]Hodiah, Bani, Beninu. [14]The leaders of the people: Parosh, Pahath-moab, Elam, Zattu, Bani, [15]Bunni, Azgad, Bebai, [16]Adonijah, Bigvai, Adin, [17]Ater, Hezekiah, Azzur, [18]Hodiah, Hashum, Bezai, [19]Hariph, Anathoth, Nebai, [20]Magpiash, Meshullam, Hezir, [21]Meshezabel, Zadok, Jaddua, [22]Pelatiah, Hanan, Anaiah, [23]Hoshea, Hananiah, Hasshub, [24]Hallohesh, Pilha, Shobek, [25]Rehum, Hashabnah, Maaseiah, [26]Ahiah, Hanan, Anan, [27]Malluch, Harim, and Baanah.

[28]The rest of the people, the priests, the Levites, the gatekeepers, the singers, the temple servants, and all who have separated themselves from the peoples of the lands to adhere to the law of God, their wives, their sons, their daughters, all who have knowledge and understanding, [29]join with their kin, their nobles, and enter into a curse and an oath to walk in God's law, which was given by Moses the servant of God, and to observe and do all the commandments of the LORD our Lord and his ordinances and his statutes.

represent the people along with an unknown number of seal impressions. Nehemiah 10:28-29 lists additional groups who take a separate pledge and constitute "the rest of the people" (Neh 10:28), which includes Levites and priests who are not among the signers, as well as gatekeepers, singers, temple servants, and "all who have separated themselves from the peoples of the lands to adhere to the law [תורה] of God" (Neh 10:28). Wives, daughters, and sons "who have knowledge and understanding" (Neh 10:28) also join in what Laird calls rites "that will reincorporate them into a new social order."[51] Like the blessings and curses found in Deuteronomy (Deut 28–29), this group enters "into a curse [אלה] and an oath [שבועה]" (Neh 10:29) and swear to follow God's torah as well as the commandments, ordinances, and statutes given to Moses. The leaders sign

F. Davies, *Ezra and Nehemiah*, Berit Olam, ed. David W. Cotter (Collegeville, MN: Liturgical Press, 1999), 123; Najman, "Notes on Nehemiah," 1702. See our commentary on Nehemiah 3 and lists.

51. Laird, *Negotiating Power in Ezra–Nehemiah*, 279.

first with their seal of approval, which implies that the people will follow them as adherents of the community's ethics. This gesture aims to unify the community in much the same way as Moses and David rallied their followers into a cohesive religious group. Since leaders sign these documents on behalf of the entire community and mandate that newcomers swear an oath to join, their actions prompt us to consider whether such actions prefer conformity over individual expression or debate.

The Hebrew for "oath" (שבועה) derives from the root שבע, meaning "to swear." It is "a sacred promise to keep one's word" that is spoken.[52] When modern people take oaths like marriage or other sacred vows, shake hands on a business deal, or make other verbal promises before God and each other, they often think very little about the theological consequences when they break them. When the people in Nehemiah's community make their oath, however, they recognize the permanence of their promise and the dire consequences for their unfaithfulness. It is no accident that the words "oath" and "curse" go hand in hand with this oral declaration of commitment.

Oaths and Curses in the Scriptures of Ancient Israel

In the Scriptures of ancient Israel, when one makes an oath there can be negative consequences like death, disgrace, illness, exile, and other unappealing and harmful actions directed at them if their oath is broken.[53] In the case of the potentially unfaithful wife (the סוטה)[54] of Numbers 5:11-31, the woman is brought to the tabernacle and made to drink a mixture of dust from the floor and holy water. The priest makes the woman take "the oath of the curse" (v. 21) to see if her uterus drops out of her body—a sign of her infidelity. Should her guilt be confirmed, she becomes "an execration among her people" (v. 27).The odds of her uterus dropping out during the ritual are slim, but the possibility of this curse is real to her and the community.[55] Daniel, in his

52. Alan C. Mitchell, "Oath," in *Eerdmans Dictionary of the Bible*, ed. David Noel Freedman (Grand Rapids: Eerdmans, 2000), 978. See Num 30:2, "When a man makes a vow to the LORD or swears an oath to bind himself by a pledge, he shall not break his word; he shall do according to all that proceeds out of his mouth."

53. The juxtaposition of oath and curse as we have in Neh 10:28 occurs in only two other places in the Hebrew Bible: Num 5:21 and Dan 9:11.

54. The Hebrew can also be spelled שׂוטה.

55. The result of drinking this liquid is debated. Rosanne Lieberman translates the first part of Numbers 5:22: "and may these waters that curse come into your bowels

prayer (Dan 9:1-19), laments that Israel has strayed from God's voice and now "the curse and the oath" (v. 11) are poured on them in the form of the calamity of exile (v. 12). The blessings and curses in Deuteronomy 27–28 are also a reminder to the community of the consequences for not maintaining their commitment to the Torah.

There are provisions in oaths to break them if the context changes. For example, when Abraham sends his servant to his kin to find a wife for Isaac, the servant takes an oath promising to succeed (Gen 24). The servant, concerned that Rebekah will not return with him, relates that he will be released from the oath because he has made the attempt (Gen 24:41). When the two spies sneak into Jericho, Rahab and the two men enter into an oath to save Rahab and her family that can be broken if she fails to lower the red cord and gather her family (Josh 2:17) or if she tells anyone about the agreement (Josh 2:20). There are times when oaths are better broken than maintained, such as when a marriage partner is abusive or a country fails to live up to its agreements.

While some interpreters regard Ezra and Nehemiah's community to be exclusive, the biblical text suggests otherwise. The community assembled for the *amanah* is open to all those willing to separate from the people of the land and live by this agreement (Neh 10:28). The changing membership of the community is illustrated by the many new names that appear on the list of signatories and the movement in and out by others.[56] Membership in this new community requires that members live by the community's ethic rather than by the values of those living around them. The acceptance of the *amanah*'s boundaries protects the community's identity and viability.

Terms of Commitment (10:30-39)

The people's pledge of fidelity and obedience occurs in 9:38 and is now forever embedded in Israel's history, a testimonial for future

to swell a stomach and make a thigh fall" (Rosanne Liebermann, "Drinkable Ink or Womb-Destroying Words? A Solution for Suspected Adultery in Numbers 5:11-31," *Postscripts* 14 [2023]: 42). Others, like Susanne Scholz, argue that no matter how you translate the Hebrew, drinking the water inscribes "reproductive deformation on her body and eras[es] her personhood" (Susanne Scholz, "Dismantling the Phallic Economy with a Hermeneutics of Reproductive Justice: A Reconsideration of Sotah in Numbers 5:11-31," *Journal of Religious Ethics* 49 [2021]: 280).

56. Davies, *Ezra and Nehemiah*, 123.

Neh 10:30-39

30We will not give our daughters to the peoples of the land or take their daughters for our sons, 31and if the peoples of the land bring in merchandise or any grain on the Sabbath day to sell, we will not buy it from them on the Sabbath or on a holy day, and we will forego the crops of the seventh year and the exaction of every debt.

32We also lay on ourselves the obligation to charge ourselves yearly one-third of a shekel for the service of the house of our God: 33for the rows of bread, the regular grain offering, the regular burnt offering, the Sabbaths, the new moons, the appointed festivals, the sacred donations, and the sin offerings to make atonement for Israel, and for all the work of the house of our God. 34We have also cast lots among the priests, the Levites, and the people for the wood offering, to bring it into the house of our God, by ancestral houses, at appointed times, year by year, to burn on the altar of the LORD our God, as it is written in the law. 35We obligate ourselves to bring the first fruits of our soil and the first fruits of all fruit of every tree, year by

generations.[57] This *amanah,* framed as a social contract and covenantal obligation, is outlined further in 10:30-39. Instructively, these verses detail how the interactions between this community and its neighbors ("the peoples of the lands") will occur. The stipulations chosen for this agreement focus on protecting Israel's identity and holiness. To begin, marrying outside one's social group (prohibition against exogamy) is perhaps the gravest perceived threat to the community's identity (Neh 10:30).[58] Ezra 9–10 outlines how these unions threaten the "holy seed" (see commentary on Ezra 9–10). While the prohibition in Ezra focuses on the "peoples of the lands," Nehemiah expands it to include marriages to the descendants of Israelites who remain in the land such as Sanballat, Geshem, and Tobiah. Following this modification comes a reinterpretation of the Sabbath in 10:31.

57. We place Neh 9:38 that addresses the אמנה in the following section with the signatures and that matches the versification in the Masoretic Text. Eskenazi, *In an Age of Prose*, 124. Jacob Myers, *Ezra, Nehemiah*, AB 14 (Garden City, NY: Doubleday, 1965), 84–88, has a long discussion about the redaction of Nehemiah 10. Myers raises the possibility that the *amanah* is a later document inserted by Nehemiah into his memoir or by a later redactor to support Nehemiah's reforms.

58. The prohibition against intermarriage is discussed in greater detail in our commentary on Ezra 9–10 and Neh 13:23-30.

year, to the house of the LORD; 36also
to bring to the house of our God, to the
priests who minister in the house of our
God, the firstborn of our sons and of
our livestock, as it is written in the law,
and the firstlings of our herds and of
our flocks; 37and to bring the first of our
dough, and our contributions, the fruit of
every tree, the wine and the oil, to the
priests, to the chambers of the house
of our God; and to bring to the Levites
the tithes from our soil, for it is the Levites who collect the tithes in all our rural
towns. 38And the priest, the descendant
of Aaron, shall be with the Levites when
the Levites receive the tithes, and the
Levites shall bring up a tithe of the tithes
to the house of our God, to the chambers of the storehouse. 39For the Israelites and the sons of Levi shall bring
the contribution of grain, wine, and oil
to the storerooms where the vessels of
the sanctuary are and where the priests
who minister and the gatekeepers and
the singers are. We will not neglect the
house of our God.

The Torah establishes Sabbath as a day set apart (קדשׁ, holy, Gen 2:2-3), by God, and prohibits human labor (Exod 20:10-11; 31:14-16; Lev 23:3). In Deuteronomy 5:12-15, this restriction is for humanitarian reasons—to allow the people of Israel, their servants, the sojourners, and the work animals to rest because they were not allowed this opportunity as enslaved people in Egypt. Whether work pertains to the physical exertion to carry out a task or the commercial exchange of goods and services, the *amanah* prohibits both on the Sabbath and other holy days.[59] As a marker of the group's identity, the prohibition distinguishes this group from those who work and participate in commerce on the Sabbath.[60]

59. For example, no kindling should be collected, fires lit, or food cooked (Exod 35:3; Num 15:32-36; Exod 16:23-29). The Talmud attempts to define "work" (see Babylonian Talmud: *Sabbath* 49b, 73a, 73b, 74a, 74b). As culture and technology change, so do the Sabbath definitions of work connected to electricity, cell phones, computers, and so forth.

60. Ostraca from the Jewish community in Elephantine provide evidence that a few people traded groceries on Sabbath without apology, and some had to fulfill military service. These inscriptions may suggest looser Sabbath laws for the greater repatriate community, but there is not enough data to draw strong conclusions one way or another. Bob Becking, "Sabbath at Elephantine: A Short Episode in the Construction of Jewish Identity," in *Empsychoi Logoi—Religious Innovations in Antiquity: Studies in Honour of Pieter Willem van Der Horst*, ed. Alberdina Houtman, Albert de Jong, Magda Misset-Van de Weg, Ancient Judaism and Early Christianity 73 (Leiden: Brill, 2008), 186–87.

Today, the observance of a Sabbath rest continues to be important as medical and psychological studies emphasize the benefits of taking a weekly break even if it is not on the seventh day of the week.[61] Still, the ability to take a day off to worship and rest could be considered a luxury, especially for those who must work multiple jobs to support themselves and their family. Without financial support systems in place for those with economic struggles, a mandatory day of Sabbath rest could present a hardship. Below, Rabbi Sonja K. Pilz offers her interpretation and reading of Kabbalat Shabbat (Welcoming Shabbat).

Kabbalat Shabbat—Welcoming Shabbat

The liturgy of *Kabbalat Shabbat*, "Welcoming Shabbat," is a "new" liturgy from the sixteenth century, created within the circles of Jewish Mysticism in the north of Israel (the Galilee). While based on older teachings of Shabbat personified as a "bride," "queen," or "lover" of either God or the People of Israel, those mysticisms made those metaphors part of their elaborate mystical theology, according to which, on Friday nights, the male (upper) and the female (lower, earthly, Torah/*Shechinah*/*Malchut*) aspects of God unite for the duration of Shabbat (roughly twenty-five hours)—a process that was to be mirrored by the union between a man and his wife. The traditional, very much embodied and nature-based liturgy of *Kabbalat Shabbat* consists of:

- an opening song (*Yedid Nefesh*, composed by Rabbi Elazar Azikri, Safed, 1533–1600)
- six psalms (95–99; 29; part of the so-called enthronement psalms), mirroring the six weekdays of the week
- the ancient prayer *Ana B'Cho'ach* ("Please, by the power . . ." ; first century)
- the song *Lecha Dodi* ("Come, My Beloved," by Rabbi Shlomo Alkabetz, Safed, 1500–1576)
- Psalm 92—the song for Shabbat
- Psalm 93

Additionally, in many Sephardi communities, the complete Song of Songs is recited on Friday night.

61. Examples, Rae Jean Proeschold-Bell et al., "Changes in Sabbath-Keeping and Mental Health over Time: Evaluation Findings from the Sabbath Living Study," *Journal of Psychology and Theology* 50 (2022): 123–38, https://doi.org/10.1177/00916471211046227; Albert Cheng, Matthew H. Lee, and Rian Djita, "A Cross-Sectional Analysis of the Relationship between Sabbath Practices and US, Canadian, Indonesian, and Paraguayan Teachers' Burnout," *JRH* 62 (2022): 1090–1113, https://doi.org/10.1007/s10943-022-01647-w.

The liturgical poem below responds to the words, structures, theological images and their blurriness, melodies, and embodied practices of those pieces of traditional liturgy.

Baruch Atah Adonai, Eloheinu Melech ha'olam, asher kid'shanu b'mitzvotav v'tzivanu lehad'lik ner shel shabbat. Blessed are You, Adonai, our God, Sovereign of Time and Space, who has hallowed us through God's directions, and directed us to light the Shabbat candles . . .

Help me illuminate the falling darkness.
Keep me awake.
Make me ready for Love.

Yedid Nefesh—Beloved of the Soul . . .
I have missed You all week.
I Am hungry and tired,
My body feels worn.
Bring out the oils and the lotions;
Let me sit at a table covered with food;
Fill my cup until it overfloweth . . .
Now I Am waiting.
I Am waiting for Love.

Psalm 95
It is hard to find words
After a week of work and
separation.
Much has been said—
Some of which with a hardened
heart.
Open My lips with a kiss,
With a song—
Let Me find the melody
That reminds Us of Love.

Psalm 96
Tonight, I will raise You in
splendor,
I will bless Your head;
I will kiss Your face.
I will reach for Your hand
Across the table,
I will cover your shoulders with
my palms . . .
I will burst into Love.

Psalm 97
Together, We rediscover
The chemistry between Our skin.
We draw images in the air
between Us
Of mountains, shores, rivers, and
flowers . . .
Saturated with Love.

Psalm 98
Our home is full
Of memories and dishes,
We found Our words again,
Our songs of love.
While darkness is still
Hovering in the corners
Our faces are lit up
Brimming with Love.

Psalm 99
I know I will never know fully
Who You Are.
However, I will continue to love
You,
And look for You in those
corners
Where darkness hovers
And Hidden Love.

Psalm 29
I am rendered helpless
By the power of love.
I am fully devoted,
To the Power of Love.

Anah b'cho'ach, g'dulat y'mincha—Please, by power of Your right . . .
The mystery.
The mystery.
That Is You.

Lecha Dodi—Come, My Beloved . . .
Get up, love,
Don't wait any longer.
Rise up, speak up,
The time has come.
Open Your arms anew,
Sweet forgiveness,
Just say, "I love you,"
Then say no more.

Let's rise together,
Let's see what we are building
In the space between Us
Which we created through love.

Come, My love,
Let's lie down together
Your left hand is under My head,
And Your right arm embraces Me.

Psalm 92
Tonight, God is neither father
nor mother,
Tonight, God is my beloved.
Where Are You, Beloved,
Among ruins and apple trees,
Don't hide Your face and soul
from Me.
You Are everywhere,
Your image is imprinted on the
surface of the earth,
And I am Your Partner.

Psalm 93
And You're here.
You're here.
My heart is singing.
I have found You—
Immersed in Love.

Rabbi Sonja K. Pilz

The concept of sabbatical rest extends to the land and includes debt forgiveness where the community "will forego the crops of the seventh year and the exaction of every debt" (Neh 10:31). Modern agriculturalists recognize the importance of rotating crops and allowing the soil a chance to rest in order to have a healthier yield in the future. In forgiving one's neighbor's debt, the community avoids food insecurity and debt slavery, thereby ensuring the overall health and well-being of the whole group. Further, the release of debt interest parallels similar legislation in Deuteronomy 15:1-6, providing financial relief to those in the community burdened by debt. In sum, the stipulations regarding Sabbath, the sabbatical year, and the release of interest debt protect the vulnerable, and model a counterculture to those who would choose wealth over care for the community's residents (Neh 5).

In Nehemiah 10:32-39, we find the creation of structures that support the service and maintenance of the Jerusalem temple and its personnel. This support includes the people's annual contributions for various religious festivals, sacred donations, and sin offerings (Neh 10:32), wood for altar fires ("wood offering"[62]) according to a scheduled rotation, and the first fruits of their crops and trees (Neh 10:34, 35). This grouping is followed by the priests' receiving the people's firstborn sons and livestock together with the first of their ground meal, grain offerings, new wine, and olive oil (Neh 10:36; see excurses on firstborn sons). These observances ensure that the Levites and priests have the food and necessities to keep their families and the temple system functioning.

In addition to these offerings are the tithes. The process of collection and those who received these gifts differs from the process found in Leviticus and Deuteronomy. In these books, every third year, the tithe is distributed to the Levites, the aliens, the orphans, and the widows who could eat their fill (Deut 26:12, cf. 14:28-29). Laity performed this collection and distribution (see also Amos 4:4). Here, the Levites perform these functions from a designated rural center with storehouses under the supervision of the Aaronide priests (Neh 10:38). Moreover, the Levites are required to offer a "tithe of the tithes" (Neh 10:38) to be deposited in Jerusalem storehouses where the singers, gatekeepers, and priests can also partake (Neh 10:39). This process turns the tithe into a quasi-tax to support the temple infrastructure now controlled by the priesthood rather than the Levites alone who have no

62. Robert Alter suggests that casting lots to decide who brings the wood makes better sense than the people presenting a wood offering that does not exist in Torah. See "Nehemiah," 854n35. Still, there is a wood offering at Qumran (Temple Scroll 11Q 19 23:2-7).

inheritance (Num 18:21-32).[63] The observances in Nehemiah 10:32-39 place the accountability and responsibility for the care of the temple and those who service it upon the people, the priests, and the Levites.[64]

What Do They Do with the Firstborn Sons?

Among the goods that the people promise to the priests are their firstborn sons (Neh 10:36). Nehemiah 10:36 does not clarify what happens to these children. Eve Levavi Feinstein notices this omission in a similar text, Exodus 22:29-30, which reads: "You shall not delay to make offerings from the fullness of your harvest and from the outflow of your presses. The firstborn of your sons you shall give to me. You shall do the same with your oxen and with your sheep: seven days it shall remain with its mother; on the eighth day you shall give it to me."[65] The "plain meaning" suggests that the son is sacrificed just as the animals will most likely be; however, the rabbis, like many modern commentaries, assume intertextual readings that keep the children alive.[66] Some suggest that these children will be consecrated (קדש) or given to the Lord as outlined in Torah (Exod 13:2; 22:29). Hannah gives her firstborn son, Samuel, to Eli the priest and he remains with him (1 Sam 1:26-28). Others suggest, based on Torah, that the firstborn son is given to the

63. Blenkinsopp, *Ezra–Nehemiah*, 318; Klein, "The Books of Ezra and Nehemiah," 820.

64. Herbert Marbury is among those who argue that the temple becomes an essential part of Judah's economic system under the Persian kings who require taxes and tributes to support their extensive military and political infrastructure. The firm commitment (אמנה), especially Neh 10:33-39, provides financial support and resources to maintain the temple's infrastructure and provide a central place for collecting tributes for the Persian king. Herbert Marbury, "Reading Persian Dominion in Nehemiah: Multivalent Language, Co-Option, Resistance, and Cultural Survival," in *The Crucial Nature of the Persian and Hellenistic Periods: Essays in Honor of Douglas A. Knight*, ed. Alice Hunt and Jon Berquist (New York: T&T Clark, 2012), 158–76. Gale Yee also recognizes the burden that this "two-tiered mode of extraction," temple and foreign taxes, has on the poor. See Gale Yee, *Poor Banished Children of Eve: Women as Evil in the Hebrew Bible* (Minneapolis: Fortress, 2003), 139.

65. Eve Levavi Feinstein, "Giving Your Firstborn Son to God," *The Torah.com*, https://thetorah.com/giving-your-firstborn-son-to-god/.

66. Feinstein, "Giving Your Firstborn Son to God." Feinstein provides a detailed discussion of how rabbinic Judaism dealt with this commandment.

priests until he is redeemed (פדה, Exod 34:19-20; Num 18:15).[67] The Torah is inconsistent with respect to the destiny of the firstborn son and substitutes the Levites for the firstborn sons (Num 3:12). Further, Feinstein reminds us that Abraham attempts to sacrifice his child (Gen 22) and Jephthah, his daughter (Judg 11:39), among others. It becomes somewhat disturbing that the repatriates unanimously agree to uphold this part of the אמנה without spelling out what this means for their firstborn sons. Even if these children are not sacrificed, the act of leaving them with the priests until they are redeemed or requiring them to give their lives in service that they might not wish to take on can be damaging and a harsh cost for both the children and their parents, especially for those without power.

The structuring of the group's social and religious life with the temple at the center exhibits multiple dependencies and a collective accountability designed to ensure communal viability and survivability. The temple was a vital extension of the community, and supporting it was essential. The pledge in 10:39 "not to neglect the house of our God" reinforces this importance. The intersection of religious commitments and communal welfare survives today as congregants in churches, synagogues, and mosques provide monetary support, gifts, and service to maintain their places of worship and to support those experiencing food insecurities, homelessness, or other disadvantages. We recognize that the availability of resources to support our religious institutions varies across the economic stratum, and there may be those who do not have the means to give.

Additionally, the readiness of this group to embrace the אמנה illustrates their willingness to privilege particular laws and adapt others to community

67. Exod 34:19-20: "All that first opens the womb is mine, all your male livestock, the firstborn of cow and sheep. The firstborn of a donkey you shall redeem with a lamb, or if you will not redeem it you shall break its neck. All the firstborn of your sons you shall redeem." Num 18:15-16: "The first issue of the womb of all creatures, human and animal, that is offered to the Lord, shall be yours, but the firstborn of human beings you shall redeem, and the firstborn of unclean animals you shall redeem. Their redemption price, reckoned from one month of age, you shall fix at five shekels of silver, according to the shekel of the sanctuary (that is, twenty gerahs)."

needs and to new situations and understandings.[68] Sara Japhet muses, "In a paradoxical way, what may be called a 'religion of the book' was not in fact 'a religion of the letter.'"[69] The same is true in our churches and synagogues as many communities choose which laws to include or which to relax or tighten to support community needs and values. While religious rituals and commitments as outlined above may be necessary for the survival and identity of Nehemiah's community, over time these rituals and commitments could become inhospitable and make it difficult for persons who may not fit within the expectations and parameters for membership in some religious communities (for example, LGBTQ+ persons).

68. The following scholars reflect on the many ways law in Ezra and Nehemiah shifts to community needs: Sara Japhet, *From the Rivers of Babylon to the Highlands of Judah: Collected Studies on the Restoration Period* (Winona Lake, IN: Eisenbrauns, 2006), 137–51; David A. Glatt-Gilad, "The Voluntary Nature of the Nehemiah Covenant in Rabbinic Literature," *The Review of Rabbinic Judaism* 20 (2017): 3–20; Eskenazi, *In the Age of Prose*, 190–91.

69. Japhet, *From the Rivers*, 151.

Nehemiah 11:1–13:31

Making, Unmaking, and Remaking

In these chapters, the people repopulate Jerusalem and the surrounding villages (Neh 11). Through the casting of lots, one-tenth of the population moves into Jerusalem to reestablish it as a holy city. In Nehemiah 12, the genealogical lists connect the temple community with the repatriates who returned under Zerubbabel and Jeshua, thereby establishing continuity and legitimacy through lineage and divine selection. This chapter concludes with a joyous celebration consisting of the dedication of the walls followed by a reaffirmation and commitment to the Torah. In Nehemiah 13, Nehemiah returns to Susa and the people backslide. Upon his return to Jerusalem, Nehemiah discovers that the people have forsaken their commitments (e.g., maintenance of the temple and its infrastructure, keeping the Sabbath, and intermarrying with the peoples of the lands). Nehemiah creates safety measures to ensure that the people begin anew and make good on their commitments. Like Ezra 9 and 10, Nehemiah ends with the same concern about foreign women and the dissolution of Jewish identity.

Repopulating the Holy City of Jerusalem (11:1-24)

Throughout Ezra–Nehemiah, Jerusalem and the temple are central to the repatriates' identity as the newly reconstituted Israel. Nehemiah 11:1-36 provides a list of leaders, temple personnel, and families who

Neh 11:1-24

[1]Now the leaders of the people lived in Jerusalem, and the rest of the people cast lots to bring one out of ten to live in the holy city Jerusalem, while nine-tenths remained in the other towns. [2]And the people blessed all those who willingly offered to live in Jerusalem.

[3]These are the leaders of the province who lived in Jerusalem, but in the towns of Judah all lived on their property in their towns: Israel, the priests, the Levites, the temple servants, and the descendants of Solomon's servants. [4]And in Jerusalem lived some of the Judahites and the Benjaminites. Of the Judahites: Athaiah son of Uzziah son of Zechariah son of Amariah son of Shephatiah son of Mahalalel, of the descendants of Perez; [5]and Maaseiah son of Baruch son of Col-hozeh son of Hazaiah son of Adaiah son of Joiarib son of Zechariah son of the Shelahnite. [6]All the descendants of Perez who lived in Jerusalem were four hundred sixty-eight valiant warriors.

[7]And these are the Benjaminites: Sallu son of Meshullam son of Joed son of Pedaiah son of Kolaiah son of Maaseiah son of Ithiel son of Jeshaiah. [8]And his brothers Gabbai, Sallai: nine hundred twenty-eight. [9]Joel son of Zichri was their overseer, and Judah son of Hassenuah was second in charge of the city.

[10]Of the priests: Jedaiah son of Joiarib, Jachin, [11]Seraiah son of Hilkiah son of Meshullam son of Zadok son of Meraioth son of Ahitub, officer of the house of God, [12]and their associates who did the work of the house, eight hundred twenty-two; and Adaiah son of Jeroham son of Pelaliah son of Amzi son of Zechariah son of Pashhur son of Malchijah, [13]and his associates, heads of ancestral houses, two hundred forty-

repopulate Jerusalem and the surrounding villages.[1] Some from the "holy seed" of Ezra 9:2 now take up residence in the "holy city" (Neh 11:1, 18). The absence of both Ezra and Nehemiah from this list suggests that the families and others in the community play a major role in this resettlement process. The holiness of Jerusalem is stressed at both the beginning and the end of the list of those repopulating the city (Neh 11:1, 18). In the book of Nehemiah, the holiness of the temple complex is greatly expanded to include the entire city of Jerusalem and all the territory within Nehemiah's reconstructed walls. To maintain the city's separateness, those who live in Jerusalem must be part of the families of Israel who can trace their lineage back to their faithful ancestors. The list distinguishes between

1. For more details about the lists and redaction history of Nehemiah 11–12, see Deirdre Fulton, *Reconsidering Nehemiah's Judah: The Case of MT and LXX Nehemia 11–12*, FAT 2.80 (Tübingen: Mohr Siebeck, 2015). The Septuagint version is shorter than the Masoretic Text version.

two; and Amashsai son of Azarel son of Ahzai son of Meshillemoth son of Immer, [14]and their associates, valiant warriors, one hundred twenty-eight; their overseer was Zabdiel son of Haggedolim.

[15]And of the Levites: Shemaiah son of Hasshub son of Azrikam son of Hashabiah son of Bunni; [16]and Shabbethai and Jozabad, of the leaders of the Levites, who were over the outside work of the house of God; [17]and Mattaniah son of Mica son of Zabdi son of Asaph, who was the leader to begin the thanksgiving in prayer, and Bakbukiah, the second among his associates; and Abda son of Shammua son of Galal son of Jeduthun. [18]All the Levites in the holy city were two hundred eighty-four.

[19]The gatekeepers Akkub, Talmon, and their associates, who kept watch at the gates, were one hundred seventy-two. [20]And the rest of Israel, and of the priests and the Levites, were in all the towns of Judah, all of them in their inheritance. [21]But the temple servants lived on Ophel, and Ziha and Gishpa were over the temple servants.

[22]The overseer of the Levites in Jerusalem was Uzzi son of Bani son of Hashabiah son of Mattaniah son of Mica, of the descendants of Asaph, the singers, in charge of the work of the house of God. [23]For there was a command from the king concerning them and a settled provision for the singers, as was required every day. [24]And Pethahiah son of Meshezabel, of the descendants of Zerah son of Judah, was at the king's hand in all matters concerning the people.

the repatriates who repopulate Jerusalem (Neh 11:1-24) and those who settle in Jerusalem's surrounding villages (Neh 11:25-36)—all validated through genealogies that connect them to the land.

The repatriates' repopulation of Jerusalem occurs in 11:1-24. Archaeologists are divided about residential life after Babylonian destruction, with some convinced of the city's emptiness and others who dispute this based on evidence of occupation.[2] One need only recall how the American West was settled on land that Indigenous peoples already occupied. While the once-bustling city of Jerusalem is certainly emptier, there are likely non-Jewish and non-repatriate inhabitants in the city whose lives are changed by the influx of this group. Nehemiah's concern

2. Hans M. Barstad argues that not all of Jerusalem is destroyed and that the emptiness of the land is a myth. Excavations at Ketef Hinnom southwest of the Old City uncovered burial caves with material culture dating post destruction. Barstad reminds us of biblical evidence that people lived among the ruins (Ezek 33:24; see "After the 'Myth of the Empty Land': Major Challenges in the Study of Neo-Babylonian Judah," in *Judah and the Judeans in the Neo-Babylonian Period*, ed. Oded Lipschits and Joseph Blenkinsopp [Winona Lake, IN: Eisenbraun, 2003], 3–20).

to revive a destroyed Jerusalem brings with it opportunities for urban renewal, increased commerce, and the reestablishment of Israel's identity and presence in this holy and ancestral city. The resettlement includes the leaders, the 10 percent chosen by lot, and some who willingly choose to put down roots with them (Neh 11:2). Still, the resettlement of the city is not without costs. The city, temple, and its occupants survive necessarily on the work and resources of other repatriates living in surrounding villages. Paradoxically, the survival of Jerusalem and the temple risks creating economic hardships for those whose labor, crops, animals, and progeny support Jerusalem's residents and temple personnel.

Casting lots to determine who lives within Jerusalem's walls indicates an effort to establish a community in the city, while also suggesting hesitancy among some within the repatriate population.[3] The reluctance to live in Jerusalem could stem from its state of disarray, a consequence of warfare and long-term neglect as described in Nehemiah 1:3. Living in a potential war zone might be unpalatable for some who may have been traumatized from dodging the perceived violence from the peoples of the lands. Further, the communal memory of exile still lingers; hence, the people's expressed relief that others also volunteered: "And the people blessed all those who willingly offered to live in Jerusalem" (Neh 11:2).

The Significance of Casting Lots

The practice of casting lots to receive revelation and determine answers to questions goes back to ancient Babylon and the practice of divination. Within the Scriptures of ancient Israel, casting lots serves several purposes, always with the assumption that God works through the process. When the community needs guidance in choosing the king, they cast lots, and Saul is selected (1 Sam 10:20-21). Further, lots choose the scapegoat for the Day of Atonement (Lev 16:8-10). In specific incidents, casting lots provides a sense of fairness under challenging situations. For example, Nehemiah's community casts lots to determine those who will live in Jerusalem (Neh 11:1); and Joshua turns to lots to apportion the land of Canaan to the Israelites (Josh 18:6-10). Casting lots determines the temple duties carried out by the priests and Levites, lots determine their roles (1 Chr 24:31; 26:13) and who will bring the wood offering

3. Bob Becking, *Ezra–Nehemiah*, HCOT (Leuven: Peeters, 2018), 295.

for sacrifices (Neh 10:34). When the sailors seek the reason for the great storm that threatens them, they cast lots, "and the lot fell on Jonah" (Jonah 1:7). In Nehemiah's community, casting lots allows leaders to pass the responsibility for difficult decisions onto God, as revealed in the dice, rather than making the choices themselves.[4]

The term המתנדבים (Neh 11:2), translated "willingly offered," is the same word used in Judges 5:2 to describe the Israelites' eagerness to volunteer for battle against King Jabin of Hazor. Similarly, Amasiah son of Zichri desires to serve Jehoshaphat and the Lord in Jerusalem while in the company of 200,000 "mighty warriors" (2 Chr 17:16).[5] Descendants of Judah and Tamar's son Perez, the "valiant warriors" in Nehemiah 11:6, also protect those living in Nehemiah's Jerusalem.[6] Here, the portrait of a fortified city with an equally strong religious presence is reminiscent of preexilic Jerusalem. For the people, this refortified Jerusalem ignites their faith and imagination where Jerusalem and its inhabitants resume their place as God's people in God's holy city.

The Portrayal of Cities

The overall portrait of biblical cities in the Scriptures of ancient Israel is one that is predominantly negative or ambivalent at best. Biblical prophets like Isaiah, Jeremiah, Ezekiel, Micah, and others often condemn foreign cities, and even Jerusalem, for idolatry, corruption, arrogance, and social injustice (e.g., Isa 13–14; 23; Ezek 16; 23:49; 34; Jer 21:4-10; 50–51). At the same time, Jerusalem is cast as a habitable city in need of protection, God's vineyard. In biblical Hebrew, cities are marked grammatically in the feminine. Metaphorically, biblical cities are sometimes

4. For more information on lots, see Julye Bidmead, "Lots," in *Eerdmans Dictionary of the Bible*, ed. David Noel Freedman (Grand Rapids: Eerdmans, 2000), 825.

5. Robert Alter, "Nehemiah," in *The Hebrew Bible: The Writings* (New York: Norton, 2019), 855.

6. Nehemiah 11:6 mentions the presence of the 468 valiant warriors of the descendants of Perez; and 11:14, another 128 valiant warriors who are counted among Jerusalem's residents.

depicted as sinful women (cf. Isa 1:21; Ezek 15:30-31; 23:44-45) or vulnerable daughters (cf. Jer 14:17; 46:16; and Isa 47:1) in need of punishment or protection. Stéphanie Anthonioz observes, "No city in the ancient Near East ever receives the treatment that daughter Zion does, who is personified to the point of becoming alive for her God and to the reader."[7] While Jerusalem in Ezra–Nehemiah is never referred to as Zion or daughter Zion, it is at times described as "wicked and rebellious" (Ezra 4:12-16; Neh 2:10, 19; 4:1-3; 6:1-2) or a place of renewed worship and devotion to God (Ezra 1:3; 3:8-13; 6:13-18; Neh 2:17-18; 6:15-16; 8:1-12; 9:1-38). This depiction of cities as places in need of God's protection or God's correction seemingly justifies military invasions and the cities' occupants as deserving of the violence inflicted on them. The feminization, in some ways, captures ancient (and even modern) cultural attitudes of women as vulnerable, unfaithful, or sinful, thereby suffering the consequences of their actions.

Today many of the world's cities are vibrant places of intercultural and creative exchange. The challenges faced by differing cultures living in close proximity to one another are real. These challenges include competition for space (housing, parking) and resources (water, food, transportation). There are cities that experience greater challenges than others with violence, poverty, militarized police forces, and neighborhoods in need of renewal. Having access to fertile land, usually more prevalent outside urban settings, provides more potential for food security. In an agrarian culture like Judah's, the desire for space and land might be more palatable for some than life in the city. Yet, the city of Jerusalem continues to be renewed under Nehemiah's leadership. Nehemiah moves the center of worship and administration back to Jerusalem from Mizpah, which had become Judah's center after the Babylonian exile.[8] In urban renewal, cities often become more economically viable as well as aesthetically pleasing to those from the middle and upper classes who swarm into this new

7. Stéphanie Anthonioz, "Cities of Glory and Cities of Pride: Concepts, Gender, and Images of Cities in Mesopotamia and in Ancient Israel," in *Memory and the City in Ancient Israel*, ed. Diana V. Edelman and Ehud Ben Zvi (University Park: Pennsylvania State University Press, 2014), 22.

8. See Jer 40–41; 2 Kgs 25:23; Neh 3:7, 15; 1 Macc 3:46 for evidence of the importance of Mizpah as a center for worship.

environment. In modern contexts we might call this gentrification—a movement into the city of those better financially and politically situated to rebuild often less affluent cities and neighborhoods.

Food Insecurity and the City

While modern cities are creative in using hydroponics, roof gardening, and a whole lot of industrious ways to grow produce, much of the food entering New York City and other major cities is grown outside their bounds. When infrastructures flow smoothly, most people are able to find the food they need to sustain themselves. During crises, however, the food chain can be at risk, which causes food insecurity, especially for those more vulnerable. Siddhartha Mahanta notes Manhattan's food supply struggle during Superstorm Sandy, where flooding and road closures threatened deliveries and excess waters destroyed stored food.[9] During the coronavirus pandemic, many people with the means started growing "victory gardens," reminiscent of those grown throughout the United States during World Wars I and II.[10]

Nehemiah singles out another group that repopulates Jerusalem—the singers (מְשֹׁרְרִים). This group, composed of male and female members (Ezra 2:65; Neh 7:67), appears several times in Ezra–Nehemiah and are sometimes listed with the gatekeepers. According to 1 Chronicles, King David, a lover of music, places Heman, Heman's brother Asaph, and other family singers in charge of the "service of song" (1 Chr 6:31-48). They serve in tandem with their "kindred" the Levites (1 Chr 6:48). Their job, among others, is to prophesy with the help of "lyres, harps, and cymbals" (1 Chr 25:1) and to make sure the songs of praise are sung in unison (2 Chr 5:12). The singers precede the ark when David moves it to Jerusalem (1 Chr 16:1-6).

9. Siddhartha Mahanta, "New York's Looming Food Disaster," *Bloomberg* (October 21, 2013), https://www.bloomberg.com/news/articles/2013-10-21/new-york-s-looming-food-disaster.

10. Tajal Rao, "Food Supply Anxiety Brings Back Victory Gardens," *New York Times* (March 25, 2020), https://www.nytimes.com/2020/03/25/dining/victory-gardens-coronavirus.html.

The singers in Nehemiah 11:22-23 descend from the guilds of Asaph and Jeduthun, which connects them to David and Solomon as well as to temple worship and the Psalms. In Nehemiah 11, these men and women play important roles in reestablishing Jerusalem and its worship as those "in charge of the work of the house of God" (Neh 11:22). For their service the text suggests that they receive support from the Persian king who commands the community to provide them daily provisions (Neh 11:23). The term "provision" (*'amanah*, אמנה, v. 23) is the same term translated in Nehemiah 9:38 as "firm agreement"—what the people sign as a promise that they will adhere to Torah and that they will maintain the house of God (see commentary on Neh 9:38–10:39). The singers are essential to maintaining the house of God and are ensured payment for the work they do on behalf of the temple. The performance of music for the temple is rewarded with a continuous living wage. The need for a living wage transcends time, as people today find themselves living below the salary they need to afford to live and eat in their communities. The greater question is what we find necessary and what we are willing to pay for. Does a church need a paid choir or choir director? Does it need a multimillion-dollar organ?

Overall, Nehemiah 11:1-24 details the lineage and leadership connections in postexilic Jerusalem, linking the leadership primarily to the tribe of Judah, the line of David, and less so to Benjamin, the line of Saul. These verses highlight the descendants of Judah—Shelah (Neh 11:5), Perez (Neh 11:4, 6), and Zerah (Neh 11:24)—establishing a direct connection to King David through Perez, son of Judah. While Tamar's name is absent as the mother of Perez and Zerah, she lurks beneath the narrative as her descendants are essential to the leadership of Judah (Gen 38), not only before the Babylonian exile, but in Persian Judah as well. First Chronicles 2:3-4 is more explicit in naming her in the genealogy of the descendants of Judah, "Now Er, Judah's firstborn, was wicked in the sight of the LORD, and he put him to death. His daughter-in-law Tamar also bore him Perez and Zerah. Judah had five sons in all." The leaders' lineage to Perez, Zerah, and David, through Tamar's historical and almost sacrificial story, cements their rightful place in Israel's story, bridging the preexilic and postexilic periods under the divine providence depicted in the Bible. In the book of Ruth, the people recognize the importance of this family and singles out Perez in her blessing to Boaz: "and, through the children that the LORD will give you by this young woman, may your house be like the house of Perez, whom Tamar bore to

Judah" (Ruth 4:12). Tamar's son, Perez, is the ancestor of the 468 valiant warriors called to protect Jerusalem and its people (Neh 11:6). Pethahiah, who advises the king of Persia (Neh 11:24),[11] is a descendant of Tamar's son Zerah. Pethahiah's name on the list speaks to the great influence he and his family have in the Persian court as he is "at the king's hand in all matters concerning the people" (Neh 11:24). As ancestors of David, Tamar and Ruth the Moabite (foreign women) have a place in David's city, Jerusalem.

As noted earlier, the holiness of Jerusalem is stressed at both the beginning and end of the list of those repopulating the city (Neh 11:1, 18). The city itself now becomes the "house of God" set apart from other cities in the region.[12] Ralph Klein notes: "In a holy city, purity of lay people is as important as the purity of priests."[13] Priests and Levites monitor all activities that take place within Jerusalem's borders and are divided into two groups—those who maintain the holiness of the temple complex (11:10) and those "who were over the outside work of the house of God" (Neh 11:16).[14]

Settled in the Surrounding Villages (11:25-36)

Intermingled in the discussion of repopulating Jerusalem in the previous section (Neh 11:1-24) are references to property inheritance and distribution. Nine-tenths of those who scatter throughout the towns settle on "their property" (Neh 11:3) or "possession"[15]—ancestral lands they reclaim even though many of them have not lived in Judah for decades. In Nehemiah 11:20, "the rest of Israel," along with priests and Levites, settle on their "inheritance" (נחלה, Neh 11:20). A נחלה is hereditary property where the stewardship of the land is passed from generation to generation and held sacred to the family.[16] For example, Naboth adamantly

11. The Persian king is the obvious monarch in this context since Yehud is colonized by Persia. Pethahiah is the name of a governor of Yehud after Nehemiah (Paul L. Reddit, *Ezra–Nehemiah* [Macon: Smith & Helwys, 2014], 317).

12. Tamara Cohn Eskenazi, *In an Age of Prose: A Literary Approach to Ezra–Nehemiah*, SBLMS 36 (Atlanta: SBL, 1988), 114.

13. Ralph Klein, "The Books of Ezra and Nehemiah," in *The New Interpreter's Bible*, ed. Leander Keck, vol. 3 (Nashville: Abingdon, 1999), 825.

14. See Becking, *Ezra–Nehemiah*, 297, for more information.

15. אחזה, *HALOT*, 32.

16. נחלה, *HALOT*, 688.

Neh 11:25-36

25And as for the villages, with their
fields, some of the people of Judah
lived in Kiriath-arba and its villages,
and in Dibon and its villages, and in
Jekabzeel and its villages, 26and in Jeshua and in Moladah and Beth-pelet,
27in Hazar-shual, in Beer-sheba and its
villages, 28in Ziklag, in Meconah and
its villages, 29in En-rimmon, in Zorah,
in Jarmuth, 30Zanoah, Adullam, and
their villages, Lachish and its fields,
and Azekah and its villages. So they
camped from Beer-sheba to the valley of Hinnom. 31The people of Benjamin also lived from Geba onward, at
Michmash, Aija, Bethel and its villages,
32Anathoth, Nob, Ananiah, 33Hazor,
Ramah, Gittaim, 34Hadid, Zeboim,
Neballat, 35Lod, and Ono, the valley
of artisans. 36And certain divisions of
the Levites in Judah were joined to
Benjamin.

refuses to give or sell his נחלה in Jezreel to King Ahab even under fear of death (1 Kgs 21:3). In Nehemiah 11:25-36 the writer lists the repatriates who live in the villages surrounding Jerusalem. The text is silent about how long-term inhabitants of the villages might welcome an influx of repatriates expecting to live in their ancestral towns—land that might be occupied by others.[17] It seems unlikely that the repatriates reclaimed the exact physical spaces of their ancestors; it is more plausible that they resettled within the general vicinity or villages once inhabited by them. With few examples, the resettled villages (11:25-36) are the same villages settled in Joshua 14–16. These villages link the present community to Joshua's assigned allotments in Canaan.

The biblical text of Joshua depicts acquiring land through inheritance as a gift and responsibility from God. In Nehemiah 11:25-36 the writer links the inheritance of the land back to Joshua with this same understanding. The land as a gift and responsibility is linked to the people's identity but not to a family's or individual's self-worth. This differs from today where property ownership is often linked to individual self-worth (e.g., credit scores, purchasing power, financial security). Still, property ownership is often difficult or impossible for persons from marginalized communities. This is illustrated through Zo Gross's words that represent the loss of a home that now belongs to someone else.

17. Israel Finkelstein is among those who note that the settlements in Nehemiah 11:24-36 look like cities settled in the Hasmonean period rather than Persian period. See Israel Finkelstein, *Hasmonean Realities Behind Ezra, Nehemiah, and Chronicles: Archaeological and Historical Perspectives*, AIL 34 (Atlanta: SBL Press, 2018). Deirdre Fulton suggests that the settlements behind the lists are likely Hellenistic or later in *Reconsidering Nehemiah's Judah*, 188.

Redlining and Housing Disparities

They may own it now, but did
they fill the flower beds to the
brim with cold earth and mulch?
Did they plant sunflowers along
each corner, ones that act like
columns holding up the sky come
August? Did they rescue the
earthworms before they dried out
along the stone walkway? Do they
know where the pets are buried
and when to leave them flowers?

It might be theirs, but were their
shoes among the many that wore
down the wood on the center
of the steps? Have their fingers
traced the banisters on the way
down? Did their pinkies grab
splinters? Did they wince when
Grandma extracted them with
her sewing needle and reading
glasses?

It is no longer ours, but did
they hear the first cries of life
echoing the halls? Hear the
frantic movements of midwives?
Did they see Grandma's smile
as Grandpa came in the room
to greet his first born? Did they
feel the soft newborn skin of my
Mother?

They may own it, but did
they join Grandpa's memorial
luncheon? Did they sweat in the
kitchen as the different cakes,
mac 'n' cheese, and pasta salad
were placed on the counters?
Did they lead hymns in the
sitting room? Did they help us
fold his clothes for donations?

We no longer own it, but do
they believe in ghosts? Ones
that appear after car crashes and
apologize for leaving you alone?
Ones that still touch your hair
in the middle of the night when
you're crying. When you're not
crying too. One that you can still
hear singing from her bedroom.
Have they felt the immortal
nature of a Mother's love?

I will never own it, but they
never heard Grandma's jokes
as she worsened and shriveled.
Never heard my sorry laugh of
reply. Never seen a Matriarch
confused in her own home.
Never heard the crack of a hip
and the sirens of an ambulance.
The silent way groceries rot and
mortgages default.

We don't live here anymore,
but have we not melded into
the very walls themselves?
Sloppy white paint might
cover the height tallies along
the washroom wall. Carpeting
can cover the living room floor
scratched up by terriers and
mastiffs and retrievers. But are
we not still here? Even after
the house is sliced into rentable
sections, after tenants haul their
furniture through the front door,
will we ever truly leave? Can a
landlord charge our spirit rent?

Can you own what you don't
belong to?

Zo Gross

Priests and Levites: Preserving the Temple (12:1-26)

Nehemiah 12:1-26 presents the last of five lists in Ezra–Nehemiah that recount the priestly and Levitical genealogies from Zerubbabel's time (Ezra 2:2, 36-39) through Nehemiah's (Neh 12:1-26).[18] The list records the heads of the priestly ancestral households through the time of Darius,[19] the Persian (Neh 12:22), and a "Book of Annals" (Neh 12:23) that records Levites through Eliashib's son Johanan (late fifth century BCE). A closer inspection of Nehemiah 12:1-26 reveals what appears to be a duplication of the names of the priests under Jeshua (Neh 12:1-7) and those under Joiakim (Neh 12:12-21).[20] As repositories for preserving memories, these lists function beyond a genealogical collection that preserves the names of temple leadership and its personnel. They were most likely inserted to create a continuous priestly genealogy to legitimize priestly authority in the restored community.[21]

Nehemiah 12:10-11 singles out the names of priests (Jeshua, Jehoikim, Eliashib, Joiada, Jonathan, Jaddua) that form a family genealogy spanning the years from Zerubbabel (520 BCE) through Jaddua (336–331 BCE). The names of these priests appear in the lists of high priests outside of Nehemiah. The narrative omits the title high priest with the exception of Eliashib (Neh 3:1, 20; 13:28), even though there is evidence that the role of the high priest expands during the Persian period and beyond.[22] The role of high priest originates with Aaron, whom Ezra calls the "head priest" (הכהן הראש, Ezra 7:5); this office becomes much more important after the demise of the Israelite monarchy, a time when priests maintained the local leadership of the temple while under the leadership of a foreign governor and king. In his *Antiquities*, Josephus (37–ca. 100 CE)

18. See Eskenazi's breakdown of the lists in *In the Age of Prose*, 111–14.

19. This ruler may be Darius I (522–486 BCE) or Darius III Codomannus (336–331 BCE), a contemporary of Jaddau who is listed last. For a helpful summary of the arguments on the identity of Darius related to these lists, see Fulton, *Reconsidering Nehemiah's Jerusalem*, 137n70. See also Joseph Blenkinsopp, *Ezra–Nehemiah: A Commentary*, OTL (Philadelphia: Westminster, 1988), 340.

20. Blenkinsopp, *Ezra–Nehemiah*, 337, compares the lists in 12:1-7 with 12:12-21 (under Joiakim), the list of signatories in 10:3-9, and a similar list in 1 Chr 24.

21. The concern for maintaining a genealogical record of priests is particularly important in the Hasmonean period when the compiler might be trying to link the priesthood back to Aaron to justify their power. See Reddit, *Ezra–Nehemiah*, 313.

22. For longer discussion of the high priest, see James C. VanderKam, *From Joshua through Caiaphas: High Priests after the Exile* (Minneapolis: Fortress, 2004); Lester Grabbe, *History of the Jews and Judaism in the Second Temple Period*, vol. 1: *Yehud: A History of the Persian Province of Judah*, LSTS 47 (London: T&T Clark, 2004), 232. See VanderKam's list of priests and sources.

Neh 12:1-26

1These are the priests and the Levites
who came up with Zerubbabel son of
Shealtiel and Jeshua: Seraiah, Jeremiah, Ezra, 2Amariah, Malluch, Hattush, 3Shecaniah, Rehum, Meremoth,
4Iddo, Ginnethoi, Abijah, 5Mijamin,
Maadiah, Bilgah, 6Shemaiah, Joiarib,
Jedaiah, 7Sallu, Amok, Hilkiah, Jedaiah. These were the leaders of the
priests and of their associates in the
days of Jeshua.

8And the Levites: Jeshua, Binnui,
Kadmiel, Sherebiah, Judah, and Mattaniah, who with his associates was in

identifies Jaddua as a high priest in Judah during Darius III Codomannus's reign and a contemporary of Alexander the Great.[23]

Egyptian priestly genealogies share similarities with those found in Nehemiah 12:10-11 and serve the same purpose: to legitimize the role of the priesthood.[24] Even though Ezra restores the Torah and is a powerful priestly presence in the reconstruction of Jerusalem and its temple worship, he is visibly absent from Nehemiah's list. Ezra–Nehemiah never identifies Ezra as a high priest, but Ezra's genealogy (Ezra 7:1-5) traces his lineage through Zadok, Phinehas, and Aaron, the chief priest.[25] Situating the names of the high priests among the other priests and Levites sends a message that these leaders, along with the entire community, are responsible for the well-being of the temple in Judah.

Sara Japhet notices that Ezra–Nehemiah tends to omit titles or political positions to shift the credit for the reconstruction away from the leaders and onto the public.[26] Still, Nehemiah's list (Neh 12:1-26) memorializes the male priesthood from Joshua through Jaddua. Later, communities record each name and read it, stamping the name into the community's memory. Women are absent from these priestly archives, but contemporary feminist theologians are creating new lists to memorialize women as spiritual leaders.

23. "Jaddua," in *Eerdmans Dictionary of the Bible*, ed. David Noel Freedman (Grand Rapids: Eerdmans, 2000), 667. See *Ant* 11:8.4-5 [326–39].

24. Kenton L. Sparks, *Ancient Texts for the Study of the Hebrew Bible: A Guide to the Background Literature* (Peabody, MA: Hendrickson, 2005), 356, 359. He also compares them with similar lists in 1 Chr 6:1-15; 6:50-53; 9:11-13; Ezra 7:1-5; Neh 11:10-14.

25. The only high priests (הכהן הגדל) named in the Hebrew Bible are Hilkiah (2 Kgs 22:4), Eliashib (Neh 3:1), and Joshua (Hag 1:1). Aaron and many of his descendants are called chief priests (הכהן הראש) (Ezra 7:5; HEB), including Seraiah (2 Kgs 25:18), Amariah (2 Chr 19:11), and Azariah (2 Chr 26:20), and others presumed to be a high priest like Zadok.

26. Sara Japhet, "Sheshbazzar and Zerubbabel—Against the Background of the Historical and Religious Tendencies of Ezra–Nehemiah," *ZAW* 94 (1982): 66–98.

Neh 12:1-26 (cont.)

charge of the songs of thanksgiving. [9]And Bakbukiah and Unno their associates stood opposite them in the service. [10]Jeshua was the father of Joiakim, Joiakim the father of Eliashib, Eliashib the father of Joiada, [11]Joiada the father of Jonathan, and Jonathan the father of Jaddua.

[12]In the days of Joiakim the priests, the heads of the ancestral houses, were: of Seraiah, Meraiah; of Jeremiah, Hananiah; [13]of Ezra, Meshullam; of Amariah, Jehohanan; [14]of Malluchi, Jonathan; of Shebaniah, Joseph; [15]of Harim, Adna; of Meraioth, Helkai; [16]of Iddo, Zechariah; of Ginnethon, Meshullam; [17]of Abijah, Zichri; of Miniamin, of Moadiah, Piltai; [18]of Bilgah, Shammua; of Shemaiah, Jehonathan; [19]of Joiarib, Mattenai; of Jedaiah, Uzzi; [20]of Sallai, Kallai; of Amok, Eber; [21]of Hilkiah, Hashabiah; of Jedaiah, Nethanel.

[22]As for the Levites, in the days of Eliashib, Joiada, Johanan, and Jaddua, there were recorded the heads of ancestral houses, also the priests until the reign of Darius the Persian. [23]The Levites, heads of ancestral houses, were recorded in the Book of the Annals until the days of Johanan son of Eliashib. [24]And the leaders of the Levites: Hashabiah, Sherebiah, and Jeshua son of Kadmiel, with their associates over against them, to praise and to give thanks, according to the commandment of David the man of God, section opposite to section. [25]Mattaniah, Bakbukiah, Obadiah, Meshullam, Talmon, and Akkub were gatekeepers standing guard at the storehouses of the gates. [26]These were in the days of Joiakim son of Jeshua son of Jozadak and in the days of Nehemiah the governor and of Ezra the priest and scribe.

Women as Spiritual Leaders

Tamar Kamionkowski reminds us: "The hereditary nature of the priesthood is deeply embedded in shared holy blood—he shares the blood of his father."[27] Hilary Lipka summarizes several theories for why Israelite women are excluded from the priesthood: they menstruate, making them periodically ritually unclean; they are needed to care for children in this agrarian context; women priests in nearby cults are used for sexual rituals; ancient Near Eastern priestesses do not sacrifice animals, which would be a major ritual in ancient Israel; they serve the goddess cults; or there are not enough jobs to go around.[28] To counter a few of these theories, priests, too, are temporarily unclean

27. S. Tamar Kamionkowski, *Leviticus*, WCS 3 (Collegeville, MN: Liturgical Press, 2018), 234.

28. Hilary Lipka, "Another View," in *The Torah: A Woman's Commentary*, ed. Tamara Cohn Eskenazi and Andrea Weiss (New York: Women of Reform Judaism, 2008), 489.

through their ejaculations, yet are allowed to serve in this role. Yet, menopausal women in Aaron's line are excluded from serving as priest. Lipka comments that, though the Bible only endorses the male priesthood, women may have leadership roles in local sanctuaries.[29] Nehemiah 12:1-26 memorializes the names of the male priests and leaders—almost in a ritual form as each name is read and remembered. Female leaders in various religious traditions expand their rituals today and add their lists and genealogies of female spiritual leaders. For example, Rosemary Radford Ruether and Elisabeth Schüssler Fiorenza are among those who remember and list, often in liturgies, women who have formed the church community—a feminist communion of saints.[30] Within the Roman Catholic Church, where an all-male priesthood is deemed legitimate, there are groups of Roman Catholic women who recognize a priestly tradition of women like the Roman Catholic Women Priests Movement—an international group of ordained women in apostolic succession.[31]

While questions remain about the historicity of this list of high priests as well as the other priests and Levites listed in Nehemiah 12:1-26, it becomes clear that the priest and Levite lists were important to Nehemiah's

29. Lipka, "Another View," 489.

30. Rosemary Radford Ruether, "Litanies of Remembrance," in *Women-Church: Theology and Practice of Feminist Liturgical Communities* (San Francisco: Harper & Row, 1985), 141–43; Elisabeth Schüssler Fiorenza, *In Memory of Her: A Feminist Theological Reconstruction of Christian Origins* (New York: Crossroad, 1983/1994); Teresa Berger, *Women's Ways of Worship: Gender Analysis and Liturgical History* (Collegeville, MN: Liturgical Press, 1999); Lorena Parrish, "Dismantling Domination through Womanist Rituals of Resistance," *Liturgy* 35 (2020): 10–18, https://doi.org/10.1080/0458063x.2020.1701897; "A Jewish Guide to Marking Transgender Day of Remembrance," *Keshet* קשת *For LGBTQ+ Equality in Jewish Life* (October 4, 2011), https://www.keshetonline.org/resources/a-jewish-guide-for-marking-transgender-day-of-remembrance/.

31. In 2002 the first Roman Catholic Women priests were ordained near the Danube River: Iris Müller, Ida Raming, Pia Bruner, Dagmar Celeste, Adelinde Roitlinger, Gisela Forster, and Christine Mayr-Lumetxberger. Roman Catholic Women Priests, https://romancatholicwomenpriests.org/. The first women Roman Catholic bishops are ordained by Roman Catholic male bishops, so they fall under apostolic succession. The Vatican Congregation for the Doctrine of the Faith declared on May 29, 2008, that the "women priests and the bishops who ordain them would be excommunicated *latae sententiae*" (automatically). Roman Catholic Women Priests reject this, insisting they are loyal members of the church who stand in the prophetic tradition of holy obedience to the Spirit's call to change an unjust law that discriminates against women.

community and served to cement their identity by connecting the priests from Aaron to the present priests. Further, this list makes connections between Zerubbabel and the Davidic line.[32] Here the Psalms attributed to David become an important part of the antiphonal singing in this new community's worship: "And the leaders of the Levites: Hashabiah, Sherebiah, and Jeshua son of Kadmiel, with their associates over against them, to praise and to give thanks, according to the commandment of David [1 Chr 15:16] the man of God, section opposite to section" (Neh 12:24).[33] The reference to David as the "man of God" in Nehemiah 12:24 bestows on him a title typically reserved for Moses and the prophets.[34] When the second temple is dedicated (Ezra 3), the people sing songs of praise and thanksgiving responsively "according to the directions of King David of Israel" (Ezra 3:10-11). Likewise, the heads of the Levites during Nehemiah's time uphold this same liturgical tradition mandated by David (Neh 12:26).

Nehemiah's account of antiphonal singing differs from Ezra's in that it does not list a specific psalm but rather notes the groups' positioning as they face one another to offer songs of praise and thanksgiving. Antiphonal singing during worship can function prophetically—to speak truth to power in God's name. It calls the community to join in a shared experience as its members express words that define the group's desired ethics and relationship with God. A glance at the psalms that are classified as "praise" or "thanksgiving" demonstrates that the psalmists celebrate God's willingness to stand with the people against oppressive forces (e.g., Pss 18; 33; 65) and to provide them daily sustenance. "Justice" and "righteousness" are common themes within these psalms sung by the community as they praise and give thanks to God (e.g., Pss 72; 82; 140).

32. First Chronicles 3:16-19 lists Zerubbabel's father as Pediah, the son of Joconiah (Jehoiachin), the king taken into Babylonian captivity in 597 BCE. Zerubbabel's continuation of the Davidic line expands into Jesus's genealogy in Matt 1:12 and Luke 3:27, although his father is identified as Shealtiel in Matthew rather than the Chronicler's Pediah.

33. Hindy Najman makes these connections in "Notes on Nehemiah," in *The Jewish Study Bible*, ed. Adele Berlin and Marc Zvi Brettler, 2nd ed. (Oxford: Oxford University Press, 2014), 1702.

34. The epithet "man of God," often assigned to Moses and other prophets, is now applied to David in postexilic texts (2 Chr 8:14; Neh 12:24, 36)—a phrase that ties him to Moses and the other Hebrew prophets, unlike in his account by the Deuteronomistic Historian (2 Samuel and 1 Kings). Rabbinic and Islamic traditions (Sifre Devarim and Surah An-Nisa 4:163, respectively) consider David to be a prophet. The Christian traditions view David as a king and priest, although he is called a prophet in Acts 2:30. See Najman, "Notes on Nehemiah," 2286 (Sifre Devarim, piska 342 on Deut 33:1, 'Avot R. Nat., version B, ch. 37).

Continually reciting these songs can have a transformative impact on communities as they embody the words in their own actions. Lorena Parrish proposes the following womanist rituals of resistance that utilize "the process of postmodern womanist reimagining as foundational to identifying and offering alternatives to oppressive language, liturgical practices, and exploitative systems that hinder the Black Church from supporting black women's and the entire black community's flourishing."[35] Not only are these liturgies prophetic, but these rituals help to form identity as theologies and ethics are repeated through word and music.

Within the book of Ezra–Nehemiah, the terms "thanks" and "thanksgiving" appear nine times, and seven of these occurrences take place in Nehemiah 12 (Neh 12:8, 24, 27, 31, 38, 40, 46). Leaders from the Levites—Jeshua, Binnui, Kadmiel, Sherebiah, Judah, and Mattaniah—are assigned to lead songs of praise and thanksgiving. Offering thanks to God is important to Israel, as we will see in their celebration and dedication of the Jerusalem walls (12:27, 31, 38, 40, 46). The joy and praise at the wall's dedication illustrate the importance of these psalms. Nehemiah 12:8 is the only place in the Scriptures of ancient Israel where the term *hodayot* (הידות), translated as "songs of thanksgiving," appears. Its appearance may be comparable to the *Hodayot*, a collection of praise hymns sung or read antiphonally by the community responsible for the Dead Sea Scrolls discovered in the caves at Qumran.[36]

Unrelenting Joy: Dedication of the City Wall, a Ritual of Purification? (12:27–13:3)

In Nehemiah 12:27–13:3 the people rededicate the walls, and the priests purify themselves, the people, the gates, and the walls. This act of purification is essential as it marks the repatriates as a holy people who now inhabit *the* holy city. Following a celebratory procession, the Torah is read (Neh 13:1-3), including Deuteronomy 23:3, which prohibits Moabites and Ammonites from entering the assembly of God. In response to this reading, the people separate from "all those of foreign descent" (Neh 13:3).

35. Parrish, "Dismantling Domination," 10.

36. Noted by Becking, *Ezra–Nehemiah*, 303. Julie Hughes connects *Hodayot* (1QH) and Neh 9:6-37 and Dan 9:4-19 based on the use of the phrase "your abundant compassion" that is repeated in this material but does not mention Neh 12:8. See *Scriptural Allusions and Exegesis in the Hodayot*, STDJ 59 (Leiden: Brill, 2006), 125. Eight copies of the *Hodayot* were discovered in 1947 within cave 1 and cave 4. See Eileen Schuller, "Recent Scholarship on the *Hodayot* 1993–2010," *CurBR* 10 (2011): 119–62, https://doi.org/10.1177/1476993X11408783.

Neh 12:27–13:3

[27]Now at the dedication of the wall of
Jerusalem they sought out the Levites
in all their places, to bring them to Jerusalem to celebrate the dedication with
rejoicing, with thanksgivings and with
singing, with cymbals, harps, and lyres.
[28]The companies of the singers gathered together from the circuit around
Jerusalem and from the villages of
the Netophathites, [29]also from Beth-
gilgal and from the region of Geba and
Azmaveth, for the singers had built for
themselves villages around Jerusalem.
[30]And the priests and the Levites purified themselves, and they purified the
people and the gates and the wall.

[31]Then I brought the leaders of
Judah up onto the wall and appointed
two great companies that gave thanks
and went in procession. One went to the
right on the wall to the Dung Gate, [32]and
after them went Hoshaiah and half the
officials of Judah, [33]and Azariah, Ezra,
Meshullam, [34]Judah, Benjamin, Shemaiah, and Jeremiah, [35]and some of the
young priests with trumpets: Zechariah
son of Jonathan son of Shemaiah son
of Mattaniah son of Micaiah son of Zaccur son of Asaph, [36]and his kindred, Shemaiah, Azarel, Milalai, Gilalai, Maai,
Nethanel, Judah, and Hanani, with the
musical instruments of David the man of

The focus of 12:27-43 is a celebratory expression of joy shared by the reconstituted community as it dedicates the Jerusalem walls. In contrast to the "great trouble and shame" Nehemiah voices upon hearing of Jerusalem's sad state (Neh 1:3), the people now offer "great sacrifices" and "rejoice with great joy" (Neh 12:43) over their accomplishments—the refortifying of the community's physical and religious structures. The Levites living in the villages are summoned to Jerusalem to fulfill their roles as the leaders of songs of praise and thanksgiving accompanied by cymbals, harps, and lyres (Neh 12:27).[37] The singers also make their way to the city for this dedication ceremony. The noun translated in Nehemiah 12:27 as "dedication" is the construct form of *chanukah* (חנכה), which is also used in the accounts of the dedications of the altar (Num 7:10), the temple (Ps 30 superscript), and the Festival of Hanukkah that celebrates the rededication of the temple in 164 BCE—all associated with a holy space.[38] Nehemiah 12:27-43, while showing signs of editing,[39] portrays a true celebration by

37. It is unclear who summons the Levites. It could be the priests or even Ezra or Nehemiah.

38. Blenkinsopp notes that the term *chanukah* is also the name of the Maccabean winter festival (1 Macc 4:52-59). See *Ezra–Nehemiah*, 344.

39. The Nehemiah Memoir reappears in Neh 12:31, which returns the narrative to the first-person voice. The presence of Ezra in Neh 12:36, as in Neh 8–10, however, might be an addition since Nehemiah and Ezra are not contemporaries.

God, and Ezra the scribe went in front of them. [37]At the Fountain Gate, in front of them, they went straight up by the stairs of the city of David, at the ascent of the wall, above the house of David, to the Water Gate on the east.

[38]The other company of those who gave thanks went to the left, and I followed them with half of the people on the wall, above the Tower of the Ovens, to the Broad Wall, [39]and above the Gate of Ephraim, and by the Old Gate, and by the Fish Gate and the Tower of Hananel and the Tower of the Hundred, to the Sheep Gate, and they came to a halt at the Gate of the Guard. [40]So both companies of those who gave thanks stood in the house of God, and I and half of the officials with me; [41]and the priests Eliakim, Maaseiah, Miniamin, Micaiah, Elioenai, Zechariah, and Hananiah, with trumpets; [42]and Maaseiah, Shemaiah, Eleazar, Uzzi, Jehohanan, Malchijah, Elam, and Ezer. And the singers sang with Jezrahiah as their leader. [43]They offered great sacrifices that day and rejoiced, for God had made them rejoice with great joy; the women and children also rejoiced. The joy of Jerusalem was heard far away.

[44]On that day men were appointed over the chambers for the stores, the

the repatriates as their mission is accomplished and they have defined who they are and their community ethic based on Torah.

Before the people celebrate, the priests and Levites purify (טהר) themselves and perform the act of purifying the people and the wall (Neh 12:30). The term translated "purified" can be translated to mean "cleanse" or "make clean" and often appears alongside the term translated in the NRSVue as "pollution" or "unclean" (טמאה). Both of these terms are related to the system of holiness in ancient Israel. Tamara Cohn Eskenazi suggests that by purifying the people (Neh 12:30), rather than the typical sacred items, the priests are "broadening the realm of the sacred."[40] As purified and holy people the repatriates can move closer to the city's holy spaces and strengthen their group identity and their relationship with their God. As holy people, they know that they matter to each other and to the Divine.

The concept of a people as holy is significant both then and now. Holiness is a state or quality of being set apart, both for individuals and religious spaces, in accordance with specific religious precepts and standards. It denotes a sacredness and purity that aligns with the beliefs and teachings of a particular religious community. The determination of what

40. Eskenazi makes the point that generally sacred items—rather than laity—are purified; Eskenazi, *In an Age of Prose*, 120.

Neh 12:27–13:3 (cont.)

contributions, the first fruits, and the
tithes, to gather into them the portions
required by the law for the priests and
for the Levites from the fields belonging
to the towns, for Judah rejoiced over
the priests and the Levites who ministered. 45They performed the service of
their God and the service of purification, as did the singers and the gatekeepers, according to the command
of David and his son Solomon. 46For in
the days of David and Asaph long ago
there was a leader of the singers, and
there were songs of praise and thanksgiving to God. 47In the days of Zerubbabel and in the days of Nehemiah all
Israel gave the daily portions for the
singers and the gatekeepers. They set
apart that which was for the Levites,
and the Levites set apart that which
was for the descendants of Aaron.

13:1On that day they read from the
book of Moses in the hearing of the
people, and in it was found written that no
Ammonite or Moabite should ever enter
the assembly of God, 2because they did
not meet the Israelites with bread and
water but hired Balaam against them
to curse them—yet our God turned the
curse into a blessing. 3When the people
heard the law, they separated from Israel
all those of foreign descent.

constitutes holiness and membership in God's community is typically defined by the community itself, based on its interpretation of religious texts such as the Torah or other sacred scriptures. This community engages in the act of setting individuals or places apart for divine purposes, such as consecrating priests or designated spaces for worship. Holiness thus emerges from the collective understanding and practices of the community, reflecting its commitment to the ideals of earlier scripture, tradition, and principles. Based on this idea of holiness, some persons are often excluded from ministerial and lay leadership because they do not fit into a prescribed paradigm of what their religious communities call holy.

Imagine how the world might change if we considered all people holy. In recent political discourse in the United States regarding the civil liberties of LGBTQ+ communities, Alexandra Ocasio-Cortez, a Roman Catholic, emphasized this understanding as she staunchly defended their rights in the face of opposition, "I know and it is part of my faith that all people are holy and all people are sacred. Unconditionally."[41]

41. Carol Kuruvilla, "Alexandria Ocasio-Cortez: Jesus Would Be Maligned as 'Radical' By Today's Congress," *Huffington Post* (February 27, 2020), https://www.huffpost.com/entry/alexandria-ocasio-cortez-faith_n_5e580e16c5b6450a30bbd0f7.

Most of the social violence we face in this world—war, poverty, racism, homophobia, intolerance of different religions—stems from the inability or unwillingness to view all people as holy. The people gathered in Jerusalem, ready to dedicate the wall, are made holy. In contrast, those also living in the land, like Sanballat, Tobiah, Geshem, and Noadiah, are not.

In 12:31-42, Nehemiah describes in detail the procession that celebrates the dedication of the walls.[42] First, he brings the leaders of Judah on top of the wall and divides them into "two great companies that gave thanks" (Neh 12:31), translated more literally by Robert Alter as "two great thanksgiving processions."[43] These companies circumambulate (walk around) on top of the walls in opposite directions (Neh 12:31). To get a sense of the size and strength of the walls, archaeologists suggest that they are wide enough for two or three people to march side by side.[44] The marchers play instruments—trumpets (Neh 12:35) and "the musical instruments of David the man of God" (Neh 12:36). Ezra leads the company that begins at the Dung Gate and marches to the right up to the Water Gate (Neh 12:36-37) while Nehemiah holds the rear of the other company that processes to the left starting at the Tower of the Ovens (Neh 12:38). Both groups end up together in the house of God (Neh 12:40). The singers sing (Neh 12:42) as those in the procession give thanks to God (Neh 12:31, 40). The choirs appear to meet face to face to sing antiphonally as suggested in Nehemiah 12:9 and Ezra 3:10-11. Nehemiah's surreptitious night walk when he first examines the broken walls (Neh 2:12-15) turns into a full display of a mission accomplished as the new Israel sings loudly and offers sacrifices and marches proudly on top of the walls, high enough to be seen and heard by those outside of the city: "The joy of Jerusalem was heard far away" (Neh 12:43). This celebration is to be compared to the celebration in Ezra 3:12-13, where the community expresses mixed emotions at the laying of the foundations.

42. This reference is the only occurrence of the term "procession" (תהלוכה) in the Hebrew Bible (*HALOT*, 237).

43. Alter, "Nehemiah," 858. Williamson labels those in the procession "two large choirs." See H. G. M. Williams, *Ezra–Nehemiah*, WBC 16 (Waco: Word, 1985), 367.

44. Nehemiah 12:31 suggests that the procession takes place on top of the wall. Blenkinsopp suggests that the walls uncovered during Kathleen Kenyon's excavations of Jerusalem (1961–1967) are wide enough to set two or three people side by side (*Ezra–Nehemiah*, 345). Fried suggests that a quickly built wall would not allow a safe procession on top of it. Instead, it makes sense that the procession takes place in front of the wall (Lisbeth S. Fried, *Nehemiah: A Commentary*, Critical Commentaries [Sheffield: Sheffield Phoenix, 2021], 343–44). While Fried's reading of the Hebrew also allows for a change of location (in front and not on top), we follow the text's description.

This community has expressed joy before—when the temple was dedicated (Ezra 6:16) and when they celebrated the Festival of the Unleavened Bread (Ezra 6:22). Further, as they restored Torah they celebrated the joy that the Torah brings (Neh 8:10). Now, as restoration is complete, the ecstasy that this community expresses on a job well done with God's support is emphasized by the multiple appearances of the terms "joy" and "rejoice": "They offered great sacrifices that day and rejoiced, for God had made them rejoice with great joy; the women and children also rejoiced" (Neh 12:43). Both the words "rejoice" and "joy" derive from the Hebrew verb שׂמח, which can also mean "mirth." The multiple uses of the adjective "great" (גדל)—"great companies" (Neh 12:31), "great sacrifices" (Neh 12:43), and "great joy" (Neh 12:43)—emphasize the magnitude of the celebration.

Processions and parades can be fun. Communities gathered to celebrate significant events can strengthen relationships and communal identity. Religious processions, like the marching of the Torah around the synagogue on Simchat Torah, magnify the importance of the scrolls for the worshiping community. Likewise, choirs and clergy processing into the sanctuary to joyful singing, raising the cross and Bible, direct the focus to symbols of Christian identity. Processional celebrations are present in other communities with the LGBTQ+ Pride, St. Patrick's Day, or Puerto Rican parades—honoring the contributions and identities of those represented. These events, when successful, are joyful and fun and pull the community together for a common cause. Nehemiah's procession does just that. Celebrating together connects the entire community to each individual member.

Parades and processions in the form of social protest are also empowering when used to raise awareness about particular communal concerns (e.g., Black Lives Matter, Selma March, March on Violence, Women's March). In other words, not all processions are celebratory: we might consider how the march in Charlottesville stoked flames of racism and white supremacy.[45] While one group celebrated and processed through the streets, the procession caused fear and unease in other groups witnessing the event.

Nehemiah 12:43 makes clear that the celebration includes women and children. This is one of the few narratives in Ezra–Nehemiah where the text intentionally mentions their presence: "the women and children also

45. Andrew Katz, "Clashes over a Show of White Nationalism in Charlottesville Turn Deadly," *Time*, https://time.com/charlottesville-white-nationalist-rally-clashes/.

rejoiced" (12:43). What remains unclear is how involved the women and children are within the rituals because of the generic "they" that runs throughout the narrative (cf. Neh 12:43, 45; 13:9). If women and children are included in the pronoun, then they march, give thanks, and offer sacrifices. They would also be among those gathered in the house of God as part of companies that assemble inside (Neh 12:40). Usually this sacred space is limited to priests, which leads some to suggest that Nehemiah and the laity in his company remain at the Gate of the Guard while the priests and Levites enter the temple.[46] Alter joins others and removes the laity by translation: "And the two thanksgiving processions stopped at the house of God."[47] The implication is that the people remain in the court outside of the temple and the priests separate from the others and enter this holy space.[48] Eskenazi argues that all of the people are purified and able to enter into the house of God, and there is enough space because the wall forms the outer boundary: "a house whose boundaries have expanded to include the city as a whole."[49]

After the procession, the narrative shifts to the ongoing needs of the community as they continue to collect contributions and care for the temple community (Neh 12:44-47). Now, "on that day," they put these commitments in place. "On that day" does little to clarify when this temple structuring takes place, but the narrative flow suggests that it occurs during the dedication of the walls. The community collects the contributions and appoints men to overlook the chambers in which they are stored together with a system for their distribution (Neh 12:44). Further, Judah rejoices that there are priests and Levites ministering to them (Neh 12:44).

The repatriates willingly bring their contributions to maintain the newly dedicated temple and the priests. But we pause to wonder if the people are truly joyfully paying their commitments or if this text functions as propaganda. There are likely members of the community who joyfully support the clergy and are grateful to have a fully reestablished

46. Williamson notes that Wilhelm Rudolph is among those who make this argument, although he believes that the laity enter the house of God. See H. G. M. Williamson, *Ezra and Nehemiah*, OTG (Sheffield: JSOT, 1987), 375–76; William Rudolph, *Esra und Nehemia, samt 3. Esra* (Tübingen: Mohr, 1949), 197–99. Jacob Wright also translates that they stop "at the house of God"; see *Rebuilding Identity: The Nehemiah-Memoir and Its Earliest Readers*, BZAW 348 (Berlin: de Gruyter, 2004), 285–86.

47. Alter, "Nehemiah," 858.

48. For a discussion on some of the arguments for assuming the laity do not enter the house of God, see Eskenazi, *In an Age of Prose*, 120–21.

49. Eskenazi, *In an Age of Prose*, 121.

priesthood and temple (Neh 12:44). Paying tribute to a good cause or to sustain one's religious community can be joyful and fulfilling, especially when giving is not an economic hardship. Some may struggle to offer their portions due to economic suffering that inevitably strike farmers and pastoralists when crops fail. Gathering all of these resources adds to the wealth and influence of the higher echelon of the priesthood in particular, as the temple also becomes the vehicle to collect and disperse tributes to the Persian rulers to whom those in Judah are beholden.[50] Nehemiah 12:47 suggests a distribution route that harks back to the days of Zerubbabel—the people give their daily portions to the singers and gatekeepers, then set aside their contributions to the Levites who bring their portions to the priests who, presumably, pay their tributes to the Persian king.[51]

The priests and Levites, as well as the singers and gatekeepers who draw from this support, continue "the service of their God"—singing songs of praise and thanksgiving—and ensure that the priesthood, laity, and city remain purified as mandated by David and Solomon and directed by Asaph (Neh 12:45-46). Maintaining the holiness of the community and its worship is of utmost importance and an ongoing process both then and today. Eskenazi shares Ezra–Nehemiah's restoration process: "Tenacity, building, and rebuilding by a faithful community, generation after generation: this is Ezra–Nehemiah's distinctive vision of restoration."[52]

The final activity of the dedication day is reading "from the book of Moses" in the presence of the people (Neh 13:1). Based on Nehemiah's exclusion of the Ammonites and Moabites in the "assembly of God" (Neh 13:1) and the subsequent retelling of the Balaam narrative, they might be reading a version of Numbers 22–24, Deuteronomy 23:3-6, which recount the story of Balaam in more detail. The stories in Numbers and Deuteronomy remind the community that a Mesopotamian prophet, Balaam, is

50. For a helpful discussion on the stratification of the Second Temple priesthood and Levites, see Herbert R. Marbury, *Imperial Dominion and Priestly Genius: Coercion, Accommodation, and Resistance in the Divorce Rhetoric of Ezra–Nehemiah* (Upland: Sopher Press, 2012), 79–109. Blenkinsopp suggests that Persian-period temples functioned like banks (*Ezra–Nehemiah*, 350).

51. Interpreters comment on the editor's remark that this process of giving contributions "in the days of Zerubbabel and in the days of Nehemiah" (12:47) infers that the text identifies these two men as contemporaries.

52. Eskenazi, *In an Age of Prose*, 122.

sent to curse the Israelites but God turns the curse into a blessing (Deut 23:4). Those persons Nehemiah struggles with the most, the Samarians led by Sanballat, as well as Sanballat's allies, Tobiah, and Geshem the Arab, become conflated with the Ammonites and the Moabites. The people get the message: "When the people heard the law, they separated from Israel all those of foreign descent" (Neh 13:3). Nehemiah's response to noncommunal members acknowledges that religious communities require boundaries that are simultaneously inclusive and exclusive. The permeabilities of these boundaries are complicated when religious identities are fragile.

"When the Cat Is Away, the Mice Will Play" (13:4-31)

We consider 13:1-3 to be part of the dedication process in 12:27–13:3. Nehemiah 13:4-31 serves as a coda to the book of Ezra–Nehemiah as one unit and demonstrates the struggle the community faces as it quickly returns to behaviors that threaten its already fragile identity. The text has three distinct sections that begin with the phrase "now before this" (13:4) or "in those days" (Neh 13:15, 23) that suggest a time well after the dedication ceremony described in Nehemiah 12:27–13:3. Also, each section closes with Nehemiah's plea that God remember him (Neh 13:14, 22, 31). Within each section, Nehemiah confronts the community for breaking the signed firm commitment (אמנה) because they forsake the temple, trade on the Sabbath, and marry outside of the community. The biblical text interweaves the language of desecration ("profaning," Neh 13:17, 18, 29) and purification (Neh 13:9, 22, 30), evil (Neh 13:17, 18, 27) and good (Neh 13:14, 31) as a way further to separate the repatriates from the people of the land living among them. The book of Ezra–Nehemiah as one unit does not end on a high note but rather describes how the community fails to live up to its agreed communal commitments and how Nehemiah attempts to reinforce the אמנה (Neh 10:30-39).[53]

We begin our examination of Nehemiah 13 with 13:4, which appears to be a continuation of Nehemiah 6:15-19, in which Tobiah received letters

53. If the Nehemiah Memoir alone recounts the reforms during Nehemiah's governorship and chapters 6 and 13 continue the narrative flow, which would be the case if chapters 7–12 are excluded, the credit for the reforms becomes Nehemiah's. By adding Neh 7–12, the editor emphasizes the community's buy-in. Eskenazi notices Nehemiah's focus at the end on struggles rather than on community success (*In an Age of Prose*, 124–25).

from the nobles "who were bound by oath to him" (Neh 6:18) and sends intimidating letters to Nehemiah (Neh 6:19).[54]

Profaning and Neglecting the Temple (13:4-14)

The great sense of commitment expressed by the people signing the firm agreement in Nehemiah 10:30-39 quickly wanes when Nehemiah journeys back to Susa and to King Artaxerxes and spends an unspecified amount of time there for an unknown purpose (Neh 13:6-7): "I was not in Jerusalem, for in the thirty-second year of King Artaxerxes of Babylon I went to the king. After some time I asked leave of the king and returned to Jerusalem."[55] The journey itself takes several months, and his commitments to the king as cupbearer may have delayed his return (see Neh 2:5).

In his absence, the priest Eliashib, who oversees the storage chambers, allows his relative and Nehemiah's sworn enemy, Tobiah, to reside in a room within the temple storage area (Neh 13:4-5). Positioning a nonpriest in the "house of God" (Neh 13:4) with the ability to influence the distribution of tithes and other temple functions is illustrative of the community's spiral into religious apostasy.

Nehemiah's anger and rapid response leads first to the removal of Tobiah's belongings (Neh 13:8) and then to a thorough cleaning of not only his room but all the chambers (Neh 13:9). While the cleansing (טהר) of the chambers suggests that Tobiah's presence defiles the entire house of God, this defilement is also temporary and removable as he defiles a place and not a people (cf. Ezra 9–10).[56] His presence disrupts the normal administrative functions and flow of God's house.

Nehemiah discovers that tithes are withheld from the Levites and singers (Neh 13:10). Withholding these tithes jeopardizes the sustainability of the place and the people as the Levites and singers leave Jerusalem to

54. Wright, *Rebuilding Identity*, 189–91. Blenkinsopp acknowledges the complicated editing of this material (*Ezra–Nehemiah*, 353). Wright also holds that all of Nehemiah's reforms that are agreed upon by the community in Nehemiah 10 are more likely put into place by Nehemiah before the wall is complete.

55. Nehemiah likely serves as governor of Judah for twelve years before he returns to Susa. Nehemiah asks for permission to leave for Yehud in the twentieth year of King Artaxerxes (Neh 2:1) and returns to him in the thirty-second year of his reign (Neh 13:6)—a total of twelve years in Yehud, more or less.

56. The term translated as "chambers" (לשׁכות) is in the plural rather than the singular in 13:5 (לשׁכה). This could indicate that the purification relates to the entire house rather than the chamber that Tobiah occupies.

Neh 13:4-14

4Now before this, Eliashib the priest, who was appointed over the chambers of the house of our God and who was related to Tobiah, 5prepared for Tobiah a large room where they had previously put the grain offering, the frankincense, the vessels, and the tithes of grain, wine, and oil, which were given by commandment to the Levites, singers, and gatekeepers, and the contributions for the priests. 6While this was taking place I was not in Jerusalem, for in the thirty-second year of King Artaxerxes of Babylon I went to the king. After some time I asked leave of the king 7and returned to Jerusalem. I then discovered the wrong that Eliashib had done on behalf of Tobiah, preparing a room for him in the courts of the house of God. 8And I was very angry, and I threw all the household furniture of Tobiah out of the room. 9Then I gave orders, and they cleansed the chambers,

secure other forms of employment.[57] Nehemiah remonstrates with the officials for not maintaining the infrastructure of the house of God (Neh 13:10-11): "Why is the house of God forsaken?" (Neh 13:11). The verb ריב (Neh 13:11), translated by the NRSVue as "contended," suggests a legal dispute between Nehemiah and the officials, similar to the lawsuit he wages on the nobles when earlier they oppressed their people by taking their land and forcing parents to traffic their children (Neh 5:7).

Although it appears that tithing continues (Neh 13:12), Nehemiah institutes reforms that provide checks and balances to ensure the integrity of the temple and its administration of these needed contributions (Neh 13:13). These checks and balances provide for skilled, committed, and faithful persons who will, together, administer the storehouses—a priest (Shelemiah), a scribe (Zadok), and a Levite (Pedaiah) along with an assistant (Hanan son of Zaccur son of Mattaniah [13:13]).[58] Nehemiah's reforms suggest that leadership within religious institutions has a fiduciary responsibility to manage faithfully the donations given by its members (tithes, offerings, etc.). Failure to account responsibly for these assets and resources, whether through mismanagement, neglect, or abuse, hinders the institution's ability (e.g., church, synagogue, mosque) to carry out its mission. This responsibility extends to the equitable distribution of resources to those who faithfully serve in paid positions within them and becomes a matter of justice when payment is withheld.

57. Levites are not to own land (Deut 14:29; 18:1-2), but the book of Nehemiah suggests otherwise (see 11:20; 12:27).

58. These three are tagged as "faithful" (אמן). See *HALOT*, "אמן," 63. The Hebrew can also be translated as "trustworthy," "firm," or "safe."

Neh 13:4-14 (cont.)

and I brought back the vessels of the house of God, with the grain offering and the frankincense.

[10]I also found out that the portions of the Levites had not been given to them, so that the Levites and the singers who had conducted the service had gone back to their fields. [11]So I contended with the officials and said, "Why is the house of God forsaken?" And I gathered them together and set them in their stations. [12]Then all Judah brought the tithe of the grain, wine, and oil into the storehouses. [13]And I appointed as treasurers over the treasuries Shelemiah the priest, Zadok the scribe, and Pedaiah of the Levites, and as their assistant Hanan son of Zaccur son of Mattaniah, for they were considered faithful, and their duty was to distribute to their associates. [14]Remember me, O my God, concerning this, and do not wipe out my good deeds that I have done for the house of my God and for his service.

Those Who Do the Work

Nehemiah recognizes that having a system of accountability increases the chances that the Levites, singers, or others who rely on the tithes and offerings will receive payment for their hard work. He acts for justice for these groups "who had conducted the service" (13:10). The Hebrew of this phrase can also be translated in such a way that the Levites and singers are "the ones who do the work." Too often, those who keep systems going—those who do the work—are undervalued and placed at risk. We wrote much of this commentary during the global COVID-19 pandemic, where many of those who "do the work" to keep food on our tables, care for the sick and vulnerable, and do other work on the front lines were not always fairly compensated for their risk of catching the virus that might kill them or take them out of the workforce or gravely impact their financial situations. The Levites and singers count on these economic resources promised to them, and Nehemiah uses his authority to ensure that these essential temple workers receive just compensation so they can continue to serve the community.

Breaking the Commitment to Sabbath (13:15-22)

The law and prophetic witness emphasize the importance of maintaining the Sabbath as holy to God. The community must not work on this day (e.g., Exod 20:10; Lev 23:3; Deut 5:14; Jer 17:21-24) or sell goods

Neh 13:15-22

15In those days I saw in Judah people
treading winepresses on the Sabbath
and bringing in heaps of grain and load-
ing them on donkeys, and also wine,
grapes, figs, and all kinds of burdens
that they brought into Jerusalem on the
Sabbath day, and I warned them at that
time against selling food. 16Tyrians also,
who lived in the city, brought in fish and
all kinds of merchandise and sold them
on the Sabbath to the people of Judah in
Jerusalem. 17Then I contended with the
nobles of Judah and said to them, "What
is this evil thing that you are doing, profaning the Sabbath day? 18Did not your
ancestors act in this way, and did not our
God bring all this disaster on us and on
this city? Yet you bring more wrath on
Israel by profaning the Sabbath."

19When it began to be dark at the
gates of Jerusalem before the Sabbath, I commanded that the doors
should be shut and gave orders that
they should not be opened until after
the Sabbath. And I set some of my servants over the gates, to prevent any
burden from being brought in on the
Sabbath day. 20Then the merchants
and sellers of all kinds of merchandise
spent the night outside Jerusalem once
or twice. 21But I warned them and said
to them, "Why do you spend the night
in front of the wall? If you do so again,
I will lay hands on you." From that time
on they did not come on the Sabbath.
22And I commanded the Levites that
they should purify themselves and
come and guard the gates, to keep
the Sabbath day holy. Remember this
also in my favor, O my God, and spare
me according to the greatness of your
steadfast love.

(Amos 8:5). To break the Sabbath commandment, a visible sign of the community's covenant with God, was to profane the day (see Isa 56:1-6; Jer 17:27).[59] In Nehemiah 13:15-22 another agreed-upon commitment, maintaining the sacredness of the Sabbath (Neh 10:31), is in jeopardy. In Judah, people press grapes, gather grain, and bring these and other goods to sell in the Jerusalem market on Sabbath (Neh 13:15). Even Tyrian merchants who live in Jerusalem (Neh 13:16) are hawking their wares within the gates of Jerusalem on Sabbath. These foreign merchants are surely a temptation to the community members who promised not to buy goods on the Sabbath (10:31).

To protect the holiness of the community and the Sabbath, Nehemiah expands the Sabbath prohibition and forbids the covenant community

59. Jeremiah warns the people of what will happen if they profane the Sabbath: "then I will kindle a fire in its gates; it shall devour the palaces of Jerusalem and shall not be quenched" (Jer 17:27).

from purchasing items, even from people outside the community (Neh 13:15)—a harsher extension of earlier Sabbath rules (Neh 10:31).[60]

Nehemiah puts an end to Sabbath markets and uses the same term ריב, "contended" (Neh 5:7; 13:11, 17), to address his complaint against the nobles. He accuses them of their complicity in endangering the holiness of the community: "Did not your ancestors act in this way, and did not our God bring all this disaster on us and on this city? Yet you bring more wrath on Israel by profaning the Sabbath" (Neh 13:18). The nobles influence and profit from trade taking place on the Sabbath day. Because they are leaders of the community, Nehemiah holds them accountable, given that their actions potentially influence the actions of others in their group.

Second, Nehemiah orders the Jerusalem gates shut from sundown on Sabbath until Sabbath ends (Neh 13:18). He ensures that the Tyrian merchants, who now settle outside of the city walls, are unable to enter the city to do business. Nehemiah positions some of his servants to keep merchants outside of the city rather than calling on the gatekeepers (Neh 13:19). These "servants" are most likely from Nehemiah's militia who are authorized to use force against the Tyrian traders if necessary.[61] Nehemiah's parting words to these traders are that if they attempt to conduct business again on the Sabbath he will "lay hands" on them (Neh 13:21). The term translated "hands" derives from the Hebrew יד, which can also be translated "power" or "strength."[62]

The threat of violence must work since the merchants remain outside the Jerusalem gates "once or twice" (Neh 13:20) before abandoning Sabbath trade for good (Neh 13:21). Once the threat dissipates, Nehemiah has the Levites purify themselves (טהר, see also Neh 13:9) and then guard the gates, not only to keep the Sabbath holy, but also to ensure the holiness of the entire city of Jerusalem (Neh 13:22).

Nehemiah acts unilaterally and expels the foreign merchants—those who do not support his Sabbath vision—from Jerusalem on the Sabbath. While maintaining that the holiness of this day and Jerusalem are important to the community's identity, Nehemiah's response toward people is violent as he changes the security infrastructure that the community agrees to and replaces the gatekeepers with his own security forces (Neh 13:22). The change in the security detail may cause distrust and fear within

60. Hindy Najman notes that the rabbis highlight Neh 13:15 as part of the early stages in Sabbath laws ("Notes on Nehemiah," 1702; m. Shab 17.4; b. Shab 123b).

61. Nehemiah enters Jerusalem with an army given to him by Artaxerxes. Robert Alter, "Nehemiah," 861; Blenkinsopp, *Ezra–Nehemiah*, 360.

62. יד, *HALOT*, 386–88.

the community as it becomes militarized. On July 8, 2020, US President Donald Trump, in response to the killing of four-year-old LeGend Taliferro by Ryson B. Ellis during a dispute with LeGend's aunt, authorized Operation LeGend, the deployment of federal law enforcement agencies throughout the country to arrest and disperse groups, often of peaceful protestors striving for racial and economic equity.[63] These forces, at times working with local police departments, were often in plain clothes and armed as they violently forced peaceful protestors into unmarked cars to be driven away.[64] The spoken fear was that the protesters threatened the safety of the cities, but mixed with this fear lurked a desire to drown out voices with a vision different from those held by US leaders. The government-ordered violence exacerbated the situation instead of creating a peaceful compromise.[65] In Nehemiah, the merchants are intimidated by the threat of violence and leave. Instead of threatening these merchants, many of whom live in Jerusalem (Neh 13:16), Nehemiah might have found a more peaceful way, in collaboration with the community, to keep the markets closed on the Sabbath and to build healthier relations with other peoples who lived among them in Jerusalem.

Who Also Lives in Jerusalem?

When Nehemiah 11:3-24 outlines the process of populating Jerusalem, the text paints a portrait of a city occupied solely by like-minded repatriates. While Jerusalem's small population probably included multiple traditions when Nehemiah enacted his reforms, we learn more explicitly that there were Tyrian merchants living in the holy city (Neh 13:16) who interacted with the other inhabitants. Tobiah, whom Nehemiah labels an Ammonite (Neh 2:10), also lived there at least for a while. The casual mention that those not included in the reconstituted Israel were inhabitants of Jerusalem suggests more intercultural interaction throughout the week than we are first led to believe by the text of Nehemiah. Further, those selling

63. "The Trump Administration's Controversial 'Operation LeGend' Program," American Oversight (November 23, 2021), https://americanoversight.org/investigation/the-trump-administrations-controversial-operation-legend-program/.

64. Chris Gelardi, "After Woman's Arrest in Unmarked Van, New York City Activists Fear Targeting by NYPD," *The Appeal* (July 29, 2020), https://theappeal.org/after-womans-arrest-in-unmarked-van-new-york-city-activists-fear-targeting-by-nypd/.

65. Operation LeGend was disbanded when President Joe Biden began his term.

wares and food relied on these interactions to feed their own families. Leaving them mostly out of the story of Jerusalem inhabitants discounts the important roles these "outsiders" served to the economy and well-being of the Jerusalem community. This happens in other historical and contemporary contexts when dominant cultures ignore the presence or contributions of those living and working among them who may be among those labeled "foreigner." Those who moved to Jerusalem from Tyre were immigrant merchants who brought fish and other goods appreciated by a city distant from the sea. Migrant workers benefit their host countries by providing services and/or goods to their hosts. Yet are often forgotten or targeted and, at times, expelled by those who fear that their values and beliefs will undermine those of the dominant culture. The converse is true when migrants operate outside the legal structure of the host country.

Expelling the Foreign Women Again (13:23-31)

Nehemiah's fear of the separated community intermarrying with the women of the land concludes the book of Ezra–Nehemiah as one unit (Neh 13:23-31). When Nehemiah learns that community members, including some priests and Levites (Neh 13:29), intermarry with women from Ashdod, Ammon, and Moab (Neh 13:23), he is enraged. Nehemiah unabashedly shares his response: "I contended with them and cursed them and beat some of the men and pulled out their hair, and I made them take an oath[66] in the name of God, saying, 'You shall not give your daughters to their sons or take their daughters for your sons or for yourselves' " (Neh 13:25).[67] The concept of pulling out the hair might be an ancient Near East-

66. This adds to the oath the people sign after Ezra reinstates the Torah into the community (Neh 10:31), although this time he extends the prohibition to the priests themselves.

67. Intermarriage appears to be widespread in the repatriate community (see the long list in Ezra 10:18-44 and Neh 13:23-31), and many purposes are proposed for why these exogamous relations occurred. For a summary of many of the major arguments, see Cheryl Anderson, "Reflections in an Interethnic/Racial Era on Interethnic/Racial Marriage in Ezra," in *They Were All Together in One Place? Toward Minority Biblical Criticism*, ed. Randall C. Bailey, Tat-Siong Benny Liew, and Fernando F. Segovia, SemeiaSt 57 (Atlanta: SBL, 2009), 47–64. She summarizes the arguments of Willa Johnson, Harold Washington, Gale Yee, Christine Hayes, and her own assessment that draw comparisons between the US anti-miscegenation laws—which prohibited interracial relationships—and the expulsion of foreign wives in Ezra and Nehemiah. These three chapters, Ezra 9–10, 13, are the most troublesome and most analyzed from Ezra–Nehemiah.

Neh 13:23-31

[23]In those days also I saw Jews who had married women of Ashdod, Ammon, and Moab, [24]and half of their children spoke the language of Ashdod, and they could not speak the language of Judah but spoke the language of various peoples. [25]And I contended with them and cursed them and beat some of the men and pulled out their hair, and I made them take an oath in the name of God, saying, "You shall not give your daughters to their sons or take their daughters for your sons or for yourselves. [26]Did not King Solomon of Israel sin on account of such women? Among the many nations there was no king like him, and he was beloved by his God, and God made him king over all Israel; nevertheless, foreign women made even him to sin. [27]Shall we then listen to you and do all this great evil and act treacherously against our God by marrying foreign women?"

[28]And one of the sons of Jehoiada, son of the high priest Eliashib, was the son-in-law of Sanballat the Horonite; I chased him away from me. [29]Remember them, O my God, because they have defiled the priesthood, the covenant of the priests and the Levites.

[30]Thus I cleansed them from everything foreign, and I established the duties of the priests and Levites, each in his work, [31]and I provided for the wood offering, at appointed times, and for the first fruits. Remember me, O my God, for good.

ern form of shaming.[68] Nehemiah's excessive violence and forced vow in response to these marriages underscore the intense fear Nehemiah shares with Ezra. Again, we must ask what it is about these foreign women that elicits such fear and violence. Nehemiah offers tangible insights into the power and influence these women bring to the community and how these unions threaten to kill Jewish culture and identity.

First, there is the threat of cultural hybridity, which gradually replaces the first language with the native language of the foreign mother (the mother's tongue). Through the maternal acts of singing, speaking, and teaching her child, the mother injects into her child her language and culture and, by extension, influences the larger community. Nehemiah is mortified when he hears Jewish children speaking Ashdodite[69] and

68. A cuneiform text dated to 420 BCE around the time of Darius II depicts this process that was also implemented in Artaxerxes's time. See Reddit, *Ezra–Nehemiah*, 333. Michael Heltzer, "The Flogging and Plucking of Beards in the Achaemenid Empire and the Chronology of Nehemia," in *Archaeologische Mitteilungen aus Iran* 28 (1995/1996): 305–7.

69. Ashdodite is not a language. Scholars argue that it can be a remnant of the Philistine language (Klein, "The Books of Ezra and Nehemiah," 848), but it could signal any non-understandable language.

languages from "various peoples" (Neh 13:24). But even worse, he observes, "They could not speak the language of Judah" (Neh 13:24). Thus, foreign women, as purveyors of their own language, exert a powerful influence in the raising of their children, an influence that is perceived by Nehemiah as a serious threat to his own culture and identity. Nehemiah expresses in his disapproval what someone will later phrase as "the hand that rocks the cradle rules the world." While these foreign women may not rule the world, Nehemiah perceives that they will have a hand in influencing his world.

Shared language and group identity go hand in hand. Jean-Pierre Ruiz underscores the importance of language to a community's identity, including Judah's. He writes, "Nehemiah regards the inability of a significant number of children of such 'mixed' marriages to speak Yehudite to be a dangerous symptom of assimilation, underscoring the important links between language and group identity."[70] While it is not explicit that mothers are the killers of the Jewish language, the text leads to this conclusion. Nehemiah perceives that Jews are losing their grasp on the Hebrew language and holds these wives accountable for this loss.

Second, Nehemiah expresses concern regarding the influence of foreign religions and their ability to dilute and even dismantle Nehemiah's religion. The ability to entirely affect the rituals, symbols, and traditions of a people is indeed powerful. While Ezra merely targets the practices of foreigners, referring to these as "abominations" (Ezra 9:1), Nehemiah is more explicit: foreign women bring with them foreign gods. He appeals to the marriage prohibition in Deuteronomy 7:3 and the example set by King Solomon in 1 Kings 11:1-8. Repeatedly, he links the religious proclivities of Solomon's foreign wives with all foreign wives, which he labels "sin" (חטא, Neh 13:26). He reasons, "Did not King Solomon of Israel sin on account of such women?" and "foreign women made even him [Solomon] to sin" (Neh 13:26; 1 Kgs 11:1-8). Although the writer of 1 Kings does not use the term חטא to characterize Solomon's misdeeds, Nehemiah equates the "sin" of Solomon (i.e., marriage to numerous foreign women) and the apostasy that followed (i.e., turning to other gods) with the sin (חטא) that potentially looms large within the foreign marriages of his day. For Nehemiah, those who do not learn from the past are destined to repeat it. That is, mixed marriages are sacrilegious, an affront to God.

70. Jean-Pierre Ruiz, " 'They Could Not Speak the Language of Judah': Rereading Nehemiah 13 between Brooklyn and Jerusalem," in Bailey, Liew, and Segovia, eds., *They Were All Together in One Place?*, 106.

Solomon and His Wives

In the Deuteronomistic historian's account of Solomon's marriages (1 Kgs 11:1-8), Solomon loves (אהב, vv. 1, 2) "many foreign women," even those from the nations listed as forbidden in Deuteronomy 7:1-6. The law forewarns: "for they [foreign women] will surely incline your heart to follow their gods" (1 Kgs 11:2; Deut 7:4). The narrative then lists a host of gods Solomon follows—Astarte, Milcom, Chemesh, and Molech—all connected to his wives. Though the Hebrew term for "sin" (חטאה) is absent in the account of Solomon in 1 Kings, Nehemiah associates his polemic with the danger of sin (חטאה) that lurks within these marriages. In 1 Kings and, by implication, in Nehemiah 13, foreign wives are blamed for leading their husbands away from God. Since Judah is sent into exile because of her unfaithfulness, falling into this same pattern of apostasy endangers the future of the community.

Nehemiah's use of ritualistic language is meant to strengthen his argument against exogamy. Speaking to those with foreign wives he asks, "Shall we then listen to you and do all this great evil and act treacherously [מעל] against our God by marrying foreign women?" (Neh 13:27). The Hebrew root מעל, which can be translated "unfaithful" or, in the NRSVue, "treacherously," is associated with ritual disloyalty and suggests legal violations against God.[71] Alternatively, מעל can be rendered "'profane,' 'desecrate,' or 'make sacrilegious'"[72]—terms related to purity (Deut 32:48-52; Ezek 15:1-8).[73] Ezra employs the usage of these terms three times (Ezra 9:2, 4; 10:6) in a similar manner. Whether these foreign women are aware of it, Nehemiah believes that they hold the power to destroy the relationship between the Israelite people and their God—which frightens Nehemiah. Nowhere is this more evident than in the intermarriages taking place within the priesthood (Neh 13:29). Nehemiah highlights the particularly troubling marriage of an unnamed son of Jehoiada, the high priest Eliashib's grandson, who marries

71. מעל *HALOT*, 613, and *BDB*, 591.

72. Elizabeth W. Goldstein, *Impurity and Gender in the Hebrew Bible* (Lanham, MD: Lexington Books, 2015), 88.

73. מעל appears in Deuteronomy 32:48-52 when God informs Moses that he will not enter Canaan because he "broke faith" (מעל) with God at the waters of Meribath-kadesh and failed to maintain God's holiness. In Ezekiel's analogy of the useless vine (15:1-8), the prophet proclaims that because of Jerusalem's faithlessness (v. 8, מעל), God will decimate her.

the daughter of his enemy Sanballat (Neh 13:28). Priestly laws mandate that the high priest must marry a virgin from his people (Lev 21:13-15). Thus, the very ones responsible for the purity and holiness of the community are themselves perceived as compromised. Finding the priesthood so closely aligned with these foreign "enemies" according to Nehemiah defiles the office and covenant of the priest (Neh 13:29). Therefore, it is perhaps not accidental that Nehemiah's last act in his memoir is to purify the priesthood: "Thus I cleansed [טהר] them from everything foreign" (Neh 13:30).

The term "purify" or "cleanse" (טהר) harks back to Ezra's נדה and טמא in Ezra 9:11. Kristin De Troyer's work on blood and its relationship to holiness reminds us that טמא (unclean) and טהר (clean) are interwoven.[74] Like נדה, the terms טמא and טהר are often bound together in the context of liminal spaces and bodily fluids that hover between life and death and cause ritual impurity, such as touching a dead body (Lev 11:32), oozing (Lev 13:6), or bodily discharges (Lev 15:13), including, as mentioned above, the blood of childbirth (Lev 12:4) and menstrual blood (Lev 15:19-31). The person who is טמא goes through a ritual purification—in the case of the menstruant, she is restored (Lev 15:28)—and is restored to a place of holiness or wholeness—the danger is gone. For Nehemiah, foreigners, especially women, threaten to sever the relationship between the newly constituted Israel and their security in the land. Their presence is a constant reminder that the danger remains so they must be purged.

We do not know if the community follows through with their resolve to divorce and cast away the foreign women and children. Merely suggesting such violence accentuates the toxic side of community exclusion. First, these women who are thrown out are likely members of the first group returning who married once they settled in the land, who Ezra–Nehemiah constructs as "other." Even if foreign, these women and children are integral members of families, contributors to society, and, presumably, loved. There is no apparent way to become members of this group. Second, Ezra imposes economic sanctions as he threatens to strip husbands of their property if they do not comply and forces them to choose between two livelihoods: the land and family (Ezra 10:8). Reading Ezra–Nehemiah's policy of family separation in the context of the United States' draconian policy that separates immigrant parents from their young children illustrates the intense brokenness and damage that such policies cost in the name of US isolationalism.

74. Kristin De Troyer, "Blood: A Threat to Holiness or Toward (Another) Holiness," in *Wholly Woman, Holy Blood: A Feminist Critique of Purity and Impurity*, ed. Kristin De Troyer et al., SAC (Harrisburg, VA: Trinity Press, 2003), 45–64.

Private Lives and Public Concerns

Nehemiah's exhortations against marrying foreign or strange women can be read as expressions of both care and fear for his community. The text presents opportunities for conversation about profound ethical questions regarding public versus private interests in marriage, community concern for children's formation, cultural preservation, and gender justice. What initially sounds like boundary policing and marking limits of tribal identity includes a curious mention of the conundrum about King Solomon. Famous for having many foreign wives, Solomon was also the epitome of cosmopolitan politics and the faithful leader, beloved of God. The history and identity of Israel includes ambiguity about foreign women. Nehemiah resolves the somewhat complicated puzzle of possible strategic advantages of mixed marriages by concluding foreign wives were the downfall of that great king, so they are obviously a temptation to be prohibited. Beware foreign women, strange seductive enticers on the slippery slope to idolatry.

Googling the term "foreign wives" was an eye-opener, as I discovered the prevalence of an apparently lucrative and bustling trade in the purchase of women mostly from desperately impoverished communities. What drives this enterprise right now? Foreign wives are marketed as exotic, docile, obedient, and low maintenance. Apparently this trope offers privileged men a bargain in comparison with the challenge of dealing with women from their own culture or economic class. A wife from one's own community would have access to more resources, like family and neighborhood networks for leveraging requests or complaints against her husband. In contrast, a wife from a foreign culture would be more dependent on her husband with less access to other support.

How does this current phenomenon of commodification of foreign wives compare with the decision of ancient Jews who married women from Ashdod, Ammon, and Moab? We can imagine the motivations included dynamics like ensuring greater dominance, access to women as a result of war, autonomy from the interference of Jewish parents or elders, or perhaps even youthful rebellion. We cannot be sure that something like romance or love was not part of the reason men chose foreign wives. Modern and postmodern Western readers might sympathize with these ancient, unconventional mixed marriages. After all, we are formed in a contemporary ideology that insists that what consenting adults do in private is no business of the public sphere or even religious authorities.

That split between private lives and public concerns lies at the heart of our difficulty in comprehending the ancient texts that suggest that the good of the community outweighs the desires of the individual. While seeking a sympathetic reading of the condemnation of mixed marriages, it is helpful to recognize our tendency to assume that marriage is a private matter. Growing up in Oklahoma, social activism connected me with a Cherokee elder whom I collaborated with on various justice issues. She was a radical leader in the American Indian Movement (AIM), and I admired her greatly. So, years ago I was shocked when I heard her say that she was against interracial marriage. My first reaction was to think that no one should interfere in a couple's decision to marry. When she explained her concern for the erasure of her people and way of life due to cultural assimilation through interracial marriage, I realized I had to think more carefully about such issues.

The community's interest in preserving its language and cultural identity requires attending to the education and formation of children. Nehemiah may sound narrow or stodgy in his insistence on reforming his people and ending mixed marriages, but there are no easy answers to the need to balance protecting cultural wisdom versus resisting bigoted tribalism. At the same time, as a feminist I have to chuckle at Nehemiah's prototypical blaming of the foreign wives and mothers. If half of the children in the community are not learning the language of their fathers, perhaps the fathers should be more involved with the tasks of raising children. Many couples raise bilingual children because both parents are attentive and present to the formation and education of their children. Nehemiah's interest in fostering the religious and cultural identity of the children in the community could be blamed on the Jewish fathers as easily as the mothers.

Despite the contemporary Western tendency to think in individualistic terms about marriage as a private, personal matter, such an approach to marriage is an anomaly for most cultures throughout history. I appreciate the reminder in this text that the community does have an important responsibility to steward the future of their children and collective identity. This is one reason for the potent battles over the institutions of marriage. The question of same-sex marriage is like a lightning rod for these issues in our own times. We struggle to articulate a consensus about the purpose of marriage and the limitations public authorities should be able to impose on couples. In this text, Nehemiah seems like the conventional voice of authority interfering with families of choice. I contend, however, that there are advantages and disadvantages in preserving cultural norms.

As a bisexual, lesbian, Christian pastor, I have spent countless hours deliberating about the institution of marriage. I sympathize with feminist and queer thinkers who are ready to abolish marriage entirely because it is typically a patriarchal, heteronormative institution. I have, however, seen the need for advocacy to protect a vulnerable partner in an intimate relationship. Prior to the legalization of same-sex marriage, I repeatedly saw situations where a gay man died, often of HIV/AIDS, and his legal next of kin came in and took property the couple shared, leaving a surviving, long-term partner homeless with no legal recourse. The institution of marriage with provisions for property and financial protection has advantages. So, doing away with marriage altogether does not appeal to me.

As a feminist, I want no part of the way this text perpetuates the narrative of women, especially foreign or strange women, causing men to sin or the nation to falter. Nevertheless, I want to be accountable to the religious and spiritual wisdom about ethical norms for my personal life. Like many, I need guidance to question and examine my own intimate partner relationships. On the other hand, since communities are notorious for getting God's wisdom wrong, especially on questions of nationalism and gender, I have a responsibility to call for reform in models of family and marriage. Nehemiah's role of prophetic critic of the social institutions like marriage is a model for standing outside conventional culture now. We should reform both public and private institutions to root out heterosexism, sexism, xenophobia, and other forms of injustice like colonialism, racism, and ethnocentrism. Perhaps persuasion, however, rather than coercion will more effectively serve to facilitate choices of intimate partners that both preserve distinct cultural identities and the healthy diversity of families of choice.

Kathleen McCallie

Pleas to Be Remembered: Nehemiah 13:14, 22, 29, 31 (and 5:19)

Running through the popular Broadway play *Hamilton* are the questions, "Who lives, who dies, who tells your story?"[75] These questions acknowledge that not all voices or deeds will be remembered, even if one creates masterpieces or makes important political, religious, or other contributions to society. Within Ezra–Nehemiah many voices are absent, particularly those of women and lower-class men and children both within and outside

75. Lin-Manuel Miranda, *Hamilton: An American Musical* (Atlantic Records, 2015).

the repatriate community. Still, the myriad lists and genealogies peppered throughout this book memorialize many in the community who built the walls or served as religious and political leaders. Surely Nehemiah, who accomplishes so much as he leads the community's efforts to reform the community, should be confident that his name will be remembered. Yet, in the midst of the conflict he faces with his enemies—Sanballat, Tobiah, and Geshem, as well as with the nobles and officials—he might be wary of how those who remember him will portray him. Does this concern lead Nehemiah to write his own memoir so he can shape his narrative?

It seems plausible that Nehemiah believes that God records for posterity the good and evil acts people commit.[76] Throughout the book of Nehemiah, Nehemiah asks God to remember him for good (טוב). First, when he lightens the people's economic burden, Nehemiah makes a request to God: "Remember for my good [טוב], O my God, all that I have done for this people" (Neh 5:19). Second, when he creates safeguards so the Levites and singers will be cared for and keeps the temple infrastructure intact, he pleads, "Remember me, O my God, concerning this, and do not wipe out my good deeds that I have done for the house of my God and for his service" (Neh 13:14). Third, when Nehemiah protects the Sabbath by setting up guards to keep the traders out of Jerusalem, he appeals to God's faithfulness: "Remember this also in my favor, O my God, and spare me according to the greatness of your steadfast love" (Neh 13:22). After Nehemiah purges the community of everything foreign and reestablishes the wood offering and first fruits, he makes one last request from God, "Remember me, O my God, for good" (Neh 13:31).[77] Ron Stanley ties Nehemiah's obsession with being remembered to his identity as a eunuch, people who are often forgotten because they do not father children to continue their name (see commentary on Neh 1:11).[78]

In contrast, Nehemiah requests that God remember his enemies' bad deeds. When Sanballat, Tobiah, and Noadiah terrorize him (Neh 6:1-14), he requests that God, "Remember Tobiah and Sanballat, O my God, according to these things that they did, and also Noadiah the prophetess

76. The concept of a book that records good and evil can be found in Dan 7:10; Mal 3:16; and Isa 65:6. See Klein, "The Books of Ezra and Nehemiah," 847. He also reminds us that after the people of Israel sin by creating a golden calf while Moses is meeting with God, Moses intervenes and asks God to forgive the people or blot him out of "the book that you have written" (Exod 32:32).

77. Neh 5:19; 13:14, 22, 31. Some link chapter 5's reforms to those in chapter 13 because they all share a desire to be remembered.

78. Ron L. Stanley, "Ezra–Nehemiah," in *The Queer Bible Commentary*, ed. Deryn Guest et al., vol. 1 (London: SCM, 2006), 268–77.

and the rest of the prophets who wanted to make me afraid" (Neh 6:14). In response to the unfaithful priests intermarrying, especially the marriage between the grandson of the high priest and Sanballat's daughter and risks the purity of the community, he prays, "Remember them, O my God, because they have defiled the priesthood, the covenant of the priests and the Levites" (Neh 13:29).

Being remembered by God for deeds, good and bad, Nehemiah's actions are remembered long after he dies. Being remembered after we die—having a legacy—is highly valued in our society as well. Many Christians remember those who are beloved in the community on All Saints Day. In Judaism, Yom HaShoah, and the tradition of Yizhor helps honor the memory of those who died during this terrible chapter in history.

Remembering in the Digital Age

With the creation of technology, remembering can be more fully experienced through audio and video that preserves ongoing memories of those who die. Hitler and his allies sought to annihilate the Jews and other groups (Roma, Sinti, disabled, Jehovah's witnesses) and their memory, yet new technology allows the narratives of survivors to endure for centuries to come. Heather Maio and Stephen Smith and the USC Shoah Foundation's Artificial Intelligence Project create holograms of Holocaust survivors who can hold conversations long after they are deceased. Maio provides rationale for this project: "I wanted to talk to a Holocaust Survivor like I would do today with that person sitting right in front of me."[79] Through intense interviews and multiple camera angles, these holograms can answer questions as the interviewer asks them, creating the feel of a real conversation.

Technology and social media allow space for voices often ignored to be shared. National Public Radio (NPR) also provides a forum to remember family stories (StoryCorps), which are archived in the Library of Congress.[80] Those voices that have traditionally been left out of the narrative are now being archived so that future generations will hear from multiple voices as histories are constructed.

79. Heather Maio quoted in "Artificial Intelligence Project Lets Holocaust Survivors Share Their Stories Forever," *60 Minutes Overtime* (April 3, 2020), https://www.cbsnews.com/news/artificial-intelligence-holocaust-remembrance-60-minutes-2020-04-03/.

80. StoryCorps, https://storycorps.org/.

Concluding Thoughts

Ezra–Nehemiah is not just about belonging and creating a community identity but also about being remembered. Reflecting on how we want to be remembered involves considering our character, relationships, contributions, resilience, and passions. People often value being seen as individuals or communities of integrity and kindness, cherished for deep and meaningful connections, and respected for their positive impact on others and the community. Demonstrating courage in challenges and pursuing passions with enthusiasm also contribute significantly to one's legacy. Thinking about these aspects help us align our daily actions with the legacy we aspire to leave, encouraging us to live intentionally and make choices that shape how we will be remembered as a community. Nehemiah demonstrates that even in the midst of challenging circumstances, one must be tenacious and bold, committed not only to the people, but to God and God's ethic (Torah). This commitment will move us past the boundaries and walls that keep us divided.

Works Cited

Ackerman, Susan. "Asherah, the West Semitic Goddess of Spinning and Weaving?" *JNES* 67 (January 2008): 1–29.

Ackerman, Susan. "Why Is Miriam Also among the Prophets? (And Is Zipporah among the Priests?)." *JBL* 121 (2002): 47–80.

Adams, Samuel L. *Social and Economic Life in Second Temple Judea*. Louisville: Westminster John Knox, 2014.

Adinkra Symbols & Meanings. September 14, 2020. https://www.adinkrasymbols.org/symbols sankofa/.

Aguilar, Grace. *The Women of Israel*. London: R. Groombridge, 1845; New York: D. Appleton, 1872.

Ahn, John J. *Exile as Forced Migrations: A Sociological, Literary, and Theological Approach on the Displacement and Resettlement of the Southern Kingdom of Judah*. Göttingen: de Gruyter, 2011.

Ainsfeld, Sharon Cohen, Tara Mohr, and Catherine Spector, eds. *The Women's Passover Companion: Women's Reflections on the Festival of Freedom*. Woodstock, VT: Jewish Lights, 2003.

Alter, Robert. "Nehemiah." In *The Hebrew Bible: The Writings*, 831–62. New York: Norton, 2019.

Altmann, Peter. *Economics in Persian-Period Biblical Texts: Their Interactions with Economic Developments in the Persian Period and Earlier Biblical Traditions*. FAT 109. Tübingen: Mohr Siebeck, 2016.

Altmann, Peter. "Tithes for the Clergy and Taxes for the King: State and Temple Contributions in Nehemiah." *CBQ* 76 (2014): 215–29.

American Oversight. "The Trump Administration's Controversial 'Operation LeGend' Program." 2021. https://www.americanoversight.org/investigation/the-trump-administrations-controversial-operation-legend-program.

Amzallag, Nissim. "The Authorship of Ezra and Nehemiah in Light of Differences in Their Ideological Background." *JBL* 137 (2018): 271–97.

Amzallag, Nissim, and Mikhal Avriel. "Psalm 122 as the Song Performed at the Ceremony of Dedication of the City Wall of Jerusalem (Nehemiah 12:27-43)." *SJOT* 30 (2016): 44–64.

Anderson, Cheryl B. "Reflections in an Interethnic/Racial Era on Interethnic/Racial Marriage in Ezra." In *They Were All Together in One Place? Toward Minority Biblical Criticism*, edited by Randall C. Bailey, Tat-Siong Benny Liew, and Fernando F. Segovia, 47–64. SemeiaSt 57. Atlanta: SBL, 2009.

Anderson, Herbert, and Edward Foley. *Mighty Stories, Dangerous Rituals: Weaving Together the Human and the Divine*. San Francisco: Jossey-Bass, 1998.

Anderson, Janice Capel, and Stephen D. Moore, eds. *Mark and Method: New Approaches in Biblical Studies*. 2nd ed. Minneapolis: Fortress, 2008.

Andrade Vinueza, Maria Alejandra. "'We Don't Want Them Here': From the Politics of Rejection to Sustainable Relationships with Immigrants." *Journal of Latin American Theology* 12 (2017): 79–99.

Angel, Hayyim. "The Literary Significance of the Name Lists in Ezra–Nehemiah." *JBQ* 35 (2007): 143–53.

Anisfeld, Sharon Cohen, Tara Mohr, and Catherine Spector. *The Women's Passover Companion: Women's Reflections on the Festival of Freedom and the Women's Seder Sourcebook; Rituals & Readings for Use at the Passover*. Woodstock: Jewish Lights Publishing, 2003.

Anthonioz, Stephanie. "Cities of Glory and Cities of Pride: Concepts, Gender, and Images of Cities in Mesopotamia and in Ancient Israel." In *Memory and the City in Ancient Israel*, edited by Diana V. Edelman and Ehud Ben Zvi, 21–42. University Park: Pennsylvania State University Press, 2014.

Aquino, María Pilar, and María José Rosado-Nunes, eds. *Feminist Intercultural Theology: Latina Explorations for a Just World*. Studies in Latino/a Catholicism. Maryknoll, NY: Orbis Books, 2007.

Aquino, María Pilar, Daisy L. Machado, and Jeanette Rodríguez, eds. *A Reader in Latina Feminist Theology*. Austin: University of Texas Press, 2002.

Astell, Mary. *Some Reflections upon Marriage*. New York: Source Book Press, 1970. Reprint of the 1730 edition; earliest ed. 1700.

Avigad, Nahman. *Bullae and Seals from a Post-Exilic Judean Archive*. Jerusalem: Institute of Archaeology, Hebrew University, 1976.

Azzoni, Annalisa. *Private Lives of Women in Persian Egypt*. Winona Lake, IN: Eisenbrauns, 2013.

Bach, Alice, ed. *Women in the Hebrew Bible: A Reader*. New York: Routledge, 1999.

Bailey, Randall C., Tat-Siong Benny Liew, and Fernando F. Segovia, eds. *They Were All Together in One Place? Toward Minority Biblical Criticism*. SemeiaSt 57. Atlanta: SBL, 2009.

Bakhos, Carol, and Gerhard Langer, eds. *The Jewish Middle Ages*. BW 4.2. Atlanta: SBL Press, 2023.

Bal, Mieke. *Lethal Love: Feminist Literary Readings of Biblical Love Stories*. Bloomington: Indiana University Press, 1987.

Bal, Mieke. "Metaphors He Lives By." *Semeia* 61 (1993): 185–207.

Baldwin, Lewis V. *Never to Leave Us Alone: The Prayer Life of Martin Luther King, Jr.* Minneapolis: Fortress, 2010.

"Bareku." In *Oxford Dictionary of the Jewish Religion*, edited by R. J. Zwi Werblowsky and G. Wigoder, 99–100. Oxford: Oxford University Press, 1997.

Barkay, Gabriel. *Ketef Hinnom: A Treasure Facing Jerusalem's Walls*. Jerusalem: Israel Museum, 1986.

Barstad, Hans M. "After the 'Myth of the Empty Land': Major Challenges in the Study of Neo-Babylonian Judah." In *Judah and the Judeans in the Neo-Babylonian Period*, edited by Oded Lipschits and Joseph Blenkinsopp, 3–20. Winona Lake, IN: Eisenbrauns, 2003.

Baskin, Judith R. "Women and Post-Biblical Commentary." In *The Torah: A Women's Commentary*, edited by Tamara Cohn Eskenazi and Andrea L. Weiss, xlix–lv. New York: URJ Press and Women of Reform Judaism, The Federation of Temple Sisterhoods, 2008.

Bass, Diana Butler. "Bad Blood: Christian Theology and Civil War." Substack newsletter. *The Cottage*. August 10, 2022. https://dianabutlerbass.substack.com/p/bad-blood.

Beavoir, Simone de. *The Second Sex*. Translated by H. M. Parshley. New York: Vintage, 1989.

Becking, Bob. "Drought, Hunger, and Redistribution: A Social Economic Reading of Nehemiah 5." In *The Historian and the Bible: Essays in Honor of Lester L. Grabbe*, edited by Philip Davies, Diana Edelman, and Lester Grabbe, 137–49. LHBOTS 539. New York: T&T Clark, 2010.

Becking, Bob. *Ezra, Nehemiah, and the Construction of Early Jewish Identity*. FAT 80. Tübingen: Mohr Siebeck, 2011.

Becking, Bob. *Ezra–Nehemiah*. HCOT. Leuven: Peeters, 2018.

Becking, Bob. "Sabbath at Elephantine: A Short Episode in the Construction of Jewish Identity." In *Empsychoi Logoi—Religious Innovations in Antiquity: Studies in Honour of Pieter Willem van Der Horst*, edited by Alberdina Houtman, Albert de Jong, and Magda Misset-van de Weg, 177–89. Ancient Judaism and Early Christianity 73. Leiden: Brill, 2008.

Begg, Christopher T. "Foreigner." In *The Anchor Yale Bible Dictionary: D–G*, edited by David Noel Freedman, Gary A. Herion, David Frank Graf, J. David Pleins, and Astrid B. Beck, 829–30. New Haven: Yale University Press, 1992.

Ben Zvi, Ehud. "Exploring Jerusalem as a Site of Memory in the Late Persian Period and Early Hellenistic Periods." In *Memory and the City in Ancient Israel*, edited by Diana V. Edelman and Ehud Ben Zvi, 197–217. Winona Lake, IN: Eisenbrauns, 2014.

Ben Zvi, Ehud. "Re-Negotiating a Putative Utopia and the Stories of the Rejection of Foreign Wives in Ezra–Nehemiah." In *Worlds That Could Not Be: Utopian in Chronicles, Ezra, and Nehemiah*, edited by Steven J. Schweitzer and Frauke Uhlenbruch, 105–28. London: T&T Clark, 2016.

Ben Zvi, Ehud, and Diana V. Edelman, eds. *Imagining the Other and Constructing Israelite Identity in the Early Second Temple Period*. LHBOTS 456. London: T&T Clark, 2014.

Berea College. "The Power of Sankofa: Know History." https://www.berea.edu/centers/carter-g-woodson-center-for-interracial-education/the-power-of-sankofa/.

Berger, Teresa. *Women's Ways of Worship: Gender Analysis and Liturgical History*. Collegeville, MN: Liturgical Press, 1999.

Berlin, Adele, and Marc Zvi Brettler. 2nd ed. *The Jewish Study Bible: Featuring the Jewish Publication Society Tanakh Translation*. New York: Oxford University Press, 2014.

Berman, Samuel A. "Midrash Tanchuma, Vayakhel 10:4." https://www.sefaria.org/Midrash_Tanchuma,_Vayakhel.10.4?ven=Midrash_Tanhuma-Yelammedenu,_trans._Samuel_A._Berman&lang=bi&with=all&lang2=en.

Berquist, Jon. *Judaism in Persia's Shadow: A Social and Historical Approach*. Minneapolis: Fortress, 1995.

Betlyon, John W. "A People Transformed: Palestine in the Persian Period." *NEA* 68 (2005): 4–58.

Betz, Eric. "Was King Solomon's Temple a Real Place?" *Discover Magazine*. December 15, 2020. https://www.discovermagazine.com/planet-earth/was-king-solomons-temple-a-real-place.

Bidmead, Julye. "Lots." In *Eerdmans Dictionary of the Bible*, edited by David Noel Freedman, 825. Grand Rapids: Eerdmans, 2000.

Biran, Avraham, and Joseph Naveh. "An Aramaic Stele Fragment from Tel Dan." *IEJ* 43 (1993): 81–98.

Bird, Phyllis A. *Missing Persons and Mistaken Identities: Women and Gender in Ancient Israel*. OBT. Minneapolis: Fortress, 1997.

Biwul, Joel K. T. "The Vision of 'Dry Bones' in Ezekiel 37:1–28: Resonating Ezekiel's Message as the African Prophet of Hope." *Hervormde Teologiese Studies* 73 (2017): 1–10.

Black Wall Street Legacy Festival. https://www.blackwallstreetlegacyfest.com/legacy.

Blenkinsopp, Joseph. *Ezra–Nehemiah: A Commentary*. OTL. Philadelphia: Westminster, 1988.

Blenkinsopp, Joseph. *Judaism, the First Phase: The Place of Ezra and Nehemiah in the Origins of Judaism*. Grand Rapids: Eerdmans, 2009.

Blenkinsopp, Joseph. "The Nehemiah Autobiographical Memoir." In *Language, Theology, and the Bible: Essays in Honour of James Barr*, edited by Samuel E. Balentine and John Barton, 199–212. Oxford: Clarendon, 1994.

Blenkinsopp, Joseph. "Trito-Isaiah (Isaiah 56–66) and the Gôlāh Group of Ezra, Shecaniah, and Nehemiah (Ezra 7–Nehemiah 13): Is There a Connection?" *JSOT* 43 (June 2019): 661–77.

Boda, Mark J. "Prayer as Rhetoric in the Book of Nehemiah." In *New Perspectives on Ezra–Nehemiah: History and Historiography, Text, Literature, and Interpretation*, edited by Isaac Kalimi, 267–84. Winona Lake, IN: Eisenbrauns, 2012.

Boer, Roland. "No Road: On the Absence of Feminist Criticism of Ezra–Nehemiah." In *Her Master's Tools? Feminist and Postcolonial Engagements of Historical-Critical Discourse*, edited by Carolyn Stichele and Todd Penner, 233–52. GPBS 9. Atlanta: SBL, 2005.

Boer, Roland. "Of Fine Wine, Incense and Spices: The Unstable Masculine Hegemony in the Book of Chronicles." In *Men and Masculinity in the Hebrew Bible and Beyond*, edited by Creanga Ovidiu, 20–33. Sheffield: Sheffield Phoenix, 2010.

Boer, Roland. *The Sacred Economy of Ancient Israel*. LAI. Louisville: Westminster John Knox, 2015.

Boer, Roland. "Thus I Cleansed Them from Everything Foreign: The Search for Subjectivity in Ezra–Nehemiah." In *Postcolonialism and the Hebrew Bible: The Next Step*, edited by Roland Boer, 221–37. SemeiaSt 70. Atlanta: SBL, 2013.

Børresen, Kari Elisabeth, and Adriana Valerio, eds. *The High Middle Ages*. BW 9.1. Atlanta: SBL Press, 2015.

Bosman, Hendrik L. "Loving the Neighbour and the Resident Alien in Leviticus 19 as Ethical Redefinition of Holiness." *OTE* 31 (2018): 571–90.

Botta, Alejandra F. "1, 2 Chronicles." In *The Old Testament and Apocrypha: Fortress Commentary on the Bible*, edited by Gale Yee, Hugh Page Jr., and Matthew Coomber, 439–66. Minneapolis: Fortress, 2014.

Boys, Mary C. "Doing Justice to Judaism: The Challenge to Christianity." *JES* 49 (2014): 107–10.

Brenner-Idan, Athalya. *The Israelite Woman: Social Role and Literary Type in Biblical Narrative*. 2nd ed. London: Bloomsbury, 2015.

Brenton, Lancelot C. L., ed. *The Septuagint with Apocrypha: Greek and English*. Peabody, MA: Hendrickson Academic, 1986.

Brettschneider, Marla, and Dawn Robinson Rose. "Meeting at the Well: Multiculturalism and Jewish Feminism." *JFSR* 19 (2003): 85–128.

Briant, Pierre. *From Cyrus to Alexander: A History of the Persian Empire*. Translated by Peter T. Daniels. Winona Lake, IN: Eisenbrauns, 2002.

Bridges, Carl. "Denarius." In *Eerdmans Dictionary of the Bible*, edited by David Noel Freedman, 338. Grand Rapids: Eerdmans, 2000.

Bright, John. *A History of Israel*. Westminster Aids to the Study of the Scriptures. 3rd ed. Philadelphia: Westminster, 1981.

Brink, Susan. "Some Cultures Treat Menstruation with Respect." *NPR*. August 11, 2015. https://www.npr.org/sections/goatsandsoda/2015/08/11/431605131/attention-trump-some-cultures-treat-menstruation-with-respect.

Brooten, Bernadette J. *Love Between Women: Early Christian Responses to Female Homoeroticism*. Chicago: University of Chicago Press, 1996.

Brosius, Maria. *Women in Ancient Persia, 559–331 BC*. OCM. Oxford: Clarendon, 1996.

Brown, F., S. R. Driver, and C. A. Briggs. *The Brown-Driver-Briggs Hebrew and English Lexicon, Coded with Strong's Concordance Numbers*. Peabody, MA: Hendrickson, 1996.

Buckley, Thomas, and Alma Gottlieb, eds. *Blood Magic: The Anthropology of Menstruation*. Berkeley: University of California Press, 1988.

Butler, Judith. *Gender Trouble: Feminism and the Subversion of Identity*. New York: Routledge, 1999.

Calduch-Benages, Nuria, and Christl M. Maier, eds. *The Writings and Later Wisdom Books*. BW 1.3. Atlanta: SBL Press, 2014.

Camp, Claudia. "Feminist- and Gender-Critical Perspectives on the Biblical Ideology of Intermarriage." In *Mixed Marriages: Intermarriages and Group Identity in the Second Temple Period*, edited by Christian Frevel, 303–15. LHBOTS 547. New York: T&T Clark, 2011.

Camp, Claudia. *Wisdom and the Feminine in the Book of Proverbs*. BLS 11. Sheffield: Almond Press, 1988.

Camp, Claudia. *Wise, Strange, and Holy: The Strange Woman and the Making of the Bible*. JSOTSup 320. Gender, Culture, Theory 9. Sheffield: Sheffield Academic, 2000.

"Camp David Being Used Less and Less by Presidents." CBS Baltimore. February 21, 2017. https://www.cbsnews.com/baltimore/news/camp-david-being-used-less-and-less-by-presidents/.

Campbell, Letitia M., and Yvonne C. Zimmerman. "Christian Ethics and Human Trafficking Activism: Progressive Christianity and Social Critique." *Journal of the Society of Christian Ethics* 34 (2014): 145–72.

Cannon, Katie Geneva. "The Emergence of Black Feminist Consciousness." In *Feminist Interpretation of the Bible*, edited by Letty M. Russell, 30–40. Philadelphia: Westminster, 1985.

Carney, Sheila. "God Damn God: A Reflection on Expressing Anger in Prayer." *BTB* 13 (1983): 116–20.

Carroll, Robert P. "Coopting the Prophets: Nehemiah and Noadiah." In *Priests, Prophets and Scribes: Essays on the Formation and Heritage of Second Temple Judaism in Honour of Joseph Blenkinsopp*, edited by Philip Davies and David Clines, 87–99. JSOTSup 149. Sheffield: JSOT Press, 1992.

Carter, Warren. "Matthaean Christology in Roman Imperial Key: Matthew 1.1." In *The Gospel of Matthew in Its Roman Imperial Context*, edited by John Riches and David C. Sim. London: T&T Clark, 2005.

Carter, Warren. *The Roman Empire and the New Testament: An Essential Guide*. Nashville: Abingdon, 2006.

Castelli, Elizabeth. "*Les Belles Infidèles*/Fidelity or Feminism? The Meanings of Feminist Biblical Translation." In *Searching the Scriptures: A Feminist Introduction*, vol. 1, edited by Elisabeth Schüssler Fiorenza with the assistance of Shelly Matthews, 189–204. New York: Crossroad, 1993.

Chapman, Cynthia R. *The House of the Mother: The Social Roles of Maternal Kin in Biblical Hebrew Narrative and Poetry*. AYBRL. New Haven: Yale University Press, 2016.

Chase-Ziolek, Mary. "Repairing, Restoring, and Revisioning the Health of Our Communities: The Challenge of Isaiah 58." *Ex Auditu* 21 (2005): 150–64.

Chazon, Esther Glickler. "Lowly to Lofty: The Hodayot's Use of Liturgical Traditions to Shape Sectarian Identity and Religious Experience." *RevQ* 26 (2013): 3–19.

Cheng, Albert, Matthew H. Lee, and Rian Djita. "A Cross-Sectional Analysis of the Relationship between Sabbath Practices and US, Canadian, Indonesian, and Paraguayan Teachers' Burnout." *JRH* 62 (2023): 1090–1113.

Chernin, Kim. "God's Bride on Pesach." *Tikkun* 18 (2003): 49–58.

Chia, Philip P. "On Naming the Subject: Postcolonial Reading of Daniel 1." In *The Postcolonial Biblical Reader*, edited by R. S. Sugirtharajah, 171–85. Malden, MA: Blackwell, 2006.

Chopp, Rebecca S. *The Power to Speak: Feminism, Language, God*. New York: Crossroad, 1989.

Christ, Carol P. "A Clash of Cultures." *Feminism and Religion* (blog). February 27, 2012. https://feminismandreligion.com/2012/02/27/a-clash-of-cultures-in-our-genes-by-carol-p-christ/.

Christ, Carol P., and Judith Plaskow. *Goddess and God in the World: Conversations in Embodied Theology*. Minneapolis: Fortress, 2016.

Claassens, L. Juliana, and Carolyn J. Sharp, eds. *Feminist Frameworks and the Bible: Power, Ambiguity, and Intersectionality*. LHBOTS 630. London: Bloomsbury T&T Clark, 2017.

Claassens, L. Juliana, and Irmtraud Fischer, eds. *Prophecy and Gender in the Hebrew Bible*. BW 1.2. Atlanta: SBL Press, 2021.

Clines, David J. A. "Nehemiah 10 as an Example of Early Jewish Biblical Exegesis." *JSOT* 6 (1981): 111–17.

Cogan, Mordechai. "Cyrus Cylinder, Fragment A." In *The Context of Scripture*. Vol. 2: *Monumental Inscriptions from the Biblical World*, edited by William W. Hallo and K. Lawson Younger Jr., 314–16. Leiden: Brill, 2000.

Cohen, Shaye J. D. *The Beginnings of Jewishness: Boundaries, Varieties, Uncertainties*. HCS 31. Berkeley: University of California Press, 1999.

Cohen, Shaye J. D. *From the Maccabees to the Mishnah*. 2nd ed. Louisville: Westminster John Knox, 2006.

Collins, John J. *The Invention of Judaism: Torah and Jewish Identity from Deuteronomy to Paul*. Taubman Lectures in Jewish Studies 7. Oakland: University of California Press, 2017.

Connell, Raewyn W. *Masculinities*. Berkeley: University of California Press, 2005.

Consolino, Franca Ela, and Judith Herrin, eds. *The Early Middle Ages*. BW 6.1. Atlanta: SBL Press, 2020.

Cross, Frank Moore. "Reconstruction of the Judean Restoration." *JBL* 94 (1975): 4–18.

Crowell, Bradley L. "Good Girl, Bad Girl: Foreign Women of the Deuteronomistic History in Postcolonial Perspective." *BibInt* 21 (2013): 1–18.

Daly, Mary. *Beyond God the Father: A Philosophy of Women's Liberation.* Boston: Beacon, 1985.

Dandamaev, M. A. "Neo-Babylonian and Archaemenid State Administration in Mesopotamia." In *Judah and the Judeans in the Persian Period*, edited by Oded Lipschits and Manfred Oeming, 373–98. Winona Lake, IN: Eisenbrauns, 2006.

Dandamaev, Muhammad A. *Slavery in Babylonia from Nabopolassar to Alexander the Great (626–331 BC).* DeKalb: Northern Illinois University Press, 1984.

D'Angelo, Mary Rose. "Women Partners in the New Testament." *JFSR* 6 (1990): 65–86.

David, Ariel. "The Mud Whisperers: Israeli Archaeologists Invent Disgusting but Effective New Way to Date Ancient Ruins." *Haaretz*. September 15, 2020. https://www.haaretz.com/archaeology/.premium-israelis-invent-disgusting-but-effective-new-way-to-date-ancient-ruins-1.9157297.

David, Janzen. "Yahwistic Appropriation of Achaemenid Ideology and the Function of Nehemiah 9 in Ezra–Nehemiah." *JBL* 136 (2017): 839–56.

Davidson, Steed Vernyl. "Authors of Biblical Books." In *The Oxford Encyclopedia of the Bible and Gender Studies*, edited by Julia M. O'Brien, 9–15. Vol. 1. Oxford: Oxford University Press, 2014.

Davies, Gordon F. *Ezra and Nehemiah*. Berit Olam. Edited by David W. Cotter. Collegeville, MN: Liturgical Press, 1999.

Davies, Philip R. "Negotiating Power in Ezra–Nehemiah." *Bib* 99 (2018): 121–24.

Davis, Ellen F. *Scripture, Culture, and Agriculture: The Agrarian Reading of the Bible.* Cambridge: Cambridge University Press, 2009.

De Troyer, Kristin. "Blood. A Threat to Holiness or Toward (Another) Holiness." In *Wholly Woman, Holy Blood: A Feminist Critique of Purity and Impurity*, edited by Kristin De Troyer, Judith A. Herbert, Judith Ann Johnson, and Anne-Marie Korte, 45–64. SAC. Harrisburg, VA: Trinity Press, 2003.

Demsky, Aaron. "Who Came First, Ezra or Nehemiah? The Synchronistic Approach." *HUCA* 65 (1994): 1–19.

Dinkler, Michal Beth. *Literary Theory and the New Testament*. AYBRL. New Haven: Yale University Press, 2019.

Douglas, Mary. "Responding to Ezra: The Priests and the Foreign Wives." *BibInt* 10 (2002): 1–23.

Dube, Musa W., ed. *Postcolonial Feminist Interpretation of the Bible.* St. Louis: Chalice, 2000.

Duchrow, Ulrich. *Alternatives to Global Capitalism: Drawn from Biblical History, Designed for Political Action*. 2nd ed. Utrecht: International Books, 1998.

Eagleton, Terry. *Ideology: An Introduction.* London: Verso, 2007.

Eagleton, Terry. *Literary Theory: An Introduction*. Anniversary ed. Minneapolis: University of Minnesota Press, 2008.

Ebeling, Jennie R. *Women's Lives in Biblical Times*. London: T&T Clark, 2010.

Edelman, Diana. *The Origins of the "Second" Temple: Persian Imperial Policy and the Rebuilding of Jerusalem*. Rev. ed. Hoboken, NJ: Taylor and Francis, 2014.

Edelman, Diana. "What Can We Know about the Persian-Era Temple in Jerusalem?" In *Temple Building and Temple Cult: Architecture and Cultic Paraphernalia of Temples in the Levant (2.-1. Mill. B.C.E.)*, edited by Jens Kamlah, 343–68. Abhandlungen des Deutschen Palästina-Vereins 41. Wiesbaden: Harrassowitz, 2012.

Enns, Elaine, and Ched Myers. *Healing Haunted Histories: A Settler Discipleship of Decolonization*. Eugene, OR: Cascade, 2021.

Eph῾al, Israel. "Esarhaddon, Egypt, and Shubria: Politics and Propaganda." *JCS* 57 (2005): 99–111.

Epp, Jay Eldon. *Junia: The First Woman Apostle*. Minneapolis: Fortress, 2005.

Eskenazi, Tamara Cohn. "Daughter-in-Law of Tobiah, Daughter of Meshullam, Wife of Jehohanan." In *Women in Scripture: A Dictionary of Named and Unnamed Women in the Hebrew Bible, the Apocryphal/Deuterocanonical Books and the New Testament*, edited by Carol Meyers, Toni Craven, and Ross Shepard Kraemer, 288. Boston: Houghton Mifflin, 2000.

Eskenazi, Tamara Cohn. *Ezra: A New Translation with Introduction and Commentary*. AB 14A. New Haven: Yale University Press, 2023.

Eskenazi, Tamara Cohn. "Ezra–Nehemiah." In *Women's Bible Commentary*, edited by Carol A. Newsom, Sharon H. Ringe, and Jaqueline Lapsley, 192–200. 3rd ed. Louisville: Westminster John Knox, 2012.

Eskenazi, Tamara Cohn. "Hassophereth/Sophereth." In *Women in Scripture: A Dictionary of Named and Unnamed Women in the Hebrew Bible, the Apocryphal/Deuterocanonical Books, and the New Testament*, edited by Carol Meyers, Toni Craven, and Ross Shepard Kraemer, 92. Boston: Houghton Mifflin, 2000.

Eskenazi, Tamara Cohn. "Imagining the Other in the Construction of Judahite Identity in Ezra–Nehemiah." In *Imagining the Other and Constructing Israelite Identity in the Early Second Temple Period*, edited by Ehud Ben Zvi and Diana V. Edelman, 230–56. London: Bloomsbury, 2014.

Eskenazi, Tamara Cohn. *In the Age of Prose: A Literary Approach to Ezra–Nehemiah*. SBLMS 36. Atlanta: SBL, 1988.

Eskenazi, Tamara Cohn. "Noadiah." In *Women in Scripture: A Dictionary of Named and Unnamed Women in the Hebrew Bible, the Apocryphal/Deuterocanonical Books, and the New Testament*, edited by Carol Meyers, Toni Craven, and Ross Shepard Kraemer, 132. Boston: Houghton Mifflin, 2000.

Eskenazi, Tamara Cohn. "Out from the Shadows: Biblical Women in the Postexilic Era." *JSOT* 54 (1992): 25–43.

Eskenazi, Tamara Cohn. "Queen, Wife of Artaxerxes." In *Women in Scripture: A Dictionary of Named and Unnamed Women in the Hebrew Bible, the Apocryphal/*

Deuterocanonical Books, and the New Testament, edited by Carol Meyers, Toni Craven, and Ross Shepard Kraemer, 287. Boston: Houghton Mifflin, 2000.

Eskenazi, Tamara Cohn. "Shelomith 4 (Ezra 8:20)." In *Women in Scripture: A Dictionary of Named and Unnamed Women in the Hebrew Bible, the Apocryphal/Deuterocanonical Books, and the New Testament*, edited by Carol Meyers, Toni Craven, and Ross Shepard Kraemer, 155. Boston: Houghton Mifflin, 2000.

Eskenazi, Tamara Cohn, and Andrea L. Weiss, eds. *The Torah: A Women's Commentary*. New York: URJ Press and Women of Reform Judaism, The Federation of Temple Sisterhoods, 2008.

Eskenazi, Tamara Cohn, and Eleanore P. Judd. "Marriage to a Stranger in Ezra 9–10." In *Second Temple Studies*. Vol. 2: *Temple and Community in the Persian Period*, edited by Tamara Cohn Eskenazi and Kent H. Richards, 266–85. LHBOTS. Sheffield: JSOT Press, 1994.

Esler, Philip Francis. "Ezra–Nehemiah as a Narrative of (Re-Invented) Israelite Identity." *BibInt* 11 (2003): 413–26.

Everhart, Janet S. "The Hidden Eunuchs of the Hebrew Bible: Uncovering an Alternate Gender." PhD diss., Illiff School of Theology and University of Denver (Colorado Seminary), 2003.

Exum, J. Cheryl. "Second Thoughts about Secondary Characters: Women in Exodus 1.8–2.10." In *A Feminist Companion to Exodus to Deuteronomy*, edited by Athalya Brenner, 75–87. FCB 6. Sheffield: Sheffield Academic, 1994.

Exum, J. Cheryl, and David J. A. Clines, eds. *The New Literary Criticism and the Hebrew Bible*. Valley Forge, PA: Trinity Press International, 1993.

Falk, Marcia. *The Book of Blessings: New Jewish Prayers for Daily Life, the Sabbath, and the New Moon Festival*. New York: Reform Judaism Publishing, 2017.

Farisani, Elelwani B. "The Ideologically Biased Use of Ezra–Nehemiah in a Quest for an African Theology of Reconstruction." In *Postcolonial Perspectives in African Biblical Interpretations*, edited by Musa W. Dube, Andrew Mũtũa Mbuvi, and Dora R. Mbuwayesango, 331–47. GPBS. Atlanta: SBL, 2012.

Faust, Avraham. "Settlement and Demography in Seventh-Century Judah and the Extent and Intensity of Sennacherib's Campaign." *PEQ* 140 (November 2008): 168–94.

Feinstein, Eve Levavi. *Sexual Pollution in the Hebrew Bible*. Oxford: Oxford University Press, 2014.

Fell, Margaret. *Women's Speaking Justified, Proved and Allowed by the Scriptures*. London, 1666.

Feminist Biblical Interpretation: A Compendium of Critical Commentary on the Books of the Bible and Related Literature. Edited by Luise Schottroff and Marie-Theres Wacker. Translated by Lisa E. Dahill, Everett R. Kalin, Nancy Lukens, Linda M. Maloney, Barbara Rumscheidt, Martin Rumscheidt, and Tina Steiner. Grand Rapids: Eerdmans, 2012.

Fensham, F. Charles. *The Books of Ezra and Nehemiah*. NICOT. Grand Rapids: Eerdmans, 1982.

Fewell, Danna Nolan, and David M. Gunn. *Gender, Power, and Promise: The Subject of the Bible's First Story*. Nashville: Abingdon, 1993.

Finkelstein, Israel. *Hasmonean Realities behind Ezra, Nehemiah, and Chronicles: Archaeological and Historical Perspectives*. AIL 34. Atlanta: SBL Press, 2018.

Finkelstein, Israel. "Jerusalem in the Persian (and Early Hellenistic) Period and the Wall of Nehemiah." *JSOT* 32 (June 2008): 501–20.

Finkelstein, Israel. "Persian Period Jerusalem and Yehud Rejoinders." In *The Crucial Nature of the Persian and Hellenistic Periods: Essays in Honor of Douglas A. Knight*, edited by Alice Hunt and Jon Berquist, 49–62. New York: T&T Clark, 2012.

Finkelstein, Israel. "The Rise of Jerusalem and Judah: The Missing Link." *Levant* 33 (January 1, 2001): 105–15.

Firestone, Reuven. "Abraham Visits Ishmael and His Wives: Between Jewish and Islamic Tradition." *TheTorah.com*. https://www.thetorah.com/article/abraham-visits-ishmael-and-his-wives-between-jewish-and-islamic-tradition.

Firth, David G. "Ezra, Nehemiah and Esther for Everyone." *JSOT* 41 (2017): 95.

Fischer, Irmtraud, and Daniela Feichtinger, eds. *Gender Agenda Matters: Papers of the "Feminist Section" of the International Meetings of the Society of Biblical Literature*. Newcastle-upon-Tyne: Cambridge Scholars Publishing, 2015.

Fischer, Irmtraud, and Mercedes Navarro Puerto, with Andrea Taschl-Erber, eds. *Torah*. BW 1.1. Atlanta: SBL, 2011.

Fisher, Eugene J. "Hebrew Bible or Old Testament: A Response to Christopher Seitz." *ProEccl* 6 (1997): 133–36.

Fitzpatrick-McKinley, Anne. *Empire, Power and Indigenous Elites: A Case Study of the Nehemiah Memoir*. Supplements to *Journal for the Study of Judaism*. Leiden: Brill, 2015.

Fleishman, Joseph. "An Echo of Optimism in Ezra 6:19-22." *HUCA* 69 (1998): 15–29.

Fleishman, Joseph. "Nehemiah's Request on Behalf of Jerusalem." In *New Perspectives on Ezra–Nehemiah: History and Historiography, Text, Literature, and Interpretation*, edited by Isaac Kalimi, 241–66. Winona Lake, IN: Eisenbrauns, 2012.

Franklin, Norma, Jennie R. Ebeling, Philippe Guillaume, and Deborah A. Appler. "Have We Found Naboth's Vineyard at Jezreel?" *BAR* 43 (2017): 49–54.

Fried, Lisbeth S. "The ʿam Hāʾāreṣ in Ezra 4:4 and Persian Imperial Administration." In *Judah and the Judeans in the Persian Period*, edited by Oded Lipschits and Manfred Oeming, 123–45. Winona Lake, IN: Eisenbrauns, 2006.

Fried, Lisbeth S. *Ezra: A Commentary*. Critical Commentaries. Sheffield: Sheffield Phoenix, 2015.

Fried, Lisbeth S. "The Land Lay Desolate: Conquest and Restoration in the Ancient Near East." In *Judah and the Judeans in the Neo-Babylonian Period*, edited by Oded Lipschits and Joseph Blenkinsopp, 21–54. Winona Lake, IN: Eisenbrauns, 2003.

Fried, Lisbeth S. *Nehemiah: A Commentary*. Critical Commentaries. Sheffield: Sheffield Phoenix, 2021.

Fried, Lisbeth S. *Was 1 Esdras First? An Investigation into the Priority and Nature of 1 Esdras*. AIL 7. Atlanta: SBL, 2011.

Friedman, Lisa. "Standing Rock Sioux Tribe Wins a Victory in Dakota Access Pipeline Case." *New York Times*. March 25, 2020. https://www.nytimes.com/2020/03/25/climate/dakota-access-pipeline-sioux.html.

Frimer, Aryeh A., and Dov I. Frimer. "Women's Prayer Services: Theory and Practice." *Tradition* 32 (1998): 5–118.

Frost, Robert. "Mending Wall." *Poetry Foundation*. https://www.poetryfoundation.org/poems/44266/mending-wall.

Frymer-Kensky, Tikva. *Reading the Women of the Bible*. New York: Schocken Books, 2002.

Fulton, Deirdre. *Reconsidering Nehemiah's Judah: The Case of MT and LXX Nehemia 11–12*. FAT 2.80. Tübingen: Mohr Siebeck, 2015.

Fulton, Deirdre. "Where Did the Judahites, Benjamites, and Levites Settle? Revisiting the Text of Nehemiah 11:25-36 MT and LXX." In *New Perspectives on Ezra–Nehemiah: History and Historiography, Text, Literature, and Interpretation*, edited by Isaac Kalimi, 197–222. Winona Lake, IN: Eisenbrauns, 2012.

Fulton, Deirdre N., and Gary N. Knoppers. "Lower Criticism and Higher Criticism: The Case of 1 Esdras." In *Was 1 Esdras First? An Investigation into the Priority and Nature of 1 Esdras*, edited by Lisbeth S. Fried, 11–29. Atlanta: SBL, 2011.

Gafney, Wilda C. *Daughters of Miriam: Women Prophets in Ancient Israel*. Minneapolis: Fortress, 2008.

Gafney, Wilda C. "A Prophet-Terrorist(a) and an Imperial Sympathizer: An Empire-Critical, Postcolonial Reading of the No'adyah/Nechemyah Conflict." *Black Theology* 9 (2011): 161–76.

Gafney, Wilda C. *Womanist Midrash: A Reintroduction to the Women of the Torah and the Throne*. Louisville: Westminster John Knox, 2017.

Galambush, Julie. *Jerusalem in the Book of Ezekiel: The City as Yahweh's Wife*. SBLDS 130. Atlanta: Scholars Press, 1992.

Gallarreta, Jose E. Balcells. *Household and Family Religion in Persian-Period Judah: An Archaeological Approach*. ANEM 18. Atlanta: SBL Press, 2017.

Garfinkel, Yosef, and Madeleine Mumcuoglu. "The Temple of Solomon in Iron Age Context." *Religions* 10 (March 2019): 198.

Gelardi, Chris. "After Woman's Arrest in Unmarked Van, New York City Activists Fear Targeting by NYPD." *The Appeal*. July 29, 2020. https://theappeal.org/after-womans-arrest-in-unmarked-van-new-york-city-activists-fear-targeting-by-nypd/.

Getty-Sullivan, Mary Ann. *Women in the New Testament*. Collegeville, MN: Liturgical Press, 2001.

Gilkes, Cheryl Townsend. *"If It Wasn't for the Women . . . ": Black Women's Experience and Womanist Culture in Church and Community*. Maryknoll, NY: Orbis Books, 2001.

Gillmayr-Bucher, Susanne, and Maria Häusl. *Prayers and the Construction of Israelite Identity*. AIL 35. Atlanta: SBL Press, 2019.

Glatt-Gilad, David A. "The Voluntary Nature of the Nehemiah Covenant in Rabbinic Literature." *The Review of Rabbinic Judaism* 20 (2017): 3–20.

"Global Passport Power Rank 2023." *Passport Index*. https://www.passportindex.org/passport-power-rank-2023.php.

"Global Passport Ranking." *The Henley Passport Index*. 2023. https://www.henleyglobal.com/passport-index/ranking.

Goldstein, Elizabeth W. *Impurity and Gender in the Hebrew Bible*. Lanham, MD: Lexington Books, 2015.

Gonzalez, Michelle A. "Latina Feminist Theology: Past, Present, and Future." *JFSR* 25 (2009): 150–55.

Good, Deirdre J. "Reading Strategies for Biblical Passages on Same-Sex Relations." *Theology and Sexuality* 7 (1997): 70–82.

Gordon, R. P. *Studies in the Targum to the Twelve Prophets, from Nahum to Malachi*. VTSup 51. Leiden: Brill, 1994.

Gosse, Bernard. "Sabbath, Identity and Universalism Go Together after the Return from Exile." *JSOT* 29 (2005): 359–70.

Gottwald, Norman K. "The Expropriated and the Expropriators in Nehemiah 5." In *Concepts of Class in Ancient Israel*, edited by Mark R. Sneed, 1–19. SFSHJ 201. Atlanta: Scholars Press, 1999.

Govier, Gordon. "Excavating the House of David." *Christianity Today* 67 (August 7, 2023): 68–71.

Grabbe, Lester L. "Chicken or Egg? Which Came First, 1 Esdras or Ezra–Nehemiah?" In *Was 1 Esdras First? An Investigation into the Priority and Nature of 1 Esdras*, edited by Lisbeth S. Fried, 31–43. AIL 7. Atlanta: SBL, 2011.

Grabbe, Lester L. *Ezra–Nehemiah*. OTR. London: Routledge, 1998.

Grabbe, Lester L. *A History of the Jews and Judaism in the Second Temple Period*. Vol. 1: *Yehud: A History of the Persian Province of Judah*. LSTS 47. London: T&T Clark, 2004.

Grabbe, Lester L. *Judaism from Cyrus to Hadrian*. Vol. 1: *The Persian and Greek Periods*. Minneapolis: Fortress, 1992.

Grabbe, Lester L. "The 'Persian Documents' in the Book of Ezra: Are They Authentic?" In *Judah and the Judeans in the Persian Period*, edited by Oded Lipschits and Manfred Oeming, 531–70. Winona Lake, IN: Eisenbrauns, 2006.

Grant, Jacquelyn. *White Women's Christ and Black Women's Jesus: Feminist Christology and Womanist Response*. AARAS 64. Atlanta: Scholars Press, 1989.

Grimké, Sarah. *Letters on the Equality of the Sexes and the Condition of Woman*. Boston: Isaac Knapp, 1838.

Gross, Carl D. "Is There Any Interest in Nehemiah 5?" *SJOT* 11 (1997): 270–78.

Guest, Deryn. *When Deborah Met Jael: Lesbian Biblical Hermeneutics*. London: SCM, 2005.

Habel, Norman C., and Peter Trudinger. *Exploring Ecological Hermeneutics*. SymS 46. Atlanta: SBL, 2008.

Haber, Susan. *"They Shall Purify Themselves": Essays on Purity in Early Judaism*. Edited by Adele Reinhartz. EJL 24. Atlanta: SBL, 2008.

Hallo, William W., and K. Lawson Younger Jr., eds. *The Context of Scripture*. Vol. 2: *Monumental Inscriptions from the Biblical World*. Leiden: Brill, 2003.

Hallock, Richard T. *Persepolis Fortification Tablets*. University of Chicago Oriental Institute Publications 92. Chicago: University of Chicago Press, 1969.

Hammer, Juliane. "Gender Justice in a Prayer: American Muslim Women's Exegesis, Authority, and Leadership." *Hawwa* 8 (2010): 26–54.

Hamori, Esther J. *Women's Divination in Biblical Literature: Prophecy, Necromancy, and Other Arts of Knowledge*. AYBRL. New Haven: Yale University Press, 2015.

Handy, Lowell, K. *Among the Host of Heaven*. Winona Lake, IN: Eisenbrauns, 1994.

Harro, Bobbie. "Updated Version of the Cycle of Socialization (2000)." In *Readings for Diversity and Social Justice*, edited by Maurianne Adams, Warren J. Blumenfeld, Carmelita Castañeda, Heather W. Hackman, Madeline L. Peters, Ximena Zúñiga, 618–25. 3rd ed. New York: Routledge, 2013.

Häusl, Maria. "Jerusalem, the Holy City: The Meaning of the City of Jerusalem in the Books of Ezra–Nehemiah." In *Constructions of Space*. Vol. 5: *Place, Space and Identity in the Ancient Mediterranean World*, edited by Gert T. M. Prinsloo and Christl M. Maier, 87–105. LHBOTS 576. New York: T&T Clark, 2014.

Häusl, Maria. " 'So I Prayed to the God of Heaven' (Neh 2:4): Praying and Prayers in the Books of Ezra and Nehemiah." In *Prayers and the Construction of Israelite Identity*, edited by Susanne Gillmayr-Bucher and Maria Häusl, 53–82. AIL 35. Atlanta: SBL, 2019.

Hayes, Christine. "Intermarriage and Impurity in Ancient Jewish Sources." *HTR* 92 (1999): 3–36.

Hays, Christopher B. "The Silence of the Wives: Bakhtin's Monologism and Ezra 7–10." *JSOT* 33 (2008): 59–80.

Hearon, Holly E., and Philip Ruge-Jones, eds. *The Bible in Ancient and Modern Media: Story and Performance*. Eugene, OR: Cascade Books, 2009.

Heger, Paul. "Patrilineal or Matrilineal Genealogy in Israel after Ezra." *JSJ* 43 (2012): 215–48.

Heltzer, Michael. "The Flogging and Plucking of Beards in the Achaemenid Empire and the Chronology of Nehemiah." *Archaeologische Mitteilungen Aus Iran* 28 (1995/1996): 305–7.

Hens-Piazza, Gina. *The New Historicism*. GBS, Old Testament Series. Minneapolis: Fortress, 2002.

Herodotus. *Darius and the Persian Empire*, 3.80-97. https://www.thelatinlibrary.com/historians/herod/herodotus5.html.

Herodotus. *The Histories*. Translated by A. D. Godley. Cambridge: Harvard University Press, 1920.

Herr, Larry G. "What Ever Happened to the Ammonites?" *BAR* 19 (November 1993): 26.

Hinson-Hasty, Elizabeth L. "Revisiting Feminist Discussions of Sin and Genuine Humility." *JFSR* 28 (2012): 108–14.

Holladay, William L., ed. *A Concise Hebrew and Aramaic Lexicon of the Old Testament*. Grand Rapids: Eerdmans, 1972.

Holloway, Steven W. "New Moon." In *Eerdmans Dictionary of the Bible*, edited by David Noel Freedman, 962. Grand Rapids: Eerdmans, 2000.

Holloway, Steven W. *Aššur Is King! Aššur Is King! Religion in the Exercise of Power in the Neo-Assyrian Empire*. CHANE 10. Leiden: Brill, 2002.

Holmgren, Fredrick Carlson. "Faithful Abraham and the 'amānâ Covenant Nehemiah 9,6–10,1." *ZAW* 104 (1992): 249–54.

Holmgren, Fredrick Carlson. *Israel Alive Again: A Commentary on the Books of Ezra and Nehemiah*. ITC. Grand Rapids: Eerdmans, 1987.

Homsher, Robert. "Mud Bricks and the Process of Construction in the Middle Bronze Age Southern Levant." *BASOR* 368 (2012): 1–27.

Hornsby, Teresa J. "Hebrew Bible and Gender." In *The Oxford Encyclopedia of the Bible and Gender Studies*, edited by Julia M. O'Brien, 323. Vol. 1. Oxford: Oxford University Press, 2014.

Hornsby, Teresa J., and Deryn Guest. *Transgender, Intersex, and Biblical Interpretation*. SemeiaSt 83. Atlanta: SBL Press, 2016.

Hornsby, Teresa J., and Ken Stone, eds. *Bible Trouble: Queer Reading at the Boundaries of Biblical Scholarship*. SemeiaSt 67. Atlanta: SBL, 2011.

Hossfeld, Frank L., and Ivo Meyer. *Prophet Gegen Prophet: Eine Analyse der alttestamentlichen Texte zum Thema: Wahre und Falsche Propheten*. Zürich: Schweizerisches Katholisches Bibelwerk, 1973.

Hughes, Julie A. *Scriptural Allusions and Exegesis in the Hodayot*. STDJ 59. Leiden: Brill, 2006.

"Humiliation and Abuse: Artifacts Made from Desecrated Torah Scrolls." Yad Vashem. https://www.yadvashem.org/artifacts/museum/desecrated-torah-scrolls.html.

Hunt Hudiburg, Alice. "Onias." In *Eerdmans Dictionary of the Bible*, edited by David Noel Freedman, 988. Grand Rapids: Eerdmans, 2000.

Ilan, Tal, Lorena Miralles-Maciá, and Ronit Nikolsky, eds. *Rabbinic Literature*. BW 4.1. Atlanta: SBL Press, 2022.

Isasi-Díaz, Ada María. *Mujerista Theology: A Theology for the Twenty-First Century*. Maryknoll, NY: Orbis Books, 1996.

Isherwood, Lisa, and Dorothea McEwan. *An A–Z of Feminist Theology*. Religious Studies. New York: Bloomsbury Academic, 2016.

Jacobson, Rolf A., and Karl N. Jacobson. "The Old Testament and the Neighbor." *WW* 37 (2017): 16–26.

"Jaddua." In *Eerdmans Dictionary of the Bible*, edited by David Noel Freedman, 667. Grand Rapids: Eerdmans, 2000.

Janzen, David. "A Colonized People: Persian Hegemony, Hybridity, and Community Identity in Ezra–Nehemiah." *BibInt* 24 (2016): 27–47.

Janzen, David. *Witch-Hunts, Purity and the Social Boundaries: The Expulsion of Foreign Women in Ezra 9–10*. JSOTSup 350. London: Sheffield Academic, 2002.

Japhet, Sara. "Composition and Chronology in the Book of Ezra–Nehemiah." In *Second Temple Studies*. Vol. 2: *Temple and Community in the Persian Period*, edited by Tamara Cohn Eskenazi and Kent H. Richards, 189–216. LHBOTS. Sheffield: JSOT Press, 1994.

Japhet, Sara. "The Expulsion of the Foreign Women (Ezra 9–10): The Legal Basis, Precedents, and Consequences for the Definition of Jewish Identity." In *"Sieben Augen auf einem Stein" (Sach 3,9), Studien zur Literatur des Zweiten Tempels: Festschrift für Ina Willi-Plein zum 65. Geburtstag*, edited by Friedhelm Hartenstein and Michael Pietsch, 141–61. Neukirchen-Vluyn: Neukirchener Verlag, 2007.

Japhet, Sara. *From the Rivers of Babylon to the Highlands of Judah: Collected Studies on the Restoration Period*. Winona Lake, IN: Eisenbrauns, 2006.

Japhet, Sara. "Law and 'the Law' in Ezra–Nehemiah." In *Proceedings of the Ninth World Congress of Jewish Studies: Panel Sessions, Biblical Studies and Ancient Near East*, edited by Moshe Goshen-Gottstein, 99–115. Jerusalem: World Union of Jewish Studies, Magnes Press, Hebrew University, 1988.

Japhet, Sara. "Sheshbazzar and Zerubbabel—Against the Background of the Historical and Religious Tendencies of Ezra–Nehemiah." *ZAW* 94 (1982): 66–98.

Jay, Nancy. *Throughout Your Generations Forever: Sacrifice, Religion, and Paternity*. Chicago: University of Chicago Press, 1992.

"A Jewish Guide to Marking Transgender Day of Remembrance." *Keshet קֶשֶׁת For LGBTQ+ Equality in Jewish Life*. October 4, 2011. https://www.keshetonline.org/resources/a-jewish-guide-for-marking-transgender-day-of-remembrance/.

Ji-Sun Kim, Grace. "Foreign Women: Ezra, Intermarriage and Asian American Women's Identity." *Feminist Theology: The Journal of the Britain & Ireland School of Feminist Theology* 22 (2014): 241–52.

Joachimsen, Kristin. "Yehudite Imaginations of King Darius and His Officials: Views from the Province beyond the River." *Religions* 13 (March 2022): 262.

Jobling, David, and Tina Pippin, eds. *Ideological Criticism of Biblical Texts*. SemeiaSt 59. Atlanta: Scholars Press, 1992.

Johnson, Elizabeth A. "God." In *Dictionary of Feminist Theologies*, edited by Letty M. Russell and J. Shannon Clarkson, 128–30. Louisville: Westminster John Knox, 1996.

Johnson, Elizabeth A. *She Who Is: The Mystery of God in Feminist Theological Discourse*. New York: Crossroad, 1992.

Johnson, Sylvester A. "New Israel, New Canaan: The Bible, the People of God, and the American Holocaust." *USQR* 59 (2005): 25–39.

Johnson, Willa M. *The Holy Seed Has Been Defiled: The Interethnic Marriage Dilemma in Ezra 9–10*. Hebrew Bible Monographs 33. Sheffield: Sheffield Phoenix, 2011.

Junior, Nyasha. *An Introduction to Womanist Biblical Interpretation*. Louisville: Westminster John Knox, 2015.

Kabiersch, Jürgen. "Esdras II: Das Zweite Buch Esdras/Esra–Nehemiah." In *Septuaginta Deutsch. Erläuterungen und Kommentare zum griechischen Alten Testament I: Genesis bis Makkabäer*, edited by Martin Karrer and Wolfgang Kraus. Stuttgart: Deutsche Biblegesellschaft, 2011.

Kamionkowski, S. Tamar. *Leviticus*. WCS 3. Collegeville, MN: Liturgical Press, 2018.

Karrer-Grube, Christiane. "Ezra and Nehemiah: The Return of the Others." In *Feminist Biblical Interpretation: A Compendium of Critical Commentary on the Books of the Bible and Related Literature*, edited by Luise Schottroff and Marie-Theres Wacker, 192–206. Grand Rapids: Eerdmans, 2012.

Karrer-Grube, Christiane. *Ringen um die Verfassung Judas: Eine Studie zu den theologisch-politischen Vorstellugen im Esra-Nehemia-Buch*. BZAW 308. Berlin: de Gruyter, 2001.

Kartzow, Marianne B., and Halvor Moxnes. "Complex Identities: Ethnicity, Gender and Religion in the Story of the Ethiopian Eunuch (Acts 8:26-40)." *Religion & Theology* 17 (2010): 184–204.

Katz, Andrew. "Clashes over a Show of White Nationalism in Charlottesville Turn Deadly." *Time*. https://time.com/charlottesville-white-nationalist-rally-clashes/.

Keefe, Alice A. "Rapes of Women/Wars of Men." In *Women, War, and Metaphor*, edited by Claudia V. Camp and Carole R. Fontaine, 79–97. SemeiaSt 61. Atlanta: Scholars Press, 1993.

Kellermann, Ulrich. *Nehemia: Quellen, Überlieferung und Geschichte*. BZAW 102. Berlin: de Gruyter, 2019.

Kelso, Julie. "Reading Silence: The Books of Chronicles and Ezra–Nehemiah, and the Relative Absence of a Feminist Interpretive History." In *Feminist Interpretation of the Hebrew Bible in Retrospect*, edited by Suzanne Scholz, 268–89. Recent Research in Biblical Studies 5. Sheffield: Sheffield Phoenix, 2013.

Kelso, Julie. "Why Should Feminists Read the Bible?" *Hecate* 33 (2007): 4–13.

Kendall, Frances E., and Charmaine L. Wijeyesinghe. "Advancing Social Justice Work at the Intersections of Multiple Privileged Identities." *New Directions for Student Services* (Spring 2017). 91–100.

Keren, Rachel. "Torah Study." *Shalvi/Hyman Encyclopedia of Jewish Women*. Jewish Women's Archive. March 20, 2009. https://jwa.org/encyclopedia/article/torah-study.

Kessler, John. "Diaspora and Homeland in the Early Achaemenid Period: Community, Geography, and Demography in Zechariah 1–8." In *Approaching Yehud: New Approaches to the Study of the Persian Period*, edited by Jon Berquist, 137–66. SemeiaSt 50. Atlanta: SBL, 2007.

King, Philip J., and Lawrence E. Stager. *Life in Biblical Israel*. LAI. Louisville: Westminster John Knox, 2002.

Kissileff, Beth. "Contemporary Reflection (Shof'tim)." In *The Torah: A Women's Commentary*, edited by Andrea L. Weiss and Tamara Cohn Eskenazi, 1160–61. New York: URJ Press and Women of Reform Judaism, The Federation of Temple Sisterhoods, 2008.

Kitzberger, Ingrid Rosa, ed. *Autobiographical Biblical Criticism: Between Text and Self*. Leiden: Deo, 2002.

Klawans, Jonathan. *Impurity and Sin in Ancient Judaism*. New York: Oxford University Press, 2000.

Klawans, Jonathan. "The Law." In *The Jewish Annotated New Testament*, edited by Amy-Jill Levine and Marc Zvi Brettler, 2nd ed., 655–58. Oxford: Oxford University Press, 2017.

Kleber, Kristin, "Taxation in the Achaemenid Empire." *Oxford Handbook Topics in Classical Studies* (online ed., Oxford Academic). April 1, 2014. https://doi.org/10.1093/oxfordhb/9780199935390.013.34.

Klein, Ralph. "The Books of Ezra and Nehemiah." In *The New Interpreter's Bible*, edited by Leander Keck, 661–851. Vol. 3. Nashville: Abingdon, 1999.

Knight, Douglas. *Law, Power, and Justice in Ancient Israel*. LAI. Louisville: Westminster John Knox, 2011.

Knight, Douglas, and Amy-Jill Levine. *The Meaning of the Bible: What the Jewish Scriptures and Christian Old Testament Can Teach Us*. New York: HarperOne, 2011.

Knoppers, Gary N. "Exile, Return and Diaspora: Expatriates and Repatriates in Late Biblical Literature." In *Texts, Contexts and Readings in Postexilic Literature: Explorations into Historiography and Identity Negotiation in Hebrew Bible and Related Texts*, edited by Louis Jonker, 29–61. FAT 2.53. Tübingen: Mohr Siebeck, 2011.

Knoppers, Gary N. "Intermarriage, Social Complexity, and Ethnic Diversity in the Genealogy of Judah." *JBL* 120 (2001): 15–30.

Knoppers, Gary N. "The Vanishing Solomon: The Disappearance of the United Monarchy from Recent Histories of Ancient Israel." *JBL* 116 (Spring 1997): 19–44.

Korada, Manoja Kumar. "Seeing Discontinuity in Chronicles–Ezra–Nehemiah through Reforms." *JETS* 61 (2018): 287–305.

Kraemer, Ross Shepard. *Unreliable Witnesses: Religion, Gender, and History in the Greco-Roman Mediterranean*. New York: Oxford University Press, 2011.

Kraemer, Ross Shepard, and Mary Rose D'Angelo, eds. *Women and Christian Origins*. New York: Oxford University Press, 1999.

Kuefler, Matthew. *The Manly Eunuch: Masculinity, Gender Ambiguity, and Christian Ideology in Late Antiquity*. Chicago Series on Sexuality, History, and Society. Chicago: University of Chicago Press, 2001.

Kuhrt, Amélie. "The Problem of Achaemenid 'Religious Policy.'" In *Die Welt der Götterbilder*, edited by Brigitte Groneberg and Hermann Spieckermann, 117–42. Berlin: de Gruyter, 2007.

Kuhrt, Amélie. "State Communications in the Persian Empire." In *State Correspondence in the Ancient World: From New Kingdom Egypt to the Roman Empire*, edited by Karen Radner, 111–40. Oxford Studies in Early Empires. Oxford: Oxford University Press, 2014.

Kuruvilla, Carol. "Alexandria Ocasio-Cortez: Jesus Would Be Maligned as 'Radical' by Today's Congress." *Huffington Post*. February 27, 2020. https://www.huffpost.com/entry/alexandria-ocasio-cortez-faith_n_5e580e16c5b6450a30bbd0f7.

LaCugna, Catherine Mowry. *God for Us: The Trinity and Christian Life*. San Francisco: HarperCollins, 1991.

Laird, Donna. *Negotiating Power in Ezra–Nehemiah*. AIL 26. Atlanta: SBL Press, 2016.

Latinas in Construction. https://www.latinasinconstruction.net/en/.

LeClaire, Jennifer. "Don't Let the Spirit of Sanballat Distract You." Jennifer LeClaire Ministries. January 4, 2013. https://jenniferleclaire.org/articles/dont-let-the-spirit-of-sanballat-distract-you/#.

Lehtipuu, Outi, and Silke Petersen, eds. *Ancient Christian Apocrypha*. BW 3.2. Atlanta: SBL Press, 2022.

Lemos, T. M. "Like the Eunuch Who Does Not Beget: Gender Mutilation and Negotiated Status in the Ancient Near East." In *Disability Studies and Biblical Literature*, edited by Candida Moss and Jeremy Schipper, 47–66. New York: Palgrave Macmillan, 2011.

Lerner, Gerda. "One Thousand Years of Feminist Bible Criticism." Chap. 7 (pp. 138–66) in *The Creation of Feminist Consciousness: From the Middle Ages to Eighteen-Seventy*. Women and History 2. New York: Oxford University Press, 1993.

Leuchter, Mark. "Ezra's Mission and the Levites of Casiphia." In *Community Identity in Judean Historiography: Biblical and Comparative Perspectives*, edited by Gary N. Knoppers and Kenneth A. Ristau, 173–95. Winona Lake, IN: Eisenbrauns, 2009.

Lev, Sarra L. "They Treat Him as a Man and See Him as a Woman: The Tannaitic Understanding of the Congenital Eunuch." *JSQ* 17 (2010): 213–43.

Leveen, Adriane. "Vayeilech, Deuteronomy 31:10-13." In *The Torah: A Woman's Commentary*, edited by Andrea L. Weiss and Tamara Cohn Eskenazi, 1235–44. New York: Women of Reform Judaism, 2008.

Levenson, Jon. *Sinai and Zion: An Entry into the Jewish Bible*. San Francisco: HarperOne, 1987.

Levering, Matthew. *Ezra & Nehemiah*. Brazos Theological Commentary on the Bible. Grand Rapids: Brazos Press, 2007.

Levine, Amy-Jill. "Bearing False Witness. Common Errors Made about Early Judaism." In *The Jewish Annotated New Testament*, 2nd ed., edited by Amy-Jill Levine and Marc Zvi Brettler, 759–63. Oxford: Oxford University Press, 2017.

Levine, Amy-Jill. "Diaspora as Metaphor: Bodies and Boundaries in the Book of Tobit." In *Diaspora Jews and Judaism: Essays in Honor of, and in Dialogue with, A. Thomas Kraabel*, edited by Andrew Overman and Robert S. MacLennan, 105–17. SFSHJ 41. Atlanta: Scholars Press, 1992.

Levine, Amy-Jill. "Multiculturalism, Women's Studies, and Anti-Judaism." *JFSR* 19 (2003): 119–28.

Levine, Amy-Jill. "The New Testament and Anti-Judaism." In *The Misunderstood Jew: The Church and the Scandal of the Jewish Jesus*, 87–117. San Francisco: HarperSanFrancisco, 2006.

Levine, Amy-Jill, and Marc Zvi Brettler. *The Bible With and Without Jesus: How Jews and Christians Read the Same Stories Differently*. New York: HarperOne, 2020.

Liddell, Henry George, and Robert Scott. *A Lexicon Abridged from Liddell and Scott's Greek–English Lexicon*. Oxford: Clarendon, 1982.

Liebermann, Rosanne. "Drinkable Ink or Womb-Destroying Words? A Solution for Suspected Adultery in Numbers 5:11-31." *Postscripts* 14 (2023): 38–64.

Liebreich, Leon J. "The Impact of Nehemiah 9:5-37 on the Liturgy of the Synagogue." *HUCA* 32 (1961): 227–37.

Lipka, Hilary. "Another View." In *The Torah: A Woman's Commentary*, edited by Tamara Cohn Eskenazi and Andrea Weiss, 489. New York: Women of Reform Judaism, 2008.

Lipman, Dov. "Time to Rejoice on Sukkot, despite Coronavirus." *Jerusalem Post*. October 1, 2020. https://www.jpost.com/opinion/time-to-rejoice-on-sukkot-despite-corona-644206.

Lipschits, Oded. "Literary and Ideological Aspects of Nehemiah 11." *JBL* 121 (Fall 2002): 423–40.

Lipschits, Oded. "The Rural Economy of Judah during the Persian Period and Settlement History of the District System." In *The Economy of Ancient Judah in Its Historical Context*, edited by Ehud Ben Zvi, Marvin Lloyd Miller, and Gary N. Knoppers, 236–63. Winona Lake, IN: Eisenbrauns, 2015.

Lipschits, Oded, and Manfred Oeming. *Judah and the Judeans in the Persian Period*. Winona Lake, IN: Eisenbrauns, 2006.

Lowe, Mary Elise. "Woman Oriented Hamartiologies: A Survey of the Shift from Powerlessness to Right Relationship." *Dialog: A Journal of Theology* 39 (Summer 2000): 119–39.

Löwisch, Ingeborg. "Miriam, Ben Amram, or, How to Make Sense of the Absence of Women in the Genealogies of Levi (1 Chronicles 5:27–6:66)." In *The Bible and Feminism: Remapping the Field*, edited by Yvonne Sherwood, 355–70. Oxford: Oxford University Press, 2017.

Magen, Yitzhak, "Bells, Pendants, Snakes & Stones: A Samaritan Temple to the Lord on Mt. Gerizim," *BAR* 36 (November/December 2010): 26–35.

Magen, Yitzhak. "The Dating of the First Phase of the Samaritan Temple on Mount Gerizim in Light of Archaeological Evidence." In *Judah and the Judeans in the Fourth Century, B.C.E.*, edited by Oded Lipschits, Gary N. Knoppers, and Rainer Albertz, 157–211. Winona Lake, IN: Eisenbrauns, 2007.

Mahanta, Siddhartha. "New York's Looming Food Disaster." *Bloomberg*. October 21, 2013. https://www.bloomberg.com/news/articles/2013-10-21/new-york-s-looming-food-disaster.

Maier, Christl. *Daughter Zion, Mother Zion: Gender, Space, and the Sacred in Ancient Israel*. Minneapolis: Fortress, 2008.

Maier, Christl. "Whose Mother? Whose Space? Jerusalem in Third Isaiah." In *Constructions of Space*. Vol. 5: *Place, Space and Identity in the Ancient Mediterranean World*, edited by Gert T. M. Prinsloo and Christl M. Maier, 107–24. LHBOTS 576. New York: T&T Clark, 2014.

Maier, Christl M., and Carolyn J. Sharp. *Prophecy and Power: Jeremiah in Feminist and Postcolonial Perspective.* London: Bloomsbury, 2013.

Maier, Christl M., and Nuria Calduch-Benages, eds. *The Writings and Later Wisdom Books.* BW 1.3. Atlanta: SBL Press, 2014.

Maio, Heather. "Artificial Intelligence Project Lets Holocaust Survivors Share Their Stories Forever." *60 Minutes Overtime*. April 3, 2020. https://www.cbsnews.com/news/artificial-intelligence-holocaust-remembrance-60-minutes-2020-04-03/.

Malamat, Abraham. "Is There a Word for the Royal Harem in the Bible? The Inside Story." In *Pomegranates and Golden Bells: Studies in Biblical, Jewish, and Near Eastern Ritual, Law, and Literature in Honor of Jacob Milgrom*, edited by Jacob Milgrom, David P. Wright, David Noel Freedman, and Avi Hurvitz, 785–87. Winona Lake, IN: Eisenbrauns, 1995.

Malbon, Elizabeth Struthers, and Edgar V. McKnight, eds. *The New Literary Criticism and the New Testament.* JSNTSup 109. Sheffield: JSOT Press, 1994.

Mansfield, Chip. "Opportunities for Women in the Construction Industry." *American Council for Construction Education.* May 31, 2023. https://www.acce-hq.org/post/opportunities-for-women -in-the-construction-industry?gad=1&gclid=CjwKCAjww7KmBhAyEiwA5-PUSg3bWcjj2BqD_YWcLVjYjmFh9IMWWGQZjbmgnu4vIz99vqLSMTA2GroCag8QAvD_BwE.

Marbury, Herbert R. *Imperial Dominion and Priestly Genius: Coercion, Accommodation, and Resistance in the Divorce Rhetoric of Ezra–Nehemiah.* Upland: Sopher Press, 2012.

Marbury, Herbert R. "Reading Persian Dominion in Nehemiah: Multivalent Language, Co-Option, Resistance, and Cultural Survival." In *The Crucial Nature of the Persian and Hellenistic Periods: Essays in Honor of Douglas A. Knight*, edited by Alice Hunt and Jon Berquist, 158–76. New York: T&T Clark, 2012.

Marchal, Joseph A. "Queer Studies and Critical Masculinity Studies in Feminist Biblical Studies." In *Feminist Biblical Studies in the Twentieth Century: Scholarship and Movement*, edited by Elisabeth Schüssler Fiorenza, 261–80. BW 9.1. Atlanta: SBL Press, 2014.

Marcus, David. *Ezra and Nehemiah*. Biblia Hebraica Qinta 20. Stuttgart: Deutsche Bibelgesellschaft, 2006.

Mark, Joshua J. "Behistun Inscription." *World History Encyclopedia*. November 28, 2019. https://www.worldhistory.org/Behistun_Inscription/.

Masenya, Madipoane J. "Proverbs 31:10-31 in a South African Context: A Reading for the Liberation of African (Northern Sotho) Women." *Semeia* 78 (1997): 55–68.

May, Vivian. *Pursuing Intersectionality, Unsettling Dominant Imaginaries*. Contemporary Sociological Perspectives. New York: Routledge, 2015.

McFague, Sallie. *Models of God: Theology for an Ecological, Nuclear Age*. Philadelphia: Fortress, 1987.

McKinlay, Judith E. *Reframing Her: Biblical Women in Postcolonial Focus*. Sheffield: Sheffield Phoenix, 2004.

McLeod, Andrew. *Holy Cooperation! Building Graceful Economies*. Eugene, OR: Wipf & Stock, 2009.

McLeod, Andrew. "Why Nehemiah?" *Nehemian Organizing: How to Rebuild a City* (blog). December 20, 2010. https://nehemian.wordpress.com/2010/12/20/why-nehemiah/.

Meacham, Tirzah. "How Pragmatism Trumps Dogmatism: Marginalization and the Masses in the Case of Coming to the Temple." In *Introduction to Seder Qodashim: A Feminist Commentary on the Babylonian Talmud V*, edited by Tal Ilan, Monika Brockhaus, and Tanja Hidde, 85–105. Tübingen: Mohr Siebeck, 2012.

Megillah 17b. *Sefaria*. https://www.sefaria.org/Megillah.17b?lang=bi.

Melcher, Sarah J. "A Tale of Two Eunuchs: Isaiah 56:1-8 and Acts 8:26-40." In *Disability Studies and Biblical Literature*, edited by Candida Moss and Jeremy Schipper, 117–28. New York: Palgrave Macmillan, 2011.

Methuen, Charlotte, Irmtraud Fischer, Mercedes Navarro Puerto, and Adriana Valerio, eds. The Bible and Women: An Encyclopaedia of Exegesis and Cultural History (BW). https://www.bibleandwomen.org.

Meyers, Carol. *Discovering Eve: Ancient Israelite Women in Context*. New York: Oxford University Press, 1988.

Meyers, Carol. "From Field Crops to Food: Attributing Gender and Meaning to Bread Production in Iron Age Israel." In *The Archaeology of Difference: Gender, Ethnicity, Class and the "Other" in Antiquity; Studies in Honor of Eric M. Meyers*, edited by Douglas Edwards and C. Thomas McCollough, 67–84. AASOR 60/61. Boston: ASOR, 2007.

Meyers, Carol. *Rediscovering Eve: Ancient Israelite Women in Context*. New York: Oxford University Press, 2013.

Meyers, Carol, Toni Craven, and Ross S. Kraemer, eds. *Women in Scripture: A Dictionary of Named and Unnamed Women in the Hebrew Bible, the Apocryphal/Deuterocanonical Books, and the New Testament*. Boston: Houghton Mifflin, 2000/Grand Rapids: Eerdmans, 2001.

Meyers, Carol L., and Eric M. Meyers. *Haggai, Zechariah 1–8: A New Translation with Introduction and Commentary*. AB 25B. Garden City, NY: Doubleday, 1987.

Miller, Shem. "The Role of Performance and the Performance of Role: Cultural Memory in the Hodayot." *JBL* 137 (2018): 359–82.

Min, Kyung-Jin. *The Levitical Authorship of Ezra–Nehemiah*. JSOTSup 409. London: T&T Clark, 2004.

Miranda, Lin-Manuel. *Hamilton: An American Musical*. Atlantic Records, 2015.

"Mishnah Rosh Hashanah 2:8." https://www.sefaria.org/Mishnah_Megillah.3.6?ven=The_Mishna_with_Obadiah_Bartenura_by_Rabbi_Shraga_Silverstein&with=all&lang2=en.

Mitchell, Alan C. "Oath." In *Eerdmans Dictionary of the Bible*, edited by David Noel Freedman, 978. Grand Rapids: Eerdmans, 2000.

Moore, Darnell L. "Guilty of Sin: African-American Denominational Churches and Their Exclusion of SGL Sisters and Brothers." *Black Theology* 6 (2008): 83–97.

Moore, James D. "Who Gave You a Decree?: Anonymity as a Narrative Technique in Ezra 5:3, 9 in Light of Persian-Period Decrees and Administrative Sources." *JBL* 140 (2021): 69–89.

Moore, Stephen D. *The Bible in Theory: Critical and Postcritical Essays*. Atlanta: SBL, 2010.

Moore, Stephen D. *Poststructuralism and the New Testament: Derrida and Foucault at the Foot of the Cross*. Minneapolis: Fortress, 1994.

Morrow, William S. "Post-Traumatic Stress Disorder and Vicarious Atonement in the Second Isaiah." In *Psychology and the Bible: A New Way to Read the Scriptures*. Vol. 1: *From Freud to Kohut*, edited by J. Harold Ellens and Wayne G. Rollins, 167–83. Psychology, Religion, and Spirituality. Westport, CT: Praeger, 2004.

Munro, Ealasaid. "Feminism: A Fourth Wave?" *Political Insight*. September 2013. https://journals.sagepub.com/doi/pdf/10.1111/2041-9066.12021.

Myers, Jacob M. *Ezra, Nehemiah*. AB 14. Garden City, NY: Doubleday, 1965.

Nadar, Sarojini. " 'Texts of Terror': The Conspiracy of Rape in the Bible, Church, and Society; The Case of Esther 2:1-18." In *African Women, Religion, and Health: Essays in Honor of Mercy Amba Ewudziwa Oduyoye*, edited by Isabel Apawo Phiri and Sarojini Nadar, 77–95. Women from the Margins. Maryknoll: Orbis Books, 2006.

Najman, Hindy. "Notes on Ezra." In *The Jewish Study Bible*, edited by Adele Berlin and Marc Zvi Brettler, 2nd ed., 1661–80. Oxford: Oxford University Press, 2014.

Najman, Hindy. "Notes on Nehemiah." In *The Jewish Study Bible*, edited by Adele Berlin and Marc Zvi Brettler, 2nd ed., 1681–1702. Oxford: Oxford University Press, 2014.

Nam, Roger. "Half Speak Ashdodite and None Can Speak Judean: Code-Switching in Ezra–Nehemiah as an Identity Marker for Repatriate Judeans and Koreans." In *Landscapes of Korean and Korean American Biblical Interpretation*, edited by John Ahn, 119–31. IVBS 10. Atlanta: SBL Press, 2019.

National Association of Black Women in Construction. https://nabwic.org/.

National Association of Women in Construction. https://www.nawic.org/.

Navarro Puerto, Mercedes, and Marinella Perroni, eds.; Amy-Jill Levine, English ed. *Gospels: Narrative and History*. BW 2.1. Atlanta: SBL Press, 2015.

Netzer, Amnon. "Esther and Mordechai." *Encyclopaedia Iranica*. Vol. 8.6, 657–58. https://www.iranicaonline.org/articles/esther-and-mordechai.

A New English Translation of the Septuagint. Edited by Albert Pietersma and Benjamin G. Wright. Oxford: Oxford University Press, 2014.

Newman, Barbara. *Sister of Wisdom: St. Hildegard's Theology of the Feminine.* Berkeley: University of California Press, 1987.

Nicol, George G. "Ezra–Nehemiah: An Introduction and Study Guide, Israel's Quest for Identity." *ExpTim* 129 (2018): 532.

Niditch, Susan. *"My Brother Esau Is a Hairy Man": Hair and Identity in Ancient Israel.* New York: Oxford University Press, 2008.

Niditch, Susan. "War, Women, and Defilement in Numbers 31." *Semeia* 61 (1993): 39–57.

Nissim, Amzallag. "The Authorship of Ezra and Nehemiah in Light of Differences in Their Ideological Background." *JBL* 137 (2018): 271–97.

Nowell, Irene. *Women in the Old Testament.* Collegeville, MN: Liturgical Press, 1997.

O'Brien, Tim. *The Things They Carried*. Boston: Mariner Books Classics, 2009.

Oded, Bustenay. "Where Is the 'Myth of the Empty Land' to Be Found? History versus Myth." In *Judah and the Judeans in the Neo-Babylonian Period*, edited by Oded Lipschits and Joseph Blenkinsopp, 55–74. Winona Lake, IN: Eisenbrauns, 2003.

Olyan, Saul M. "Purity Ideology in Ezra–Nehemiah as a Tool to Reconstitute the Community." *JSJ* 35 (2004): 1–16.

Omar, Dullah. "Truth and Reconciliation Commission Website, South Africa." http://www.justice.gov.za/trc/.

Pakkala, Juha. *Ezra the Scribe: The Development of Ezra 7–10 and Nehemiah 8*. BZAW 347. New York: de Gruyter, 2004.

Pakkala, Juha. "Nehemiah (Book and Person)." In *Encyclopedia of the Bible and Its Reception*, edited by Constance M. Furey, Joel Lemon, Brian Matz, Thomas Römer, Jens Schröter, Barry Dov Walfish, and Eric Ziolkowski, 50–72. Vol. 21. Berlin: de Gruyter, 2023.

Parrish, Lorena. "Dismantling Domination through Womanist Rituals of Resistance." *Liturgy* 35 (2020): 10–18.

Passoni Dell'Acqua, Anna. "Prayers of Jewish Women: Studies of Patterns of Prayer in the Second Temple Period." *Bib* 90 (2009): 274–78.

Patta, Debora, S. Carter, J. Guzman, and K. Breen. "Candy Company Mars Uses Cocoa Harvested by Kids as Young as 5 in Ghana: CBS New Investigation." *CBS News*. November 29, 2023. https://www.cbsnews.com/news/children-harvesting-cocoa-used-by-major-corporations-ghana/.

Patterson, James. "The American Nehemiad, or the Tale of Two Walls." *Journal of Church and State* 57 (2015): 450–68.

Patton, Cheryl. "What Made Nehemiah an Effective Leader?" *Journal of Applied Christian Leadership* 11 (2017): 8–14.

PBS. *Finding Your Roots*. https://www.pbs.org/show/finding-your-roots/.

Peckruhn, Heike. "Disability Studies." In *The Oxford Encyclopedia of the Bible and Gender Studies*, edited by Julia M. O'Brien, 101–11. Vol. 1. Oxford: Oxford University Press, 2014.

Penchansky, David. "Deconstruction." In *The Oxford Encyclopedia of Biblical Interpretation*, edited by Steven McKenzie, 196–205. New York: Oxford University Press, 2013.

Perdue, Leo G., and Warren Carter. *Israel and Empire: A Postcolonial History of Israel and Early Judaism*. Edited by Coleman A. Baker. London: Bloomsbury T&T Clark, 2015.

Piazza, Michael S. "Nehemiah as a Queer Model for Servant Leadership." In *Take Back the Word: A Queer Reading of the Bible*, edited by Robert Goss and Mona West, 115–23. Cleveland: Pilgrim Press, 2000.

Plaskow, Judith. "Anti-Judaism in Feminist Christian Interpretation." In *Searching the Scriptures: A Feminist Introduction*, vol. 1, edited by Elisabeth Schüssler Fiorenza with the assistance of Shelly Matthews, 117–29. New York: Crossroad, 1993.

Porten, Bezalel, J. Joel Farber, Cary J. Martin, Günther Vittmann, et al. *The Elephantine Papyri in English: Three Millennia of Cross-Cultural Continuity and Change*. 2nd ed. Studies in Near Eastern Archaeology and Civilisation. Atlanta: SBL, 2011.

Powery, Emerson B. "Under the Gaze of the Empire: Who Is My Neighbor?" *Int* 62 (2008): 134–44.

Proeschold-Bell, Rae Jean, Beth Stringfield, Jia Yao, Jessica Choi, David E. Eagle, Celia F. Hybels, Heather Parnell, Kelly Keefe, and Sara Shilling. "Changes in Sabbath-Keeping and Mental Health over Time: Evaluation Findings from the Sabbath Living Study." *Journal of Psychology and Theology* 50 (2022): 123–38.

Pui-lan, Kwok. *Postcolonial Imagination and Feminist Theology*. Louisville: Westminster John Knox, 2005.

Rabarijaona, Brigitte. "Women in the Book of Nehemia." In *Gender Agenda Matters: Papers of the "Feminist Section" of the International Meetings of the Society of Biblical Literature*, edited by Irmtraud Fischer and Daniela Feichtinger, 115–24. Newcastle-upon-Tyne: Cambridge Scholars, 2015.

Rainey, Brian. "'Their Peace or Prosperity': Biblical Concepts of Hereditary Punishment and the Exclusion of Foreigners in Ezra–Nehemiah." *Journal of Ancient Judaism* 6 (2015): 158–81.

Rambo, Shelly. *Spirit and Trauma: A Theology of Remaining*. Louisville: Westminster John Knox, 2010.

Rampton, Martha. "Four Waves of Feminism." October 25, 2015. https://www.pacificu.edu/magazine/four-waves-feminism.

Rao, Tajal. "Food Supply Anxiety Brings Back Victory Gardens." *New York Times*, March 25, 2020. https://www.nytimes.com/2020/03/25/dining/victory-gardens-coronavirus.html.

Redditt, Paul L. *Ezra–Nehemiah*. Macon: Smith & Helwys, 2014.

Redditt, Paul L. "Sanballat." In *Eerdmans Dictionary of the Bible*, edited by David Noel Freedman, 1165. Grand Rapids: Eerdmans, 2000.

Redditt, Paul L. "Tobiah" in *Eerdmans Dictionary of the Bible*, edited by David Noel Freedman, 1317. Grand Rapids: Eerdmans, 2000.

Reeser, Todd W. *Masculinities in Theory: An Introduction*. 2nd ed. Newark: Wiley-Blackwell, 2023.

Refugees International. "The Trump Zero Tolerance Policy: A Cruel Approach with Humane and Viable Alternatives." July 31, 2018. https://www.refugeesinternational.org/reports-briefs/the-trump-zero-tolerance-policy-a-cruel-approach-with-humane-and-viable-alternatives/.

Ress, Mary Judith. *Ecofeminism in Latin America*. Women from the Margins. Maryknoll, NY: Orbis Books, 2006.

Rich, Adrienne. *Blood, Bread, and Poetry: Selected Prose, 1979–1985*. New York: Norton, 1986.

Rienzi, Greg. "Other Nations Could Learn from Germany's Efforts to Reconcile after WWII." *Johns Hopkins Magazine* (Summer 2015). https://hub.jhu.edu/magazine/2015/summer/germany-japan-reconciliation/.

Ringe, Sharon H. "When Women Interpret the Bible." In *Women's Bible Commentary*, edited by Carol A. Newsom, Sharon H. Ringe, and Jacqueline E. Lapsley. 3rd ed. Louisville: Westminster John Knox, 2012.

Ringrose, Katherine. *The Perfect Servant: Eunuchs and the Social Construction of Gender in Byzantium*. Chicago: University of Chicago Press, 2004.

Ritmeyer, Leen. "The Water Gate of Jerusalem." *Ritmeyer Archaeological Design*, June 22, 2011. https://www.ritmeyer.com/2011/06/22/the-water-gate-of-jerusalem/.

Ritmeyer, Leen, and Kathleen Ritmeyer. *Jerusalem in the Time of Nehemiah*. Jerusalem: Carta, 2014.

Robinson, George. *Essential Judaism: A Complete Guide to Beliefs, Customs, and Rituals*. New York: Pocket Books, 2000.

Roman Catholic Women Priests. https://romancatholicwomenpriests.org/.

Rom-Shiloni, Dalit. *Exclusive Inclusivity: Identity Conflicts between the Exiles and the People Who Remained (6th–5th Centuries BCE)*. LHBOTS 543. London: Bloomsbury, 2013.

Rooke, Deborah W. *Embroidered Garments: Priests and Gender in Biblical Israel*. King's College London Studies in the Bible and Gender 2. Sheffield: Sheffield Phoenix, 2009.

Rudolph, William. *Esra und Nehemia, samt 3. Esra*. Tübingen: Mohr, 1949.

Ruether, Rosemary Radford. *Sexism and God-Talk: Toward a Feminist Theology*. Boston: Beacon, 1993.

Ruether, Rosemary Radford. *Women-Church: Theology and Practice of Feminist Liturgical Communities*. San Francisco: Harper & Row, 1985.

Ruiz, Jean-Pierre. "'They Could Not Speak the Language of Judah': Rereading Nehemiah 13 between Brooklyn and Jerusalem." In *They Were All Together in One Place? Toward Minority Biblical Criticism*, edited by Randall C. Bailey, Tat-siong Benny Liew, and Fernando F. Segovia, 79–95. SemeiaSt 57. Atlanta: SBL, 2009.

Rushton, Kathleen P. "The Woman in Childbirth of John 16:21: A Feminist Reading in (Pro)Creative Boundary Crossing." In *Wholly Woman, Holy Blood: A Feminist Critique of Purity and Impurity*, edited by Kristin De Troyer, Judith A. Herbert, Judith Ann Johnson, and Anne-Marie Korte, 77–96. SAC. Harrisburg, VA: Trinity Press, 2003.

Rutledge, David. *Reading Marginally: Feminism, Deconstruction and the Bible*. BibInt 21. Leiden: Brill, 1996.

Sadler, Rodney S. *Can a Cushite Change His Skin? An Examination of Race, Ethnicity, and Othering in the Hebrew Bible*. LHBOTS 425. London: T&T Clark, 2005.

Sakenfeld, Katharine Doob. *Just Wives? Stories of Power and Survival in the Old Testament and Today*. Louisville: Westminster John Knox, 2003.

Schneiders, Sandra M. *The Revelatory Text: Interpreting the New Testament as Sacred Scripture*. Rev. ed. Collegeville, MN: Liturgical Press, 1999.

Scholz, Susanne. "Dismantling the Phallic Economy with a Hermeneutics of Reproductive Justice: A Reconsideration of Sotah in Numbers 5:11-31." *Journal of Religious Ethics* 49 (2021): 270–89.

Scholz, Susanne, ed. *Feminist Interpretation of the Hebrew Bible in Retrospect*. Recent Research in Biblical Studies 5, 8, 9. Sheffield: Sheffield Phoenix, 2013, 2014, 2016.

Scholz, Susanne. "From the 'Woman's Bible' to the 'Women's Bible,' The History of Feminist Approaches to the Hebrew Bible." In *Introducing the Women's Hebrew Bible*, 12–32. IFT 13. New York: T&T Clark, 2007.

Schottroff, Luise. *Lydia's Impatient Sisters: A Feminist Social History of Early Christianity*. Translated by Barbara and Martin Rumscheidt. Louisville: Westminster John Knox, 1995.

Schuller, Eileen M. "Recent Scholarship on the *Hodayot* 1993–2010." *CurBR* 10 (2011): 119–62.

Schuller, Eileen M. "Women in the Dead Sea Scrolls: Research in the Past Decade and Future Directions." In *The Dead Sea Scrolls and Contemporary Culture: Proceedings of the International Conference Held at the Israel Museum, Jerusalem (July 6–8, 2008)*, edited by Adolfo D. Roitman, Lawrence H. Schiffman, and Shani Tzoref, 571–88. STDJ 93. Boston: Leiden, 2011.

Schuller, Eileen, and Marie-Theres Wacker, eds. *Early Jewish Writings*. BW 3.1. Atlanta: SBL Press, 2017.

Schüssler Fiorenza, Elisabeth, ed. *Feminist Biblical Studies in the Twentieth Century: Scholarship and Movement*. BW 9.1. Atlanta: SBL Press, 2014.

Schüssler Fiorenza, Elisabeth. *In Memory of Her: A Feminist Theological Reconstruction of Christian Origins*. New York: Crossroad, 1983/1994.

Schüssler Fiorenza, Elisabeth. *Jesus: Miriam's Child, Sophia's Prophet; Critical Issues in Feminist Christology*. New York: Continuum, 1994.

Schüssler Fiorenza, Elisabeth. *The Power of the Word: Scripture and the Rhetoric of Empire*. Minneapolis: Fortress, 2007.

Schüssler Fiorenza, Elisabeth. *Wisdom Ways: Introducing Feminist Biblical Interpretation*. Maryknoll, NY: Orbis Books, 2001.

Schutte, P. J. W. "When *They*, *We*, and the *Passive* Become *I*—Introducing Autobiographical Biblical Criticism." *HTS Teologiese Studies / Theological Studies* 61 (2005): 401–16.

Schwartz, Regina M. "Holy Terror." In *'Holy War' and Gender: Violence in Religious Discourses = 'Gotteskrieg' und Geschlecht*, Berliner Gender Studies 2, edited by Christina von Braun, Ulrike Brunotte, and Gabriele Dietze, 13–22. Berlin: LIT, 2006.

Segal, Michael. "Numerical Discrepancies in the List of Vessels in Ezra I 9-11." *VT* 52 (January 2002): 122–29.

Seitz, Christopher R. "Old Testament or Hebrew Bible? Some Theological Considerations." *ProEccl* 5 (1996): 292–303.

Seltzer, Sarah. "Did *Star Wars* Toymakers Intentionally Exclude Rey?" *Flavor Wire*. January 22, 2016. https://www.flavorwire.com/557366/did-star-wars-toymakers-intentionally-exclude-rey.

Shepherd, David. "Prophetaphobia: Fear and False Prophecy in Nehemiah VI." *VT* 55 (2005): 232–50.

Sherwood, Yvonne. *A Biblical Text and Its Afterlives: The Survival of Jonah in Western Culture*. Cambridge: Cambridge University Press, 2000.

Sherwood, Yvonne. "Introduction." In *The Bible and Feminism: Remapping the Field*, edited by Yvonne Sherwood with the assistance of Anna Fisk. New York: Oxford University Press, 2017.

Siedlecki, Armin. "Ezra–Nehemiah in Reception History." In *The Oxford Handbook of the Historical Books of the Hebrew Bible*, edited by Brad Kelle and Brent Strawn, 526–36. Oxford: Oxford University Press, 2020.

Siegert, Folker. *Zwischen Hebräischer Bibel und Altem Testament. Eine Einführung in die Septuaginta I*. Münsteraner Judaistische Studien 9. Munster: LIT, 2001.

Slezak, Michael. "Eve's Closest Relative Found." *New Scientist* 224 (October 11, 2014): 8–9.

Smith, H. Clay. "Reconsidering the Composition of Ezra–Nehemiah in Light of 2 Maccabees 1:10–2:18." *JBL* 141 (2022): 257–76.

Smith, Mark S. "In Solomon's Temple (1 Kings 6–7): Between Text and Archaeology." In *Confronting the Past: Archaeological and Historical Essays on Ancient Israel in Honor of William G. Dever*, edited by Seymour Gitin, J. Edward Wright, and J. P. Dessel, 275–82. Winona Lake, IN: Eisenbrauns, 2006.

Smith-Christopher, Daniel L. *A Biblical Theology of Exile*. OBT. Minneapolis: Fortress, 2002.

Smith-Christopher, Daniel L. *The Religion of the Landless: The Social Context of the Babylonian Exile*. 2nd ed. Eugene, OR: Wipf & Stock, 2015.

Snyman, Gerrie. "Collective Memory and Coloniality of Being, and Power as a Hermeneutical Framework: A Partialized Reading of Ezra–Nehemiah." In *Postcolonial Perspectives in African Biblical Interpretation*, edited by Andrew M. Mbuvi, Musa W. Dube, and Dora Mbuwayesango, 359–85. GPBS 13. Atlanta: SBL, 2012.

Sohn-Kronthaler, Michaela, and Ruth Albrecht, eds. *Faith and Feminism in Nineteenth-Century Religious Communities.* BW 8.2. Atlanta: SBL Press, 2019.

Sojourner Truth. "Ain't I a Woman?" Modern History Sourcebook. https://sourcebooks.fordham.edu/mod/sojtruth-woman.asp.

Solvang, Elna K. "The First Orientalist? Fantasy and Foreignness in the Book of Esther." In *In the Wake of Tikva Frymer-Kensky*, edited by Steven Holloway, Jo Ann Scurlock, and Richard Beal, 199–216. Gorgias Précis Portfolios 4. Piscataway, NJ: Gorgias Press, 2009.

Southwood, Katherine. "'And They Could Not Understand Jewish Speech': Language, Ethnicity, and Nehemiah's Intermarriage Crisis." *JTS* 62 (2011): 1–19.

Southwood, Katherine. *Ethnicity and the Mixed Marriage Crisis in Ezra 9–10: An Anthropological Approach*. Oxford Theological Monographs. Oxford: Oxford University Press, 2012.

Southwood, Katherine. "Ezra–Nehemiah." In *Fortress Commentary on the Bible: The Old Testament and the Apocrypha*, edited by Gale Yee, Hugh R. Page Jr., and Matthew J. M. Coomber, 467–85. Minneapolis: Fortress, 2014.

Southwood, Katherine E. "The 'Foreigner' and the Eunuch: The Politics of Belonging in Isaiah 56:1-8," *BibInt* 30 (2020): 437–59.

Sparks, Kenton L. *Ancient Texts for the Study of the Hebrew Bible: A Guide to the Background Literature*. Peabody, MA: Hendrickson, 2005.

Srulevitch, Andrew. "Why Is Putin Calling the Ukrainian Government a Bunch of Nazis?" ADL (March 4, 2022). https://www.adl.org/resources/blog/why-putin-calling-ukrainian-government-bunch-nazis.

Stanley, Ron L. "Ezra–Nehemiah." In *The Queer Bible Commentary*, edited by Deryn Guest, Robert E. Goss, Mona West, and Thomas Bohache, 268–77. Vol. 1. London: SCM, 2006.

Steiner, Richard C. "Bishlam's Archival Search Report in Nehemiah's Archive: Multiple Introductions and Reverse Chronological Order as Clues to the Origin of the Aramaic Letters in Ezra 4–6." *JBL* 125 (2006): 641–85.

Stern, Ephraim. "Between Persia and Greece: Trade, Administration and Warfare in the Persian and Hellenistic Periods (539–63 BCE)." In *The Archaeology of Society in the Holy Land*, edited by Thomas Levy, 432–45. London: Leicester University Press, 1998.

Stone, Ronald H. "Reinhold Niebuhr and the Feminist Critique of Universal Sin." *JFSR* 28 (2012): 91–96.

StoryCorps. https://storycorps.org/.

Strong, John T. "Mizpah." In *Eerdmans Dictionary of the Bible*, edited by David Noel Freedman, 908. Grand Rapids: Eerdmans, 2000.

Sumi, Cho, Kimberlé Williams Crenshaw, and Leslie McCall. "Toward a Field of Intersectionality Studies: Theory, Applications, and Praxis." *Signs: Journal of Women in Culture & Society* 38 (Summer 2013): 785–810.

Ta'anit 29a. *Sefaria.* https://www.sefaria.org/Taanit.29a.17?lang=bi&with=all&lang2=en.

Tadmor, Hayim. "Was the Biblical sārîs a Eunuch?" In *Solving Riddles and Untying Knots: Biblical, Epigraphic, and Semitic Studies in Honor of Jonas C. Greenfield*, edited by Ziony Zevit, Seymour Gitin, and Michael Sokoloff, 317–25. Winona Lake, IN: Eisenbrauns, 1995.

Taitz, Emily, Sondra Henry, and Cheryl Tallan. *The JPS Guide to Jewish Women 600 B.C.E.–1900 C.E.* Philadelphia: JPS, 2003.

Taylor, Marion Ann, and Agnes Choi, eds. *Handbook of Women Biblical Interpreters: A Historical and Biographical Guide.* Grand Rapids: Baker Academic, 2012.

Thiessen, Matthew. "The Function of a Conjunction: Inclusivist or Exclusivist Strategies in Ezra 6.19-21 and Nehemiah 10.29-30?" *JSOT* 34 (2009): 63–79.

Thorpe, J. R. "This Is the Actual Reason Pad Commercials Use That Weird Blue Liquid." *Bustle.* October 20, 2017. https://www.bustle.com/p/why-do-period-product-commercials-use-blue-liquid-the-practice-has-a-long-bizarre-history-2957963.

Throntveit, Mark A. *Ezra–Nehemiah.* IBC. Louisville: Westminster John Knox, 2012.

Thurston, Bonnie. *Women in the New Testament: Questions and Commentary.* Companions to the New Testament. New York: Crossroad, 1998.

Tiemeyer, Lena-Sofia. "Ethnicity and the Mixed Marriage Crisis in Ezra 9–10: An Anthropological Approach." *JTS* 64 (2013): 598–601.

Tolbert, Mary Ann. "Social, Sociological, and Anthropological Methods." In *Searching the Scriptures: A Feminist Introduction*, vol. 1, edited by Elisabeth Schüssler Fiorenza with the assistance of Shelly Matthews, 255–71. New York: Crossroad, 1993.

Tollefson, Kenneth D., and Hugh G. M. Williamson. "Nehemiah as Cultural Revitalization: An Anthropological Perspective." *JSOT* 17 (1992): 41–68.

Torrey, Charles Cutler. "Sanballat 'the Horonite.'" *JBL* 47 (1928): 380–89.

Trible, Phyllis. *God and the Rhetoric of Sexuality*. OBT. Philadelphia: Fortress, 1978.

"Tukulti-Ninurta I." CDLI Wiki. https://cdli.ox.ac.uk/wiki/doku.php?id=tukulti-ninurta_i.

Ulrich, Dean R. "David in Ezra–Nehemiah." *WTJ* 78 (2016): 49–64.

Ulrich, Eugene, John W. Wright, Robert P. Carroll, and Philip R. Davies, eds. *Priests, Prophets, and Scribes: Essays on the Formation and Heritage of Second Temple Judaism in Honour of Joseph Blenkinsopp.* JSOTSup 149. Sheffield: JSOT Press, 1992.

Ungnad, Arthur. "Keilinschriftliche Beiträge zum Buch Esra und Ester." *ZAW* 58 (1941): 240–44.

UNICEF. "Child Labour." June 2023. https://data.unicef.org/topic/child-protection/child-labour/.

US Department of Justice. "Attorney General Announces the Zero-Tolerance Policy for Criminal Illegal Entry." April 6, 2018. https://www.justice.gov/opa/pr/attorney-general-announces-zero-tolerance-policy-criminal-illegal-entry.

Ussishkin, David. "On Nehemiah's City Wall and the Size of Jerusalem during the Persian Period: An Archaeologist's View." In *New Perspectives on Ezra–Nehemiah: History and Historiography, Text, Literature, and Interpretation*, edited by Isaac Kalimi, 101–30. Winona Lake, IN: Eisenbrauns, 2012.

VanderKam, James C. *From Joshua to Caiaphas: High Priests after the Exile*. Minneapolis: Fortress, 2004.

Vander Stichele, Caroline, and Todd Penner, eds. *Her Master's Tools? Feminist and Postcolonial Engagements of Historical-Critical Discourse*. Atlanta: SBL, 2005.

Vatican. "Saint Esdras, Scribe." https://www.vaticannews.va/en/saints/07/13.html.

Vermeulen, Karolien. *Conceptualizing Biblical Cities: A Stylistic Study*. London: Palgrave Macmillan, 2020.

Viezel, Eran. "Ezra (Book and Person), Rabbinic Judaism." In *Encyclopedia of the Bible and Its Reception*, edited by Brennan Breed, Constance M. Furey, Peter Gemeinhardt, Joel Marcus LeMon, Thomas Römer, Jens Schröter, Barry Dov Walfish, and Eric Ziolkowski, 632–34. Vol. 8. Berlin: de Gruyter, 2014.

Wafawanaka, Robert. "In Quest of Survival: The Implications of the Reconstruction Theology of Ezra–Nehemiah." In *Postcolonial Perspectives in African Biblical Interpretations*, edited by Andrew M. Mbuvi, Musa W. Dube, and Dora Mbuwayesango, 349–58. GPBS 13. Atlanta: SBL, 2012.

Walker, Alice. *In Search of Our Mothers' Gardens: Womanist Prose*. New York: Harcourt Brace Jovanovich, 1967, 1983.

Wallenstein, Peter. *Tell the Court I Love My Wife: Race, Marriage, and Law—An American History*. New York: Palgrave Macmillan, 2002.

Warnock, Raphael. "ICYMI: Senator Reverend Warnock Responds to Horrific Shooting in Midtown Atlanta, Calls on Congress to Turn Prayer into Action." *Reverend Raphael Warnock*. https://www.warnock.senate.gov/newsroom/press-releases/icymi-senator-reverend-warnock-responds-to-horrific-shooting-in-midtown-atlanta-calls-on-congress-to-turn-prayer-into-action/.

Warrior, Robert Allen. "Canaanites, Cowboys, and Indians." *USQR* 59 (2005): 1–8.

Washington, Harold C. "Israel's Holy Seed and the Foreign Women of Ezra–Nehemiah: A Kristevan Reading." *BibInt* 11 (2003): 427–37.

Wassersug, Richard J., Emma McKenna, and Tucker Lieberman. "Eunuch as a Gender Identity after Castration." *Journal of Gender Studies* 21 (2012): 253–70.

Waters, Matthew W. *Ctesias' Persica and Its Near Eastern Context*. Wisconsin Studies in Classics. Madison: University of Wisconsin Press, 2017.

Watkins, Durrell. "Ezra–Nehemiah." In *The Queer Bible Commentary*, edited by Mona West and R. E. Shore-Goss, 235–41. 2nd ed. London: SCM, 2022.

Wearne, Gareth. "What Was the Book of Moses in 4QMMT?" *CBQ* 82 (2020): 237–55.

Weems, Renita J. *Just a Sister Away: A Womanist Vision of Women's Relationships in the Bible.* San Diego: Lura Media, 1988.

Weinraub, Bernard. "Trove of Judaica Preserved by Nazis to Tour U.S." *New York Times.* September 20, 1983, sec. U.S. https://www.nytimes.com/1983/09/20/us/trove-of-judaica-preserved-by-nazis-to-tour-us.html.

Werblowsky, R. J. Zwi, and Geoffrey Wigoder, eds. *The Oxford Dictionary of the Jewish Religion.* New York: Oxford University Press, 1997.

Whitters, Mark F. "The Persianized Liturgy of Nehemiah 8:1-8." *JBL* 136 (2017): 63–84.

Williams, Delores S. *Sisters in the Wilderness: The Challenge of Womanist God-Talk.* Maryknoll, NY: Orbis Books, 1993.

Williams, Delores S. "A Womanist Perspective on Sin." In *A Troubling in My Soul: Womanist Perspectives on Evil and Suffering*, edited by Emilie Maureen Townes, 130–49. Bishop Henry McNeal Turner Studies in North American Black Religion 8. Maryknoll, NY: Orbis Books, 1993.

Williamson, H. G. M. "Ezra and Nehemiah, Books of." In *DBI*, edited by John H. Hayes, 375–82. Vol. A–J. Nashville: Abingdon, 1999.

Williamson, H. G. M. *Ezra and Nehemiah.* OTG. Sheffield: JSOT, 1987.

Williamson, H. G. M. *Ezra–Nehemiah.* WBC 16. Waco: Word, 1985.

Williamson, H. G. M. "Prophetesses in the Hebrew Bible." In *Prophecy and Prophets in Ancient Israel: Proceedings of the Oxford Old Testament Seminar*, edited by John Day, 65–80. LHBOTS 531. New York: T&T Clark, 2010.

Williamson, H. G. M. "Sanballa (Person)." In *The Anchor Yale Bible Dictionary: O–Sh*, edited by David Noel Freedman, Gary A. Herrion, David F. Graf, John David Pleins, and Astrid B. Beck, 973–75. New Haven: Yale University Press, 1992.

Williamson, H. G. M. "Sanballa (Person)." In *The Anchor Yale Bible Dictionary: O–Sh*, edited by David Noel Freedman, Gary A. Herrion, David F. Graf, John David Pleins, and Astrid B. Beck, 973–75. New Haven: Yale University Press, 1992.

Wittig, Monica. "One Is Not Born a Woman." In *Women's Studies: Essential Readings*, edited by Stevi Jackson, 22–25. New York: NYU Press, 1993.

Wright, Jacob. *Rebuilding Identity: The Nehemiah-Memoir and Its Earliest Readers.* BZAW 348. Berlin: de Gruyter, 2004.

Wright, Jacob L., and Michael Chan. "King and Eunuch: Isaiah 56:1-8 in Light of Honorific Royal Burial Practices." *JBL* 131 (2012): 99–119.

Wright, Jacob L., and Tamara Cohn Eskenazi. "Contrasting Pictures of Intermarriage in Ruth and Nehemiah." *TheTorah.com.* https://www.thetorah.com/article/contrasting-pictures-of-intermarriage-in-ruth-and-nehemiah.

Xenophon. *Cyropaedia.* In *The Project Gutenberg Ebook of Cyropaedia.* Translated by Henry Graham Dakyns. https://www.gutenberg.org/files/2085/2085-h/2085-h.htm.

Yamauchi, Edwin M. "Archaeological Backgrounds of the Exilic and Postexilic Era, Part 4: The Archaeological Background of Nehemiah." *BSac* 137 (1980): 291–309.

Yamauchi, Edwin M. "Was Nehemiah the Cupbearer a Eunuch?" *ZAW* 92 (1980): 132–42.

Yap, Timothy. "The House That Built Me: The 'House of God' and Its Role in the Construction of Fear in Nehemiah 6.1-15." *JSOT* 46 (2022): 408–20.

Yee, Gale A. " 'He Will Take the Best of Your Fields': Royal Feasts and Rural Extraction." *JBL* 136 (2017): 821–38.

Yee, Gale, ed. *Judges and Method: New Approaches in Biblical Studies.* Minneapolis: Fortress, 1995.

Yee, Gale. *Poor Banished Children of Eve: Women as Evil in the Hebrew Bible*. Minneapolis: Fortress, 2003.

Yee, Gale. " 'She Stood in Tears Amid the Alien Corn': Ruth, the Perpetual Foreigner and Model Minority." In *Off the Menu: Asian and Asian North American Women's Religion and Theology*, edited by Rita Nakashima Brock, Jung Ha Kim, Kwok Pui-lan, and Seung Ai Yang, 45–65. Louisville: Westminster John Knox, 2007.

Younger, K. Lawson, Jr. "The Deportations of the Israelites." *JBL* 117 (1998): 201.

Zierler, Wendy. "Torah Study 'For Women.' " In *New Jewish Feminism: Probing the Past, Forging the Future*, edited by Elyse Goldstein, 102–12. Woodstock: Jewish Lights Publishing, 2009.

Zulu, Edwin. "Interpreting the Exodus among the Ngoni People." *Scriptura* 108 (2011): 365–80.

Index of Scripture References and Other Ancient Writings

Other Ancient Texts

Extrabiblical Writings

Index of Subjects

Authors

Deborah Ann Appler is the professor of Hebrew Bible/Old Testament at Moravian Theological Seminary in Bethlehem, Pennsylvania, an ordained elder in the Eastern Pennsylvania Conference of the United Methodist Church, and an Earth Keeper for the UMC Board of Global Ministries. Her research, publications, and teaching seek to encourage conversations around community justice, especially as these issues appear in biblical texts and intersect with gender, sexuality, elder issues, and food justice. She participated in several archaeological excavations, including Jezreel, Megiddo, and Ramat Rachel to better understand the history and culture behind biblical texts.

Terry Ann Smith is the associate dean of institutional assessment and associate professor of biblical studies at New Brunswick Theological Seminary in New Brunswick, New Jersey. Her research interests and publications focus on inspections of the Hebrew Bible that expose normalized inequitable distributions of power and privilege as these intersect categories of ethnicity, class, and gender. As an ordained Baptist minister, she is particularly interested in contextualized socio-political readings of biblical texts that foster conversations which address the theological, practical, and ethical applications of the Bible by the church.

Volume Editor

Amy-Jill Levine is Rabbi Stanley M. Kessler Distinguished Professor of New Testament and Jewish Studies, Hartford International University for Religion and Peace; University Professor of New Testament and Jewish Studies Emerita, Mary Jane Werthan Professor of Jewish Studies Emerita, Professor of New Testament Studies Emerita, Vanderbilt University. Her recent publications include *The Gospel of Luke* (with Ben Witherington III, the first biblical commentary by a Jew and an Evangelical Christian), *The Jewish Annotated New Testament Second Edition* (co-edited with Marc Brettler), *The Bible With and Without Jesus: How Jews and Christians Read the Same Stories Differently* (with Marc Brettler), *The Pharisees* (co-edited with Joseph Sievers); and in the Beginner's Guide series, *Sermon on the Mount, Light of the World, Entering the Passion of Jesus, The Difficult Words of Jesus, Witness at the Cross, Signs and Wonders, The Gospel of Mark,* and *The Gospel of John.*

Series Editor

Barbara E. Reid, general editor of the Wisdom Commentary series, is a Dominican Sister of Grand Rapids, Michigan. She is the Carroll Stuhlmueller, CP Distinguished Professor of New Testament Studies, and president emerita of Catholic Theological Union (the first woman who held the position). She has been a member of the CTU faculty since 1988 and also served as vice president and academic dean from 2009 to 2018. She holds a PhD in biblical studies from The Catholic University of America and was president of the Catholic Biblical Association in 2014–2015. Her most recent publications are *Luke 1–9* and *Luke 10–24*, co-authored with Shelly Matthews (WCS 43A, 43B; Liturgical Press, 2021); and *At the Table of Holy Wisdom: Global Hungers and Feminist Biblical Interpretation* (Paulist, 2023).